The Making of Citizens

The Making of Citizens

Cities of Peasants Revisited

BRYAN R ROBERTS

A member of the Hodder Headline Group
LONDON • NEW YORK • SYDNEY • AUCKLAND

First published in Great Britain 1995 by
Arnold, a member of the Hodder Headline Group
338 Euston Road, London NW1 3BH

Copublished in the USA by Halsted Press,
an imprint of John Wiley & Sons, Inc.,
605 Third Avenue,
New York, NY 10158-0012

British Library Cataloguing in Publication Data
A catalogue record for this book is available from the British Library

Library of Congress Cataloging-in-Publication Data
Roberts, Bryan R., 1939–
    The making of citizens: Cities of peasants revisited/Bryan
  Roberts.—2nd ed.
      p.   cm.
    Rev. ed. of: Cities of peasants. 1978.
    Includes bibliographical references and index.
    ISBN 0-340-60478-6 (pb)
    1. Urbanization—Latin America.   I. Roberts, Bryan R., 1939–
  Cities of peasants.   II. Title.
  HT127.5.R62   1995
  307.76′098—dc20   95-21065
                                                              CIP

ISBN 0 340 65264 0 HB
ISBN 0 340 60478 6 PB
ISBN 0 470 23531 4 HB (in the USA only)
ISBN 0 470 23530 6 PB (in the USA only)

1 2 3 4 5 95 96 97 98 99

Typeset in 10/12pt Sabon by
Phoenix Photosetting, Lordswood, Chatham, Kent
Printed and bound by
J. W. Arrowsmith, Bristol, UK

Contents

Preface   vii

1 Urbanization and Underdevelopment   1

2 Urbanization and Underdevelopment Before the Modern Period   28

3 Urbanization and Industrialization   55

4 Migration and the Agrarian Structure   87

5 The Urban Economy and the Organization of the
  Labour Market   113

6 The Nature of Urban Stratification   134

7 Urban Poverty, the Household and Coping with Urban Life   157

8 The Development of Citizenship   184

Epilogue   208

Bibliography   212

Index   253

Preface

This book began with the decision of Arnold to bring out a second edition of *Cities of Peasants*, originally published in 1978. I am grateful to Laura McKelvie for the encouragement she gave me to undertake the challenge. Since most of the writing for that book had been done in the mid-1970s, I found myself faced with the interesting but daunting task of reviewing almost 20 years of change in Latin American urbanization. The basic issue was to decide whether a simple updating was needed, adding new references and tables, but leaving the basic argument untouched, or whether the original should be rewritten, using new arguments to suit new circumstances. At first, I inclined to the latter option since my continuing work on development problems suggested that there was something of a 'sea change' in the nature of urbanization in Latin America. The global context differed in that the Latin American economies had become more open than previously and, after the debt crisis, more dependent on external finance. Also, these had become increasingly sophisticated urban societies where employment concentrated in the white-collar services, individualized patterns of consumption predominated and most people participated fully in a global media-based culture. The title, in particular, seemed inappropriate to a reality that appeared to have more in common with a post-modern world of cultural and social fragmentation than with a pre-modern world of peasant urbanites.

As I began to rethink the issues and take account of the new data, I revised my initial opinion, deciding that there were more continuities than I had supposed. The specificities in Latin America's current development could still be explained in terms of the long and perhaps illusory roads to modernization imposed on these societies from the time of their first insertion into the capitalist world economy. Since, in essence, this is the argument of *Cities of Peasants*, it meant that the challenge I faced was not to provide a new theoretical approach but to develop my original argument. This focused on the internal logic of capitalist development in each country and its consequences for class formation. The present book is, as a result, an even more historically-based account than was its predecessor, since the contrast between the contemporary period and the earlier one is an essential part of my sociological argument. As a result, much of the earlier book is retained, but there is also much that is added. However, the reader should remember that this volume is not a definitive review of the literature on development issues in Latin America since inevitably I have been selective.

I would like to thank the Center for Social Theory and History at the University of California, Los Angeles, and its director, Robert Brenner, for the opportunity to present a paper that initiated my rethinking of *Cities of Peasants*. I owe a basic debt to the commentators, John Friedmann and Susan Hecht, who challenged my argument that there was a uniform sea change in Latin American development. This led me to rethink my argument along the lines of the present book, for whose limitations, they are, of course, not responsible. Much of my account of the changes in rural structure since the 1970s is informed by my continuing association with Norman Long and my collaboration with him over the chapter on the Agrarian Structures of Latin America, in the *Cambridge History of Latin America 6*. My debt is an even more specific one to Orlandina de Oliveira with whom I have worked over the past six years in analysing trends in urbanization and labour markets in Latin America. I owe her especial thanks for allowing me to use some of the material that we have collected and written together and which can be found in our chapter on Urban Social Structure and Change in the *Cambridge History of Latin America 6*. I need also to thank the graduate students in my seminar, an Introduction to the Sociology of Latin America, who wrote bibliographic essays that helped me considerably both in updating the literature on development trends in Latin America and in providing a critical input. Last, there is the help that I have received from Harley Browning. *Cities of Peasants* owed a great deal to his intellectual input and encouragement. It is fitting that almost 20 years later this new account should carry a similar debt. Then, I was a visitor at the Population Research Center of the University of Texas, using his hospitality and the excellent resources of the University to complete the earlier book. Now, as a colleague at the same University, I have had even more opportunity to benefit from his help and friendship.

Bryan Roberts
Department of Sociology
Population Research Center
University of Texas at Austin

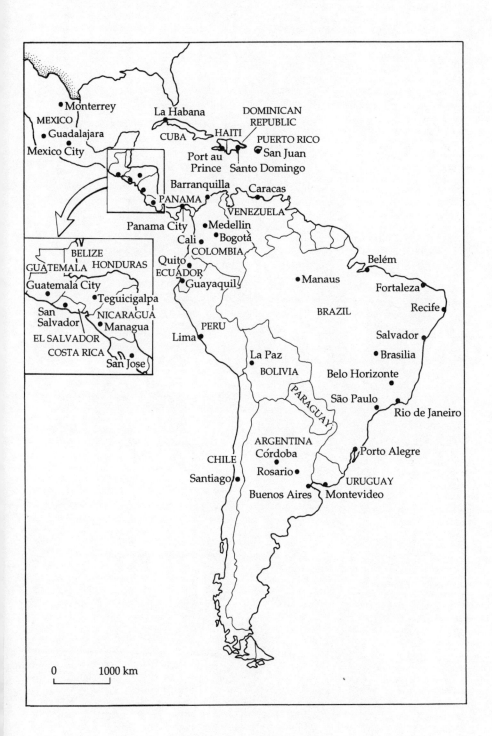

Monterrey
MEXICO
Guadalajara
Mexico City

La Habana
CUBA
HAITI
Port au
Prince
Santo Domingo

DOMINICAN
REPUBLIC
PUERTO RICO
San Juan

BELIZE
GUATEMALA HONDURAS
Guatemala City
Teguicigalpa
San
Salvador
NICARAGUA
Managua
EL SALVADOR
COSTA RICA
San Jose

Barranquilla
PANAMA
Caracas
Panama City
VENEZUELA
Medellin
Cali
Bogotá
COLOMBIA
Quito
ECUADOR
Guayaquil

Belém

Manaus

Fortaleza
Recife

BRAZIL

Salvador

PERU
Lima

La Paz
BOLIVIA

Brasilia

Belo Horizonte
PARAGUAY
São Paulo
Rio de Janeiro

ARGENTINA
Córdoba
CHILE
Rosario

Porto Alegre

Santiago
Buenos Aires
URUGUAY
Montevideo

0   1000 km

1

Urbanization and Underdevelopment

The themes of this book are the urban problems of underdeveloped countries and the changes in these problems since the mid-1970s when *Cities of Peasants* was written. Now, as then, most of the examples will be taken from one part of that world – Latin America. This restriction is necessary if we are even to attempt to come to grips with the complexity of our theme since comparisons have more meaning when examined within a broadly uniform economic context shaped by a similar history of colonial dependence on Europe, later to be replaced by increasing economic and political dependence on the United States. The analysis that I will use requires a certain historical depth and attempting to provide it for one continent, let alone two or three, is a daunting task.

In the period following the Second World War, underdeveloped countries urbanized rapidly so that their urban population doubled in the 30 years to 1975. In the 15 years to 1990, the urban population had doubled again, reaching some 40 per cent of the population of all underdeveloped countries. In some countries, the proportions living in towns of 20,000 or more have attained the high proportions common in the advanced industrial world. Population is also concentrated in relatively few urban centres which have high rates of growth, often in excess of 5 per cent a year, and seven of the world's ten largest cities are located in underdeveloped countries (United Nations, 1993).

Urban growth continues to be accompanied by poverty. Contrasts between wealth and poverty, between 'modernity' and 'traditionalism' are as sharp in the mid-1990s as they were in the mid-1970s. Modern skyscrapers, sumptuous shopping, office and banking facilities still coexist with unpaved streets, squatter settlements and open sewage. The difference is that the areas occupied by these uses have expanded to cover large areas of the countryside, creating severe pressure on water resources and demands for energy that contribute to environmental pollution. Rapid rates of urbanization, combined with high rates of population growth, result in particularly high comparative rates of contamination in the largest cities. Thus, Jimenez and Velasquez (1989) report higher concentrations of sulphur dioxide in the atmosphere of metropolitan Manila than in New York, Los Angeles or Chicago and higher concentrations of particulate matter than in Tokyo, New York or London.

In the central streets of the cities of the underdeveloped world, the elegantly dressed are waylaid by beggars and street vendors; their shoes are shined and their cars are guarded by urchins from an inner city slum whose earnings are a vital part of the family budget. One paradox of contemporary population movements and the interdependence of national economies is that these scenes have become familiar in the metropolises of the developed world. There, immigrants from the developing world can be seen peddling their services or selling prepared food in the streets of cities like New York.

Observers in the 1990s are less likely than in the 1970s to see the solution to the problems of urban growth in underdeveloped countries as that of providing stable, well-paid industrial employment. Indeed, many fear that this type of employment is abandoning the cities of the developed world and is being relocated to developing countries where labour is cheaper. However, the multinational companies that open up manufacturing units in developing countries usually do not locate in the major cities of these countries. The major cities are viewed as being chaotically organized, with problems of congestion and too many conflicting regulations concerning labour and production. Instead, the new foreign investment in manufacturing often goes to 'green field' sites with access to transport infrastructure and close to intermediate size cities. As in the mid-1970s, the cities of the underdeveloped world are seen as overpopulated with high levels of unemployment or underemployment. The concentrations of jobs in 'non-productive' activities in government and in the informal sector, particularly in commerce and personal services, are often cited as one of the evils of contemporary 'underdeveloped' urbanization. In the course of this book, I shall argue that while this emphasis on urbanization without industrialization is misleading, the major cities of the developing world are, like their counterparts in the developed world, increasingly service-based economies in terms of the growth of employment and of contribution to the gross national product.

Part of the dynamic of this service growth is complementary to the growth of the manufacturing sector, providing the financial and technical services that are integral to the growth and productivity of that sector (Fajnzylber, 1990). There is continuing debate, as we will see, as to whether this development increases or decreases equity in income distribution. In developing countries, to the possible effects of industrial restructuring on income polarization are added those of a sizeable, informally organized, sector of petty commerce, small-scale manufacturing and personal services. This sector, as we will see, is at least as large as it was in the mid-1970s. We will consider later the significance of the 'informal' sector for poverty and its alleviation, arguing that, though the components are different, contemporary forms of poverty are as integral parts of the current pattern of economic growth of the Third World as were their counterparts in the 1970s.

Although 1940 is a somewhat arbitrary date to use as the beginning of this 'urban explosion', it is significant in the sense that it marks the definitive shift of underdeveloped economies towards industrial production following the curtailment of external supplies of manufactures as a result of the war. Many underdeveloped countries, especially in Latin America, had already begun to develop a local industry long before 1940, but it was with the Second World War, and especially with the expansion of international trade after it, that underdeveloped countries began to industrialize rapidly. These are also the years in which the pace of urbanization increased dramatically. In later chapters I shall examine how and why this process of industrialization occurred and illustrate its extent by examples from Latin America where, in almost every country by 1970, industry contributed a greater share of the gross national product than did agriculture.

I shall examine the contradictions present in an urban situation in which increasing industrial growth and concentration is accompanied by an inadequate urban infrastructure and by the continuing poverty of much of the urban population. One of these contradictions is a process of capital accumulation in the cities of the underdeveloped world which is based on access to cheap and abundant labour, not only to power the factories but to provide complementary services and ancillary manufacturing.

The inconsistencies of contemporary urban capitalist development are not only, or even mainly, internal to industry but appear in many facets of urban life. The city must provide the basic facilities that workers and their families need for survival – housing, shops and markets, transport and public services such as health, water and electricity. Indeed, creating and maintaining urban labour power involves more than providing material facilities. Specialized schooling and training facilities are needed to prepare people for the different types of jobs created by a complex production system. Even maintaining order and fostering a sense of civic responsibility and work discipline are necessary preconditions for industrial production. These processes provide for the reproduction of labour power in the sense of maintaining a supply of labour both physically able to work – in that, for example, workers are healthy and live near their places of work – and prepared, culturally and ideologically, to work under the prevailing conditions of capitalist production.

Private enterprise is rarely able or willing to provide directly for the reproduction of urban labour power. The nature of the facilities needed are such that they must often be provided collectively and through the agency of the state. Moreover, private enterprise normally puts pressure on the state to provide the infrastructure that contributes directly to its own profitability (good roads, telecommunications and so on) and, at times, to take over the less profitable but necessary branches of production. As cities increase in size, the costs of providing an adequate urban system rise considerably and the social pressure to do something about them also increases, if only in order to avoid the dangers of epidemic, traffic chaos and so on. However, investment in the social and physical infrastructure of the city is not directly profitable and private enterprise is reluctant to pay the taxes needed for such an investment.

The state is thus faced with conflicting pressures of ensuring the profitability of industry by providing the needed infrastructure and by keeping taxes low and of meeting (or at least appearing to meet) the demand of urban residents for 'non-productive' investment in housing, schools and other social services. This type of analysis became a relatively familiar one in the literature on urbanization in Europe in the 1970s, in which the urban system is seen as one of the major arenas for the class struggle (Pickvance, 1976; Castells, 1977). The contradictions in many cities of the underdeveloped world are sharper because capital is comparatively scarce and less easily transferred for investment in the urban infrastructure. Also, though the urban poor are an integral part of the urban capitalist system, few of them are employed in large-scale enterprises and they do not form an important part of the internal market for consumer goods. In the period of large-scale rural-urban migrations, from the 1940s to the 1970s in Latin America, the poor literally built their own cities, occupying land, installing basic facilities and constructing their own housing. Under these conditions, it follows that the urban system in underdeveloped countries, as initially organized, excludes much of the population from any substantial material benefits. We have therefore to examine the conditions under which the state comes to rely on coercion as a means of capitalist development or, alternatively, seeks to integrate the urban population through democratic politics or through direct improvement in their standards of living.

Though these issues continue to be important in the period after the 1970s, changes in the international context have brought new issues to the fore and given a different cast to old ones. Urbanization in developing countries is occurring in a significantly different context in the present period to that which prevailed as recently as the early 1970s. This demarcation is heuristic, since these changes in the world economy are gradual and cumulative. However, the financial restructuring occasioned by the oil 'crises' of the early 1970s appears to be a turning-point in development policies. I will focus on Latin America, contrasting the contemporary phase of urbanization with that from the 1940s to the 1970s dominated by import-substitution industrialization (ISI). The ISI phase of urbanization in Latin America refers to the period of rapid urban growth from approximately the 1930s to the 1970s. National development policies promoted industrialization through tariffs and subsidies with the aim of supplying the domestic market and reducing dependency on the export of primary products.

The world economy is now more integrated than in the ISI phase, merging markets for capital, commodities and labour, that were previously fragmented by national boundaries, and creating a new international division of labour (Frobel et al., 1980; Bornschier and Chase-Dunn, 1985). National and even city-level urban processes are now much more closely tied than before to this evolving world system, its interdependencies and division of labour (Timberlake, 1985, 1987). The significance of these developments will be assessed later on in this chapter. They raise the question of whether or not we are witnessing a new stage in development requiring a different analysis from that of the period from the 1940s to the 1970s.

My answer will be a qualified 'no'. The theme running throughout the discussion in the following chapters and linking the historical analysis of urbanization with that of the contemporary urban structure remains, as in *Cities of Peasants*, class and class conflict. Class alliances and conflicts comprise the dialectic process by which change takes place; the emergence of new forms of production creates new class interests and threatens those interests tied to an established and perhaps superseded form of production. The struggle of different classes to expand and defend their interests results in social and political institutions (political parties, employers and workers' associations, new forms of legal contract or of regulation of work) that contribute to the form of later economic development. In the contemporary period, the strengthening of civil society is part of this same process. The identities on which struggle and organization are based may look somewhat different to those of the past, as when, for example, gender and ethnicity appear to supplant traditional class identities such as those of peasant or industrial worker as bases for political protest. Yet what matters is the degree of pressure for change that these new forms of identity bring. This depends on the alliances that can be made across different groups, their degree of cohesion and the opportunities that different types of political structure provide for them to exercise influence.

By focusing on the class struggle it becomes easier to recognize the specificity of each country's and each city's development, enabling us to compare, for example, the problems of manufacturing cities with those of cities that are mainly commercial and administrative centres. Although cities in the underdeveloped world may seem to be facing similar problems and seeking similar solutions to those problems, the manner of fostering and coping with economic development is, in fact, quite different from country to country. Some countries, though fewer than in the past, have conservative, authoritarian military regimes. There are also civilian governments with widely differing degrees of popular support. The extent to which the state intervenes in the urban economy and provides urban infrastructure also differs from country to country.

By limiting myself to Latin America, I will not be able to take proper account of the diversity of patterns of contemporary urbanization in developing countries. This diversity is linked, in part, to differences in the histories of their integration into the world system. Other developing countries have been, for instance, less committed to ISI, resulting in marked differences in timing and levels of urbanization. In the last section of this chapter,

I consider briefly the diversity of patterns of urbanization in developing countries and suggest ways in which these differences are likely to affect their 'responses' to the new order. Also, I will attempt to place contemporary urbanization in its historical context by considering the experiences of developing countries when they began to urbanize rapidly. These experiences show diverse patterns indicating that there is no one pattern of urbanization that developing countries must follow if they are to develop economically. There are also, as we will see, some important demographic differences beween urbanization in developing countries and that of the developed world. First, we need to consider the theoretical issues in the study of urbanization and development and some of the changes in these issues that have occurred since *Cities of Peasants* was written.

Urbanization and Development

Urbanization, in the modern period, has entailed a profound process of social and economic transformation. Agriculture has become a less direct source of livelihood and a steadily decreasing proportion of the population in both developed and underdeveloped countries is employed on the land. Urbanization has also implied an increasing territorial division of labour. Agricultural areas become specialized in the production of certain crops to provide foodstuffs for urban populations at home and abroad; towns and cities specialize in branches of industrial activity. Urban and rural areas become increasingly interdependent economically and this interdependence leads to an international division of labour as each nation specializes in different branches of production for export.

Specialization and interdependence are thus the by-products of industrialization and it is this pattern of urbanization that distinguishes the modern period from earlier ones. As Lampard (1965) indicates, there is a long history of urban civilization in which cities served as residences of elites, craftsmen and traders and as centres for the organization and appropriation of the agricultural surplus; it is only factory-based industrialization that has given rise to an incessant urbanization based on increasing specialization and interdependence.

One of the most common approaches to economic development stresses the necessary contribution that urban industrialization makes to economic development. The approach here is to measure economic development in terms of growth in national productivity and rise in per capita income. From this perspective, the concentration of people in urban-industrial places contributes to economic development by reducing over time the proportion of the population in a nation's economy engaged purely in agricultural subsistence. Thus, Rosenstein-Rodan's (1943) programme for promoting urban industrialization in the depressed areas of eastern and south-eastern Europe after the war was echoed later in the declarations of leaders of underdeveloped countries that were seeking to escape dependence on the industrialized countries. Nkrumah in Ghana and the Economic Commission for Latin America, were some among many who wished to embark upon a pattern of urban industrialization similar to that of the developed world (Brookfield, 1975). It was recognized that increases in the urban population might not at first be absorbed into industrial employment; but it was claimed that the availability of such labour stimulated industrial investment.

Other commentators have stressed the advantages of urbanization from a sociological and psychological perspective. Levels of education are thought to improve with urbanization, if only because the urban milieu combats illiteracy. Likewise, various patterns of traditional behaviour are thought to be less likely to persist in an urban environment (Inkeles, 1960; Sjoberg, 1965). Kinship structures or ritual observances might persist, but it has been held that, unless they are compatible with the new forms of economic organization and an urban style of living, their function will merely become ceremonial (Hawley, 1971).

These perspectives can all best be regarded as theories of modernization. What modernization perspectives have in common is a view of development as a convergent and evolutionary process in which simpler forms of organization are increasingly absorbed into more centralized and complex ones (Moore, 1977). Such a focus means that an implicit model of necessary stages in urbanization is often used to evaluate the significance of variations in urbanization throughout the world. Reissman (1964) has analysed urbanization in underdeveloped countries as a replication, albeit in a more concentrated and uneven form, of the urbanization experience of the European nations at the time of their urban industrialization. The factors that he identifies as complementing each other in this development process are urban growth, industrialization, the presence of middle classes and nationalism. Imbalance between these factors, such as urban growth without industrialization, is conceived as creating social problems and constitutes a hindrance to progress at the next stage. Societies in these phases of development are described as transitional to more complex forms of organization.

Concepts such as transition and convergence have, however, a limited usefulness in understanding the experience of urbanization. From the perspective of this book, development is more usefully seen as an interdependent process in which some countries and regions acquire a predominant place within the division of labour, using coercion to organize production elsewhere, as in the case of colonialism, or through control of capital or advanced technology and markets. The division of labour that results is unequal in terms of the relative advantages that each part derives: the dominant partner reserves for itself the most lucrative activities using the other as a source of cheap raw materials or foodstuffs and as a market for manufactures. This situation is expressed in two related concepts, that of dependency and that of the world system.

The first analyses of dependency, for example by Frank (1971) and Amin (1973), who uses the term neo-colonialism, stressed the structural relationship by which the advanced capitalist world at once exploited and kept the Third World underdeveloped. Underdevelopment can thus be seen as being produced and maintained by the way in which capitalist expansion occurred in Latin America, Africa or Asia. The dominant capitalist powers (first England and then the United States) encouraged the transformation of local political and economic structures, both directly and indirectly, to serve their interests. Colonial territories were organized to produce the commodities needed by the metropolis, first precious metals and some agricultural products (such as sugar) and then, increasingly, the gamut of primary products needed for industrial expansion and feeding the urban populations of the advanced capitalist world. Characteristically, the dependency situation is one in which the local population does not have sufficient control over its resources to be able to extract better terms of exchange with the dominant powers or to sustain a locally based pattern of balanced economic development (Amin, 1974). A colonial power is able to reorganize native society to the economic advantage of the metropolis, thereby creating a kind of vassalage. Thus, Spain reorganized village life in Mexico and Peru to provide labour for the mines from which it extracted its richest treasure.

However, the situation of dependency is not simply produced by colonialism; it is also an internal structure of class relationships which works to the economic advantage of the metropolis and to the progressive underdevelopment of the periphery. At the periphery, there is a disarticulation of the economy, with sectors only marginally engaged in exchange with each other (Amin, 1974). Foreign merchants and financiers provide a market for the primary materials and the locals use the revenues to purchase luxury goods from the advanced capitalist world. This free trade makes it difficult for local industry to develop in the face of competition from foreign imports; but the protection of local industry is rarely to the advantage of local oligarchies which derive their wealth from the export economy. Even with formal independence, a former colony can, in these ways, remain securely tied to the interests of the colonial power.

From this point of view, the chain of exploitative relationships that links the metropolitan country to the major city and dominant classes of the dependent country extends from these classes to traders and producers located in provincial towns right down to the peasant producer or to the landless rural worker (Stavenhagen, 1965). At each stage of appropriation or expropriation there must always be a class of people who derive advantage from their situation and are prepared to act as agents in channelling the local resources to the metropolis. The surplus that remains in the dependent country does little to stimulate development: the lifestyles and values of the dominant classes of landowners and merchants entail, it is claimed, that this surplus is consumed in luxury expenditures rather than productive investments.

This analysis of dependency rests on an analysis of the logic of capitalist development. Capitalism is to be seen as becoming a dominant world economic system from the sixteenth century onwards, with the expansion of capitalism as conterminous with that of colonialism and underdevelopment. The problems of Latin America from the colonial period onwards, for example, are thereby to be understood in terms of the way in which capitalism has penetrated that continent. Even apparently traditional institutions, such as the *hacienda* or Indian community, can be seen to have been shaped by capitalist expansion; it can be argued, therefore, that such institutions are not simply the survival or transplant of non-capitalist forms of organization and production, such as feudalism or primitive communism.

This perspective is similar to the line of analysis developed by Wallerstein (1974a) in his concept of the modern world system. Wallerstein, however, extends the dependency perspective by recognizing that the world system is more complex than is suggested by the polar contrast of dependent and metropolitan countries. Thus he stresses three types of position within the world system: core, semi-periphery and periphery. In his view, the world system is based on the specialization of different regions at different stages and under different aspects of the production process. In the early modern period, Wallerstein distinguishes between the core industrial regions, such as England, semi-peripheral regions specializing in commerce and in organizing the production of primary products, such as Spain, and peripheral regions, such as Latin America and Eastern Europe, which were organized to provide primary products for the core countries. This specialization affects the relative capacity of the economic and political elites of different countries to consolidate their internal power and extend it externally. For example, England's core position depended on the economic capacity of its merchant capitalists and industrialists to finance and organize overseas trade using, for example, loans to foreign governments or to the landed elites of foreign countries as a means to that end; but it also depended on securing state backing for their project, particularly through English naval control of the sea lanes.

Inevitably, these relative capacities will change over time as the balance of economic or military advantage shifts as a result of technological innovation, of processes of change internal to a country or of global conflicts and alliances. Thus, from the world system perspective, countries can change their relative position and are not doomed to perpetual economic stagnation and underdevelopment, as the early dependency perspectives appeared to suggest.

The position of a region within the world system has, argues Wallerstein, systematic consequences for the nature of class organization since labour relations are organized differently in core, semi-periphery and periphery. In the core, the growth of industrialization and commercial agriculture makes wages the predominant form of labour relation, giving rise to the classic conflicts of early capitalism between the wage-earners – the proletariat – and the owners of the means of production – the bourgeoisie. The transition to the wage relation is much weaker in the semi-periphery since both industry and commercial agriculture are less well developed and elites obtain their wealth from commerce, colonial extraction or extensive landholdings that they do not directly farm. The predominant form of labour relations are non-wage ones, such as tenancy and sharecropping. In the peripheries, in contrast, even commerce is weakly developed because their role in the world system – that of providing precious metals or other primary products – provides little stimulus to the development of internal markets. Indeed, to extract resources cheaply means that labour will be obtained by various forms of coercion, such as obligating the population to provide labour for mines or *haciendas*. Readers need to consult Wallerstein's accounts (1974a, b, 1979, 1980) of the evolution of the world system to obtain a complete picture of the various mechanisms by which he suggests that position in the world system results in differences in class organization and labour markets. From this perspective, the impact of the world system reaches even to household organization (Smith and Wallerstein, 1992).

The world system approach has been used to understand contemporary urbanization. Thus, studies of urbanization in non-core countries have shown that the world system and its processes affect the urban hierarchies and internal urban processes of individual countries (London, 1980; Bornschier and Chase-Dunn, 1985; Nemeth and Smith, 1985). Variables associated with non-core position, such as degree of multinational penetration, have been shown to correlate positively with rapid urban growth, employment concentration in the tertiary sector and, negatively, with economic growth (London, 1987; London and Smith, 1988; Bradshaw, 1987). In these studies, the impact of external economic dependency is, following Lipton (1977), shown to affect urbanization and development mainly through intermediate, internal processes, such as patterns of investment which disrupt the agrarian structure, result in 'urban bias' and produce an over-inflated tertiary sector.

The Sources of Diversity

Studies focusing on the structure of dependency or on that of the world system have tended to overlook those local-level forces making for change in the situation. Dependency 'theory', as Fernando Cardoso (1977) points out, has become reified in some hands as a purely mechanical analysis of the ways in which external agents, such as foreign governments or multinational corporations, dominate local politics and economic life. Yet

substantial transformations have occurred in the economic and social structures of almost all underdeveloped countries, despite the unevenness of this
development, and these transformations must be analysed in terms of the
internal processes of change as much as of the external context. For this reason I use the term 'development' in this book, as well as the apparently more
neutral terms 'growth' or 'change'. Provided that we remember that no optimistic view of progress is implied by its use, the term development has the
advantage of drawing attention to the increasing specialization and differentiation that is taking place within even the most underdeveloped countries.

To obtain a clearer idea of the local forces of change, we need to consider
more closely the mechanisms by which inequality between regions and
between classes are sustained. Friedmann (1972a, b), for example, emphasizes the political dimensions that are important for regional development
and stresses the concentration of power that develops in the economically
most dynamic regions. He calls these regions core regions and examines the
processes whereby such regions organize the production of peripheral
regions; this organization has the effect of concentrating resources at the
core and creating a progressive economic and political dependence of the
periphery on the core. His major point is that the dominance of core regions
is a self-reinforcing process since innovations in technology or culture tend
to be developed first in core regions. Proximity to centres of decision-making, the presence of a highly developed consumer market and the presence
of organizational resources for innovations are among the many factors that
can be cited to explain this concentration of innovation. Economic advantages accrue to the earliest innovators and all innovation tends to reinforce
and extend the control of the core over the periphery. More traditional competitors at the periphery will be forced out of business and less productive
enterprises will be displaced from the core to the periphery.

The dominance of the core tends to produce or reinforce what appears to
be inefficiency or traditionalism at the periphery. Indeed, the dynamism of
the core depends, in great part, on creating conditions of scarcity at the
periphery. Thus Friedmann argues that, in the case of Chile, the predominance of Santiago has deprived provincial city government of any financial
resources; in this situation, local government appears inefficient since it does
not provide adequate urban services or foster local economic development.
Taxes and local banking deposits channel capital to Santiago, where it pro-
motes the economic growth of the core region. In the face of the dominance
of the core, the dominant provincial classes in many countries may espouse
regionalism, stressing the traditional virtues or ethnic characteristics of their
region as a means of challenging the dominance of the core. These potential
conflicts between periphery and core may in the long run limit the expansion of the core, giving rise to counter-elites at the periphery and perhaps to
the eventual withdrawal of the periphery from the influence of the core
(Friedmann, 1972a).

We will look, in subsequent chapters, at the systems of production that emerge in dependent countries and regions as a result of capitalist expansion. These systems of production are based on differences in the labour, capital and technological requirements of different commercial crops, raw materials or manufactures. Associated with these systems of production are particular types of class formation and class conflict. This form of analysis stresses that dependency is not a uniform condition but includes many different situations of dependency. One of the most complete versions of this approach is that given by Cardoso and Faletto (1979), in an essay entitled *Dependency and Development in Latin America*. They argue that within the constraints of the international capitalist system an uneven development has taken place within Latin America. They have succeeded in showing that this development varied economically and politically as a result of the specificity of the class struggle and that this was based on differences in the organization of production.

Hirschman (1977) provides specific suggestions as to how different forms of production can influence class organization and class struggle. He is interested in the direct backward and forward linkages generated by both primary and manufacturing production, but he extends the linkage concept to include the consumption patterns generated by a form of production and to take account of whether or not production stimulates the development of the state's fiscal mechanisms. Certain forms of production lend themselves more easily to state taxation than others: for example, their ownership and control may be in foreign hands, as in enclave production, and they represent a visible target for a government seeking revenue. Other products, and coffee is often such a case, are owned nationally and by a relatively large number of influential landowners. In this case, the state may find it hard initially to tax production in face of the opposition of the dominant local classes, although, as happened with coffee in Brazil, the need of producers to seek guaranteed prices in the face of world market fluctuations became an important factor in stimulating the development of the state's fiscal mechanisms.

Hirschman's suggestions are not meant to be applied mechanically; his major point is that we should pay more attention to the dialectic process that is involved in the expansion of any system of production. This production creates new class interests and the possibility of clashes among them. An expanding system of production entails clashes of interests between those committed to the new production and those whose position is threatened by its growth. For example, labour may be attracted away from older forms of production by higher wages and these older forms may also find that the policies advocated by the new interests, such as tariff reform, are counter to their own. Likewise, Hirschman stresses the social and political factors in development, even to the point of identifying the advantages of primary products which do *not* create opportunities for linkages, such as a demand for sophisticated processing plant or equipment. His argument is that, in the early stages of development, such linkages would inevitably be controlled by the foreign investors of capital, relegating the grower of the product to the agricultural role. In contrast, where the product requires only a few simple operations (drying and bagging, for instance) and its value per unit of weight justifies the grower himself transporting it to market, then the grower is more likely to extend his interests into commerce and transport. The profits of such a product would thus contribute to a more widespread local development.

I will extend this approach further in this book by taking into account the types of labour required for different forms of primary and industrial production, the political institutions needed to obtain such labour and the implications these have for the development of the class struggle. Obtaining labour also involves the struggle to gain labour's willing compliance with the system, such as the readiness of labour to acquire the qualifications needed for new types of work or to use their initiative to benefit the firm. For some theorists, notably the French 'regulation' school, the mode by which workers are regulated becomes the defining feature of new forms of capitalist organization. For example, the forms of regulation appropriate for Fordist production, based on the discipline of the assembly line, seniority and wage scales, give way to those appropriate to contemporary post-Fordism with its emphasis on worker flexibility, teamwork and concern for quality control (see Castells, 1977; Lipietz, 1988; Harvey, 1990). Following this line of analysis, we will explore the ways in which changes in aspirations, in family authority structures and in popular culture interact with changes in the organization of capitalism *within* underdeveloped countries. My concern is less with the ways in which the advanced capitalist world continues to exploit underdeveloped countries (continuity within change according to Frank), than with the patterns of social, economic and political life that have resulted from the exigencies of capitalist expansion in unevenly developed economies.

A New Stage in Urbanization?

We need to consider the possibility that development and urbanization are entering a new stage that is, in certain respects, qualitatively different from that of the period from the 1940s to the mid-1970s. This most recent stage in capitalist development, often labelled the post-modern stage, can be characterized in various ways. For Harvey (1990) it represents a peculiarly intensive phase of the time-space compression that has characerized capitalist development since the beginning of the modern period. For Soja (1989), in partial contrast, it is a period characterized by the predominance of the spatiality of capitalism over its temporality. Time is compressed by modern 'instantaneous' communications and improved transport. National boundaries increasingly lose their economic significance and hitherto fragmented markets, financial and commodity, become integrated on a world scale. The unevenness of capitalist development becomes an increasingly important basis of capital accumulation since time-space compression facilitates the incorporation of previously underexploited spaces into high technology production and services.

There is no sharp break with the past since market integration, improved communications and the exploitation of the unevenness of capitalist development are characteristics of the period following the Second World War and earlier. However, it is in recent years that these trends have combined to create what is likely to be a new stage in development. This stage is based, it is argued, on supranational financial agencies, on microprocessor-based technologies that facilitate the coordination of production and of service delivery on a world-wide scale and of the evolving role of the multinational corporation in internationalizing production as well as consumption patterns (Canak, 1989). Flexible systems of production and circulation enable firms to concentrate on essential functions in which quality is a prime consideration, while relegating routine operations to subcontracting and outside suppliers. Linked to these developments are the emergence of commodity chains in which the different units of the chain are distributed globally according to the comparative advantage that each site offers (Gereffi and Korzeniewicz, 1990). This spatial dispersion of interdependent production and service activities is accompanied by an increasing centralization of capital ownership. This centralization is managed by an integrated system of financial markets based in a few major cities. These markets concentrate private wealth whatever its national origin.

Under these circumstances, capital is increasingly 'footloose' and not easily controlled by national governments. The bargaining power of governments at local or national level is consequently reduced vis-à-vis the concessions demanded by capital in terms of regulation or fiscal obligations. One consequence is to emphasize government fiscal austerity and cut-backs. The bargaining power of labour is also reduced. Employers reduce their labour force to compete in global markets. The workers that are retained are often reorganized in ways that weaken collective bargaining – 'quality control' teams in which the management-worker divide is blurred, profit sharing and other incentives that individualize the worker's position.

Various studies have shown the implications of the current transformation in the world economy for urban development at the core (Noyelle and Stanback, 1984; Sassen-Koob, 1985; Hill, 1986; Feagin, 1988). Multinational corporations operate a global strategy in which their various divisions are divided spatially: headquarters in one city, regional headquarters in another and manufacturing or service delivery plants in yet other cities. Corporations operating a world strategy have no strong commitment to place and relocate different divisions according to the most cost effective strategy: where certain types of labour are cheaper, are more available or where favuorable tax or other concessions are obtained. In this way, the strategies of the automobile corporations changed the face of Detroit, displacing factories from the central areas and renewing them as corporate headquarters (Hill, 1986). .

These corporate strategies make the uses of urban space more volatile than in the past, with the processes most intense in such world cities as New York or Los Angeles, followed by second-level cities such as Houston or Detroit (Soja, 1986, 1987; Feagin, 1988; Sassen-Koob, 1988). The effects on labour markets are equally systematic, resulting in different occupational structures between cities at different levels of the hierarchy. Those of the 'world' cites, such as New York or London, and particularly those of their centres, tend to polarize between well-paid professional and technical jobs, mainly concentrated in producer services, and low-paid, unskilled jobs in personal service occupations, 'sweat-shop' manufacturing and domestic outwork (Sassen, 1991). In the United States, these low-paid jobs have been filled by the 'new' waves of immigrants from developing countries, particularly from Latin America. Intermediate-paying manual jobs in manufacturing or clerical jobs, such as those in data processing, are displaced to smaller towns or suburban locations or to low labour cost countries, such as Mexico (Noyelle and Stanback, 1984). In this context, Sassen (1995) shows how 'local' labour markets are created that span international boundaries, such as those between the United States and Mexico, dramatically demonstrating the consequences of global interdependence for labour mobility.

There is also a perceptible polarization in labour markets. Job growth is fast in those jobs that pay high salaries and demand high qualifications. It is equally fast in those jobs that pay low salaries and demand few qualifications. In contrast, the intermediate-paying jobs, those traditionally identified with the skilled worker and, in the US, with high school graduation, stagnate. In terms of the theory of a new stage, this polarization is not a temporary aberration but an integral part of economic restructuring.

The rapid growth of high-paying jobs results not only from the demand for highly qualified people in high-tech production but also from the importance of the 'control' services, such as financial and other professional services, in the new pattern of 'flexible' accumulation. New technology in communications contributes to income and occupational polarization, adding high-paid jobs in the computer-related professions and low-paid jobs in mass retailing and assembly line manufacturing through efficient central inventory control of spatially dispersed operations. The expansion of low-paying jobs occurs primarily among employees of retailing chains and fast-food outlets and in low-cost personal services: cleaners, janitors and domestic servants. By 1993, the retailing giant, Walmart, had become the single largest employer of labour in the United States but with an average income for employees that was below the national average wage. In contrast, the types of production and services, including government services, that once paid intermediate-level wages are retrenching employment. Furthermore, cheap imports are replacing intermediate-paying jobs in some sectors or these are being located abroad where wages are lower. In her writing, Saskia Sassen provides an image of the two worlds of New York created by these processes: the daytime world of the professionals and technicians that occupy the skyscapers and night-time world of the cleaning and custodial staff that occupy them at night.

These processes in the core are likely to have their counterparts in the periphery. Thus major cities of Latin America, such as Sao Paulo in Brazil or Mexico City, show, as we will see, signs of specializing in services, particularly the 'control' ones of finance and corporate headquarters, and serve as organizational centres for regional economies in which other cities specialize in manufacturing or distribution. Moreover, the cities of the developing world are themselves part of financial, production and distribution networks whose centres are the cities of the developed world (see Sassen, 1993, for a global account of these interrelations).

Developing countries are drawn into the new division of labour, but their place within it is ambivalent. Some become locations for export industries on the basis of their comparative advantage in low labour costs and high degrees of control over labour; but these opportunities are limited by new, flexible production technologies in the core countries which are reconcentrating production in new and old regions of the developed world (Schoenberger, 1988).

The problem of competitiveness in the world economy is sharpened under these conditions, particularly because the 1970s and 1980s witnessed deteriorating terms of trade for the natural resources of developing countries, their main source of a trade surplus. Developing countries are now less able than before to shelter their industries behind tariff protection and must, instead, find specializations which allow them to compete in manufacturing exports with other countries. Competitiveness in manufacturing depends, however, on a combination of factors that are part economic, part social and part political. Increasing productivity depends on technological innovation and this, in turn, is linked to improved educational standards, to the preparedness of entrepreneurs to invest in new areas, to the selective encouragement of key export sectors and to economic policies that promote cooperation between government, business and labour sectors (Fajnzylber, 1990). In the debates over the best policies to ensure growth, there is greater ambivalence than in the 1960s over the role of the state. Even those favouring state intervention recognize the need to adapt public policy to promote competitiveness in a global economy.

This ambivalence fosters an approach to underdevelopment that is sharply different to the 'developmentalist' policies previously dominant: instead of state-directed economic intervention aimed at promoting industrialization and modernization, economic liberalism dominates international trade policies and the internal economic policies of underdeveloped countries. One of the major mechanisms by which this pattern of integration affects urbanization is through the financial dependence of developing countries on developed countries. Loans are tied to policy requirements which severely limit the capacity of the governments of developing nations to intervene in urbanization and ameliorate its negative consequences. These loans are tied to austerity measures that, as Walton and Ragin (1989) argue, affect urban populations most harshly. Equity financing, which is an increasingly important part of foreign investment in developing countries, means that governments are closely dependent on international market pressures. Appropriate free market policies help ensure massive inflows of funds, but these will be withdrawn quickly if governments appear to interfere unduly in markets or at the first signs of economic or political crisis. These conditions sharpen the debate over the trade-off between equity and growth by discouraging policies designed to redistribute income because they might deter investment. I am in agreement with Fajnzylber's (1990) position that sustainable growth depends on equity in income distribution and access to services. Equity is needed to avoid social conflict and mobilize a population behind the effort to upgrade qualifications and adapt to new technologies.

As markets liberalize and governments seek private investment, business interests, both national and international, are likely to become more insistent in the demands they make of government. These demands include a pro-business fiscal policy, modern infrastructure, including an education system geared to the needs of business, and regulations that enable them to implement new and more flexible forms of labour organization. In the 1990s, the international pressures on the governments of developing countries are considerably greater than was the case earlier. The dependency of developing countries on external finance makes them more sensitive than in the past to these external demands. These differ in force with those coming from international economic organizations, such as the IMF or the World Bank, having the greatest weight. Less noticed but also influential, however, are the large numbers of non-governmental organizations (NGOs), both religious and secular, that operate programmes of direct assistance to local populations within developing countries. Not only do they help local groups to organize and make demands on government, but NGOs can influence governments directly, particularly those governments whose reliance on aid or trade agreements makes them sensitive to international public opinion.

Diverse as the sources of demands on governments in developing countries are, they exercise a similar pressure for accountable government. For the international economic organizations, accountability may be defined narrowly in terms of following economically rational policies that make the market work more efficiently, whereas for non-governmental organizations accountability is more likely to mean sensitivity to the needs of the poor and an end to human rights abuses. The sheer number of citizen groups and the liberalization of markets also ensures that social and economic actors are less likely than in the past to see a general advantage in making deals with government to meet their specific needs. Consequently, coercion or patronage politics are unlikely to be enough to maintain order and promote development. As higher proportions of the urban population are born and raised in the cities, educated to aspire to higher standards of living and gain confidence in participating in organizations to defend or improve their urban situation, the demands on government increase. Though many of these demands come from the 'new' middle classes of office workers, technicians, managers and professionals, we will see that some of the strongest have originated among a working class whose members, women as much as men, have built up an experience of organizing to improve their precarious living conditions (Blondet, 1991; Jelin, 1987, 1990).

The various sets of actors are likely to prefer to work with impartial and predictable rules for resource allocation since these enhance their capacity to enter into long-term strategies and diminish their dependence on the whims of government personnel. We do not know whether these changes in the relationship of state to civil society alter the power of different social and economic actors. Only research will tell whether, for example, multinational companies have more or less power to influence the policies of developing countries in the second period as compared to the first. My argument, to be developed in the final chapter, is that the trend towards a more integrated world economy and more liberalized national economies has been accompanied by an increasingly, though chaotically, organized civil society in many developing countries. In these countries, the demands of various groups, such as entrepreneurs, neighbourhood associations, women's groups and ecological groups, combine with international pressures to force governments towards a more efficient, systematic and impartial administration of resources.

External and internal determinants of change are increasingly intertwined. There is, as we will see, still considerable diversity in the situation of developing countries, but this diversity is, in part, the product of the interaction between the external constraints of an increasingly global economy and culture and the particular histories of developing countries. There are two aspects of the intertwining of the external and internal that we will need to consider. The first is the renewed emphasis on decentralization and local autonomy that is based, on the one hand, on a rejection of bureaucratic centralization and, on the other, on a desire to see more community control of resources. This concern with decentralization has attracted support from commentators of very different economic and political persuasion. Thus, Friedmann (1989) calls for a revival of the *barrio* economy in Latin America in order to restore some degree of control over their lives to the urban poor (see also the essays in Sachs, 1992). However, this emphasis is also echoed by neo-liberal commentators concerned to diminish or eliminate state bureaucratic regulation. Thus, De Soto's (1989) call for another path (*El*

Otro Sendero) is basically a call for state non-interference in the economy in order to enable (small-scale) entrepreneurial initiative to flourish.

The second are the issues of the global environment. These range from population questions to protecting the natural environment and the avoidance of global warming. The concern of governments of the developed world with these issues has led to increasing pressures on countries of the developing world to plan population growth, to diminish contamination in the cities and to preserve rain forests (see Sachs (1993) on the politics of environmental concerns). In Latin America, these issues have been a major source of external pressure and intervention. Their significance is to create a development agenda that is an increasingly international one in which groups in developing countries ally with those in developed countries, often bypassing local states and political agendas. The internationalization of local development agendas, including those of human rights, has in this way become one of the most significant changes in the context of development in the contemporary period.

New issues there are in plenty, but my sense is that the underlying theme, that of the contradictions in capitalist development, is the same as it was in the mid-1970s. Latin America is not witnessing a new stage in capitalist development but the fulfillment of the nineteenth-century agenda described by Marx in his account of the increasing centralization of capital and of the integration of markets on a world scale. The project of capitalist modernization proceeds apace in Latin America and arouses similar passions for and against as it did in the mid-1970s. The population of Latin America is as committed now as it was then to improving its standard of living and defines that standard of living in similar mass consumption terms. There are, as we have noted, differences in the rapidity with which people are affected by global changes and, certainly, mass media creates a sense of participating in a global culture that was not present to the same extent before. Yet the concerns of the urban poor today and the strategies that they use to survive are similar to those recorded in the 1960s and 1970s: preoccupation with food and shelter, the acquiring of basic amenities and the uses of family and community resources to these ends.

One change that will be documented in the chapters to follow – the broadening of political participation – is essentially part of the project of modernization so long delayed in underdeveloped countries. And, as in the case of the developed world, there is no reason to expect that political participation and democracy will resolve class conflict or issues of equity. What is happening is, to my mind, not so new as to require a different theoretical focus, such as the preoccupations of some analysts of post-modernity with cultural fragmentation and the absence of structures. The tensions between individual and collective interests identified in the 1970s are still present in the 1990s. The fear of poverty is as much a preoccupation of the majority of the population as it was in early periods of urbanization. Though some of the bases of collective identity and action may have changed, I do not detect any fundamental shift in what people want and in the mix of individual and collective strategies that they use to obtain their ends.

Urbanization in Historical and Comparative Perspective

This final section provides an overview of some of the major trends in urbanization, comparing the experiences of the United States, France and Britain in the late nineteenth century and surveying the experiences of the developing world in the last 40 years. The aim is to remind ourselves of the historical and comparative context of urbanization in the developed and developing worlds, thus setting the scene for the subsequent discussion of the Latin American cases. We will see that there is no single pattern of urbanization since urbanization reflects a country's specific development path. However, the manner in which developing countries were brought into the world economy shaped, and continues to shape, their pattern of urbanization.

There are important differences in urbanization, even among the advanced capitalist countries, that reflect contrasting patterns of economic development (see Roberts, 1978a). We can appreciate some of the major differences by comparing the cases of Britain, France and the United States, whose patterns of urbanization differed sharply from each other in the late nineteenth century (Table 1.1). These differences shaped the nature of urban politics, of urban stratification and of urban problems in the three countries contributing, it could be argued, to distinctive national cultures.

British urban-industrialization of the nineteenth century was preceded by an almost complete commercialization of agriculture (Landes, 1970). With the advantage of being the first industrial nation, industrial production for a world-wide market absorbed labour and concentrated wage workers in towns and factories throughout the country, but also contributed to the consolidation of London as the dominant centre of government services and even industrial employment (Dyos, 1971). By 1900, Britain had a much higher proportion of its population living in large cities than did France or the United States and London's role as primate city had been strengthened.

Though nineteenth-century French economic development was rapid, it was based to a much greater extent than that of Britain on small-scale craft industry, specializing in luxury products, such as jewellery, glass, porcelain, watchmaking and silk weaving. The French population had low rates of natural increase, while the predominance of small-scale, peasant agriculture supported an extensive rural population and an urban system based on small market towns and regional centres. By 1900, when France was a major industrial power, only 11 per cent of its population was living in large

Table 1.1. Growth of European, United States and Mexican cities between different time periods[A]

	Rate of population growth of country	Rate of urbanization[B]	Growth of largest city	Annual growth rate next 3 cities	% living in cities at start of period	% living in cities at end of period	Index of 3 city primacy at start[C]	Index of 3 city primacy at end
United States 1860–1900 (15 cities)	2.2	1.1	2.7	3.3	10	14.6	1.2	1
France 1860–1900 (6 cities)	0.1	1.1	1.2	1.2	7	11	2.3	2.2
Britain 1860–1900 (11 cities)	1.2	0.5	1.8	1.5	29.8	36.8	2.2	2.5
Mexico 1940–1980 (8 cities)	3	1.6	4.9	4.7	21.9	42	2.6	2.6

[A]For France and Britain, these are cities with a population of 250,000 or more in 1900. For Mexico it is cities with more than 250,000 in 1980.
[B]Urbanization is the annual rate of growth of the proportion living in cities with respect to the total population.
[C]This is the ratio of the largest city to the next three largest cities.
Sources: Mitchell, 1976, Table B4; 1983, Table E9; Garza and Departamento del Distrito Federal, 1987.

cities. Also, the growth of the French cities was slower than that of their British counterparts. Paris was the dominant city and the primacy of the urban system changed little between 1860 and 1900.

Urbanization in the United States contrasts sharply with that of the two European countries. In the nineteenth century, United States economic development was based on the extension of the agricultural frontier and on an industrialization closely linked to agricultural production. Employment in manufacturing and construction had a lesser importance than it did in Britain and employment in the distributive services a greater importance (Browning and Singelmann, 1975). Cities in the United States were bridge-heads for the settlement of the moving frontier (Wade, 1959).

In this context, the proportion of the total population that lived in large cities was small in 1860 and remained small by 1900. No single city dominated the urban system and since the capital, Washington, was not the largest city, the US urban system had neither the levels of economic nor political centralization that characterized Britain and France. However, the rate of population growth, fed by massive immigration from Europe, was high and so was the rate of urban growth. The large United States cities of the late nineteenth century may have represented a small fraction of the nation's population, but they were growing at unprecedentedly high rates with all the attendant problems of overcrowding, lack of infrastructure and social problems.

The waves of immigration from Europe created ethnic distinctions in the cities of the northern United States that supplanted the class distinctions of the European cities. However, the social and spatial mobility of the European ethnic groups meant that ethnicity did not become permanently associated with underprivilege, thus attenuating any ethnic-based class conflict (Lieberson, 1980; Thernstrom, 1964). These conflicts would arise later with the mass migration of African-Americans to northern and mid-western cities that led to a racially-based underprivilege based on prejudice and limited opportunities for social mobility.

The comparison with Mexico serves as a preliminary reminder of some of the differences between European and United States urbanization and that of developing countries in the twentieth century. Population growth is higher in Mexico as is the rate of urbanization. Consequently, the pace of growth of the large cities is extremely high, surpassing even that of the United States. Moreover, Mexico already had a high level of urban concentration by 1940, so that by 1980 the proportion of the population living in very large cities was approaching half the population. Note that Mexico, like the two European countries, has a primate urban system. The predominance of Mexico City remained unchanged between 1940 and 1980.

These historical comparisons should not lead us to overlook the interdependent nature of the urbanization process in different parts of the world. Urbanization is essentially the product of capitalist development and expansion. The contrasts in the development patterns of Spain, Portugal, Britain, the other European powers and the United States are significant because these countries had a major impact on the economies of the underdeveloped world. From the sixteenth century onwards, Britain and the other European powers directly influenced the urbanization of developing countries through imperialism and through investments in transport and infrastructure designed to facilitate the extraction of primary products. The impact of this influence changed over time and with the characteristics of the colonial power. The influence of the United States came later, but by the 1940s the United States had become the dominant trading partner in Latin America and US capital was to become a major source of investment throughout the developing world.

The European and United States forms of economic imperialism were to have a very different impact on the underdeveloped world. Economic imperialism can be defined for our purposes as the search for, and creation of, overseas markets for the products and investments of the metropolitan country (see Brookfield, 1975 for a short review of the different perspectives on economic imperialism, contrasting the emphasis on the search for new markets (Luxemburg) with that on the export of capital (Lenin)). The difference between the European powers and the United States was due, in part, to the different stage of capitalist development at which they were dominant. Britain, for example, was dominant at the stage when industrial production was relatively small-scale and fragmented. The United States, in contrast, dominated the monopoly stage of capitalist development, primarily after the Second World War. In this stage capital was concentrated and centralized first through large industrial conglomerates and banking institutions and, subsequently, through multinational corporations. This international context must be kept in mind when we consider the internal transformations taking place in the underdeveloped countries, since the change in the dominant capitalism has, as its counterpart, a change in the organization and control of production in underdeveloped countries.

The legacy of the different forms of imperialism account, in part, for differences in the contemporary pattern of urbanization in developing countries. The data in Table 1.2 are estimates and should be treated with caution, but they provide a reasonably reliable guide to the differences in the gross patterns of urbanization in major regions of the world. Remember also that there are important variations within the regions. The classifications used in Table 1.2 are based on contrasts in the timing and mode of incorporation into the world economy. These two variables provide a preliminary understanding of the key historical experiences affecting urbanization in the developing world, particularly the varieties of agrarian transformation. I refer to the transformation of existing rural social relations through proletarianization and through breaking down subsistence production.

Incorporation produced many variations in this process, as Wallerstein (1974a, 1980) shows, at times reinforcing existing relationships, at others

Table 1.2. Annual rates of urbanization in the developing world: 1950–1990

Rates of urbanization	Type 1		Type 2		Type 3	Type 4		Type 5
	Temperate South America[A]	Tropical & Middle America[B]	China	Southern Asia[C]	North Africa[D]	Tropical Africa[E]	South-east Asia[E]	South Korea
1950–60	1.2	2.1	5.5	0.8	2	2.3	1.7	2.6
1960–70	0.7	1.8	0	1.2	1.9	2.7	1.4	3.8
1970–80	0.6	1.4	1.7	1.6	1.1	2.8	1.7	3.3
1980–90	0.4	1.1	2.9	1.6	0.9	3	1.8	2.4
Total population growth, 1950–1990	1.6	2.5	1.8	2.2	2.3	2.7	2.2	1.9
% urban population 1990	85.9	70.8	26.2	26.4	43.8	27	28.8	72.1
% total population in urban agglomerations, 1990[G]	40.9	28.9	8.9	9.5	18	6.7	10.4	49.2
% urban growth due to natural increase 1950–1990[H]	69.6	63.1	45.8	62.9	63.1	49.2	57.2	38.3

[A]Temperate South America includes Argentina, Chile and Uruguay.
[B]Tropical and Middle America are the other countries of South America, Central America and Mexico.
[C]Southern Asia includes Afghanistan, Bangladesh, Bhutan, India, Iran, Maldives, Nepal, Pakistan and Sri Lanka.
[D]North Africa includes Algeria, Egypt, Libya, Morocco, Sudan and Tunisia and Western Sahara.
[E]Tropical Africa is all of Africa excepting North Africa and Southern Africa (Botswana, Lesotho, Namibia, South Africa, Swaziland).
[F]Southeast Asia includes Brunei, Cambodia, East Timor, Indonesia, Kampuchea, Laos, Malaysia, Myanmar, Philippines, Singapore, Thailand, Vietnam and Brunei.
[G]Agglomerations are cities with 1 million inhabitants or more in 1990.
[H]This is proportion of urban growth accounted for by vegetative population growth.
Source: United Nations, 1993, Tables A-2, A-4, A11, A16.

introducing archaic ones, as in the 'refeudalization' of Central Europe. Latin America was the area that was earliest incorporated into the European world economy through a radical restructuring of rural social relationships that, over time, generalized wage labour and stimulated the purchase of manufactured commodities. It shows the highest current levels of urbanization and initially high but declining rates of urbanization (Table 1.2).

Four other types of incorporation can be identified from among the geographical groupings in Table 1.2. The first of these types (China and Southern Asia) is the early incorporation of countries, such as China and India which had well-developed internal markets but whose economies were not fundamentally restructured by economic imperialism. In both these countries, internally generated economic changes were slow and colonialism or, in the case of China, neo-colonialism brought no radically new sets of social and economic relationships (Raza et al., 1981; Skinner, 1977). Both the rates and levels of urbanization are low, though the rates of urbanization in China have fluctuated sharply due, in part, to policy changes that encouraged, for a period, the movement of population from the cities to the countryside.

The experiences associated with the third type, those fitting the countries of North Africa, are similar since they, too, were subject to colonialism and without fundamental restructuring, and rates of urbanization are low in this type also. The contrast with China and India is that lacking large internal markets, various countries of this type have been heavily dependent on external trade, resulting in the moderately high levels of urbanization associated with an old urban culture. Janet Abu-Lughod (1980) points out that the focus of urban growth has alternated between coast and interior in North Africa depending on the international context and whether interior or Mediterranean trade routes were favoured.

In the fourth type, colonialism brought a partial restructuring of local economies, resulting in 'islands' of export agriculture or mining amidst subsistence cultivation. The countries of Sub-Saharan Africa and South-east Asia fit this type, though to varying degrees. The level of urbanization is low, but the rate of urbanization is high (for more detailed accounts see Gugler and Flanagan, 1978, and Hart, 1987, for Africa and, for Asia, Armstrong and McGee, 1985, who provide a typology of urban trajectories, and Nemeth and Smith, 1985).

The fifth type also shows high rates of urbanization. It is the most recent form of the incorporation of independent states into the capitalist world economy, that associated with the political economy of the cold war. These are the 'new' Asian countries, of which South Korea is the example in Table 1.2, which became significant locations of foreign investment in the 1950s and 1960s. Though Korea has a long history as an independent state and was colonized by Japan, its incorporation into the capitalist world economy is closely linked to two phenomena, considerable economic and military aid and its proximity to Japan, as it seeks markets and outlets for investment (Nemeth and Smith, 1985; Deyo, 1986).

These different development histories continue to affect the demographic components of contemporary urbanization. Note the differences between the eight regions in Table 1.2 with respect to the importance of migration to urban growth. In the 'old' urban regions such as temperate South America, rural-urban migration contributed a relatively small part to urban growth so that in the period 1950–90 an estimated 30 per cent of urban growth was due to migration. In contrast, South Korea's economic growth has resulted in rapid urbanization in recent decades and in rural-urban migration contributing possibly over 60 per cent of urban growth. Thus, the extent to which rural-urban migrants are a significant characteristic of urban society depends on the stage and pace of urbanization which, in turn, reflects the ways in which different countries have been incorporated historically into the world economy.

Types of historical experience are also significant in forming the social actors in urban development. As Henderson (1986) argues, it is the nature of the state and the balance of social forces within it that, in practice, mediate the impact of the world system on urban development. Non-core countries vary widely in the developmental priorities of their governments with respect, for instance, to housing and urban welfare provision, partly because of variations in the relative strength of the various class groupings that affect these priorities.

Two variables are crucial, and I introduce them to indicate the need to further differentiate the types outlined above. One is the centralization of the state and its capacity to administer its territory in the face of centrifugal forces such as regionalism. The other is the strength of the 'challenge' that the state faces from the emerging urban classes – the working class and also the emerging middle classes.

The contrast between Latin America and South Korea is instructive in this respect. South Korea was born as a highly centralized state, inheriting the traditions of the Japanese colonial bureaucracy. An early and radical agrarian reform destroyed regional agrarian elites, weakening traditional forces that might be opposed to changing the economic status quo (Kang, 1989). Also, Korea industrialized later than Latin America and on the basis of substantial rural to urban migration. The urban working classes in Korea are, then, more 'immature' than those of most Latin American countries and in the face of a strong, authoritarian state have, until recently, been unable to organize to obtain better conditions of work and pay (Deyo, 1986).

Korea became one of the 'developmental' states *par excellence*, as Evans (1989) argues. The state maintains close ties with nationally owned conglomerates that dominate the economy and selectively encourages the growth of dynamic export sectors through financial mechanisms. South Korea, in contrast to the Latin American countries, has, since the 1960s, managed to achieve high rates of economic growth, based on international competitiveness in manufactures, while increasing equity in income distribution (Fajnzylber, 1990; Lee, 1992).

The Latin American states have been independent nations for over a century, but centrifugal forces, generated by regionally based, mainly landed, economic interests, have been strong, though that strength varies considerably from country to country. In Evans' terms, the Latin American states are too embedded in their societies, managing only a partial autonomy. Also, the challenge that the Latin American states have faced from the urban classes has been more powerful than in the case of Korea. Most Latin American countries acquired substantial urban populations earlier than did Korea and in some, such as Argentina, Mexico and Brazil, industrialization had begun by the late nineteenth century.

Also, first European then United States consumption patterns had a pervasive influence throughout Latin America. Thus, it became the region of the developing world whose cultures, whether those of elites or popular classes, most aspired to imitate the lifestyles of the developed capitalist countries. Fajnzylber (1990) points to the difficulties that Latin American consumer aspirations create for producing sustained economic growth since they undermine the austerity that he identifies as an essential element of growth with equity. In South Korea, I suggest, austerity results, in part, from endogenous cultural traditions that were less affected than those of Latin America by incorporation into the capitalist world economy.

Conclusion

This chapter has introduced the basic concepts that will guide the analysis in the remainder of the book. The notions of dependent development and of core-periphery will be used to explore both the relationship between Latin American countries and the advanced capitalist countries and that between dynamic regions and less developed ones within the same country. The basic challenge, however, is to take account of the specific development path of each country while keeping in mind the general forces that determine that development. I have suggested that the analysis of the class struggle, as it develops around the expansion of capitalist production, is the best means to achieve this end. The analysis of the European and US patterns of industrialization and urbanization has served to remind us that there is no single path to economic development. These cases have also illustrated the ways in which political and social forces shape economic development, creating the context which defines and limits the action of the market. Indeed, the expansion of British and American interests overseas is one of the most important contextual elements to keep in mind when, in the remainder of the book, we concentrate on the internal processes of change in underdeveloped countries.

|2|

Urbanization and Underdevelopment Before the Modern Period

This chapter is an outline of the historical origins of the contemporary patterns of urbanization in Latin America. I shall first examine the role of the colonial city in the development of the Latin American economies. This is a convenient step in the argument because it enables us to explore the early effects of European overseas expansion on underdeveloped countries. Also, we can evaluate the historical significance of the traditional practices and archaic institutions that are often thought to be an obstacle to economic development. I shall look at the kinds of changes that occurred even in the slowly moving colonial economy and estimate the extent to which these changes shaped the pattern of change to come, particularly the fragmentation of the subcontinent into a large number of independent states.

The following section will concentrate on the changes which occurred in the nineteenth century when Latin America became more closely connected economically to Europe. It is in this period that contemporary patterns of urbanization in Latin America were shaped as the expansion of primary production for export transformed the agrarian structure. This focus will enable us in the concluding section to examine the divergences in development between regions and subregions of the continent which resulted from the characteristics of the dominant classes, of the labour supply and of the system of production.

With the Spanish and Portuguese conquests, Latin America became a peripheral part of a European economy which was becoming predominantly capitalist in terms of its basic ethos and overall organization. The role of Latin America in this economy was to provide commodities, especially precious metals, needed by the core countries and to produce them as cheaply as possible. Its incorporation into the European economy radically changed social and economic structures of the whole subcontinent. To provide the labour needed to extract export commodities and to service clergy, landowners and the colonial administration, people were redeployed and village economies reorganized. This exploitation of the economy was based, in the main, on what might be termed pre-capitalist forms of production such as forced labour in the mines and workshops, large landholdings worked by tied labour and sharecropping in its various forms.

These aspects of the colonial experience fit Wallerstein's account of the role of the periphery in the expansion of the modern world system in the sixteenth and seventeenth centuries. However, my perspective is closer to that taken by Stern (1988) in his debate with Wallerstein (1988) over the explanatory power of the world system approach. Stern argues that local level forces produced change in Latin America despite the constraints of the world system and, even under colonialism, were as important as the world system in shaping the various paths of development experienced by the different regions of Latin America. I will examine the implications of the core-periphery relationship for the patterns of urbanization that developed in the colonial period and lasted until the early twentieth century.

The analysis of urbanization in different periods provides insight into the economic and political contradictions that developed within Latin America and became potential sources of internally generated transformations. These include the conflicts of interest between the Spanish and, to a much lesser extent, the Portuguese state and colonial elites. In the nineteenth century, there were conflicts between traders and manufacturers interested in developing an internal market and those landholders who depended on keeping the native population tied to its customary position as providers of cheap labour and tribute.

Class interests and class struggles took on different forms in different regions according to the dominant forms of economic enterprise developed in them, and they varied too according to the possibilities of economic expansion and the problems encountered in obtaining labour. We shall see how these factors produced the fragmentation of Latin America into distinct national and subnational units. For more comprehensive accounts, readers can consult Leslie Bethell (ed.), *The Cambridge History of Latin America*, Vols 1–3 on the history of colonial Latin America and from Independence to c. 1870, William Glade (1969), Celso Furtado (1976), and Victor Bulmer-Thomas (1994) on the Latin American economies, and Fernando Cardoso and Enzo Faletto (1979) for an analysis of class and class conflict in producing divergent patterns of development.

The Colonial Period

Urban development was an integral part of both Spanish and Portuguese colonization and the system of cities that developed had as its main object the control and administration of the new domains. Some cities, such as Salvador in Brazil, La Havana in Cuba, Callao in Peru and Veracruz in

Mexico, were established at points which facilitated sea communication with Europe; others, such as Mexico City, Santiago de los Caballeros in Guatemala, Cuzco and Quito, were based on existing urban centres, and in some cases, like Puebla in Mexico and Arequipa in Peru, the cities were founded in locations where there were dense indigenous populations. A comprehensive review of the stages of urban settlement, detailing the urban plans and the differences between Spanish and Portuguese settlement, is provided by Hardoy (1975), who stresses the extent to which the location and design of early urban settlements were experimental; by the mid-sixteenth century, however, a uniform pattern was followed throughout Spanish America and this was reinforced by crown legislation.

Morse (1962, 1971a, 1992) provides a useful characterization of this urban system, contrasting the centripetalism of the European town, which concentrated and organized the commerce of a region, with the centrifugal-ism of the Latin American town, which served to control and administer resources based in the countryside. Morse also discusses the modifications to this characterization that a more complex analysis of urbanization in Latin America would require; for example, colonial towns in Latin America were never simply centres of control and administration but were often developed as part of more comprehensive plans of regional development that included the mining and farming areas (Morse, 1971a).

One of the most striking examples of a colonial town that fostered the commercialization of a wide area is Potosi in present day Bolivia. For many years after 1545 the Potosi mines produced more than half of the world's output of silver and, with a population estimated at over 100,000 people by the end of the sixteenth century, it was the largest city in South America (Hanke, 1956). Assadourian's (1977) analysis of the town's mining econ-omy suggests that it made extensive use of wage labour and stimulated craft and commercial foodstuff production over a large distance (see also Stern, 1988). Apart from the forced labour of Indian villages (the mining mita), the city attracted migrants on a more or less permanent basis from all over the vice royalty of Peru. This type of town development suggests that, even in the sixteenth century, integration into the European economy favoured commodity circulation and undermined the self-sufficiency of local agrarian structures in Latin America.

It is clear, however, that the development of the urban system in colonial Latin America gave primacy to the political and fiscal needs of the empire (Glade, 1969). The urban hierarchy of city and village, often imposed upon pre-existing native jurisdictions and urban institutions, preserved and enforced status distinctions between categories of the population. The cate-gories of Indian, slave, mestizo (of Spanish and Indian parents) mulatto (of Spanish and black parents), and Spaniard had different sets of rights and obligations in terms of tribute, forced labour, taxes, military service, trading and debt contraction. Glade contrasts this form of colonization with Turner's characterization of the North American frontier as a source of economic and political autonomy and innovation. In Spanish America there was merely a geographical and not an institutional frontier since the process of settlement or the opening up of new lands did not free the colonial population from centrally imposed legal and economic restraints.

In this situation, towns in Spanish America (even less perhaps than those in Europe at this period) did not serve to generate economic progress in a 'backward' countryside (Merrington, 1975). The town jurisdiction was not restricted to a specific urban area but included the surrounding countryside up to boundaries of the next urban jurisdiction; towns owned their hinterlands both in the sense of economic proprietorship and in the sense of politico-administrative control (Portes and Walton, 1976). These towns became dominated by the landed classes who resided in them and who used municipal jurisdictions to consolidate and enlarge their estates, often at the expense of native communities (Glade, 1969). The *vecinos* (chartered land proprietors), with rights to participate in municipal government, were few in the early period; in 1561, for example, the municipality of Lima was estimated to have 99,000 inhabitants in both city and hinterland but of these no more than 40 had the title of *vecino* (Portes and Walton, 1976).

Brazil represents a somewhat different case in this period since the Portuguese did not impose as extensive or rigid a system of state control on their dominions as the Spaniards did. There was no densely settled indigenous population in Brazil, nor at first did Brazil seem to offer good prospects of yielding precious metals or other valued commodities. Sugar production for the European market soon developed in the north-east on the basis of imported black slaves. England and other European powers were given important trading concessions. Colonization in Brazil was entrusted much more to private initiative than was the case in Spanish America; moreover, commerce figured prominently in the early economy. Portuguese settlement concentrated along the littoral and mainly in the north; this settlement was managed through relatively independent colonies which were often promoted as business ventures (Glade, 1969).

The relative decentralization of early colonial Brazil meant that towns did not acquire the degree of political and administrative pre-eminence enjoyed in Spanish America. One consequence of lasting significance was that the large plantation acquired considerable importance in north-eastern Brazil as a centre for local administration, economic life and as a place of residence for the wealthy (Schwartz, 1984). The structuring of the economy and polity of the north-east of Brazil around the plantation contrasted with the town-based developments that occurred in the central south with the discovery of gold in Minas Gerais in the eighteenth century. Rio de Janeiro became the administrative centre of Brazil in 1763 as the nearest port to the thriving gold region. A system of towns developed in the interior of the central south stimulating commerce and agricultural production.

The regulation of political and economic life in Latin America by Spain, and to a lesser degree by Portugal, did not mean that the local economies were totally subordinated to the metropolises. Assadourian (1973, 1992) shows how misleading it is to characterize the colonial economy in Latin America as consisting simply of the export of primary products and the import of those commodities (textiles, metal implements, luxury goods) demanded by the colonial middle and upper classes, with the mass of the population subsisting on crafts and foodstuffs produced for domestic consumption. The export mining sector generated backward and forward linkages within the colonies as did others sectors such as transport and leather manufacture. There was a substantial amount of interregional trade taking place within colonial Latin America, both medium- and long-distance. It was this trade rather than either the local or the international markets that Assadourian (1982) views as the main force of change in the colonial economic system. It was based on a large variety of commodities in which production was relatively specialized and regionalized (wine, wheat and corn, potatoes, hides, coarse textiles). The most intense exchanges occurred within regions such as that of colonial Peru, but trade also moved between Peru, other regions of Spanish America and even Brazil. The relative weakness of the Spanish and Portuguese economies, coupled with administrative regulation, did at least afford some protection to trade and manufacture within the colonies, which was to be lost with the coming of independence: 'Breaking in pieces the colonial mediations and articulations, with cannons, guns and banners of liberty, our poor and heroic national revolutions go forward to receive the fighter's reward, the technically more refined domination of the English' (Assadourian, 1973).

One of the clearest examples of the internal transformation of the colonial economy is the impact of mining on the Mexican Bajio in the eighteenth century (Brading, 1971; Wolf, 1957). The requirements of the mines provided a stimulus to other forms of commercial enterprise. Mining products were transformed and handled by large numbers of animals and men who needed to be fed; *haciendas* developed in the Bajio plain to meet these needs. The *haciendas* used labour tied through debt peonage; these peons purchased clothing and other goods in the *hacienda* stores. The labour power of both the commercial *haciendas* and of the mines provided a market for manufacturers, especially textiles. The population growth of the Bajio urban centres was rapid in this period: by 1803, Queretaro had 50,000 inhabitants and, in the same year, Guanajuato was estimated to have 71,000 inhabitants, making it the second largest city in Latin America after Mexico City (Wolf, 1957; Morse, 1974, Tables 1–7).

The Bajio case also illustrates the basic limitations imposed by the colonial system of government on capitalist development. Government officials saw the population of the Bajio towns as a dangerously volatile element in colonial society, for ethnic and status distinctions among them had become blurred as a result of common working conditions (Wolf, 1957). Riots in the mining towns at the end of the eighteenth century led the government to impose restrictive legislation on the free economy of the towns in the interests of public order. This policy should not be seen simply as the reaction of a backward colonial government. As Brading (1971) shows, even the dominant classes in the colonial economy – the large merchants and landowners – had little interest in free economic exchange. To obtain labour or to sell goods within a predominantly subsistence economy required non-market mechanisms of compulsion; these mechanisms, by imposing legal and status constraints on the local population, further restricted the impact of market forces on local production. It has been argued, in this respect, that the form of corporate organization of Indian communities in Mexico and Peru was less a legacy of pre-colonial society than a response to the requirements and pressures of the colonial system (Wolf, 1957; Samaniego, 1974). This was the enduring contribution of the colonial period to the development of the post-independence states of Latin America. It produced a situation in which, as many commentators have pointed out, non-capitalist forms of production and apparently 'archaic' social formations, such as the Indian community and its rituals, were reinforced but with a changed function as a result of the incorporation of Latin America into the capitalist world economy (Wolf, 1957; Frank, 1971; Laclau, 1971; Mallon, 1983; Stern, 1982; Spalding, 1984; Long and Roberts, 1984).

This is the context in which the relationship between urbanization and underdevelopment was established. The internal dynamic of economic transformation in Latin America became linked to the needs and expansion of the European market. Within this territorial division of labour the towns and cities of Latin America had only a limited generative role. As points of initial settlement and conquest and subsequently as centres of administration and of the export trade, towns spread rapidly throughout Latin America in the colonial period. By 1630 there were, according to Hardoy (1975), at least 165 'cities' in Spanish America, but the urban population remained relatively small. By the end of the eighteenth century, Mexico City had over 100,000 inhabitants and six cities had over 50,000 inhabitants – Rio and Salvador in Brazil, Puebla and Guanajuato in Mexico, La Havana in Cuba and Lima in Peru. In general, the concentration of population in urban centres was low; according to the figures assembled by Morse (1974, Table 10), Brazil had some 5 per cent of its population concentrated in its four largest cities in 1803. Aggregating Morse's data for some 30 of the largest cities in Latin America at this time, we find that they contain only about 7 per cent of the population of the continent.

Thus, though the conquest and economic colonization of Latin America were accomplished through a network of urban centres, for most of the colonial period these centres were relatively unimportant in terms of population concentration. It is this fact that gives substance to Morse's characterization of the urban system as centrifugal: cities and towns served merely as administrative centres and as bridgeheads to settlement, while the bulk of the population and the main economic activities lay outside them. The colonial city, Brading (1976) argues, was an alien enclave 'with an elite which in dress, culture and ethnic background differed from the rural masses'. The city was the centre of conspicuous consumption by the elite: the dress, style of life and ornate palaces of the wealthy were one of the chief means of consuming the residue of the colonial economic surplus left to it. This type of expenditure extended also to the church and the religious orders – the major landholders in Spanish America by the end of the colonial period. Thus, Brading calculates that most of the *hacienda* agriculture of the rich Oaxaca valley in Mexico was devoted to providing an income to support the secular priests of Oaxaca and, above all, a large convent in which nuns maintained separate suites of rooms, servants and private dining facilities.

This use of revenue from agriculture or mining meant that the urban economy had a large service sector providing employment for domestic servants, shopkeepers, street vendors, musicians, barbers and so on. Much of this employment was casual, with people moving back and forth from city to countryside. Transport required a large labour force to attend the mule trains and to cart produce and people; in the Argentinian town of Mendoza this 'floating' transport workforce made up 10 per cent of the total (Halperin, 1970). Despite the 'splendour' of the colonial city, contemporaries frequently remarked on the disorderliness, filth and poverty of the majority of the population (Brading, 1976).

There was a certain amount of urban artisan industry, though the importance of this in the urban economy appears to have varied from one place to another. Textiles in Peru were largely produced in the countryside, whereas in Mexico they came from towns such as Puebla or Mexico City. Likewise, Brading reports 8,157 artisans and another 1,384 men engaged in textiles and other productive industry for Mexico City, while in Lima at the same date (1790) there were 1,007 artisans and 60 *fabricantes*; in Lima, clergy and the religious orders numbered 1,306 males and females, and in Mexico City, 1,134.

Though the colonial city played only a marginal role in the expansion of a market economy, it was an integral part of the colonial economic system. As Cardoso and Singer have pointed out, the towns were the organizing and control centres that made possible commercial agriculture and mining (Cardoso, 1975a; Singer, 1973). Despite the apparent isolation and self-sufficiency of the Brazilian sugar plantation, plantation production also depended on a strong urban system. The existence of communities of escaped slaves and the constant danger of slave revolts made planters dependent on the legal and coercive backing of the government (Singer, 1973). The profits of the colonial economy were distributed by means of these urban centres to government, merchants and the church and were protected from pirates and smugglers within the more easily defendable and taxable cities. Mines and plantations depended in the long run on a strong central authority prepared to enforce labour services, impose order and quell revolt. In effect, the situation that developed in Latin America towards the end of the colonial period was almost that of a city-state system; poor interregional communications and a weakly developed interregional division of labour meant that the commercial and landed interests of the different regions depended on the political and administrative power of their local city. Halperin (1970) emphasizes the internal fragmentation of Spanish America produced partly by the difficulties of transport. He cites the high costs of overcoming distance, such as those involved in transporting wine overland from San Juan to Salta in Argentina, a journey of 40 days. The attempts by the Spanish government to impose a more effective central control, by-passing regional centres and regional elites, threatened to undermine the local basis of power and profit. Likewise, the economic interests of the elites of the major colonial centres such as Mexico City and Lima were opposed to those of the less important cities, since they had more direct access to crown monopolies and to the other perks of centralization.

Singer argues that the implication of such a centrifugal city system was the fragmentation of Spanish America into a large number of independent states. These independent states were essentially city states, based upon one of the predominant colonial urban centres. The scope of influence of these urban centres defined the new national units; thus, the antagonism between Buenos Aires and the interior provinces of the old vice royalty of the Rio de Plata led eventually to the fragmentation of the vice royalty between Uruguay, Paraguay, Bolivia and Argentina.

The persistence of Brazil into the nineteenth century as a single territorial unit is at first sight surprising given the size of the country and the existence of regional economic differences. There were important seccessionist movements in the early nineteenth century but these ultimately collapsed as local elites preferred to pursue their interests independently rather than exhaust themselves in long campaigns (Singer, 1973). As late as 1932 the state of Sao Paulo had its own army and fought the federal forces and those of neighbouring states in an ill-fated attempt to defend local interests against federal encroachment. The maintenance of union in Brazil in the nineteenth and early twentieth centuries was made possible by permitting a considerable degree of autonomy to regional elites. Portugal was a relatively weak colonial power and tended to respect local jurisdictions. The central authority was an arbiter between regional elites, and the imperial bureaucracy provided a degree of administrative stability without threatening the control of land and labour by the elites (Halperin, 1970; Cardoso and Faletto, 1969). Since Brazilian society was concentrated near the coast, communication between even the most remote regions was easy enough. Thus, centrifugal forces were weaker in Brazil than in Spanish America.

The pattern of urbanization is only one factor in the complex events which shaped Latin America in the period of independence. The purpose of placing such emphasis on urbanization is to show the importance of the partial and fragmented nature of economic development in the continent for its subsequent evolution. Singer criticizes commentators like Quijano and

Castells, who to his mind place too much emphasis on external factors in explaining the fragmentation of Latin America (Singer, 1973; Castells, 1972; Quijano, 1968). While recognizing that external interests like Britain's played an important part in the balkanization of Latin America, Singer makes the point that it is the internal structure – and in particular the local class struggles based on the requirements of local systems of production – that made external interests so successful. This class struggle against the colonial power united the diverse regional centres of Spanish America; after independence, however, the class struggle became particularized, depending upon the economic configuration of each of the independent states.

Increasing Integration into the European Economy

In the nineteenth century the patterns of urbanization in Latin America changed as the continent became more closely integrated into the European and later the North American economy. The general factors at work were, first, the new technologies of the Industrial Revolution, which raised the productivity of European industry and enabled it to market widely used goods (non-luxury textiles, tools and so on) far more cheaply than the traditional craftsmen of underdeveloped countries could supply them in their own localities. Secondly, new forms of transport substantially lowered the costs of carrying goods overseas or inland (Dyos and Aldcroft, 1969). The time (hence the costs) needed to cross the Atlantic was reduced substantially during the course of the century and regular services could be provided that were not dependent on the vagaries of wind power. Atlantic grain freights fell from 8 shillings a quarter in 1863 to 1s.3d. in 1901 and the Lancashire–Shanghai freight costs fell in approximately the same proportion (Dyos and Aldcroft, 1969). British naval control of the seas ensured that merchant ships travelled more or less unmolested – a situation in striking contrast with earlier centuries when privateers constantly interrupted the galleon trade.

Towards the end of the nineteenth century, railway development in Latin America was reducing the costs of bulk transport of primary products and manufactured goods. In comparison to mule trains and carting, the railway was capable in certain circumstances of reducing the cost of transporting minerals, for example, to as little as a fifth of the rate of animal transport (Miller, 1976). Finally, the Industrial Revolution in Europe and its accompanying growth of urban populations created a new and continuously expanding demand for non-precious minerals and foodstuffs that could be produced in both the tropics and temperate zones.

These changes in technology and patterns of consumption were occurring throughout the nineteenth century and help to explain the timing and nature of economic change in the different subregions and countries of the continent. It was not until the end of the nineteenth century that even the most economically powerful of the Latin American republics, such as Argentina, had fully developed their export economies. Before analysing these divergences in the next section, we need to identify the general trends in urbanization that accompanied them and affected the whole continent.

The initial consequence of independence in Spanish America appears to have been a decrease in the degree of urbanization amounting to what Morse (1992) describes as a 'ruralization'. Morse's statistics suggest that during most of the nineteenth century a lower proportion of Latin America's population was living in the major cities than was the case at the end of the eighteenth century (Morse, 1974, Table 10; Wibel and de la Cruz, 1971). The conditions created by the struggle for independence explain some of this decline, but disturbances of the early independence period were partially offset by the growth of towns offering greater security. Alejandra Moreno Toscano shows how Mexico City and other towns grew in this period through immigration from the rural areas (Moreno Toscano, 1972; Moreno Toscano and Aguirre, 1975). A decline in the degree of urbanization in the nineteenth century is also observable in Brazil, which did not experience the turmoil of the independence movements in Spanish America (Morse, 1974).

Changes in the patterns of urbanization in the nineteenth century are most convincingly explained by the economic processes that were affecting the whole of Latin America in this period. The early nineteenth century in Latin America shows a more intensive exploitation of agricultural resources. Though this exploitation still needed the organization and political support of the towns, the urban infrastructure required was in certain respects a simpler one since the bureaucracy of colonialism was no longer necessary. As political control became regionalized, fewer officials were required. More importantly, the opportunities for commercial agriculture were diversifying, stimulating the colonization of new regions and giving rise to increasing production. The colonial period in Latin America had been one in which staple commodities for export had been precious metals and sugar; in the eighteenth and nineteenth centuries cacao, cotton, coffee, leather, tallow, wheat and non-precious metals were added.

The closer articulation with the European economies may also have affected urbanization by undermining the basis for local manufacturing production. Glade (1969) cites some political propaganda written about 1818 in Mexico which claimed that the opening of the port of San Blas in western Mexico had put some 12,000 persons in the regional craft guilds out of work. The regionalization of Latin America and the diversification of exports changed this situation in two important ways: more people were themselves able to afford cheap mass-produced foreign goods and exporters of primary products found themselves at loggerheads with domestic industry which demanded tariff protection. The landed elites were in effect recruited into this exchange system both as suppliers of primary products and as agents of European or North American importing houses. Substantial profits were derived from the sale of imported manufactured products to the plantations, mines and towns of their region. This close identification of local elites and foreign interests was sealed often enough through intermarriage with foreigners, especially Europeans. Moreno Toscano and Florescano (1974) provide an account of the effect of these processes on Mexican regional development in the nineteenth century.

Class interests developed in the port, frontier and commercial cities based on importing foreign manufactures (such as cotton cloth) or even staples such as cotton itself. These imports worked against the industrial interests of regions such as Puebla and Tlaxcala which specialized in cotton manufacture and in the production of cotton (Moreno Toscano, 1972). When merchants were unable to persuade the government to lower tariffs, they achieved their objective by extensive contraband. Increased competition in the internal market eventually destroyed much local industry (Moreno Toscano and Florescano, 1974).

The impact of competition was probably felt most in the larger cities such as Puebla or Mexico City. There are no adequate data on the relative rates of small-town growth for most of the nineteenth century; it seems likely that the expansion of the export economy stimulated regional economies and the growth of smaller towns, if only because the transport of goods by mule train brought business to them simply through servicing the traffic involved. Offsetting this diversification of local economies was the tendency for export production to be based on relatively self-sufficient economies within plantations, *haciendas* or mines. Halperin (1963) reports the way in which the early nineteenth-century expansion of livestock farming in Argentina served to weaken the small town economy in its vicinity. The livestock *hacienda* became a self-sufficient unit of production in which everything was consumed on the spot; illicit trading in any product was suppressed. Limited investment and innovation in ranches and associated industries (salting and tanning plants) retarded local commercial or service functions. Thus, depending on the structure of exports and the means of handling them, local economies might diversify and expand or stagnate.

As we shift our attention to the late nineteenth and early twentieth century, it is easier to identify a number of trends. This was the time when most Latin American countries were strengthening the control of the central government over provincial centres and when the penetration of remote areas by railway brought these within the system of ports and capital cities. The dominant trend in urbanization in Latin America in the late nineteenth century is the increasing primacy of the urban system – the situation in which the largest city is many times larger than the next largest cities (see Gilbert, 1992a, Browning, 1958, 1972a, and Morse, 1974, 1992, for a general discussion of primacy with reference to Latin America).

Morse (1992) views the imbalances in the urban systems of Latin America as the outcome of the increasing reliance on a plantation economy. The major city acted as a nodal point of the plantation economy and, within the city, administrative, commercial and other service activities developed. As a place of government, the major city attracted elite groups and became the place of residence of the land owning and merchant class. The purchasing power of these countries also became concentrated in the primate city, stimulating further commercial and service activity, construction and some local industrial production. This growth produced migration from the less prosperous agrarian zones. Once a primate city had emerged, moreover, the process of agglomeration tended to become cumulative since other places were starved of the resources needed to follow suit. For example, Mexico City had been relatively stagnant for much of the nineteenth century in the face of the rise of regional centres profiting from the liberalization of trade (Moreno Toscano, 1972). By the end of the century, and as a result of the centralization produced by the development of a railway network based on the capital, Mexico City recovered its economic predominance. In 1900, it was three times as large as the next biggest city, whereas in 1852 it had been just over twice as large (Boyer, 1972, Table 9).

The degree of primacy in the different Latin American countries is also related to the extent of their connection with the world economy. McGreevey suggests that there is a correlation between exports per capita and the degree of primacy (McGreevey, 1971b). Cuba, Argentina and Chile had the highest per capita exports in the 1870s and their city-size distributions had shifted from a log normal distribution to one of primacy far more sharply than those of the other five countries surveyed (Mexico, Columbia, Venezuela, Brazil and Peru). By 1920, most Latin American countries had primate urban systems. Argentina then had the highest primacy of the major countries, whether measured by comparing the size of Buenos Aires with that of the next largest city or with that of the next three largest cities (Browning, 1972a, Table 2). Cuba, Mexico and Chile also had high primacy by this date on both indexes (Morse, 1974, Table 10; Browning, 1972a, Table 2). Peru and Uruguay were similar to these other countries; by 1900 almost one-third of the total Uruguayan population lived in the capital city (Glade, 1969). Although Brazil appears to be an exception to this trend since Rio's predominance had declined by 1920, a bi-primary index (Rio and Sao Paulo compared to the next three largest cities) shows very high primacy (Browning, 1972a, Table 3). The two major countries in which primacy was less evident by 1920 are Columbia and Venezuela (Browning, 1972a, Table 2; Morse, 1974, Table 10).

We can now compare this pattern of primacy in 1920 with that of British and United States investment immediately before this date. British investments in Latin America in 1913 were concentrated as follows: 37.34 per cent in Argentina, 23.21 per cent in Brazil, 16.21 per cent in Mexico, 6.65 per cent in Chile, 4.81 per cent in Uruguay, 4.46 per cent in Cuba, 2.67 per cent in Peru, 1.04 per cent in Guatemala and the rest distributed between the other nine independent countries (Glade, 1969, Table 7.1). United States investments in 1914 were concentrated in Mexico (52.4 per cent), Cuba (17.3 per cent) and Chile (10.6 per cent) (Glade, 1969, Table 7.2).

Foreign investments, especially British, were deployed in ways likely to increase pimacy by helping to provide the administrative and economic infrastructure for exports; this infrastructure was concentrated in the major city through which exports were channelled. US investments were placed in productive enterprises such as mining in Mexico and Chile or plantations in Cuba, but these actually did little to stimulate provincial economic development. Instead, the product was directly transported out by rail and stimulated, in return, imports of manufactured products which were consumed in the major cities. The absence of any pronounced primacy in Venezuela and Colombia in the nineteenth century on the other hand was due to the relatively weak incorporation of these countries into the world economy. This and poor internal transport diminished the primacy effects of the plantation and mining systems in both countries (Galey, 1971; Friedel and Jimenez, 1971). By 1920, however, the absence of primacy in Colombia can be accounted for by a regional pattern of urban development.

Cesar Vapñarsky's (1975) analysis of primacy and the distribution of urban places in Argentina provides a useful way of relating this discussion of the determinants of primacy to the overview, in the next section, of the regional divergences in urbanization. Vapñarsky points out that both high and low primacy is compatible with two very different forms of internal urbanization. As we have seen, in a situation in which there is little internal economic integration and the urban centres have only weak economic relationships among themselves, then one urban centre can become dominant and monopolize the external trade of the whole country. However, primacy can still emerge despite increasing internal economic integration and the rise of hierarchically organized urban systems in various regions. In this case, the primate city (for instance, Buenos Aires in the twentieth century) owes its predominance not to the lack of dynamism among potential competitors but to the continuing advantages of its historic role as the accumulator of the nation's economic resources. This is to suggest that export-led development of underdeveloped countries tends to produce primacy irrespective of the degree of their internal economic integration or development. Likewise, low primacy can be explained either in terms of a high degree of internal economic integration and a relatively low dependence on exports or in terms of a very low degree of economic integration and a relatively low dependence on exports. This last situation is, in fact, the one that McGreevey (1971b) suggests as characterizing the colonial situation in Latin America, where he finds that urban places exhibit a log normal distribution (a balanced distribution without excessive concentration in a few places).

Export dependence does not necessarily imply the absence of strong economic and social organization outside the main city. This economic organization may give rise to class interests distinct from those present in the primate city and these interests may be sufficiently organized to exercise a significant independent effect on the development of the national polity and economy. It is this perspective which is explored in the following section in an attempt to counteract the tendency in some analyses to view economic dependency as a uniform phenomenon.

Divergent Trends in National and Regional Development

The economic forces operating upon Latin America in the nineteenth century made for the creation of export-orientated economies trading in primary products, but the problems of developing these economies were, as Cardoso and Faletto (1969) have pointed out, less economic than political. Basically, these problems were similar to those of the colonial period: sufficient labour had to be secured for the expansion of the plantation system or mining and land had to be made available. Both needs required 'political' rather than 'economic' solutions in countries in which, as we have seen, a free market in labour and land had not developed. Coercion at local and national level was necessary to secure labour and to 'open up' new lands for cultivation, usually by appropriating them from existing users. To obtain these ends, the economically dynamic classes (foreigners and nationals linked to the export economy) needed to ally themselves with more traditional interests, such as the military, governmental officials or landowners with unproductive land. The composition of these alliances and these classes differed from country to country and contributed to divergences in their patterns of development. Perhaps more significant still for these divergences were differences in local endowments of labour and land and in the system of export production.

Following this line of analysis, Cardoso and Faletto (1969) provide a general picture of the different paths of development taken by Latin American countries in the nineteenth century. Among the most important variables they perceive are: (a) the economic dynamism of the export staple(s) and its likelihood to encourage economic diversification, giving rise to new social groups and to the beginnings of an urban-industrial economy; (b) the relative cohesiveness of the dominant class and the capacity of this class to fashion the institutions of the national state to its economic ends; and (c) the strength of foreign interests. They contrast the development paths of Brazil and Argentina and point to the relative cohesiveness of the dominant classes in Argentina based on the efficient commercial exploitation of land for the export market (cattle and cereals) and also to the relative fragmentation of those classes in Brazil. The dominant classes in Brazil represented distinctive and powerful regional economic interests in such states as Minas Gerais, Sao Paulo and Rio Grande do Sul; moreover, the planters of the north-east retained considerable local power. In this situation, the dominant classes in Argentina were able to effect a relatively more thoroughgoing modernization of the economy and society than was possible in Brazil. Cardoso and Faletto also explain how in some countries (mainly in Central America) cohesion of the dominant classes is high but local export interests are relatively inert and often subordinate to what might be described as foreign enclave production.

An economic enclave exists when a system of production has no linkages into the economy of the region or nation in which it is located. An example of this is Klaren's (1973) description of the sugar plantations of the north coast of Peru, where the cane was milled on the plantation, the sugar was exported along the company's railway and port and the workers' subsistence was provided through the company store. Though an enclave rarely exists in pure form (largely because the wages of workers are spent in the surrounding economy and the enclave gives contracts for construction work or the like), it represents a type of production which, while under foreign control, does little to diversify the local economy or contribute to capital formation within it. The relative dominance of enclave production in a nation's economy consequently hinders the development of a national bourgeoisie.

We can advance this analysis by examining briefly the concrete relationship between systems of production, the rise of the state and class conflict in four Latin American countries (Argentina, Brazil, Mexico and Peru) used by Cardoso and Faletto to illustrate differences in nineteenth-century development. Argentina was the most urbanized and modernized of Latin American countries; Brazil, though more unevenly developed with strong regional elites, had the economically dominant form of production in local hands; Mexico was an 'intermediate' case where foreign ownership of production was important but where a strong national state developed and national interests remained strong in certain sectors of the economy; Peru was the classic case where foreign interests owned the bulk of export production.

Argentina exhibited considerable internal economic development, including industrialization, by the beginning of the twentieth century, based on its staple exports of wheat and meat. This pattern was reflected in a pattern of urbanization in which a primate city (Buenos Aires) existed within a fairly well integrated regional system of towns. In the material that follows, I want to draw attention to two factors that influenced this pattern of development – the system of production of the staple crops and the constant need to obtain and control labour.

We can look first at the expansion of livestock farming in the beginning of the nineteenth century, which depended on finding ways of recruiting and stabilizing the labour force (Halperin, 1963). The *hacendados* came to dominate local society, acting as magistrates and using legislation against vagabondage to discipline their workers. Control of government in Buenos Aires assured the livestock owners control of their labour; it also enabled them to extend their grazing grounds as new territory was 'rescued' by government action from marauding Indian groups. Livestock investment in one form or another became the basis of the power of post-independence elites in Argentina. These elites were closely allied with foreign merchants – particularly the British – who organized the commercialization and financing of the livestock operation and also the importation of manufactured products, particularly cloth.

In other regions of Argentina, landholders emerged with a similar interest in the control of labour and in obtaining finance for their operations. Jorge Balan (1976) has analysed the case of the sugar producing area of Tucuman, in the north-west of Argentina at the end of the nineteenth century: plantations were large and processing was centralized in modern mills which provided the goods and services required by the workers. Small-town commerce and industry were undermined by this economy and wealth became concentrated in the city of Tucuman. Tucuman was the residence of the planter elite and served as the commercial centre for sugar and as a transport node. The profits of production were not invested in developing local industry and their developmental impact on the region was slight. There was little consciousness of regional interests because of the polarized situation of sugar cane production and the lack of a plurality of regional interests (Balan, 1976). However, Tucuman had an important impact on national developments and the two presidents of Argentina between 1874 and 1890 (the period in which large-scale international migration began) were from Tucuman. Balan points out that the success of the sugar economy depended on the political power of the sugar elite. In the absence of an abundant cheap labour supply locally, the planters relied on various forms of coercion to obtain labour; they also needed railways to market the sugar. The Tucuman planters thus became active in national politics, both by consolidating their local power and obtaining the railway and by forming alliances with financial groups in Buenos Aires which invested in sugar production.

The international migrations that populated the Pampas and were the basis for the rapid growth of Buenos Aires were also conditioned by the cohesion and political power of these dominant classes. One of the aims expressed in government circles and by the newspapers of Argentina for encouraging immigration was that it would serve to populate the interior in ways similar to the homestead policies of the United States (Scobie, 1964). It is historically doubtful whether the Homestead Act of 1862 had the effect on the settlement of the American West that Argentinian observers supposed, and it is certainly the case that very few of the millions of migrants that came to Argentina at the end of the nineteenth century and the begin-

ning of the twentieth became homestead farmers. Under pressure from large
landowners and land speculators, the government did not enact any effective homestead legislation until it was too late to help the immigrant and it
gave little support to colonization. Instead, the immigrants were used,
directly and indirectly, to open up farming lands and develop large-scale
wheat farming for the benefit of large landed and commercial interests.
Land appreciated so enormously in value with the extension of the railways
and with colonization that landowners could retain their land, renting it on
short-term contracts to immigrants. Labour for the harvests was partly provided by seasonal migrations from Italy.

Although Scobie (1964) emphasizes the poverty of the wheat farmers and
their economic dependence on the four big wheat exporting firms in Buenos
Aires, the expansion of wheat cultivation undoubtedly stimulated economic
development at the local level. Argentinian wheat farming did not produce
the extensive economic linkages that occurred in the mid-west of the United
States, but the system of wheat production, based on small-scale commercial producers dependent on the market for many commodities, was conducive to regional development. Gallo (1974) shows how the province of
Santa Fe expanded on the basis of wheat farming and of foreign immigration. Towns, as well as cities, grew fast, literacy rates improved and the
socio-occupational structure diversified. Gallo compares this wheat zone
with a wool producing zone to show that in the wool zone there was a more
scattered population and proportionately less industrialization. Elsewhere,
as in Mendoza, small-scale commercial farming based on wine began to
flourish by the end of the nineteenth century giving rise to a diversified economic structure and a well integrated network of towns and cities (Balan,
1976).

The cohesion of the dominant classes centralized political and economic
control in Buenos Aires. The expansion of the export economy generated
the resources that permitted the rapid growth of Buenos Aires in construction, service employment and, by 1895, industry. Though the most important industries were linked to agriculture, industrial production increased
over eight times between 1895 and 1914 (Cortes Conde and Gallo, 1967).
In the circumstances, it is not surprising to discover that so many immigrants either stayed in Buenos Aires, their port of arrival, or ended up there.
The conditions of life on the Pampas were not attractive and the government did little in the early period to encourage people to move out of the
city. By 1914, Buenos Aires had 1,576,000 inhabitants, or approximately
20 per cent of the total national population (Lake, 1971). At this date, more
than 2,300,000 of the country's population had been born abroad and three
out of four adults in Buenos Aires were foreigners (Scobie, 1964). The abundant labour supply encouraged investment in manufacturing and provided
the means to build the railways, to man the docks and develop the city.
Balan (1973) lays stress on the economic dynamism of Buenos Aires in this
period, arguing that its growth was due to the expansion of economic

opportunities in the city rather than to the failure of agricultural settlement policies.

My argument here is that the development of a strong, centralized state is partly to be explained by the extent to which the dominant classes needed to control and develop central government to expand their economic interests. Control of labour and the sponsoring of international migration usually require the agency of a strong central government. In the Brazilian case, however, it was the state of Sao Paulo, and not the federal government, that organized the massive European immigrations needed to power the coffee boom. To achieve this, Sao Paulo developed a powerful government apparatus by the beginning of the twentieth century. Indeed, so effective was this apparatus that Robert Shirley (1978) argues that this was one of the main reasons for the orderliness of Sao Paulo's growth when contrasted with that of Manchester, England. For a long time coffee production had been a more attractive proposition than sugar, as indicated by the increasing transfer of the slave population from the north-east to the coffee areas of the central south (Leff, 1972). Stolcke (1988) describes the various strategies, such as sharecropping, used by the coffee planters to secure a labour force in the face of the emancipation of the slaves. Most of these strategies left direct control of production in the workers' hands enabling them to resist the owners' demands for increased productivity. Only mass immigration from Europe would enable owners to overcome this obstacle to increased profitability by providing ample supplies of wage labour.

At the end of the nineteenth century, the rate of immigration into Brazil, mainly to Sao Paulo state, sometimes exceeded immigration into Argentina and averaged over 100,000 immigrants a year between 1888 and 1897 (Graham, 1972). The fluctuations in immigration into Brazil were closely related to economic conditions in Italy and in the United States, the alternative destination for immigrants. When coffee prices fell and production slowed down, many immigrants left Brazil for Italy or Argentina; between 1902 and 1910 more than 330,000 immigrants arrived in the Sao Paulo port of Santos, but as a consequence of re-embarkation the total gain for the period was only 16,667 (Dean, 1969).

Conditions of work on the coffee plantations were bad and pay low; consequently, there was a substantial turnover in labour as migrants returned to Italy, sought opportunities elsewhere in the rural areas or went to the city (Hall, 1974). The profits of the coffee economy and the attractiveness of investment in coffee were to a considerable extent due to the presence of this abundant, cheap labour force (Lopes, 1977). The system of production of coffee, however, does not seem to have stimulated a rapid urban or industrial development of Sao Paulo state. After 50 years' expansion of the coffee frontier in Sao Paulo, the non-agricultural labour force in the state was only 37 per cent of the whole in 1920; only 4 per cent of the state's population lived in the capital in 1890, and 11 per cent in 1900 (Katzman, 1977, 1978). Likewise, the early growth of the city of Sao Paulo was, in comparison with the federal capital, Rio de Janeiro, predominantly based on service rather than industrial employment. In 1893, approximately 63 per cent of the labour force of Sao Paulo was employed in transport, commerce and domestic service, and scarcely 7 per cent in manufacturing industry (Fausto, 1976).

Over time, the growth of the coffee economy did become the basis for rapid urban and industrial growth. The coffee plantations remained in national hands even though the financing and exporting of coffee were controlled by foreign companies. The planters were resident in the state and pushed for the development of the necessary infrastructure – roads, railways and power plants (Dean, 1969). The availability of a literate and abundant labour force in the city and towns, as well as on the plantations, encouraged investment in the production of goods that could compete relatively easily with imports (construction materials, drinks, textiles and shoes).

The cities of the central south, Rio de Janeiro and Sao Paulo, grew more rapidly than those of the north-east. By 1900, the combined population of Rio and Sao Paulo was almost three times greater than that of Salvador and Recife, whereas in 1819 the latter had a larger combined population (Conniff, et al., 1971). Sao Paulo's growth between 1872 and 1900 was 8.3 per cent a year compared with Rio's annual rate of 3.7 per cent in the same period. In 1890, 22 per cent of the city of Sao Paulo's population was foreign born, while in the state of Sao Paulo, 5.4 per cent was foreign-born (Fernandes, 1969). By 1920, 36 per cent of Sao Paulo's population of 579,033 people was foreign born and 18 per cent of the state's population was born abroad (Graham, 1972, Table 8).

Although occurring at a slower pace than in Argentina, the diversification of the economy in Brazil was also based on an export crop. What was to differentiate the Brazilian experience, however, was the persistence of powerful and distinct regional interests alongside the dominant interest (Sao Paulo coffee exports were responsible for something like 65 per cent of the value of the country's exports). The regionalism of the dominant classes in Brazil was based, until the 1930s, on the relative self-sufficiency of the regional systems of political and economic organization. The three most economically dynamic states – Sao Paulo, Minas Gerais and Rio Grande do Sul – maintained a high degree of internal elite cohesion and counterbalanced each other in the federal system (Love, 1975; Wirth, 1975).

The coffee boom reinforced the underdevelopment of the north-east. Commercial enterprises and labour were tied to the north-east in a situation in which the rates of return on their dominant activities were declining. The relatively low rates of out-migration were partly due to transport costs. The supply of labour was generally assured and fixed in the north-east by paternalistic relationships between planter and dependent peasantry, but the supply also depended on political power. The landed elites of the north-east maintained control of regional administration well into the twentieth century, and even during the Vargas regime of the 1930s they sought to retain their influence in national politics to avoid labour legislation hostile to their interests (Lopes, 1976).

Low rates of out-migration meant that there was little stimulus to rationalize production, to convert to new crops or to consolidate holdings (Leff, 1972). The disadvantages of the north-east in these respects were increased by membership of the same political unit as the central south. The north-east was unable to adjust exchange rates to protect its sugar and rice and, since these rates were based on the saleability of coffee, Brazilian sugar was priced out of many markets.

Thus, the emergence of more dynamic economic activities in other parts of Brazil did not produce structural change in the depressed areas of the north-east. Instead, involution occurred and the dominant system of production was maintained, but with an increase in subsistence and labour-intensive activities.

Diverse and often conflicting interests among regions meant that the dominant economic groups (the Paulista coffee interests) could not pursue as coherent a project of economic modernization at the national level as could their Argentinian counterparts. Alliances and counter-alliances were to characterize Brazilian federal politics and to lead, as we shall see in the next chapter, to a somewhat different approach to industrialization than was to be the case in Argentina.

We can now look at two cases – Mexico and Peru – in which the dominance of foreign interests in production was more pronounced than in the case of Argentina and Brazil, with economic enclaves such as mines, sugar plantations and cattle ranches directly linked by rail and ship to the foreign metropolis. The pattern of urbanization associated with enclave production is usually seen as one in which the primate city grows as a service centre to the export economy, in which there is little industrialization and in which regional urban centres decline or stagnate. In Mexico and Peru, the situation was more complex and mercurial than this model suggests. The class conflicts arising from the expansion of export production became significant factors in shaping national development in both countries. Each had substantial indigenous populations so their capacity for providing labour to power the export industries was quite different from that of Argentina and Brazil. However, the supply of labour in Mexico differed from that in Peru, which meant the development of relatively strong and weak central governments, respectively.

Mexico's pattern of economic development and urbanization in the nineteenth century (Moreno Toscano, 1972) showed marked regional differentiation. The by-passing of the Mexico City-Veracruz trade axis after independence created opportunities for both legitimate and illicit trade among the small ports and regional centres. Guadalajara, situated to the north-west of Mexico City and beyond the capital's sphere of influence, was well placed to take advantage of commerce on the Pacific coast and to organize the trade of the diversified agriculture of its region. In Guadalajara, the urban growth of the nineteenth and early twentieth centuries was based on small and medium sized enterprises and a dispersed structure of ownership. Although the region of Guadalajara did contain large landholdings, it was also an important area of small and medium sized farms, of commerce and of craft production. Guadalajara was also the fastest growing Mexican city in the last half of the nineteenth century, far exceeding Mexico City though remaining by 1900 about a third of the capital's size of 345,000 (Boyer, 1972, Table 2).

Other nineteenth-century examples of regional urban development in Mexico were the rise of the northern industrial centre of Monterrey and the growth of Merida in the Yucatan. The stimulus for both these regional centres was the American Civil War. In Monterrey's case the Civil War led to a substantial rise in commerce through Texas to the Mexican Gulf ports which stimulated cotton production in the nearby states. In the Yucatan, cotton production also began on a large scale with the Civil War. Both centres developed independently of Mexico City and their growth continued in the late nineteenth century on the basis of new forms of production – sisal in the Yucatan and manufacturing in the Monterrey area. Merida's growth in the late nineteenth century was second only to that of Guadalajara while Monterrey's growth in the early twentieth century was equally fast (Boyer, 1972).

The development of the Mexican railway system reinforced certain features of this regional pattern of urbanization (Moreno Toscano, 1972). The railways favoured export crops and indirectly undermined local systems of small-scale foodstuffs production (Moreno Toscano, 1972). Thus, the ending of mule transport and the carriage trade deprived many small urban centres of their means of livelihood. The railways made possible, however, the rise of other centres based on export production: the cattle and cotton producing areas of the north of Mexico were centralized through a contiguous group of cities – Torreon, Lerdo and Gomez Palacio. This urban group was not part of Monterrey's zone of influence and both zones became closely and independently integrated into the US market by means of the Mexico-United States railways network. Rail links to the sea and to the hinterland contributed to Merida's dominance in Yucatan. Also, new cities began to emerge to service areas producing tropical export crops: Uruapan, Ciudad Guzman and Cordoba are examples that Moreno Toscano (1972) has used to illustrate the changes in Mexico's pattern of urbanization.

Friedrich Katz (1974) has traced the social and political implications of this regional differentiation and attributed them to factors such as the abundance or scarcity of local labour, the type of production and the quality of the land. He surveys the forced labour practices of the sisal and other export crop *haciendas* in the south of Mexico where, in the absence of local labour, outside labour was tied through debt and physical coercion. He has contrasted this situation with that of the sugar *haciendas* of the centre of Mexico in which such practices were unnecessary owing to the abundance of seasonal labour produced by dispossessing villages of their lands. In the north of Mexico, the mines, cattle ranches and export crop *haciendas* had to offer the workers relatively favourable wages and, in other cases, share-cropping facilities in order to offset the competitive labour market which included the southern United States.

In the centre and south of Mexico, the significance of state power for the expansion of export production is well brought out by Wallace Thompson's account of the situation in 1921: 'So valuable did this labour become that bribery and government coercion, special detectives and policemen had to be called in to capture and return the peons who ran away from their contracts and judges and mayors of towns were induced to arrest the runaways' (Katz, 1974). In the north, landed and mining interests had less reliance on state coercion and, to a greater extent than the landowners of the south and centre, the northern elites joined in the revolutionary uprisings against the Porfirian regime (Katz, 1974).

The importance of the export industries did not, however, weaken industrialization. In the later nineteenth century there was a substantial industrialization that received support and tariff protection from the Porfirian regime (Haber, 1992). By the turn of the century, Mexico was one of the most industrialized of Latin American countries. With the success of the revolution the newly dominant classes inherited and strengthened central government and continued to use it to industrialize.

In Peru, the dominant export enterprises (sugar, cotton and mining) developed in areas away from the major concentrations of population; although dispossession of land did occur, its impact was less than it was, for example, in creating the sugar *haciendas* of the Morelos region of Mexico. Moreover, the supply of labour for the export enterprises came mainly from free peasant communities. These communities had reached a point at which their increasing numbers on limited land had forced the peasants to seek work further afield to supplement their local craft and agricultural activities (Long and Roberts, 1978, Mallon, 1983). Although the *enganche* (a form of debt labour) was used to recruit labour for the mines and plantations, there is little evidence that such enterprises had any need to invoke the law or the government to enforce these contracts (Scott, 1976). Instead, the process of recruitment was handled by intermediaries who were usually the richer farmers or traders from the villages. In this context there was less pressure from the dominant foreign or national interests to strengthen central government: the mines and plantations provided most of their own infrastructure and local development (roads and irrigation) was left, for the most part, to the initiative of local communities.

The expansion of sugar exports did lead, however, to new forms of class conflict in one of the most important of the sugar areas of the north coast – the Chicama valley (Klaren, 1973). This valley was dotted with small but flourishing towns which had developed on the basis of Indian communities whose communal landholdings had been partly redistributed with the lib-

eral reforms of independence. In the same valley there were over 50 small
and medium sized sugar *haciendas* and *fundos*. The towns prospered on
commerce and on independent farming of crops such as corn, wheat, rice
and other staples. By 1920, travellers commented upon the extent to which
these towns had decayed and attributed their decline to the expansion of
sugar cultivation (Klaren, 1973). Sugar cultivation had, in this period,
become concentrated into large combines; over 50 sugar holdings had been
concentrated by 1927 into three largely foreign-owned companies. The concentration of holdings was accompanied by increasing production for
export; whereas the old *haciendas* often left a substantial part of their land
uncultivated, the new companies brought all land under cultivation. To do
this, they secured control of water resources for irrigation, thus depriving
the independent towns of an adequate supply. This concentration of land-
holding ended by undercutting the fortunes of the provincial capital,
Trujillo. In the first stage of the expansion of the sugar industry, Trujillo and
other urban centres had prospered, supplying food to the workforce of the
plantations and distributing imported manufactures; but, in due course, the
large plantations became self-sufficient. The largest of these, Casa Grande,
operated its own port facilities through which goods were directly imported.
Soon the competition from the plantation's stores was arousing bitter hostility from Trujillo merchants (Klaren, 1973).

These events created a significant regional dimension in Peruvian politics.
The large corporations that controlled the plantations needed government
approval to consolidate their operations; for example, Casa Grande's port
operation was a government concession. Representatives of the companies
were active in Peruvian national politics to keep government from interfer-
ing with new economic interests. At the same time, the activities of the companies aroused hostility from other regional groups; local merchants and
professionals were opposed to the foreign-owned monopolies and were
joined in opposition by railway workers whose jobs were threatened by the
plantation's own railway operations and by the workers in the sugar mills
and cane fields. These workers had become increasingly conscious of their
class position through claims for better working conditions and wages
(Klaren, 1973).

Klaren attributes the origins of the powerful populist political party,
APRA, to this conjuncture of class interests on the north coast of Peru.
However, even in Peru the expansion of export production often stimulated
a region's urban growth. In other areas where enclave production was
strong, as in the mining towns of the central region of Peru, miners'
incomes and revenues from contracts for food supplies, transport and construction for the mining company substantially raised regional income
levels (Long and Roberts, 1984). This flow of cash made possible the diversification of village economies and the expansion of crafts; many of these
activities were essentially new ones, such as repair workshops for cars and
trucks.

I have stressed this expansion of opportunities created by the export economy since it would be difficult otherwise to understand why the dominant agro-mining classes in Latin America who were opposed to tariff protection for industry should receive such substantial popular political support. In Argentina, even those classes not directly linked to the agro-exporting economy still supported a policy of free trade on the grounds that it helped agriculture and promoted 'healthy' competition for local manufacturers. This explains why labour unions in Argentina at the end of the nineteenth century were against tariff protection for industry, as were most of the urban middle classes (Cortes Conde and Gallo, 1967).

Ethnicity and Inequality

The immigration of Europeans, the bringing of large numbers of Africans to work as slaves on the plantations and the presence of diverse indigenous cultures created the bases of multi-ethnic nations in Latin America. Colonization and the nineteenth-century social and economic structures that replaced those of the colony forged a persisting link between the status of being Indian or of being of African descent and occupying an economically and socially marginal position in the new nations.

The Indian populations of Latin America have retained a sense of their cultural identity to the present, but this identity has been as much a source of stigma and disadvantage as it has been a basis for resistance to elite domination or the formation of multi-ethnic nations (Urban and Sherzer, 1991). With independence and the emergence of nation states, the ethnic difference between governing elites and indigenous populations was seen by those elites as an obstacle to progress. Part of the issue was the supposed ignorance and superstition of the indigenous population, who lacked literacy in Spanish or Portuguese and were strangers to European culture. For instance, the Bolivian Census of 1900 noted that its estimate of 48.4 per cent of the population being Indian (Indígena) indicated that the 'Indian race' was in the process of gradual extinction, adding (my translation) 'if this may be a good is a question of the reader's judgement, considering that if there has been a factor holding back our civilization, it is due to the indigenous race, essentially unamenable to any kind of innovation and to any progress' (*Censo General de Bolivia*, 1904).

Furthermore, indigenous cultures posed a particular threat to elite projects of nation building in that they fostered local and regional allegiances, not national ones. The nineteenth-century liberal constitutions further undermined the collective identity of indigenous peoples by favouring individual rights to property over collective ones, by enshrining Spanish and Portuguese as the official languages and by promoting central power against regional autonomy. Most of the Latin American constitutions of the nineteenth and early twentieth centuries made no mention of indigenous populations or their rights. Instead, the indigenous population was subsumed into the general class of *campesino*.

In this context, Indian ethnic identity was formed through the particular relations between the indigenous peoples of Latin America and their nation-states (Urban and Sherzer, 1991). These relations varied by historical period and by region, consisting of different mixes of three policies: acculturation, repression/elimination or paternalistic protection. Where the indigenous population was numerous and provided a labour force for the elites, acculturation interspersed with repression was usually the dominant relationship. Conversion to Catholicism, intermarriage with Europeans and forced participation in the market economy produced substantial *mestizo* populations even in the countries of densest pre-Colombian indigenous settlements: Mexico, Central America, Colombia, Ecuador, Peru and Bolivia. The extent of acculturation varied according to the distance of the Indian populations from the centres of colonial power. Mallon (1992) contrasts the co-optation of Indians in central Mexico with the bi-polar situation of Peru where the highlands were Indian and the coast white, black and *mestizo*. By 1940, for instance, those speaking an Indian language had become a small minority in Mexico. The Mexican Census of that year reported 15 per cent of Mexico's population as speaking an Indian language and half of these also spoke Spanish (Direccion General de Estadistica, 1943).

Government protection of Indian populations became more common in twentieth-century Latin America, but it was extended most readily where these populations were a relatively small minority of the nation and occupied lands that were not commercially important. As in the case of Mexico's *Instituto Indigenista*, this state protection was often paternalistic, allowing little autonomy to Indian groups, especially in their external relations. Elimination, amounting to genocide, has also been practised to deal with political opposition among Indians in those states in which they are numerous and, for that reason, feared by the dominant *mestizo* elite: El Salvador in 1932 and Guatemala between 1979–84 (Adams, 1991). The Guatemalan case is the clearest example of the persistence of Indian identities in the face of the attempts of the state to incorporate the Indian populations as subordinate members of the nation through simultaneous policies of repression and acculturation (Smith, 1990).

Indigenous populations were eliminated and driven onto marginal lands in those countries where they were relatively few in number, not easily incorporated as a labour force and posed an obstacle to the expansion of commercial farming, as happened in nineteenth-century Argentina and Chile. In Brazil, in contrast, the size of the country and the concentration of the non-indigenous population along the coast meant that indigenous peoples could survive in the interior, with some tolerance from the state, until the frontier expansions of the mid-twentieth century (Maybury-Lewis, 1991).

In this context, to be Indian and to retain an indigenous language and customs meant being rural and, from the point of view of elites, backward. By the mid-twentieth century, identifiable 'Indian' populations survived mainly in economically poor rural areas. The collective identity of Indian populations was weakened by their fragmentation into village communities that were often hostile to each other and differentiated by dialect and customs. The external relations that each community had with the state, the market and landowners contributed to this differentiation and was also a source of internal division. Even in Mexico, after a Revolution that emphasized the pre-Colombian origins of the nation, to be classed as Indian was to be classed as poor and uncultured. Friedlander (1975) shows how in one 'Indian' village of Mexico there was little sense of a collective Indian identity. The traditions that the villagers had were not pre-Conquest but were adapted from the customs of the colonial and post-colonial elites. Villagers put little emphasis on their 'Indian' identity because, for them, it was a derogatory term.

Wasserstrom (1983) shows, in contrast, the considerable resilience of Mayan communities and Mayan culture in Central Chiapas. In Chiapas, Indian communities may be poor and rarely organize collectively in defence of their interests, but this, as Wasserstrom argues (1983), is not a question of world view or of anything inherent in community organization but of the external relations, particularly with the state, to which they are subject. The Chiapas area became in 1994 and 1995 the centre of world attention as a result of the *Zapatista* movement which seized temporary control of the provincial capital demanding respect for the rights of Indian communities and more democracy both locally and nationally.

The other major components of race/ethnic differentiation in Latin America have been the populations of African descent. These have been concentrated in Brazil where slave labour was the basis of the sugar economies of the north-east. By 1850, almost half the population of Brazil was classified as 'Black', and were concentrated in the north-east. However, there are also significant Black populations in those other countries that needed labour for the plantation economy and did not have a ready supply of indigenous labour: some of the Central American countries, Venezuela and Ecuador.

Being Black, like being Indian, has meant disadvantage in Latin America. In Brazil, the racist doctrines that dominated elite thinking at the end of the nineteenth century depicted Blacks as genetically inferior and a handicap to progress (Skidmore, 1974). Progress was associated with the disappearance of Blacks through miscegenation, leading to a 'Whitening' of the population. The numerical inferiority of Whites, who in 1872 were 38.1 per cent of the population of Brazil, contributed to the acceptance of a mixed category unlike the situation in the United States where any drop of Black blood tended to fix the individual as 'Black' in the eyes of others. By 1980, 'Whites' were classed as 54 per cent of the Brazilian population, 'Browns' as 39 per cent and 'Blacks' as 6 per cent (Wood and Carvalho, 1988, Table 6.1).

Conclusion

I have argued that it is the particular way in which capitalism has expanded overseas that has produced economic and social backwardness among the local population in terms of the persistence of archaic institutions and an uneven pattern of development in which vast cities exist alongside stagnant provincial economies. We have also found, however, that economic growth has important transformative effects even when it is based on the export of primary products and confined to forms of production which do not develop strong linkages into the local economy. We must, then, pay particular attention to the way in which capitalism expands within underdeveloped countries, and not simply focus on the mechanisms through which the dominant world economies have extracted a surplus from underdeveloped countries.

For this reason, the emphasis in this chapter has been on the various patterns of development that are possible when countries occupy a similar, subordinate position within the world economy. Latin American countries in the nineteenth century were underdeveloped in terms of their low levels of productivity in agriculture and in industry and in terms of the poverty of the mass of their inhabitants. It is important, however, to recognize that economic growth did take place throughout the continent. This growth created new opportunities for national and foreign entrepreneurs; but in order to make use of these opportunities the entrepreneurs had to bring new social and political forces into play. Labour had to be recruited and when it was not available locally it was brought from abroad. European immigration, slavery and the migration of indigenous groups to the mining camps and plantations contributed to the ethnic diversity of Latin America and to ethnic-based inequalities.

Political institutions had to be shaped to serve the needs of the new production. Rival elites had to be conciliated or defeated. These processes constitute the dynamic of the situation of dependency in Latin America. The forces that are brought into being by the drive to expand production are not passive participants in the next stage of the development struggle; and it is to this participation and its impact on industrialization that we now turn.

|3|

Urbanization and
Industrialization

In this chapter the analysis departs from the historically-based discussion of the uneven pattern of capitalist development in Latin America to a consideration of contemporary patterns of urban life. This transition will be made through surveying the stages in Latin America's industrial development in this century. Urban-based industrialization has become the dominant economic force in Latin America, gradually displacing in importance the rurally based agro-mining sector. The growing importance of industry raises two crucial issues for the development of my argument. First, we need to examine the way in which industrialization created new situations of dependency by altering the role of underdeveloped countries from one of suppliers of raw materials and foodstuffs to one of consumers of imported technology. Consequently, much of the analysis in this chapter is aimed at uncovering the internal and external factors that have shaped industrialization in such a way that it is not a force enabling Latin America to rival economically the advanced capitalist countries. Secondly, we need to examine the new political and social forces brought into play by industrial development since these forces have helped to mould contemporary developments by introducing new forms of class conflict and new class alliances and by influencing state policy.

In the twentieth century, the export sector continues to be an important source of foreign earnings and of finance for industrial development in underdeveloped countries; but developing the internal market for manufactured products becomes an increasingly significant economic strategy for national governments and for national and foreign entrepreneurs. This strategy was modified in the 1980s and 1990s as the external, rather than the internal market, for manufactured goods became the priority of many governments and entrepreneurs. An important stimulus for adopting this new priority is the deterioration of the exchange terms for agricultural and mining products and the persistence of substantial import deficits in manufactured goods despite 50 years of industrialization (Fajnzylber, 1990).

These changing priorities have social and political implications which we will begin to explore in this chapter.

Capital-intensive industrialization, adopted in different degrees throughout Latin America, brings some convergence in the pattern of urbanization and in the nature of urban social and political organization, as indicated, for example, by the prevalence of populism. Different levels of economic development entail, however, that the trends are not similar throughout the region and that diversity persists as countries tackle, with different degrees of success, the economic and social problems accompanying industrialization. By the 1990s, economic and social priorities came increasingly into conflict leading both to similarities and differences in government responses as internal demands for an improved standard of living clashed with external insistence on austerity policies to reduce internal consumption and make economies more competitive in the world market.

We will be examining a crucial stage in dependent development which, to different degrees, is affecting the rest of the underdeveloped world in the contemporary period. In making any comparisons it will, of course, be necessary to keep in mind the sharp differences in the level of industrialization *within* the Third World. There are still a number of African countries in which agriculture makes up more than half the gross domestic product and relatively few in which industry, including mining and construction, is a more important contributor than agriculture. In contrast, only three of the Latin American economies (Nicaragua, Guatemala and Paraguay) generate more of their gross domestic product in agriculture than in industry and in none of these cases does agriculture contribute more than a third of GDP (World Bank, 1994a, Table 3). Industrialization has led to a substantial growth in the modern service sectors: financial, insurance, real estate, professional and technical. More indirectly, industrialization has stimulated the expansion of the social services such as health and education as states seek to provide the social infrastructure for industrial growth. The modern service sectors produce an increasing amount of the gross domestic product and generate substantial amounts of employment. They become the basis of a 'new' middle class in developing countries that contrasts with the 'old' middle class of liberal professionals, small-scale traders and independent artisans.

The industrialization of underdeveloped countries thus means that new social and economic forces are brought into play: an industrial working class, an industrial bourgeoisie committed to the expansion of an internal market, an expanded commercial, administrative and professional middle class. 'Traditional' groups may, however, still be numerically important and retain their political and economic power. In the twentieth century, industrialization and the conflicts that it entails have become a crucial issue for the dominant political and economic elites. In place of the transient populations of mining camps and plantations, many of which preserved links with village economies, governments and elites face the 'problem' of a massive, permanent urban population whose presence is necessary to the expansion of the economy. Not only does this permanently resident population raise for the elites the spectre of working-class organization and of overt class conflict: it also involves costs in social and material infrastructure (housing, welfare and sanitation) that both governments and the dominant elites are loath to pay.

The General Context of Industrialization in the Twentieth Century

In their first analyses, the Economic Commission for Latin America (ECLA, 1957) drew attention to two associated structural changes in Latin America – industrialization and urbanization. The ECLA report estimated that the rate of urbanization in the decade 1945–55 was probably more rapid than in previous decades and attributed this very largely to the role of industrial expansion in economic growth from 1945–55. An analysis by Schnore (1961) also suggested a close association between urbanization and industrialization in Latin America and other underdeveloped countries. Industrialization did not come as rapidly, or as early, in some countries as it did in others; but the tendency for the centre of economic gravity to shift from agriculture towards manufacturing is unmistakable.

From the 1940s until the 1970s, the trend in all Latin American countries was similar: in each decade, agriculture contributed a lower percentage of the gross domestic product while manufacturing, with some fluctuations, contributed a higher percentage. In some countries, the predominance of manufacturing was observable by 1940: Chile had a higher percentage of its net domestic product at factor cost generated by manufacturing in that year than was generated by agriculture (United Nations, 1948). By 1945, Argentina, which had been a wheat and animal products exporting economy, had almost as much of its gross domestic product generated by manufacture as by agriculture (United Nations, 1948). The estimates given by the United Nations of the industrial origin of the gross domestic product of Latin American countries show how this trend has affected even the less developed countries: the share of agriculture in the gross domestic product of Bolivia dropped from 32 per cent in 1958 to 14 per cent in 1972 and, in this latter year, manufacturing also contributed 14 per cent of the domestic product. In Brazil, the agricultural share declined from 28 per cent in 1948 to 12 per cent in 1973, while manufacturing increased its share in those years to 19 per cent. In Peru, agriculture contributed 35 per cent of the gross domestic product in 1950 and 16 per cent in 1972, whereas manufacturing contributed 15 and 21 per cent in those years respectively (United Nations, 1975, 1967). In the 1970s, production in manufacturing continued to grow at a faster pace than in agriculture, a trend that was also true of Africa and Asia; but in the 1980s, the growth of manufacturing in Latin America and sub-Saharan Africa slowed appreciably. In both regions, the growth in the agricultural product, though slow, was faster than that of manufacturing (World Bank, 1994a, Table 2). By 1990, the share of manufacturing in the gross domestic product of Latin America was lower than it was in 1970.

The UN and World Bank estimates should be taken only as rough guides to change in the economic structure of Latin America; in all countries, it is the service sector of the economy (trade, transport and communications, government, real estate and finance) that contributes the highest percentage to the gross domestic product. What these statistics indicate is a change in the dynamic of underdeveloped economies: increasingly, both foreign and local investment is channelled into manufacturing industry rather than into agricultural enterprises. Agriculture does not necessarily decline in this period and, indeed, both the ECLA statistics and those of the World Bank indicate that the agricultural product continues to increase throughout the underdeveloped world, though at rates barely above those of the increase in population (ECLA, 1957; United Nations, 1975, World Bank, 1994a, Table 2). However, agriculture begins to contribute less to the creation of new jobs and to income opportunities than do those sectors of the economy linked to urban industrial expansion. ECLA (1965, Table 4) estimated that between 1925 and 1950, the agricultural sector in Latin America absorbed 40.3 per cent of the net increase in the economically active population, whereas between 1950 and 1960 agriculture absorbed only 26.7 per cent of the increase.

In many Latin American countries industrialization had begun before the end of the nineteenth century. We saw in the last chapter how a strong export economy led to economic diversification and industrialization in Argentina but to a lesser extent in Brazil. Under the rule of Porfirio Diaz (1876–1911) in Mexico there was substantial industrial growth fostered, in part, by government policies of tariff protection and subsidy (Haber, 1992). Even in Peru, where the export economy was weaker than in these other countries, there was a significant spurt in industrialization at the turn of the century (Thorp and Bertram, 1976). In the 1920s, the Antioquia region of Columbia was to industrialize rapidly with Medellin as its base. Economic development in Antioquia was based on coffee produced by small-scale farmers who required local arrangements to finance, commercialize and store the crop. This situation had produced, by the early twentieth century, a thriving urban system with the city of Medellin at its head. A market was created for textiles and other mass consumption goods and capital was accumulated locally and invested in local enterprise (Friedel and Jimenez, 1971). Medellin became an important industrial centre producing textiles, beverages and processing food. Monterrey in Mexico also industrialized rapidly in the same period, helped by its location, close to the US-Mexican border, and the investment of US capital (Balan et al., 1973; Walton, 1977). These well known cases of early industrialization emphasize the fact that, in most Latin American countries, industrialization had begun before the end of the boom period in the export of primary products.

Some of the reasons for the increase in industrial growth in the twentieth century were outlined in the first chapter: foreign investment began to concentrate in manufacturing. Between 1912 and 1929, 32 US companies opened branches in Brazil. Unlike British investments, these companies were mainly industrial and aimed at exploiting the internal market. Some of the engineering companies were linked to the export of products from the United States to Brazil (Singer, 1975a; Graham, 1973). External events, such as the Great Depression and two world wars, stimulated the local production of needed industrial goods.

Also, in the first half of the twentieth century the dangers of relying on the export of primary products became increasingly apparent. There was, in this period, a substantial growth in export competition for Latin American products, especially from those underdeveloped areas which were more directly under the control of the colonial powers (Glade, 1969). British planters first experimented with rubber in Brazil and then transplanted it to Malaya, where it could be grown under colonial protection (Singer, 1975a). Rubber from South-east Asia destroyed the Brazilian rubber boom and growing supplies of sugar from the European beet industry, as well as from the Carribean and from Asia, severely depressed world sugar prices. Copper, cacao and coffee were produced in Africa and competed increasingly with Latin American products.

The development of chemical industries in the advanced countries began to replace the demand for natural fibres and nitrates. The increase in these different forms of competition combined with climatic variability to make concentration on the exports of primary products an unstable and risky basis for national prosperity. The benefits of free trade and of the 'natural' exchange of primary for manufactured products were increasingly questioned as the European powers and the United States adopted more restrictive commercial policies (Glade, 1969). Tariff and quota systems closed markets to Latin American products. Under these conditions, it is not surprising that even those Latin American economic interests based on the export of primary products began to seek means of diversifying the internal economy.

The social forces produced by the development of the export economy in the nineteenth century added a strong impetus to industrialization. Plantations and mines had increasingly militant workforces and, in times of recession, their interests combined with those of the urban working and middle classes to attack the stranglehold of foreign interests on national economies. Foreign-owned railways and telegraphs, foreign managers and technicians were evident restrictions on the possibilities of native enterprise and limited the chances of social mobility.

In all countries that were strongly articulated with the world economy by the beginning of the twentieth century, nationalism became a strong force for promoting industrialization and diminishing dependence on the external market. Peron came to power in Argentina in the 1940s with a policy of nationalizing key foreign enterprises and promoting industrialization. In the 1930s, Vargas in Brazil also pursued a nationalist, pro-industrial policy as was the case with Cardenas in Mexico in the 1940s. Although Peru had not industrialized to the extent of these other countries, the APRA political party, based on the sugar economy of the north coast, became a powerful force towards nationalizing foreign-owned enterprises and creating local industry. I shall examine these political movements in greater depth in a later section; for the moment it is enough to note that the conjunction of economic and political forces in the early twentieth century created the basis for industrialization.

The industries established in the first part of the century produced simple consumer goods, construction materials and tools; ECLA (1965) listed the following industries as comprising this early stage of development: textiles and leather, food and beverages, simple chemical preparations, basic pottery, china and glassware and wood processing. These industries had already begun to develop in some countries at the end of the nineteenth century and by the 1940s this stage of industrialization was well advanced in many Latin American countries. Some countries, notably Argentina, Brazil and Mexico, began to move into what ECLA labels the third phase of industrialization, with the development of the rubber, steel and cement industries and petroleum refining. The chief characteristic of the early stages of industrialization was that industry, even factory industry, was small scale and used simple processes, permitting local capital to promote industrialization. Also, the form of production was relatively labour intensive, enabling the manufacturing sector to absorb manpower on a fairly intensive scale from 1925 to 1950

Though factory production tended to displace domestic industry in some lines of production (such as textiles), this was offset by the expansion of small-scale artisan production in urban centres, often in competition with factory production (ECLA, 1957). Since even simple manufactured goods had previously been imported, there were in effect opportunities for import substitution for both factory and artisan production. From 1925 to 1950, both factory and artisan production absorbed part of the increase of the economically active population.

The Different Paths of Economic Development

Although the conditions favouring economic development were present in most Latin American countries in the first part of the twentieth century, significant differences appeared both in the extent of development and in the role of the state in development. The nature of exports, particularly the internal and external linkages they generated, their diversification, their regional concentration and the relative importance of the internal market are some of the crucial economic factors that shaped subsequent development paths. Demography, particularly the impact of international migrations, also influenced subsequent development. Some countries, Argentina, Uruguay, Chile and south central Brazil, populated their cities and rural areas with European migrants who, of necessity, depended on the market for their survival. The impact of these immigrants was heightened by their eventual concentration in the large cities which as national or regional capitals were the major arenas of economic and political decision-making.

In the twentieth century, Latin American countries fall into three broad groupings with respect to urbanization and economic growth. Table 3.1 averages the figures for the countries in each category, but there is practically no overlap between individual countries in the different categories on either urbanization or level of per capita income. The first grouping consists of those countries which had high levels of urbanization and per capita income by the 1940s. These are the three countries of the southern cone, Argentina, Chile and Uruguay, which are similar to each other in their high levels of development on these two indicators and in their relatively slow rate of growth subsequently.

The three countries were heavily populated by European migrations at the end of the nineteenth century and the beginning of the twentieth century. Agriculture was substantially commercialized and none of them had a

Table 3.1. The pace of development in Latin America

Countries	Beginning of period[1]		End of period[2]		Rates of growth[3]	
	% in cities of 20,000+	Per capita income constant $ (1980)	% in cities of 20,000+	Per capita income constant $ (1980)	Urbanization	Per capita product
Early developers[A]	39.0	2193	69.9	2789	1.5%	0.7%
Fast developers[B]	15.9	1121	52.9	2258	3.0%	2.0%
Slow developers[C]	11.7	796	25.8	1008	2.0%	0.7%

[1]Beginning is 1940 for urban population and 1960 for per capita income.
[2]End is 1980 for urban population and 1988 for per capita income.
[3]Rates are 1940–80 for urbanization and 1960–88 for per capita income.
[A]Argentina, Uruguay and Chile.
[B]Brazil, Colombia and Mexico.
[C]Bolivia, El Salvador, Guatemala and Honduras.
Sources: ECLAC, 1993; InterAmerican Development Bank, 1989.

large peasant population. Venezuela has several of the characteristics of this first group. Oil revenues had made it the richest per capita Latin American economy by 1960 and the proportion of its population living in cities of 20,000 or more were as high as those of Argentina by 1980. However, both its urbanization and economic growth were more recent than those of the other three countries of the first group.

After mid-century, a group of countries both urbanized rapidly and had high rates of economic growth. These countries are the three largest Latin American countries in population: Brazil, Mexico and Colombia. By the 1980s, they had attained levels of per capita income approximating those of the early developers and had more than half their populations living in towns and cities of substantial size. All three countries have considerable natural resources and a regional diversity which, from early in the century, contained areas of modern as well as traditional agriculture. They had a diversified urban system that included important industrial centres such as Sao Paulo in Brazil, Medellin in Colombia and Monterrey in Mexico as well as the national capitals and provincial administrative centres.

In contrast with this group are the slow developers, Bolivia and El Salvador, Honduras, and Guatemala in Central America. All of these are relatively small countries and undoubtedly their size and lack of resources have limited their development. Nicaragua also fits this category, but the *Sandinista* revolution of 1979 and the United States-imposed blockade led to a different trajectory characterized by, on one hand, the rapid extension of agrarian reform, health and educational services and, on the other, by economic collapse with a negative per capita growth rate between 1960–88 of −0.7 per cent (InterAmerican Development Bank, 1989).

These countries were among the least urbanized and economically developed countries by mid-century. Their subsequent rates of change were also relatively slow so that by the 1980s they remained mainly rural with low levels of per capita income. The slow developers had entered the world economy as exporters of primary materials – agricultural in the case of Central America and minerals in the case of Bolivia. Their specialization in this role had barely changed by the 1980s, providing a weak stimulus for industrialization and for the development of the internal market.

Three of the five countries that do not fit into the above categories are small in population and occupy a special position in terms of strategic resources. Panama, as a result of the canal, early became an entrepôt of hemispheric trade, resulting in high levels of urbanization by mid-century and moderate levels of urban and economic growth thereafter. Ecuador and Paraguay benefited from oil and hydroelectric resources respectively, enabling them to emulate the growth patterns of the fast developers, but from a lower starting level. By the 1980s, the pace of their development had put them in an intermediate position between the fast and slow developers. Peru and Costa Rica provide more interesting exceptions. Peru conforms to the slow development pattern in terms of low initial levels of urbanization, low initial per capita levels and low per capita growth thereafter. It departs sharply from it, however, in having one of the highest rates of urbanization in the region between 1940 and 1980. In terms of the relation of *per capita* growth to urbanization, Peru is the most extreme case of 'overurbanization' in the region.

Costa Rica contrasts in that it has the most balanced pattern of growth in Latin America in terms of rate of urbanization and rate of economic growth. By 1980, Costa Rica had 34 per cent of its population in cities of 20,000 plus, mainly in the capital, San José. It was, relative to other Central American countries, ethnically homogeneous and moderately prosperous, with a substantial proportion of its rural population consisting of independent, small-scale, commercial farmers.

The influence of these economic and demographic differences lies in the particular ways they shape alliances in each country between landed interests, the urban middle classes, the nascent industrial bourgeoisie, their workers and, at times, the peasant populations. We can use Cardoso and Faletto's account (1979) of responses to industrialization in Latin America to illustrate the links between different patterns of development and political processes. First, they examine the case of Argentina, an early developer, as an example of industrialization undertaken primarily by a national bourgeoisie and without economic intervention by the state to any significant degree. This response they call 'liberal' industrialization and it is based almost entirely upon private enterprise. The preconditions for this type of industrialization are the existence of an internal market and of a vigorous, dominant, agro-exporting class. This class is linked through the financial system to the industrial bourgeoisie and to the internal market. Under the conditions of the 1920s and 1930s these classes sponsored industrialization based on Buenos Aires that was sufficient to absorb most of the available labour force as an industrial working-class.

The second type of industrialization is 'national populist'. This is the case of Brazil, a fast developer, and occurred when there was no hegemonic class. The economically dominant classes (the coffee and industrial interests of Sao Paulo) have never been strong enough to neutralize the power of the traditional agrarian interests. Nor have they been able to provide sufficient industrial employment to absorb the increase in numbers of the urban and rural population produced by the expansion of the export economy (for example, through the international migrations and the rapid turnover of labour on the plantations). Under these conditions, the state, from 1930 onwards, has assumed an important role in constituting the industrial system. The state has provided not only the infrastructure and institutional regulation required by the system but has set up public enterprises itself. This state intervention was 'imperative for a country that was urbanizing, whose previous agrarian economy had deteriorated and which did not have a capitalist sector which had accumulated sufficiently to respond rapidly to massive employment needs' (Cardoso and Faletto, 1969). In Brazil, the industrial working class has thus remained numerically less important than in Argentina down to the middle of the present century. Also, Brazil's industrialization has taken place in a context in which the mass of the population were rural workers and peasants, or the urban poor employed in the services and in artisan industry.

State-sponsored industrialization acquired an even more predominant role than in Brazil in the cases of Chile and Mexico, an early and a fast developer respectively. This type of industrialization is brought about by what Cardoso and Faletto call the developmentalist state. This type occurs in those countries in which the dominance of the enclave economy prevented the rise of a strong national bourgeoisie thus impeding the 'liberal' industrialization of the Argentinean type or even its more limited equivalent, that based on a regional bourgeoisie with national pretensions – the case of Sao Paulo in Brazil. However, the expansion of the export economy in Chile and Mexico stimulated the growth of administrative and other services to varying degrees and created in the urban centres both a middle and a working class. With the crisis in the export economy, it was therefore the state that took control in promoting industrialization, both because the groups that controlled the state needed a means of rapid capital accumulation and because this policy expanded employment opportunities for the middle and working classes.

The role of the state in industrialization depends, in part, on the existence of strong central government; it also depends on the strength of the class interests supporting or opposing its policies. Early and fast developers are likely to differ in the strength of class organization. In Chile, an early developer, working-class (based on mining) and middle-class organization had time to develop prior to industrialization and class-based politics ensured more overtly nationalistic economic policies.

We can contrast both Mexico and Chile with the case of Peru, a slow developer, in which the enclave economy was also dominant. In Peru, central government was relatively weak until the 1960s and the urban middle and working classes were neither numerous nor strongly organized. In this situation, the favourable opportunities for industrialization in the early twentieth century were neglected by governing elites (Thorp and Bertram, 1976). This last analysis would apply also to situations such as those of the Central American republics and Bolivia.

My aim here is not to provide a comprehensive account of the variations in the recent economic history of Latin American countries but rather to illustrate the type of analysis and the type of variables that can be used to understand why countries faced by a powerful force for convergence – that of urban industrialization – may still diverge in their pattern of political and economic development. This 'mixed' situation of divergence within an overall trend to convergence is represented by the political phenomenon of populism. Populism, in Di Tella's (1965a) definition, represents an alliance of classes in which, under an anti-status quo leadership drawn predominantly from the elites and middle classes, important segments of the working class are given access to political power. Di Tella (1990) distinguishes between two main types of populism: the first is the middle-class populist party, such as APRA in Peru in which charismatic leadership and middle-class organizers, often students and teachers, bind urban and rural trade unions into a strong party; the second type, the 'Peronist', has relatively weak middle-class membership, but strong trade union support for the charismatic leader and some support from elites (such as military and industrialists). Populism characterizes most of the recent civilian regimes in Latin America up to the 1960s, including, for example, Peron in Argentina (1943–5; 1974–6), Vargas, Kubitschek and Goulart in Brazil (1930–64), the APRA-Prado coalition in Peru (1955–60), the MNR in Bolivia (1952–64), and the PRI ruling party of Mexico.

Populism is a phenomenon that is based on the rapidity of urbanization and the unevenness of industrialization in Latin America (Germani, 1966, 1968; Weffort, 1973; Di Tella, 1990). In part, its appeal is to populations uprooted mentally and physically by dramatic changes in living and working conditions. The massive movement of people into the cities is one aspect of these changes, but the impact of urbanization will also be felt in rural areas as economic change disrupts traditional farming practices. These populations are socially mobilized, to use Di Tella's (1990) term for this process of uprooting; but they have not, as yet, established their own autonomous organizations. The rapid growth of cities, due largely to migration, creates an urban working class with little political experience and which traditional political institutions are unable to accommodate. Moreover, this working class is responsive to the appeal of populist politicians who offer social welfare and jobs and stress patriotic themes such as the nationalization of foreign enterprises. The populist political style is continuous with older traditions: the personalistic appeals and patronage of regional, landowning elites: the *caudillos, caciques* and *coroneles* of Latin America (De la Torre, 1992).

There are, however, other dimensions to populism. Populism represents a particular strategy of economic development based on expanding personal consumption, and thus the market for industrial products, while controlling and limiting the demands of the working classes. The low-income groups incorporated by populist regimes are not economically marginal populations but those that are most necessary to the growth of industrial capitalism. Industrial capital supports, directly or indirectly, populist regimes because such regimes solve the problems confronting capital at a particular stage of its development. This stage occurs at a time when industrial interests are becoming predominant in the economy but when their power is not sufficiently consolidated to enable them either to incorporate other groups through economic benefits or to coerce them through control of the state apparatus. One of these other groups is likely to be the landowners producing for the export economy. This class loses some of its authority as a consequence of the crisis in the export sector in the early part of the century; but it remains a major source of finance for industrialization. The other group is the working class created by the industrialization process.

Lopes (1961) provides a case study of the dilemmas that the increasing concentration of industry has entailed for industrialists in Brazil. In the early industries in the Minais Gerais and Sao Paulo regions, industrialists used paternalistic techniques to control workers and keep wage demands to an acceptable level. Workers were housed on company property which at times formed a textile colony made up of ex-workers from the owner's plantation. Owners and administrators provided welfare benefits and acted as godparents to their workers. However, as more industries were developed and concentrated in the towns, competition between industrialists led them to seek to save on labour costs as far as possible thus ending many paternalistic favours. Also, the workers came into contact with each other and could move from factory to factory in search of better conditions. This process led both to an increasing organization of the working class and to an increasing recognition on the part of the employers that they needed to combine and seek government help to resolve their labour problems. By the 1930s, Sao Paulo industry was beginning to export to other states of the federation and was restricted by interstate customs duties; on this count, too, industrialists became more conscious of the need to strengthen federal power (Love, 1975).

The increasing concentration of working-class populations occurred in situations in which there already existed traditions of radical working-class political movements. In both Argentina and Brazil, immigration from Europe had, to an extent, entailed the importation of European socialist and radical traditions (Hall, 1974; Germani, 1966). However, even in countries such as Peru, without such immigration, there was an upsurge of working-class radical political movements in the early years of the twentieth century; indeed, the origins of APRA, though responding mainly to local conditions, were partly based on European revolutionary socialism (Yepes, 1974; Klaren, 1973).

The early working-class political movements in the cities of Latin America were relatively weak, however, even in those cities where there was a sizable industrial working class. Anarcho-syndicalists in Sao Paulo failed, in the 1930s, to organize the immigrant working class, despite bad working conditions and in the face of severe police repression (Fausto, 1976). In Argentina, the labour movement of the 1930s and 1940s was strong and resisted government control, but did not present a unified electoral front (Di Tella, 1990). One factor in the political weakness of the working class was the geographical mobility of labour; both in Argentina and Brazil mass migrations provided a readily exploitable force. Hall (1974) points out that this mobility took place on a scale comparable to that of the United States and, citing Thernstrom and Knights (1970), argues that it had a similarly devastating effect on working-class consciousness.

Other factors, such as an industrial workforce which, in the early stages, had high proportions of women and children, need also to be considered; above all perhaps was the strength of state repression. Labour militants in early nineteenth-century England battled with a relatively ineffective police force and an army whose resources were tightly stretched (Foster, 1974). Those of Latin American cities were faced, even in the early twentieth century, with a large-scale, relatively professionalized repressive apparatus. Robert Shirley (1978) contrasts Manchester and Sao Paulo in this respect, showing that although both cities had approximately the same population (600,000), Manchester had, in 1898, 1,037 police and Sao Paulo, in 1920, had 8,814.

Despite its political weakness, the industrial working class was still a formidable force, especially in countries that had industrialized early. The Labour movement was particularly strong in Chile and Argentina before 1940, but trade union organization was occurring throughout the region. Since working-class militancy was identified by industrialists and other sectors of the urban middle class as a potential threat to their well-being, they were forced to choose between supporting the repression of the labour movement or tolerating it when it was a subordinate part of a governing coalition. The latter choice attracted the emerging commercial-industrial elites when they needed to build coalitions to pressure central and local governments; to develop industry they needed a favourable tariff policy and assistance in providing the roads, energy sources and other infrastructure. This assistance from government implied the gradual taking away of resources from the landed elites, either through taxation or tariff policies. Elite toleration of the labour movement was always provisional. Thus, Peron's support from industrialists fluctuated sharply and, in his early years of power, he relied heavily on union support (Horowitz, 1990). The shifts that industrialists and the urban middle classes made between repression and toleration accounts for much of the political instability of Latin America to the present.

The populist alliance emerged under such conditions. Populist regimes collaborated in industrializing their countries; Peron's early period of power was one of rapid, government-assisted industrialization based on national entrepreneurship. Vargas in Brazil also sponsored the industrialization of Sao Paulo and its region. The working classes were incorporated directly, through unions and political parties affiliated to the regime; working-class interests were protected through labour legislation on minimum wages, social welfare and job security. Although the traditional landed classes were increasingly marginal to the alliance between organized labour and industrial-commercial interests, they, too, received some consideration under populist regimes. Labour legislation was not vigorously applied to the rural areas or not applied at all, enabling the commercial agricultural interests to continue their use of cheap, seasonal labour or labour tied to farms by sharecropping and other interests (Lopes, 1976; Weffort, 1973).

The success of populism rested to a great extent on the capacity of industrialization to create employment in the cities. In the 1940s there is evidence that urban growth in both Argentina and Brazil was accompanied by a substantial increase in employment in the transformative sector of the economy (Balan, 1973; Faria, 1976; Germani, 1966). In this situation, most of the urban classes derived advantages from urban industrialization. The middle classes received profits and high salaries from the increase in industrial productivity and the increasing demand for commercial and other services which it entailed. The working class, many of whom were of rural or immigrant origin, could also feel themselves to be in a better situation.

Thus, Weffort (1973) emphasizes the importance of the individual social mobility which accompanies this stage of urban growth, as opportunities in manufacturing and in allied sectors of the economy expand as fast as does the urban population, with urban wages higher than those in the rural areas. Industry is heterogeneous in terms of levels of technology and size of enterprise creating a variety of working-class situations and many opportunities for social mobility within the urban economy. Workers with some years of urban experience are able to find relatively well-paid employment in the more advanced sectors of industry; these workers are 'replaced' in their previous, low-paid jobs by recent migrants from the countryside.

The contrast with the European working class in its formative stage is thus twofold: in Latin America there is a greater heterogeneity of working situations within industry and, linked to this, the working class in Latin America is confronted by an industrial bourgeoisie that is only in the process of establishing itself. The middle classes have only a weakly developed, independent productive base. Most of them are dependent on the services or, directly, on state employment, and the agrarian-based export sector still provides the finance to expand these employment opportunities.

In other countries of Latin America, populism was not to be as powerful a political force as in Argentina and Brazil. In some countries, the low levels of industrialization meant that the political contradictions to which populism is a response were not as sharp. Thus, in Peru the traditional agro-mining exporting elites maintained themselves in power until the 1960s and the Peruvian populist party (APRA) was only to achieve office with Alan García in 1982. Indeed, its access to power in the period 1956–60 was possible only through an alliance with its hitherto inveterate enemy – the Peruvian oligarchy.

Likewise, in those countries where the state has taken an early and preponderant role in fostering industrialization, populism has a distinctive character. In Mexico, for example, strong labour unions were created under Cardenas, partly to offset foreign pressure against attempts to extract better returns from foreign enterprises in Mexico. Entrepreneurial, middle-class and peasant organizations were similarly created and brought within the organization of the ruling party, the PRI. Thus Mexican 'populism' is not so much a response to the existing contradictions of industrialization as a vehicle through which the state has organized the politics of economic development, granting access to groups when their collaboration becomes crucial to that development.

Stressing the way in which populism served to co-opt the working classes in Latin America should not obscure the importance and growing independence of the labour movements. Indeed, despite the limits it placed on political participation, populism enabled working-class political organization to develop and gain self-confidence. Thus, Gutiérrez and Romero's (1992) analysis of the development of political and social citizenship in Buenos Aires from 1912 to 1955 emphasizes both the limitations of a citizenship that was handed down by the state and its contribution to convincing the working class of the legitimacy of their rights. Expectations were raised under populist regimes and workers demands were incorporated into government policy even when this threatened the interests of industrialists, as happened with Vargas in Brazil (Dutra Fonseca, 1989).

The Transition to the Second Stage of Industrialization

It was in the context of populist regimes seeking to industrialize that the Economic Commission for Latin America's (ECLA) early assessments of what needed to be done to promote further development were made. ECLA and its executive secretary in the 1950s and 1960s, Raul Prebisch, played a central role in influencing Latin American economic and social policies. ECLA was more active and prominent in policy debates in its region than were the other regional commissions of the United Nations, due, in part, to the prestige of Prebisch (see Love, 1994).

The Commission was not entirely homogeneous in its viewponts and prescriptions for action, but it sought an alternative mode of economic development to that of dependency on the export of primary products. The role of Latin American countries as exporters of minerals and agricultural products and as importers of manufactured products was identifed by ECLA as a prime cause of the slow rates of economic development in the continent. Part of the argument was that increasingly unfavourable terms of trade of primary products with respect to the manufactured exports of developed countries inhibited capital formation in underdeveloped countries. This made necessary some degree of protection and subsidization for nascent industry if underdeveloped countries were to protect income and employment (Baer, 1962). ECLA's policy recommendations emphasized a state-induced industrialization, but one that strengthened internal capacities to export as well as to substitute for imports, thus building up a long-term comparative advantage (Thorp, 1992). In these respects, ECLA's early recommendations are not too different from those of commentators of the 1980s, such as Fajnzylber, who emphasize the need to develop a comparative advantage in manufactured exports to offset the relative decline in export revenues from primary products.

However, the social structural implications of reliance on the primary sector were also identified as harmful to development. Primary sector exports were seen to be based, in part, on a structure of land tenure that inhibited agrarian development. Thus, in order to produce for export, large estates maintained a dependent group of labourers and peasants and limited the land available for local foodstuffs production. ECLA (1957) pointed out that the poverty of the Latin American countryside inhibited the development of small and medium sized towns. Productivity was shown to be low and to be associated with widespread underemployment of males (Table 3.2). Note that in the 40 intervening years to 1990, productivity in agriculture appears to have declined further despite the decrease in the proportion employed in agriculture. We will return to this point in the next chapter.

Industrialization was favoured by ECLA as a way of retaining a greater part of the profits of the export sector. Industries created job opportunities and stimulated a rural-urban migration which could reduce pressure on land and permit higher productivity in agriculture. Employment in industry was also regarded as absorbing 'unproductive' employment in the existing commercial and service sector of the urban economy. Indeed, by 1956 ECLA was already signalling some of the dangers of the expansion of the service sector of the Latin American economies, though it viewed this as a transitional problem. Basing its comparisons on the situation in the advanced capitalist world, ECLA pointed out that in a 'properly' balanced development, such as that in Western Europe, the service to manufacturing employment ratio was close to 1; only in those countries with exceptionally high productivity, such as the United States, did the service to manufacturing employment ratio reach 1.5. Thus, Latin America's ratio of 1.39 in 1950 was seen to be excessive.

Some of the cityward migration was viewed as being absorbed in marginal activities which served to depress productivity; such service employment was characterized by ECLA (1957) as 'overburdening' the urban population and as being 'excessive'. A similarly disapproving note entered into its characterization of small-scale industry, which was seen as diminishing productivity in its sector: 'a vast mushroom growth of small, inefficient workshops, which can operate at a profit owing to the ample supply of cheap labour, provided by the steady immigration of rural population to towns and by the already existing stock of marginal population' (ECLA, 1957). This early characterization of certain types of employment as marginal and harmful to the development of the modern economy anticipates, as we shall see in later chapters, the debates over the informal economy. ECLA blamed this employment situation on the underdeveloped nature of the agricultural sector and on the slow progress of industrialization.

Table 3.2. Latin America: gross product per employed person and percentage distribution of total gross product by sectors c. 1950 and c. 1990

Sector	% of GDP[A] c. 1950	% of labour force c. 1950	% of GDP[A] c. 1990	% of labour force c. 1990	Indices of labour productivity c. 1950[B]	Indices of labour productivity c. 1990[B]
Agriculture	25	53	11	25	47	44
Mining	4	1	4	1	400	400
Manufacture	18	14	25	17	128	147
Construction	5	4	6	5	125	120
Other activities (commerce & services)	44	28	52	52	175	100

[A]Percentages do not add up to 100, because the contribution of housing rents and utilities are not included.
[B]GDP divided by labour force and multiplied by 100. Average productivity of all sectors = 100.
Sources: For 1950 figures, ECLA, 1957, Table 16; for GNP estimates for 1990, Wilkie et al. 1993, Table 3426. Estimates of labour force 1990 are my own, based on available 1980 figures and trends in available 1990 censuses.

By the 1960s, however, a noticeable change had taken place in ECLA'S analysis; there was by then some disappointment with the poor performance of industry in increasing employment opportunities. Such 'advanced' Latin American countries as Argentina, Chile and Uruguay were singled out for their slow rates of economic growth and for the 'exorbitant' expansion of service employment. In the 1966 report, industrialization, involving techno-logically sophisticated plant which required relatively little labour and the high-income concentration and mass poverty in Latin American countries, was seen to inhibit the expansion of the market for labour-absorbing indus-try. The analysis of the possibilities of expanding employment opportunities also changed radically from 1956; in 1966, the best chances to expand pro-ductive employment were seen to rest with agriculture and construction. Even small-scale industry received a grudging acceptance (ECLA, 1965).

The analyses and policy recommendations of ECLA reflect the general tenor of critical thinking about the problem of underdevelopment in the immediate post-war period. The emphasis on the nationalist solution to underdevelopment was stressed, in this same period, in Africa and Asia. Among intellectuals and policy makers, nationalism and the institutions of the nation-state were seen to provide a possible basis for internal unity and for an economic restructuring that would reduce dependence on the advanced capitalist world. Difficulties facing such a restructuring were rec-ognized, but in general these were viewed as obstacles to change that could be overcome with concerted effort from government and an aware citizenry. This ideology was indeed an integral part of the populist political philoso-phy. It received support from theories of modernization that emphasized the importance of internal, and state-induced processes, such as education and industrialization, to change values and favour economic growth (Inkeles, 1960; Rostow, 1956). Thus, many of the obstacles were identified with reformable aspects of the internal structure of the new nations. One of ECLA'S major recommendations, for example, was for an agrarian reform which would make possible the development of small-scale commercial agriculture (Faria, 1976).

External Dependence and Capital-Intensive Industrialization

A major reason for disillusion, even within ECLA itself, with the policy of import-substitution industrialization (ISI) was the evidence that it did not promote independent economic development. Debate continues as to why ISI failed in its objectives, but two sets of factors appear crucial. First, high tariffs and overvalued currencies combined with the demands for a 'Western' standard of living by the urban middle and upper classes to create incentives to produce consumer durables for the domestic market. This diverted resources from the development of intermediate and capital goods industries and from the inputs needed to raise productivity in agriculture (Thorp, 1992; Griffith-Jones and Sunkel, 1986). The emphasis on the production of consumer durables, such as automobilies, domestic appliances and televisions, resulted in the dominance of these sectors by multinational companies since they were the only available source of investment capital and technological know-how. Brazil's economic boom of the 1960s was in great part based on the expansion of the automobile industry and on the manufacture of other durable consumer goods (Oliveira, 1972). Traditional industrial production also became more capital intensive, with both textiles and the food processing industries installing technologically sophisticated machinery which, while increasing output, reduced the labour requirements of a plant. The multinationals have tended to exploit existing technology, contributing little to research and development within Latin America and importing the machinery needed for production as well as many intermediate inputs. Paradoxically, then, ISI policies meant to increase economic independence resulted in dependence on foreign technology and capital. This pattern, argue Griffith-Jones and Sunkel (1986), increased the external vulnerability of the Latin American economies by making them, by the 1970s, dependent on imports to maintain even essential production.

The second set of factors arose from an unsympathetic international context in which Latin America, unlike Europe, received no significant financial aid from the United States to restructure post-war economies. The financial resources for growth and development in Latin America were to come from foreign direct investment, mainly that of multinational companies. When United States official aid agencies began to contribute in the 1960s, the amount of net assistance was less than half the profit remittances from Latin America to the US, a possible factor claim Griffith-Jones and Sunkel (1986) in the support of US multinationals for the Alliance for Progress.

High rates of urbanization did little to increase agricultural productivity, as its continuing decline by 1990 shows; while the employment structure of the cities became even more weighted to the 'unproductive' tertiary sector (Table 3.2). Note, in this respect, how the index of productivity in commerce and the services is below that in manufacturing by the early 1990s. The data should be treated with caution since it is notoriously difficult to measure productivity in the services and the 1950s data are not fully comparable with those of the 1990s. However, the relative decline of productivity in commerce and the services makes sense. By the 1980s, these sectors had become increasingly heterogeneous, including government, producer services and a host of informal activities in small-scale commerce and personal services. In contrast, manufacturing was probably less heterogeneous in the 1990s than in the 1950s when small-scale, craft-type workshops still abounded. Though employment in non-government modern services has grown fast from the 1960s onwards, its growth is matched by that of services of low productivity such as 'informal' personal services and petty trade.

Moreover, the economic development that did occur, as measured by rate of growth in the national and per capita product, produced increasing inequalities in income distribution (Foxley, 1976). An explanation for these trends is provided by examining, as do Cardoso and Faletto (1979) and Anibal Quijano (1973, 1974), the internal implications of the economic dependence of underdeveloped countries on the advanced capitalist world.

First, the economies of the advanced capitalist nations are in a constant process of change. Consequently, the nature of their articulation with underdeveloped countries changes significantly over time. We noted earlier that the dynamic of the first phase of economic imperialism to affect Latin America (Britain's) is different from that of American economic imperialism. Such changes in articulation set the conditions of exchange which promote or limit development within underdeveloped countries.

In the twentieth century, American investments have concentrated increasingly in industrial production; their location has shifted over time from extractive industry to manufacturing and, within manufacturing, have become concentrated in technologically sophisticated products such as durable consumer goods. From this perspective, the urban industrialization of underdeveloped countries does not reduce dependence but is a process closely tied to the economic development of the advanced capitalist world.

Quijano (1973, 1974) analyses the changes in the advanced capitalist economies which fostered the pattern of industrial urbanization in Latin America and other underdeveloped countries. After the Second World War, and partly as a consequence of technological developments produced by that war, the most advanced capitalist economies accelerated their rate of technological innovation. This meant in part that the market for the sophisticated products of these economies was concentrated in the advanced capitalist countries themselves; underdeveloped countries provided only a limited market and then only where there was a sufficiently concentrated high-income population.

This changing emphasis of the advanced capitalist economies meant that it became more advantageous for certain sectors of capital to transfer their production activities to underdeveloped countries. With high costs of labour in the developed world, products destined for the general market in underdeveloped countries could be produced profitably in those countries, especially with the protection of tariff barriers. Local production did not compete with the sophisticated technology of advanced capitalism and, in fact, provided a market for machinery and new production processes. Interlocking production activities became possible, as when the simpler parts of an electrical appliance are manufactured locally and the more complicated ones made in the developed countries. Thus, a complex pattern of economic interdependence has emerged in which the advanced capitalist countries retain the most productive economic activities such as those asso-

ciated with the latest technological innovation (like electronics), but delegate more routine production to poorer countries where costs may be lower.

Fernando Cardoso, in an article entitled 'Dependency Revisited' (1973),
argues that a new pattern of economic dependence is constituted by the tripartite alliance between state companies, multinational corporations and
the local companies associated with both. The multinational corporation is
the organizational means whereby advanced capitalism overcomes the limitations of its territorial bases. It becomes possible to make use of cheaper
costs of production in certain countries or to establish subsidiaries as the
only way of getting at local markets, while retaining substantial control over
the production process. Though Latin American governments restricted
direct foreign control of production in key sectors of the economy, the technology on which production is based remained directly under the control of
the parent company. The restrictions on control were, in fact, the basis for
the tripartite alliance which, at first sight, might appear strange given the
nationalism of many Third World regimes. Technologically based production creates complementarities of interest between local elites and foreign
ones because the former can derive their profits from direct production,
while the latter can derive theirs from the use of their technologies in production (Alavi, 1972). In a similar fashion, Paul Singer indicates that it is to
the advantage of multinational corporations to allow firms not directly controlled by them to use their innovations in production because this enables
the multinationals to extend the scale of their operations (Singer, 1973). For
this reason, branches of production highly dependent on technological
advance can be taken over by the public sector or 'let out' to national entrepreneurs without opposition from the foreign monopolies. In return for providing the know-how, the monopolies derive royalties, rights to market the
product or concessions in other branches of production.

In this situation there are few disadvantages to multinational corporation
investment in industrial expansion in underdeveloped countries. Such
investment does not compete with the home products of the foreign company within the international division of labour produced by the activities
of the multinational corporation. Indeed, certain underdeveloped countries
may export the industrial products of the 'multinationals' elsewhere; thus,
the Brazilian car industry exports to the rest of Latin America and that of
Mexico is a substantial exporter to the United States. Such exports are often
more profitable for the parent company than direct export from the home
country, where costs of production and transport are higher.

The emergence of the multinational and the changing characteristics of
the advanced capitalist economies are part of the explanation for the
increasing predominance of foreign corporations in industrial production in
Latin America and elsewhere in the Third World. Brazil, which had at first
espoused an explicitly nationalistic policy of industrialization, has become
increasingly dominated by multinational corporations which control most
industrial sectors, often in association with the state (Souza and Affonso,

1975). In Argentina by 1959, of the 100 enterprises with the highest sales receipts, 55 were multinational corporations and of the top ten corporations, eight were multinational (Arias, 1971). In Peru, the relatively rapid industrialization by the 1950s and 1960s was a phase in which foreign-controlled companies became increasingly predominant (Thorp and Bertram, 1978).

By the 1990s, most United States foreign direct investment in Latin America was concentrated in manufacturing or in finance, insurance and real estate. The automobile industry, in particular, was entirely controlled by affiliates of the largest transnational automakers and its production was concentrated in Brazil and Mexico which between them accounted in 1983 for 79 per cent of the number of vehicles produced and assembled in Latin America (Jenkins, 1984). Jenkins provides an account of the post-war changes in the automobile industry and the strategies of the transnationals that have resulted in the increasing integration of production of vehicles and autoparts on a hemispheric and global basis. With integration and trade liberalization, the transnational companies have even greater leeway in deciding where to produce and what to produce, severely limiting the capacity of Latin American states to make their own plans for manufacturing exports. Foreign affiliates play a key role in production and export within Latin America so that they contribute about 30 per cent of production and between 30 and 40 per cent of total exports by value (SALA, Vol 30, pt 2, Table 3017).

US companies and their affiliates increased their share in total manufacturing exports from 7 per cent in 1966 to 15 per cent in 1986, with the increase being more dramatic in certain countries, such as Mexico, where the US share rose from 9 per cent to 29 per cent (SALA, Vol 30, pt 2, Table 3020). In the Mexican case, much of this export volume is produced by the foreign-owned, in-bond industry (the *maquiladora* plants) located on the northern border that produce televisions, computer equipment, textiles, and autoparts (see Sklair, 1993, for an analysis of the *maquila* industry and its workforce). The automobile industry dominated by US and Japanese companies is also a major source of exports of autos and motors to the United States and Canadian markets. Shaiken (1990) provides case studies of these export industries showing how they have successfully implemented high-technology production, including the use of robots and total quality control, despite the relative lack of industrial experience on the part of their workers. These export industries have only limited economic linkages with the local economy. The in-bond industries, until recently, could only export their product but, in their case, as with the automobile plants, relatively few of their inputs were derived locally. Wages are not high, particularly in the new auto and *maquila* industries of the north of Mexico, even when compared with those of older plants in the centre of the country (see Wilson, 1992, the essays in González-Aréchiga and Barajas, 1989, and Carrillo, 1990, 1993, for an analysis of the regional impact of the export industries and differences in wages and work organization between the new industries and their counterparts in the traditional industrial heartlands of the centre of Mexico).

There is one final paradox to explain, that of the sudden death, in the 1980s, of the economic nationalism that appeared so well entrenched in Latin America. Ironically, in 1994, it was the lot of Fernando Cardoso, perhaps the most perspicacious commentator on the evolving nature of dependency, to announce his intention, as newly elected President of Brazil, to remove the last major restrictions on foreign investment. These events are less suprising, however, if put in the context of the 1970s and 1980s and the changes in the balance of internal and external forces. By this period, Latin American countries had acquired a desperate need for foreign investment as a result of a distorted structure of production that depended on considerable inputs of foreign capital and intermediate goods, a decaying industrial infrastructure in need of modernization and limited sources of domestic capital resulting from external indebtedness and capital flight.

The internal forces that might have resisted the opening to foreign investment were weakened by the recessions that had accompanied the debt crises: the trade unions in both public and private sectors struggled unsuccessfully to maintain their members' standard of living in the face of layoffs; national entrepreneurs faced sharp drops in demand and punitive interest rates. Furthermore, governments and large sections of the population saw few alternatives to opening economies to international trade and investment if these economies were to be reactivated and social disorder avoided. Unlike the recessions of the 1920s and '30s, those of the late 1970s and '80s had an impact on countries that were mainly urban and whose population was consequently highly dependent on the market and the subsidies that had reduced the cost of urban living. In the 1980s, austerity measures linked to loans from the international agencies produced considerable unrest, the so-called IMF riots that were common in Latin America as elsewhere in the developing world (Walton and Ragin, 1989).

The opening of economies became an increasingly favoured internal policy in the absence of any other viable means of obtaining foreign capital for development. Multinational corporations had been shifting their investments to the developed world and were less interested than before in the protected markets of developing countries. Other sources of external finance for development, such as loans from multinational commercial banks, inter-government aid and loans from international development agencies dried up as a result of the debt crisis. The debt crisis was, in part, the responsibility of these other sources of external finance, particularly the multinational banks who competed to find profitable outlets for loans in a rapidly growing financial market stimulated by the recycling of petrodollars and the growth of the Euro-currency market (Griffith-Jones and Sunkel, 1986). Even in the oil exporting countries of Latin America, such as Mexico, this shift in external finance led to a debt crisis as governments and the private sector used easy access to external funding to cover balance of payments deficits and to import non-essential goods. Griffith-Jones and Sunkel (1986) point to the lack of public control and supervision of this lending, either by governments, whether of developed or developing countries, or by international agencies, such as the International Monetary Fund. Capital flight increased in this situation as some in Latin America took advantage of unrestricted convertibility and overvalued currencies to invest abroad at higher real levels of return.

At the same time, changes in the world economy favoured the opening of the Latin American economies, making it likely that initiatives in that direction would have positive results for economic growth. The increasing integration of world financial and commodity markets and production systems provided new potential sources of external finance. Equity finance was one method by which both national and foreign investors bought stock in newly privatized companies, such as the Mexican Telephone Company, providing the finance needed to improve and expand the system. Also, improvements in communications technologies made it feasible for multinational corporations to organize production in spatially dispersed sites and to coordinate elaborate commodity chains linking suppliers and customers in different countries (see Gereffi and Korzeniewicz, 1990). By the 1980s, there was a clear shift in the strategy of multinational corporations towards using developing countries to produce for a world market and not just for the internal market. These trends had been developing even under ISI, as in the case of the in-bond industrialization programme on the northern border of Mexico which began in the 1960s, where US and Japanese multinationals established electronics and textile plants to take advantage of cheap Mexican labour and exported the product to the US market.

The ending of ISI and the opening of the Latin American economies to free trade and foreign investment are developments with important consequences for politics and society. These will be explored in subsequent chapters, but we can note some of the economic consequences at this point. Encouraging free trade means that local industry must be competitive at a world level. This inevitably entails a drastic process of industrial restructuring as inefficient enterprises collapse and efficient ones seek greater productivity through technology and reducing labour inputs. In Mexico, competition from cheap imports of textiles and shoes has, for instance, put many small and medium size enterprises out of business. There are possible compensations since any increase in the volume of internal and external trade will generate employment and generate dynamic linkages with other sectors of the economy. Also, Latin American industry can develop comparative advantages in certain branches of production and build up a powerful export base. There is evidence that this is happening both in Mexico and in Brazil where some industrial enterprises have even established subsidiaries abroad. However, the present period of economic opening is a volatile one, as shown by the 1995 economic crisis in Mexico which reverberated throughout Latin America. Restructuring inevitably destabilizes labour markets since the new economic opportunities are often in different places to the old, stimulating inter-urban migration. Also, the new employ-ment opportunities are for different categories of worker than those whose jobs are lost, whether in terms of skill levels, age or gender.

The pace of change is likely to be accelerated by the deregulation that accompanies the current opening of the economies of the developing world and by unrestricted flow of foreign capital. The uncertainties accompanying these changes are not unique to Latin America but, like many other devel-oping countries, they are made more intense by the rapid shift from state regulation of internal markets to deregulation.

The experience of some of the newly industrializing nations of Asia has, however, been different and a brief consideration of their case helps illumi-nate the factors that account for this divergence. South Korea had only a brief period of import-substitution industrialization and, by the 1960s, was already concentrating on the export of manufactures. Its ability to do this was made possible by a set of factors that were absent in Latin America. Internal consumption per capita in South Korea is lower than in Latin America, both of consumer durables and of foods requiring high energy inputs, such as meat (Fajnzylber, 1990). Consequently, the structure of internal demand allows resources to be concentrated on exports. A more equal distribution of land in South Korea, the consequence of radical land reform, meant that rapid urbanization both supplied an abundance of labour to industry and raised productivity in the countryside.

A strong authoritarian state, Peter Evans' (1989) example of the devel-opmentalist state *par excellence*, ensured that wage demands by both work-ing and middle classes were kept low. Indeed, income distribution in Korea became more even during its rapid period of urbanization and industrializa-tion. Also, its key position in the cold war gave South Korea unusual access to US aid and a certain freedom from pressures to open its markets to for-eign direct investment, a freedom which Latin America did not enjoy. In South Korea external investment was channelled through the state which used it to invest in the infrastructure to support rapid private sector indus-trialization. The combination of these factors meant that even when there was a deterioration in South Korea's terms of trade in the 1970s, foreign debt did not halt growth or distort the economy.

Regional development and industrialization

Capital-intensive industrialization reinforces an uneven pattern of devel-opment, as can be seen in the problems of regional development. Although the picture is at first sight a pessimistic one, this is partly because

I have made somewhat rigid assumptions about the nature of capital-intensive industrialization, seeing it as necessarily resulting from the types of
goods produced under the demand structure of societies in which income is
highly skewed. However, Kirsch (1973) points out that the same product is
often produced under widely differentiated technological conditions in
Latin America and that certain basic industries such as food, beverages,
tobacco and even textiles are at times more capital-intensive than consumer
durable or capital goods industries in the same country. There is also the
point that I shall take up in Chapter 5: it is by no means certain that the
structure of consumption would be significantly altered by a policy of
income distribution (Kirsch, 1973; Wells, 1976). These caveats imply that
provincial economies may expand even when subordinated to the industrialization of core regions. Also, deliberate policies aimed at fostering more
labour-intensive production or at redistributing income may both increase
employment and provide the basis for industrial growth and diversification.

In the second chapter I discussed the regional inequalities that develop
during earlier stages of underdevelopment. In the analysis of 'internal colonialism', the provinces are seen to be exploited by means of their own urban
centres to the benefit of the dominant commercial and landed classes residing in the largest cities (Stavenhagen, 1965; Gonzalez Casanova, 1965). In
these Mexican studies, the treatment of the mass of the local population as
an ethnic group (Indian) with characteristics and rights distinct from those
of the dominant groups was shown to facilitate exploitation. Such practices
have continued into the contemporary period and are one of the means
whereby capitalist enterprises secure relatively cheap labour power.

The period of capital-intensive industrialization has, however, changed
the nature of the articulation between the capital city and other large cities
and provincial places (Morse, 1971b). Rapid urbanization and the development of capitalist production in agriculture have increased the importance
of the internal market for both agricultural and industrial production.
Improvements in communications and the penetration of government, commerce and the mass media to even the remotest areas of a country are other
factors increasing economic and political integration.

In such a situation, internal colonialism is an inadequate concept to
explain contemporary provincial underdevelopment. In the post-war period
regional inequalities in income distribution and in social welfare appear to
have grown in most Latin American countries (Griffin, 1969; Foxley, 1976).
These inequalities are not, however, the result of segregating provincial populations from the 'benefits' of economic development by maintaining their
relative isolation and by enforcing local commercial or political monopolies;
rather, these persisting and increasing inequalities are the results of the types
of economic integration generated by capital-intensive industrialization.

This concern with the ways in which economic development generates
regional inequalities is an old one. To some economists such inequalities
represent the first stages of economic development as a dynamic metropoli-

tan centre begins to generate growth for the whole country (Wingo, 1969; Friedmann, 1969). In the United States regional inequalities grew in the first stages of economic development and were subsequently evened out. In underdeveloped countries, this issue is an immediate one in that regional inequalities in economic growth contribute to population concentration in a few urban centres.

Even commentators like Wingo, who stressed the advantages of spatially concentrating economic development, urged governments to take concerted steps to promote a more balanced regional economic development. The persistence of regional inequalities has led John Friedmann, for example, to modify his optimism about the generative effects of planned large-city growth. In his later works, as we saw in the first chapter, Friedmann (1972a, b) has stressed the ways in which economic development projects can perpetuate the economic dependence of peripheral regions on central ones.

In exploring the impact of capital-intensive industrialization on provincial development, it is important to remember that this impact will vary depending on the strength of the articulation between the region and the economic centre. In Lopes' (1977) analysis of regional agrarian development in Brazil, the patterns of change differed markedly, for example, as between the Sao Paulo region and the north-eastern region. In the Sao Paulo area, agriculture is becoming transformed in a capitalist direction, with a rural proletariat that provides occasional labour power for the capitalist farms. In contrast, in the north-east and on the frontier, peasant farming provides a low-cost agricultural product (rice and beans) for the low-income populations of the cities; but food for high income tastes in the north-east is often imported from the capitalist farms of the central south. The limited high-income market of the north-eastern cities is in turn a result of the peripheral role of these cities with respect to Sao Paulo and the cities of the central south of Brazil. As Faria (1976) shows, the north-eastern cities have a greater proportion of 'marginal' economic activities as a direct consequence of their increasing integration into the national economic system.

Such regional inequalities are reinforced by the implantation of capital-intensive production in peripheral regions. Singer points out that such implantations are most likely to benefit the central regions. Factors such as congestion and high land prices may make it profitable for a Sao Paulo enterprise to locate in a less-developed area. This location policy will not, however, diminish the dependency of the north-east on the central south, but change that dependency from a commercial to a financial one (Singer, 1973). Thus, the major part of the profits of the enterprise will be appropriated by the banking institutions of Sao Paulo. The location of the enterprise in an industrial park means that construction materials, machinery and so on are likely to be imported from the central south.

The recent population and economic growth of Manaus, in Amazonia, has, likewise, increased a periperal region's dependency on central regions. Despres (1991) describes the way the establishment of a free trade zone in the city has led to substantial industrial and population growth. However, unlike the region's rubber-based economy of the past, the new economy is purely urban, with some 44 per cent of the the state of Amazonas' population now concentrated in the city, as opposed to approximately 20 per cent at the height of the rubber boom. Manaus' economy is heavily dependent on investment, inputs and consumption from the centre-south, primarily Sao Paulo, or from outside the country. The top positions in government and in the private sector are filled by migrants from the centre-south who look upon their stay in Manaus as a temporary step in their careers. Despite 20 years of government plans to promote a self-sustaining regional development, Manaus' industrial growth has promoted few linkages with the mainly extractive economies of the surrounding rural areas.

This form of 'enclave' production is thus unlikely to generate much local development; the technology involved will be too sophisticated to permit complementary industries to be developed locally. Furthermore, the dependence of the firms on decisions made in Sao Paulo subordinates an important element of a region's economy to external interests. Such developments can harm a region's development in the long run; the setting up of capital-intensive industry raises local prices of commodities, land and housing. These increases may make it more difficult for the subsistence or near subsistence producer to survive locally, especially when the industry does not provide economic opportunities for such producers. Out-migration may increase, reinforcing the enclave effects of the implanted industry. The results may be that, while the Sao Paulo interests derive considerable profits from their ventures, the possibilities of local accumulation may actually decrease.

These dilemmas are spelled out in Barkin's (1975) account of regional development in Mexico. He argues that despite considerable investments in regional production and infrastructure by the Mexican government, the result has been to increase regional underdevelopment. He admits that government projects increase local productivity and improve the infrastructure in ways that benefit local inhabitants through the provision of better communications, health facilities and schools. However, the major beneficiaries of the development programmes are the large-scale capitalist farms. These farms were in a position to take advantage of the improved possibilities of production and could most easily shift production when the market changed. The large farms had better access to credit than the small peasant (*ejidal*) farmers. Government agencies were reluctant to extend credit to the small farmer, since such credits provide a low return on capital.

In contrast, Barkin shows that most government investment went to the richer, industrialized regions of Mexico and into large-scale irrigation projects which benefited the large farms most. He outlines some of the local consequences of these development programmes in the Tepalcatepec river basin project in the states of Michoacan and Jalisco to the west of Mexico City: population in the zone grew by slightly less than the rate of natural increase between 1950 and 1970, but the employment structure of the population changed appreciably. The population became increasingly based on agricultural wage labour or urban employment, often in the service sector of the economy. The small farmer found it increasingly necessary to rent his land and to work as a day labourer to sustain his family; temporary migrant labour from other regions of the country came to work on the harvests of the large farms. The region's towns grew rapidly on the basis of the commerce linked to large-scale agricultural production; the towns became centres for the sale of agricultural machinery, seeds and fertilizer and provided a range of services. Barkin comments that this pattern of development increased the economic dependence of the area on Mexico City, through the centralization of financial control and of policy making in the capital. Many of the large commercial firms were foreign owned and almost all were centred in Mexico City, increasing the outflow of capital.

The pattern of development described by Barkin appears not to have changed substantially in subsequent years. In his survey of a decade of regional planning in Mexico, from 1978 to 1988, Garza (1989) concludes that two major negative tendencies of regional development persist: regional inequalities continue to increase as does economic concentration in the Mexico City metropolitan area and its immediate periphery. Indeed, between 1970 and 1990, when Mexico City's share of the national population began to decline, the capital increased its percentage of the national Gross Domestic Product from 29 per cent to 31 per cent. Garza and his colleagues (1989) provide detailed information on the various planning and investment programmes of the Mexican government and their impact on their regions, such as the policy of installing industrial parks in provincial cities to encourage decentralization (see also, Garza and Sobrino (1989) for a case study of the relative failure of planned industrialization in the state of Sinaloa in north-western Mexico). They evaluate the attempts to manage urban development in the major metropolitan areas. Their general conclusion is that planning has failed in the face of the powerful political and economic forces arrayed against it: landowners, including *ejidatarios*, seeking to sell poor agricultural land for urban development, land speculators, the construction industry and national and foreign entrepreneurs to whose advantage it is to locate their enterprises in or close to Mexico City.

The tendency of the state to contribute to regional dependence and inequality by the pattern of its investment appears to be a general one in Latin America. This is one of the conclusions reached by Webb (1975) in analysing public policy and regional incomes in Peru. Webb demonstrates the difficulties in attempting to correct imbalances without major social investments. The few social investments made in education and health, for example, redounded to the advantage of the urban populations and of those employed in the modern sector of the economy. Webb's conclusion is that regional inequalities in income and welfare have increased from 1960 to 1971. Slater (1985) extends the analysis to the 1980s providing case studies of regional development in Peru. He shows the difficulties in correcting regional imbalances and redistributing income to the lowest-income sectors in face of the 'natural' tendency of governments to favour capital-intensive industrialization policies.

In this context, it is unlikely that urbanization contributes to a more balanced regional development. The growth of provincial urban centres may lead to a more balanced urban hierarchy, but productive investment is likely to continue to concentrate in the largest cities. Gilbert (1974) provides for Colombia and Garza (1985) for Mexico a detailed account of the forces which lead to such concentration. Capital-intensive industrialization concentrates in centres with ample consumer markets, a skilled labour force and a developed infrastructure; the structure of government employment and the increasing expenditures of local government also reinforce the advantages of the existing large urban centres. In the case of Mexico City, Garza argues that government has, in effect, subsidized the city's growth by providing cheap public transport and other infrastructure such as electric and water supplies. Mexico City enterprises make higher profits than their counterparts in provincial cities, an important factor in attracting industry to the capital. However, Garza (1985) calculates that it is government subidies more than the internal characteristics of the enterprises that account for these higher profits.

Capital-intensive industrialization leads to the concentration of employment in manufacturing and construction in the largest cities of an underdeveloped country. In contrast, the growth of provincial urban centres is more likely to be based on the expansion of employment in commerce and in other service sectors. Jobs in these sectors are likely to be in smaller enterprises or to be in self-employment. This is Faria's conclusion for Brazil and it fits much of the existing Latin American data. Thus, the city of Huancayo in Peru has an employment structure which is highly concentrated in smaller enterprises and in the service sector when compared with Lima. Huancayo has a large proportion of government employment and is the place of residence of government employees, such as teachers, who work in the villages of the region as well as in the city. The relatively high incomes of government employees are one of the mainstays of the city's economy; government employees have the highest average income of any occupational groups in the city. Many employees do not permanently reside in the city and the highest officials maintain a residence in Lima and make minimal investments in Huancayo (Roberts, 1976a). Thus, despite the contribution of government to the regional economy, the gains to the region are offset by the relative lack of local commitment on the part of these elite groups. They are not a source of capital accumulation and development for the region. Indeed, a concrete expression of Huancayo's contemporary dependency on Lima is the fact that many of its most prominent citizens (including its mayor) have been migrants who, in the course of their careers, will pass on to the national capital (Roberts, 1976a).

It would be unwise, however, to assume that provincial regions are stagnant economically and unimportant elements in national decision-making. The truth of the matter is that we often do not know enough about political and economic processes at the provincial level; the focus of studies of underdevelopment has been excessively on key metropolitan areas, their economies and politics. This focus will be one that will dominate the rest of this volume as we examine the way in which population has concentrated in large urban centres. Consequently, we must keep in mind not only national differences in the situation of underdevelopment, but also those that are produced by the territorial division of labour within countries. Small towns, provincial centres and national metropolises differ from each other in their occupational and income distributions, in their polities and in their urban culture. Had we the time and space, it would be possible to show that many of these differences are understandable in terms of the structure of interdependence produced by the uneven industrial development of the contemporary period.

Conclusion

L atin America's historical role as an exporter of raw materials and of foodstuffs, stimulated in the course of this century an extensive industrialization which has concentrated economic opportunities in the major cities of the region. Variations between countries in the degree of industrialization can, to a certain extent, be explained by the characteristics of the dominant classes and by the presence or absence of a strong, centralized state. Industrialization has, in turn, brought new forces into play, such as an organized working class and an industrial bourgeoisie. The political strength of these forces was limited by an uneven pattern of development in which agriculture remained controlled by traditional landowners and which, in the cities, resulted in a large service sector, often dependent on government. The inability of any one class to establish a clearly dominant position in this situation meant the emergence of the populist 'solution' to economic modernization by which, through limited concessions, the industrial working class was incorporated into the structure of government.

Industrialization has brought important changes in the economic relationships with developed countries. In a continent lacking in capital and with consumer preferences similar to those of the developed world, industrialization followed the capital-intensive pattern of more advanced countries. The dependence of underdeveloped countries has become technological. Foreign companies set up operations within the underdeveloped country producing basic consumer goods and importing their technology. These companies profit from the cheaper production costs of underdeveloped countries to export their manufactures to both the developed and underdeveloped world. The effects of this situation of technological dependence on economy, politics and lifestyles will be further explored in the following chapters; but one of its most evident consequences is the stagnation of provincial regions in the face of the concentration of economic growth in a few large cities.

It is at this point that we can appreciate the forces making for convergence in the patterns of urbanization in the underdeveloped world. To the extent that the economic dynamic of underdeveloped economies depends on emulating the consumption patterns of the advanced capitalist world, then the spatial representation of those patterns is likely to dominate. The concentration of middle- and high-income populations in a few urban centres makes investment in capital-intensive consumer goods industries attractive. These industries are located in, or close to, the centres of population and contribute to the attraction of the large cities for rural migrants. Improvements in urban infrastructure such as roads, lighting, sanitation and housing are part of the dynamic of this industrialization, extending the market for consumer durables such as automobiles and domestic appliances.

The increasing complexity of the urban environment in the large cities of Latin America is an important reason for technological dependence on the advanced capitalist nations. New and more sophisticated systems of communication and the means of keeping order increase reliance on foreign technicians and on advanced technology. The contrast between the large cities with their skyscrapers, sophisticated highway systems and ultramodern facilities and the small towns and villages of Latin America is a striking testimony to the urban basis of technological dependence.

|4|

Migration and the Agrarian Structure

The importance of industrialization in shaping the economy and society of underdeveloped countries must be set within a context in which a large proportion of the population still works in agriculture and lives in small towns and rural villages. In the next three chapters, I will focus on contemporary urban life in underdeveloped countries, but before making this shift in perspective, we need to consider the processes by which agricultural pursuits have become increasingly replaced by urban ones. I have argued that it is economic expansion, not stagnation or traditionalism, that is the basis of the contemporary problems of underdeveloped countries. This argument applies to the agrarian structures of underdeveloped countries which have long been affected and partially transformed by market forces. The agrarian structures of Latin America have, perhaps, been more deeply affected by external political and economic forces, and for a longer period, than have those of most underdeveloped areas, with the result that village-level society has been fragmented, social and economic relationships individualized and a labour supply made available for capitalist expansion (De Janvry and Garramon, 1977). However, the transformation of the agrarian structure in a capitalist direction has only been partial with peasant farming persisting in most parts of Latin America despite the expansion of large-scale commercial agriculture. Indeed, by the 1980s, peasants represented a larger proportion of the agricultural labour force than they did in the 1960s (De Janvry et al., 1989, Table 3).

I have touched on some of these themes in previous chapters and in the present one I will limit myself to a brief analysis of the economic diversity of rural Latin America and of the economic activities of its rural population. These activities are, I will claim, part of the flux of both urban and rural life, contributing to a geographical mobility and occupational diversity that are important factors in blurring class boundaries and limiting class organization. To understand urban economic activity and social stratification requires us, then, to develop an idea of the total field of action, rural as well as urban and, at times, international, within which urban populations move and survive. However, like their urban counterparts, the rural economies of Latin America have been changing in recent decades in directions that tend to diminish the intensity of rural-urban relations and the flow of rural-urban migration. We must then modify the account given in *Cities of Peasants* of the significance of migration for urban life by taking account of the differences between the present historical period and that of the mid-1970s (see Long (1977) and Long and Roberts (1994), for a full analysis of the dynamics of change in the agrarian structure).

We must remember that the importance of agricultural employment varies from country to country. By 1990, only 10 per cent of employment in Argentina, for example, was agricultural, whereas in Brazil, Colombia and Mexico agricultural employment was between 20 and 30 per cent of the total, and over 40 per cent of the total in Guatemala, Honduras, Bolivia and Paraguay (Table 4.1).

This section provides a brief overview of rural-urban migration. Though the contribution of rural-urban migration to the current rates of growth of cities is less than in the past, migrants and the children born to them in the city are a significant element in cultural, political and economic change. The sheer volume of movement makes urban migration one of the most evident 'problems' of underdeveloped countries; it has been estimated, for example, that between 1970 and 1980 net migration added some 300,000 to greater Sao Paulo each year from cities, towns and villages throughout Brazil (Martine, 1989).

The urban impact of these movements depends in part on the characteristics of the provincial areas from which the city draws its population. For example, the manner in which migrants cope with urban life is affected by the resources that they bring to the cities – the educational skills, the financial and material capital or the social capital of a network of friends and kin who provide lodgings and information about jobs. In turn, these resources vary from one area to another, depending on the level and type of their economic development and their social and cultural structure. Thus, the nature of the hinterland from which a city draws its population is one source of variation in the social structures of cities in underdeveloped countries.

Patterns of Migration and their Significance for Urban Growth

Industrialization initially entails a certain convergence in the patterns of migration throughout the underdeveloped world; for example, migration movements become a preponderantly rural-urban movement of a relatively permanent kind (Balan, 1973). This migration pattern contrasts with those

Table 4.1. Rural population and agricultural employment in Latin America, 1970–1990

Countries	Numbers of rural population			% Rural population			% Agricultural population		
	1970	1980	1990	1970	1980	1990	1970	1980	1990
Argentina	5178	4836	4493	22	17	14	16	13	10
Bolivia	2562	3114	3515	59	56	49	52	46	42
Brazil	42346	40952	36926	44	34	25	45	31	24
Colombia	9142	9568	9696	43	36	30	39	34	27
Costa Rica	1044	1300	1606	60	57	53	43	31	24
Chile	2354	2090	2029	25	19	15	23	17	13
Ecuador	3659	4308	4610	60	53	44	51	39	30
El Salvador	2175	2645	2875	61	58	55	56	43	37
Guatemala	3382	4330	5569	64	63	61	61	57	51
Honduras	1868	2346	2894	71	64	56	65	61	55
Mexico	20623	22561	23169	41	34	27	44	37	23
Nicaragua	1093	1306	1479	53	47	40	52	47	38
Panama	802	983	1139	52	50	47	42	32	25
Paraguay	1480	1835	2247	63	58	52	53	49	46
Peru	5619	6127	6509	43	35	30	47	40	35
Uruguay	503	430	343	18	15	11	19	19	14
Venezuela	2924	2513	1843	28	17	9	26	16	11
Total	106754	111244	110942	43	35	29	40	32	25

Sources: For rural and urban: United Nations, 1993; for structure of labour force, 1970 and 1980, ECLAC, 1993, Tables 18, 19; for 1990, Wilkie et al., 1993, Table 1310, corrected with available national censuses.

patterns previously predominant in Latin America which included substantial international migrations, seasonal and other temporary labour migrations and rural-to-rural migrations as well as cityward migration. One of the major reasons for the preponderance of urban migration is that industrialization begins to unify the internal market of underdeveloped countries, bringing even the more remote and less developed regions into direct economic dependence on the major urban centres. The improvement of internal communications is part of this process, so that regional identities and economic commitments are increasingly eroded by these centralizing forces. In the past, as we have seen, regionalism was often reinforced by the weakness of the economic and political links with the national capital and by direct economic links between a region of a country and foreign economies.

The overall trend in cityward migration until the 1970s is increasingly to concentrate populations in the large cities of Latin America. Robert Fox (1975, Table 5) shows that in the six major Latin American countries of his survey, the large cities (250,000 and more) increasingly concentrate the urban population; in 1960, they contained 63.5 per cent of the total urban population and by 1980 he estimated that they were likely to contain 69.6 per cent. The shift from economies orientated to the export of primary products to those which were internally focused and based on urban indus-trialization thus intensified population concentration in Latin America. Browning (1972a) shows that up until the 1960s there was an increasing trend towards urban primacy in all but one of the eight major Latin American countries. The exception to the trend is Brazil, but in this case the exception is produced by the emergence of a bi-city primacy (Rio and Sao Paulo).

In the 1980s, the patterns of migration appeared to have changed and become less centripetal in nature. Rural-urban migration lessened in impor-tance, while inter-urban migration and, in some countries, international migration gained in importance. The lessening of rural-urban migration was, in part, due to the declining proportions of the region's population liv-ing in rural areas. By 1990, for example, only 23 per cent of the Latin American population was classed as rural (Table 4.1). Economic changes combined with declines in fertility (more pronounced in the major metro-politan areas) to diversify the urban system. The largest cities have the low-est rates of natural increase and their large population base means that migration from a shrinking rural population is unlikely to add significantly to their growth. In contrast, medium-size and smaller cities, particularly in areas of low levels of economic development, as in the north-east of Brazil, are likely to have higher rates of natural increase and to gain more from migration.

By 1980, and more so by 1990, the primacy of many urban systems had declined. Portes (1989) reviews the trends in primacy up to the 1980s and finds evidence of a general decline in primacy in Latin America. The increas-ing disadvantages of agglomeration lead to some deconcentration of indus-trial activities and a movement of population from the crowded metropolises. These movements are usually to the peripheries of the large cities and have resulted, for example, in new industrial nucleii within a hun-dred miles or so of Sao Paulo and Mexico City. In Mexico and Brazil, it is the secondary cities that have been growing faster than the primary ones in recent decades. Thus, in Brazil, Martine (1992) shows that, in contrast to previous decades, the cities of more than a million people grow less fast than smaller urban centres and become a smaller proportion of the urban popu-lation. In Brazil, the fastest growing cities of the 1980s are cities peripheral to Sao Paulo, those serving the agricultural frontier in the north and centre-west of the country, and 'spa' cities; the latter trend Martine (1992) attrib-utes to the wealthy elderly seeking the Brazilian equivalent of Florida. My calculations show that in Mexico from 1980 to 1990 the annual rate of growth of intermediate-size cities, between 100,000 and 1 million, (3.2 per cent) was substantially faster than that of the four major metropolises: Mexico City, Guadalajara, Monterrey and Puebla (1.4 per cent). The fastest growing cities in Mexico are the border cities where the *maquila* industry is located, cities of the interior that are locations of export or tourist industry and cities peripheral to Mexico City.

A striking phenomenon of the 1980s in Mexico is the net out-migration of inhabitants of Mexico City to cities on its periphery, such as Toluca, Querétaro and Puebla, and to cities on the northern border of Mexico, such as Tijuana and Ciudad Juarez. As we have seen, the crises of many Latin American economies in the 1980s severely impacted the cities, leading many of their inhabitants to move elsewhere in search of work or a cheaper cost of living. Also, the lack of opportunities in the cities are likely to have deterred rural-urban migration, but this issue needs further research. Economic crisis did, however, increase international migration to the United States from Mexico and Central America. Though this migration is still predominantly from rural areas, it begins to include many urban inhabitants (Cornelius, 1991a, b). In the case of Mexico City, it often includes those who had originally migrated there from a rural area and who, when faced with lack of economic opportunities in the city, took the further step of moving to the United States.

Contemporary international migration is different in several important respects from the international migrations that we reviewed in earlier chapters where the 'surplus' populations of Europe came to the Americas and helped develop labour-short economies (Massey, 1989). Most contemporary international migrants originate in developing countries and come to developed countries, such as the United States, whose ecomomies are expanding slowly and offer immigrants few opportunities other than unskilled labour. We will consider later in this chapter some of the implications of these changes in the nature of international migration.

A key consideration to bear in mind is the changing demographic situation. Population growth in underdeveloped areas has been high, but is now beginning to decline in many places. In tropical and middle America and tropical Africa, where the rates of growth were fastest, population increased at approximately 2.7 per cent annually from 1950 to 1990, and the annual rates of growth in southern and south-eastern Asia were approximately 2.3 per cent in the same period. In contrast, population increase in England and Wales in the period of the Industrial Revolution – say 1801–51 – was approximately 1.5 per cent a year. The high rates of population increase in underdeveloped countries result from the reduction in mortality consequent on improvements in health, sanitation and medical facilities, while countervailing trends reducing the birth-rate appear later. It is only in the 1980s that birth-rates have declined markedly as a result of the social and economic changes accompanying urbanization and industrialization. In Latin

America, fertility rates (births per women aged 15–49) dropped from 5.0 in 1970–75 to 3.1 in 1990–95, though the impact of this drop on natural increase is offset somewhat by an increase in life expectancy in the same period from 61 to 68 years (World Bank, 1994b, Table 2.2).

In this situation, migration from rural areas can contribute substantially to urban growth without depopulating the rural areas. Table 4.1 shows that, despite the rapid urbanization of Latin America, the absolute size of the rural population kept on increasing up to 1980. Indeed, since productivity in agriculture was low in 1950 and declined further by 1990, rural out-migration did not even remove the economically 'surplus' rural population. The trend among large-scale commercial farming operations was toward a drop in the demand for permanent labour. The dense concentrations of rural population were usually in poor, dry-farming zones where there were few employment opportunities in agriculture. Rural population increase was, under these conditions, absorbed by households relying more than previously on combining various farm and non-farm activities. Thus, a detailed analysis of demographic change over 20 years in a highland village of Peru – the Ayacucho community of Quinua – shows the difference between births and deaths resulted in a 1.2 per cent annual growth rate in 1960, and 2.8 per cent in 1980 (Mitchell, 1991). In this village, agriculture was only one part of the population's subsistence activities that included a thriving craft industry in pottery, trade and labour migration.

Too much should not be made of the often mentioned 'peculiarity' of contemporary urbanization in underdeveloped countries, the lack of rural depopulation. In nineteenth-century Europe rural depopulation also was not significant in the early stages of urbanization. In England, agricultural employment and production probably continued to increase during the first half of the nineteenth century (Saville, 1957). In Germany, the small amount of rural depopulation at the end of the nineteenth century is accounted for by the 'promotion' of rural villages to urban status and thus their inclusion by the census-takers under urban population (Weber, 1899). What is significant about the Latin American data is that in many countries rapid urbanization is accompanied by an increasing population pressure on a rural structure in which land is unevenly distributed and which, for most of the population, is insufficient to meet even subsistence needs.

De Janvry and his collaborators assembled data on sixteen Latin American countries to show that between 1950 and 1980 the average size of small farms declined from 2.4 to 2.1 hectares (De Janvry et al., 1989). They point out that this decline in land size means that the peasantry is increasingly 'cornered', dependent on non-farm sources of income but often unable to abandon subsistence farming for the lack of full-time wage employment opportunities, either locally or through out-migration. It is worth noting, in this context, that agrarian reform in Latin America did little to alleviate land shortage (see the analysis of the various agrarian reform programmes in

Latin America in Long and Roberts, 1994). Despite the effects of the Mexican Revolution in redistributing land, land concentration persisted: in 1960, agricultural units of less than five hectares made up 77.3 per cent of the total of over 1,000,000 private landholdings, but controlled only 10.8 per cent of the total cultivated land. Units of over 400 hectares were 0.2 per cent of the total number of units and 35.5 per cent of the over 13,000,000 hectares cultivated (CIDA, 1970). Even when *ejidal* land (redistributed as social property with agrarian reform) is included, 2,000 landholdings of over 400 hectares still make up 20.4 per cent of the area cultivated. In Chile, agrarian reform was reversed under the Pinochet government, returning expropriated land to its original owners. In Chile, as elsewhere in Latin America, it is the medium-size capitalist farm that increasingly predominates, not the large estate, but the peasantry remains equally marginalized (see the essays in Kay and Silva, 1992).

In the years of most rapid urbanization, 1950–1970, urban growth rates were particularly high because of the combination of high rates of natural increase of the urban population and large numbers of rural-urban migrants. In Latin America and in other underdeveloped regions, there is little difference in the rates of natural increase between urban and rural populations; cities, particularly in the early stages of rural-urban migration, have a higher proportion of young adults than the countryside – a fact that increases crude birth rates and decreases crude death rates – and public health is generally better in cities. Another factor offsetting the tendency of the urban milieu to depress birth rates is, as Faria (1976) points out, the informal economic organization of cities in underdeveloped countries. This informal organization makes it possible to use child labour at an early age, but entails economic insecurity in old age, thus making children an economic and social asset. However, with the slow-down in the growth of the Latin American cities from the 1970s onwards, the associated set of factors reducing birth rates have begun to predominate: a later average age of marriage, higher educational levels among men and women and more opportunities for women to work outside the home, leading to higher rates of female economic participation, even among married women.

The importance of migration in urbanization must not obscure the equally important fact that the population of even a fast-growing city is often mostly born in that city. Natural increase has accounted for most urban growth in Latin America between 1950 and 1990, and the contribution of natural increase is particularly strong from the 1970s onwards (Table 1.2). George Martine (1972) provides a case study on the growth of Rio de Janeiro since 1920, showing the decreasing importance of migration in that city's growth over time.

In the period 1920 to 1940, internal migration accounted for at least 60 per cent of Rio's growth to 1,764,100; international migration accounted for another 15 per cent and natural increase for the remainder (Martine, 1972). By 1950, the city's population was 2,377,450; 69.1 per cent of the increase was accounted for by internal migration and 4.1 per cent by immigration. In 1960, a population of 3,281,910 had increased 45.6 per cent through migration and 45.2 per cent by natural increase. By 1970, natural increase accounted for 57 per cent of population growth.

In Guatemala City, approximately 40 per cent of the city's growth between 1950 and 1964 was due to immigration (Roberts, 1973a). About one-third of Mexico's urban population growth from 1960 to 1970 was the result of migration and, in contrast to previous decades, between 1950 and 1970 natural increase was more important than migration in the growth of urban population (Cornelius, 1975; Unikel, 1975). The Mexican censuses of 1980 and 1990 show that cities of more than 100,000 inhabitants grew at a annual rate of 2.1 per cent, just half their rate of growth in the previous three decades. The annual rate of increase of Mexico's total population in 1980 to 1990 was 1.9 per cent, also substantially lower than in previous decades, but suggesting that the cities grew mainly by natural increase. Mexico City's rate of growth for this period was, in fact, less than population growth, suggesting a substantial out-migration from the city.

The preponderance of migration in urban growth is thus likely to occur mainly in the first stages of rapid urbanization when the large size of the rural population can sustain high rates of transfer to the urban population and when population increase in both urban and rural areas is high. Perceptions of the migrant 'problem' in urban growth are thus likely to vary for demographic reasons by historical period. The fears of the influx of rural migrants that beset many urban natives in the 1950s and 1960s may be less present today in those countries which are urbanizing slowly and at a time when the rates of population growth are in decline. Even within rapidly urbanizing countries, the importance of migration to urban growth will vary according to how recently established the urban centre is or to differences between cities in their rates of growth. By the end of the 1980s, the large majority of the population of Mexico City was born in that city; in contrast, migrants made up the majority of the population of the fast-growing industrial cities of Mexico's northern border.

The contribution of migration to urban growth is, however, a cumulative one; children of migrants born in towns or cities are counted as part of the natural increase of urban places. Consequently, even in those countries in which net migration contributes a minor fraction of urban population growth, the migration experience may still be an important one in the urban social structure. Lowder (1973) has calculated, for example, that in Lima, Peru, the chances of a child who was born in the city having both parents who were also born there is less than one in ten. Furthermore, since migrants are disproportionately drawn from those age groups who are economically active (14–60), the adult and working population of a city may be predominantly migrants even when the majority of the population has been born in the city, since a large part of this majority is likely to be made up of children under 14.

Internal migration is also more significant to urban growth than it might appear from the statistics. As we noted above, the urban populations of Latin America are, in some respects, floating populations. A city grows not only through the addition of the newly born or the migrant to an existing stable population, but also through the increasing flows of people who pass through the city and who are recorded as the resident population at the census points. Even those born in a city may not have resided there for their whole lives; many will have left to work elsewhere, often in other urban areas, before returning to their native city.

Changes in the Agrarian Structure

The persistence of a large and growing rural population in the face of inadequate land resources and the substantial economic and social changes accompanying urbanization and industrialization is the problem posed by Singer (1973) when he remarks that the basic issue of internal migration is *not* why so many people leave the land but why more people do not do so. In this section, my aim is to explain the presence of two apparently conflicting trends in the agrarian structure – one towards an increasing 'peasantization' of the rural economy that acted to retain population on the land and to create strong rural-urban linkages and the other towards an increasing proletarianization that tended to expel population and to weaken rural-urban linkages.

These trends vary in their scope and nature from one country to another and from one region of a country to another, depending on the nature of the local agrarian structure and the impact upon it of the changes in the national and international economy. At least four types of agrarian structure can be identified in different areas and countries of Latin America by the mid-twentieth century (see Long and Roberts (1994) for a full discussion of these types). The first type is the agrarian structure dominated by large-scale commercial production found mainly in the southern cone countries, such as cereal and cattle production in the Pampas of Argentina. The various types of farming unit common in this type of production supported a large, but frequently transient population of permanent and temporary labourers, tenants and small proprietors (Taylor, 1948). A second type is the economic enclave based on mining or plantation agriculture exemplified by the banana and sugar plantations in Central America, the Caribbean, the Morelos region of Mexico, northern Peru and north-west Argentina, and mining enterprises in highland Peru and Bolivia. The labour for the enclaves is often provided by labour migration from areas of subsistence farming. Thirdly, small-scale, market-orientated farming dominated some regions in most countries of Latin America: the Antioqueño region of Colombia, the

Mendoza region of Argentina, parts of Rio Grande do Sul, Santa Catarina, Paraná in southern Brazil and much of the western area of Mexico. A fascinating case study of a farming area of this type is Daniel Nugent's (1994) account of the town of Namiquipa, in the state of Chihuahua, Mexico. The settlement was originally founded as a means of populating Mexico's northern frontier and as a defence against Indian raids. From the mid-nineteenth century onwards, townspeople defended their small-holdings not only against Indian attack but against the attempt of the state following the Mexican Revolution of 1910 (which townspeople supported) to impose central control through the *ejido* system of social property.

Perhaps the most common type was that of subsistence farming interspersed with estates of low productivity. Though rarer in the southern cone, with the exception of Chile, this type was frequently encountered to the north in the areas of pre-Hispanic settment in Bolivia, Peru and Ecuador. They were found in the northern areas of Brazil where the decline of the sugar economy had resulted in subsistence farming even on large estates and were common in Central America and Mexico.

The predominance of one form of agrarian structure or another is an important source of variation in rural-urban relationships and in the characteristics of migration. Areas of capitalist farming, for example, directly 'expel' more people than do areas of peasant farming through consolidating land and through mechanization, resulting in a permanent out-migration. In some areas of Latin America, the increasing commercialization of agriculture may not result in a lessening of the demand for labour, but instead creates a resident rural proletariat which works on nearby farms for a wage or migrates from place to place in search of seasonal agricultural work (D'incao e Mello, 1976). Such rural workers will often live in the towns. These trends have been analysed for Brazil by Lopes (1976), for Mexico by Bartra (1974), for Peru by Greaves (1972), and for Chile by Rodriguez (1987). This transformation of the agrarian structure is the classic case of capitalist development as described for England by Marx; it occurred even in those counties such as Lancashire where domestic industry (handloom weaving) predominated (Marshall, 1961; Roberts, 1978b). This trend means that when the rural population eventually migrates to urban areas there are few economic ties binding urban populations to their rural origins.

The processes of agricultural modernization have an important impact on the peasantry that contribute, indirectly, to out-migration of both a permanent and temporary kind. The higher productivity of capitalist farming areas means severe market competition for peasant farming, while modernization is likely to reduce the demand for temporary or seasonal labour previously supplied by peasant farmers. Earning less for their products on the market and deprived of essential supplementary sources of income, the population of poor, dry-farming areas becomes a major source of urban and international migration, as Arroyo (1989) shows for the rural areas of western Mexico and Martine (1987) for Brazil. Martine points out that when the peasant farming system in Brazil began to break down, out-migration was substantial since the small, peasant farm was highly efficient in its use of labour. The intensive use of labour on the peasant farm results in a high value of production per hectare, enabling relatively large numbers to subsist on small amounts of land. When demography and external economic pressures make this system unworkable, the effect is like a dam breaking, releasing, as it were, a flood of labour onto the market.

The peasant population has supplied most migrants in Latin America. This population is a key source of labour for the other types of production, providing temporary labour to plantations, commercial farms and even to areas of small-scale, market-orientated farming. Also, areas of peasant production present a complex set of economic and social relationships in which family enterprises span rural and urban locations, with town migrants retaining rights to land and aiming to return eventually. Peasant (subsistence) farmers not only survive in the present period but have increased in number since the 1940s, providing food for the large urban centres and a subsistence base for those working seasonally in commercial agriculture or, even, in urban employment. Migrant labour is common among them as is trade and craft work complementary to agriculture. Relatively few peasant households depend exclusively on agriculture for their survival. Many are semi-proletarians in that they engage in occasional wage labour, but full-time wage labourers are sparse in the countryside. Indeed, by the 1980s, peasant farmers were 65 per cent of the agricultural population compared with 61 per cent in the 1960s and have increased in absolute numbers (De Janvry et al., 1989).

We can understand the persistence of the peasantry by reminding ourselves of the impact of the export economy on the rural areas of Latin America. Subsistence farming, whether in independent village communities or on land rented or sharecropped from *haciendas*, increasingly changed its nature as a consequence of the articulation with capitalist forms of production. From at least the time of the Spanish conquest, subsistence farming in Latin America was not a natural economy based on the self-sufficiency of agricultural and craft production at village level. Very few subsistence farmers could hope to survive entirely from the product of their land or from domestic industry; increasingly in all parts of Latin America, wage migration became a permanent part of the village economy. Likewise, village households increasingly diversified their economic activities. Women and children might engage in small-scale trading or artisan activities to complement the family budget, men might permanently engage in seasonal migration to plantations or urban centres. Trading and artisan activities became tied into regional and even national networks of exchange.

The processes through which this diversification occurred are not difficult to identify. In part, they result from increasing demographic pressure on existing land. The best lands were occupied by the large enterprises and, with division of inheritance, each generation had less land resources available. Demographic pressure is only part of the explanation, however, because we need to know why so many stayed on the land despite the increasing difficulty of making a living.

Expedients such as temporary migration were an integral part of the survival of the household economy. A husband's or wife's wage labour was generally sufficient to complement small-scale farming or craft activities, but given the low wages of the plantations or mines it was often not enough to provide an attractive basis for the permanent migration of the whole family. The 10,000-strong workforce of the smelting plants of *Cerro de Pasco* Corporation in central Peru was essentially made up of 'temporary' migrants from the nearby villages of the Mantaro valley (Laite, 1981). These worked in the smelters for an average of two to three years and, if married, left their families behind in the villages to which they, too, eventually returned. In the Bolivian mines, in contrast, the greater distance from the sources of labour supply appear to have resulted in a more permanent settlement of workers and their families (Boeger, 1994).

In the rural economy, the defection of one member of a household to seek work permanently outside could have serious consequences for the viability of the household and its family commitments. In this situation, the costs of more permanent or long-distance migration were greater since these included the loss in labour suffered by the village-based household enterprise, whether in farming, crafts or commerce. One of the reasons why even the younger members of poor households in the Mantaro valley of Peru did not migrate at the turn of the century was their responsibility for older kin; unless younger members worked as sharecroppers or as peones, there would be no one to take responsibility for their older kin.

Wages earned in the mines or plantations, money made from trade and so on became one of the main bases for the diversification of village economies. It provided capital on a small scale for investments in trade, craft production, fertilizer and seed and by so doing made possible the intensification of subsistence exploitation. Larger numbers of people survived on a fairly constant set of resources, not only by increasing their labour input but also by making such a labour input feasible through an increased use of cash to underpin the new ventures.

In certain respects, this process is akin to that described by Geertz when he discussed what he terms the agricultural involution of the village economy in Indonesia (Geertz, 1963a). There, too, the plantation economy uses the labour of the villages and the village economy intensifies its input of available labour to raise food production marginally. Geertz's point is that the process of involution – increasing attention to detail through a high labour input for only a small increase in production – destroys the dynamic of capital accumulation at the village level; productivity is not raised per capita and thus there are few opportunities for local entrepreneurs to accumulate and begin to set in train a rationalization of local production leading to the predominance of capitalist agricultural production. In this context, the increasing commercialization of agricultural production does not necessarily dispossess the peasant farmer of his land or displace agricultural labour; instead, village land becomes one part of a household economy that includes migration as an integral feature of its own survival.

Household-based enterprises persist in the rural areas because access to land provides a secure basis for utilizing all available labour to obtain a certain standard of subsistence; these enterprises produce goods at competitive prices by the working of long hours, using unpaid household labour and accepting low standards of subsistence. It is this kind of farming enterprise that I include under the term 'peasant'. It is the peasant sector of the rural economy which is expanding most rapidly, numerically, in many underdeveloped countries. Even in those countries where capitalist farming is expanding rapidly, such as Brazil, peasant farms are increasing through the colonization of new lands and the renting of land from *latifundia*. Many *latifundia* in north-eastern Brazil produce crops that compete with the more efficient capitalist production of the central south zone and have substantially reduced the number of their *colonos* (tied labourers) and the area of land under cultivation. In this situation, peasant farmers survive because they provide a low-cost product, such as beans and rice, or become colonists on the Amazonian frontier opening up land that the capitalist enterprise may subsequently take over (Lopes, 1976, 1977; Schmink and Wood, 1992).

Also, industrialization is often accompanied by the increasing diversification and commercial vitality of the rural, household-based economy. Kemper and Foster (1975) demonstrate the increasing diversification of the village economy in their well documented study of developments over 40 years in the village of Tzintzuntzan in Mexico. Out-migration from the village was relatively rare prior to 1945, but subsequently increased to reach a peak in the 1960–69 period. Tzintzuntzan became linked by good roads to the urban centres. This integration into the national economy was accompanied by increasing sales of urban products in the village and an increasing commercialization of agriculture. During this period, the population of the village increased despite out-migration from 1,003 in 1930 to 2,169 in 1970; moreover, the period of most rapid population increase in the village (3.2 per cent per annum between 1950 and 1960) was also a period when the village economy was closely articulated to the national urban economy. The local economy became increasingly diversified as the number of full-time farmers decreased and the number of craftsmen and small traders increased.

A similar process occurred in the village of Muquiyauyo, in the Mantaro valley of central Peru, despite severe land shortage. In the period from about 1940 to 1960 the local economy increasingly diversified as it became more closely integrated, through migration, into the national economy; the numbers of local stores, craftsmen and farmers making a surplus increased substantially (Adams, 1959; Grondin, 1978a, b; Laite, 1981). Muquiyauyo's population grew from just over 1,000 at the turn of the century to 3,500 in 1960.

The dynamic of small-scale production is akin to that of competitive capitalism. Small-scale enterprises survive in the face of modern capitalist expansion by a high degree of exploitation of labour and a readiness to undertake the riskier and less profitable branches of production and services (Roberts, 1975; Singer, 1973). Bartra (1974) terms a similar process in Mexico 'permanent primitive accumulation'. The logic of this form of agrarian transformation is that of the small trader, transporter or industrialist seeking to sell or obtain products in geographical areas and among sectors of the population which are relatively isolated from modern capitalist enterprise. The presence of this process is one of the most crucial variables affecting the pattern of internal migration.

The most successful rural entrepreneurs are those most likely to leave, especially in the early stages, since their activities (or those of their parents) will have generated the capital and skills to make migration feasible. Moreover, their commercial activities will have brought them into contact with the urban centres and provided knowledge of urban job opportunities. The greater economic opportunities offered by the large cities are sufficient reason why such groups should wish to transfer their enterprise or acquired skills (such as educational attainment). The more successful or better educated represent those groups who are most 'free' to undertake the movement. Their local labour is less necessary to the survival of the household unit or can be more easily replaced by hiring others. Other areas of a country become involved in cityward migrations as they become internally transformed by economic diversification. This description fits the pattern of rural out-migration in Brazil where, as Martine (1989) puts it, '(out-migration) is not directly proportional to the relative levels of poverty/development of different subregions, but to the *timing* and the pace of penetration of capitalist forms of agricultural production.' Those that leave these more remote or 'backward' areas are likely to be those with superior skills or resources in comparison with the population of origin.

Poor farmers are incorporated into local enterprises to provide occasional labour in the fields and to aid with local crafts or trading ventures. In certain cases, farmers are attracted from poorer agricultural regions to work in more prosperous regions, cultivating on a sharecropping or rental basis the fields of those who have migrated to live in the city (Roberts, 1976b; Long and Roberts, 1984). In this way, the agrarian structure retains an increasing population while making such a population increasingly mobile.

This description is complicated by the likelihood that in certain regions members of the poorer, more subsistence-based strata of the agrarian population will at times be forced by the development of capitalist production in agriculture to undertake long-distance migration; also, poorer families may move by stages to work in other villages, small towns or provincial centres. The permanent long-distance migration of the poorest is, however, less likely to take place than that of the more skilled and prosperous since they will not have the contacts or resources to survive easily in the competitive job market of the big cities. Massey and his colleagues (1987) describe these processes as they affect villages in the centre-west of Mexico whose inhabitants migrate internationally as well as internally. Migrants, whether to Mexican cities or to the United States, tend to be better educated and less poor than non-migrants. Interestingly, migrants to the Mexican cities appear to be somewhat more highly educated and skilled than those to the United States, presumably because migrants find that there is a greater payoff for skill and literacy in the Mexican urban labour markets than in those of the United States where the demand is mainly for unskilled labour. Nugent (1994) describes the long-term involvement of people from Namiquipa in temporary migration to the United States. This migration enabled many to continue subsistence farming, but by the 1980s agriculture in the township had become more commercialized, the numbers of landless labourers had grown and, it appears, temporary migration was being replaced by permanent out-migration.

A further complication is that some of the areas that provided the earliest city migrants may subsequently prove attractive areas to which migrants return. These areas are economically diversified and may have been completely transformed in the direction of petty commodity production; as such, they provide a range of small-scale economic opportunities that city migrants may eventually consider as offering more secure or profitable opportunities than does the city. For this pattern to occur, however, it is necessary that such areas do not become completely transformed by modern capitalist production. Lopes' (1979) description of the increasing capitalization of agriculture in the area of Sao Paulo demonstrates that there are decreasing economic opportunities in this area other than those of wage labour.

Seeing internal migration as a product of local enterprise rather than of local stagnation helps to differentiate the stages of internal migration and the characteristics of those migrating. When the agrarian structure is transformed through the agency of small-scale enterprise, internal migration is a manifestation of the progressive and cumulative incorporation of provincial areas into the dominant national urban economy. This incorporation is one that is organized by the economic activities of provincials; it is not a disorganized response to external pressures. The recognition that internal, cityward migrations are, under certain conditions, socially and economically organized movements helps to explain, as we will see, the high degree of organization displayed by migrants in the cities. The peasant, semi-proletarian character of many regions of Latin America has influenced the development of the cities, placing, I suggest, unusual emphasis on networks of kin and fellow villagers in migrant adaptation to the city. In turn, weak industrialization created urban labour markets that encouraged individual and family initiative to survive in the cities. Members mixed wage employment, unpaid wage labour and self-employment of various kinds. They profited from kin-based economic networks that, at times, linked city and country-side, as Smith (1984) shows for highland Peruvian migrants in Lima.

Rural-urban migration in most of Latin America was usually direct migration to the large cities from small as well as medium-size places (Roberts, 1978a). Few of the migrants coming to the cities had prior experi-ence of full-time wage work in the countryside, though migrant labour to mines and plantations gave some experience of labour organization. For example, in the early twentieth century, recession in the mining regions of the north of Chile led to migration to Santiago and brought workers with experience of political organization to the capital, including women work-ers (Valdes and Weinstein, 1993).

These patterns of migration also need to be compared with patterns else-where that differ in terms of the proletarian origins of urban migrants. In Northern Europe, for example, the population that flocked to the cities appears to have substantially been a proletarian one (Tilly, 1984). However, the agrarian structure of Southern Europe, particularly the south of Italy, was peasant and semi-proletarian (Lopreato, 1967). In the south of Italy, weak industrialization, peasant migration to the cities and the importance of networks in subsistence appear to have been factors in shaping the urban cultures of the south as compared to the north of Italy (Mingione, 1994).

By the 1980s, family-based peasant farming was under severe threat as a viable and widespread source of livelihood in Latin America as a result of the cumulation of difficulties it faced: declining size of landholdings, inade-quate credit and infrastructure, an urban bias that kept food prices low, often through imports, at the expense of the small farmer and competition from modernized estates and small- and medium-size farms run as capitalist enterprises. Lack of opportunities in the rural areas reinforced the perma-nence of out-migration.

As migration became a permanent affair, household and community organization was restructured, though to different degrees, depending on the intensity of national economic changes and on social class position. Out-migration, by permanently removing whole households or members of households, usually young adult males and females seeking education or work in the urban centres, restructured inter- and intrahousehold coopera-tion. The households that remained, while more likely to contain male and female heads permanently committed to the local economy, were less likely to have additional labour resources. Though the locality might contain more households than previously, each rural household by the 1980s had a smaller number of members.

This both reduced the possibilities of interhousehold cooperation and increased the need for those households with more land to employ wage labour. The farming strategy of such households was inevitably geared to maximizing the profits to be gained from farming and associated activities. The hunger for cash and out-migration also severely reduced the amount of able-bodied labour available to the subsistence economy. Thus, in a long-term study of back-and-forth migration between a Peruvian highland village and a coffee colonization area, Collins (1988) shows that migrants became more firmly embedded in the cash economy of the coffee area, resulting in their increasingly withdrawing labour from the agricultural and craft activities of the home village. Hence, the highland village economy was starved of labour and was sustained, with difficulty, mainly by older people. The combination of all these factors resulted in a process of social differentiation in the rural sector based on the increasing specialization and commoditization of the household.

The impact of these changes is often generational. As each generation reached adulthood, its pattern of agricultural work was shaped by the opportunities available at the time. It was the children of the generation of the 1930s and the 1940s, not their parents, who felt the full brunt of the breakdown of family-based agriculture where that had occurred. They were a transitional generation for whom temporary work opportunities, either in agriculture or outside of it, became a permanent way of life in many parts of Latin America.

They remained in the rural areas because their parents still worked there while they, unlike the subsequent generation, had not been fully caught up in the increasng flow of cityward migration. The temporary work opportunities, taken up in early adulthood, were not replaced by a stable attachment to land, either as a smallholder peasant or as a permanent worker. In the subsequent generation, work opportunities in agriculture for those few children who remained were more stable, even though they were as likely to be wage workers as smallholders. These generational changes are described in detail by Vanegas (1987) in her account of the change in the nature of work opportunities in the fruit-growing area of the Central Valley of Chile. There was a substantial increase in temporary work among the transitional generation who reached adulthood in the 1950s, but permanent wage work predominated among the modern generation of males. An important factor underlying these trends is declining fertility, meaning that the families of recent generations are smaller and have fewer children seeking work. Smaller households and permanent out-migration are also likely to mean that the migrant networks that connect village and city are now less dense than in the past.

The Characteristics of Migrants and of Migration Movements

Studies of the individual characteristics of migrants and the nature of their movements are numerous, but their findings are complex and often contradictory, warning us, as Morse (1971a, b) and Gilbert (1974) have pointed out, of the dangers of generalizing without discriminating carefully between migrants of different socio-economic backgrounds and between different urban and rural contexts (see Gugler's (1992) overview of urban-rural migration in developing countries). With this caveat in mind, I will examine the extent to which the processes of rural economic diversification described in the last section explain the characteristics of migrants and the pattern of their movements. I will qualify this perspective by introducing a time perspective. Migration is influenced by the particular stage and intensity of the industrial development through which a country is passing. Also, migration necessarily changes the social structure of both rural and urban areas in terms of both age and sex distribution and educational and occupational qualifications, creating a new situation for future migrations.

The change from temporary labour migration to mines and plantations to a more permanent rural-urban migration was a slow and often partial one. Even in those cases in which the plantation or mine economy was in relative decline and economic expansion was occurring in the urban industrial sector, it often took time for internal migrations to reflect these changes. Merrick and Graham (1979) survey the long-run changes in population redistribution in Brazil, contrasting, among other periods, 1940–50 with 1950–60, and 1960–70. In the first period, despite the poverty of the north-eastern region, the rate of net out-migration from this region was lower than that of Minas Gerais which, although poorer than the southern area to which its migrants went in search of work, was wealthier than the north-east. It is only in 1950–60 that the rate of out-migration from the north-east became greater than out-migration from Minas Gerais.

A substantial proportion of north-eastern migration is long-distance migration to the economically developing areas of the central south. Graham (1970) attributes the change in migration patterns between the earlier and the later period to the greater rate of economic growth in the second period, with industrialization proceeding faster than the expansion of agricultural production both in aggregate and on a per worker basis. He also emphasizes the improvements in road networks and in transport that facilitated long-distance migration.

In the first stages of urban-industrial expansion it is, then, not necessarily the poorest areas in a nation which have the most substantial out-migration rates but those areas close to the expanding economic centres. The costs of transport and the risks of seeking work far from home counter the attraction of substantially higher incomes. Studies in Chile, Colombia and Mexico and estimates from Brazil show that initially most migrants come from the areas close to the expanding centres (Herrick, 1965; Simmons and Cardona, 1972; Balan et al., 1973; Martine, 1989, 1992). This migration pattern is similar to that of England during her industrialization where, also, there was little long-distance migration of poor farmers from the south to the north of England.

Census data on immigration to Lima in Peru since 1940 show some of the social and economic factors underlying and modifying this short-distance migration (*Censo Nacional*, 1940; Cuadro 145). In 1940, the departments (administrative regions) that contributed most migrants to Lima were the neighbouring departments of Ancash, Junin and Ica, the northern department of La Libertad (centre of the sugar industry) and the southern department of Arequipa. All these departments had been substantially affected by the expansion of capitalist enterprises linked to the export economy and were, with the exception of Ancash, among the departments with the highest literacy rates and the highest proportion of people living in urban places. More densely populated and poorer departments, such as Puno in the southern highlands, sent very few migrants to Lima. In the censuses since 1940 other departments have come increasingly to contribute to Lima's growth and these departments are among the remotest and poorest in the country, such as Ayacucho, Huancavelica and Puno. A similar trend is found in the contribution of various regions of Mexico to the growth of the capital city; it is only in the 1960s and 1970s that migrants from poorer and more isolated regions such as the state of Hidalgo appear in substantial numbers in Mexico City. By the 1980s, even migrants from the most remote villages are found in Latin America's metropolises, usually occupying unskilled positions in domestic service, construction or the 'informal' economy. This trend is also apparent in international migration from Mexico to the United States. The first international migrants, at the end of the nineteenth century, came from the predominantly *mestizo* states of the west of Mexico where agriculture was already highly commercialized (Gamio, 1930; Taylor, 1932). In the 1980s, Indian migrants from economically isolated villages in the state of Oaxaca were migrating to the major Mexican cities and were forming visible migrant communities in the Mexican border cities and in California (Hirayabashi, 1993; Nagengast and Kearney, 1990).

The gradual inclusion of more remote and poorer regions in migration to the major urban centres suggests that contemporary rural-urban migrations are selective processes (Gilbert, 1974). Browning argues that migrant selectivity is a general feature of the first stages of urbanization and summarizes data from a variety of Latin American countries and from Africa to show that in the early stages of migration out-migrants are disproportionately concentrated in the young adult age groups, are more likely to be single than the populations of origin, are better educated and are more likely to have non-agricultural occupations than the populations of origin (Browning, 1972). Migrants to the metropolitan centres in many Latin American countries have been drawn disproportionately from urban as opposed to rural places (Elizaga, 1971; Herrick, 1965).

The major contrast that Browning finds between Latin American and African migration is that cityward migration in Latin America is often predominantly female, whereas in Africa it was until recently predominantly male (Caldwell, 1969; Gugler, 1992). Female migration to cities in Latin America is encouraged by the multitude of jobs available for women in domestic and other service activities (Herrick 1965; Degregori et al., 1986).

Browning (1971) uses data from a detailed survey of the migration and occupational histories of males in Monterrey, Mexico, to demonstrate that over time the selectivity of migrants decreases; the more recent migrants are more like the populations of origin in terms of marital status, education, work experience and so on. The argument is that early out-migration disproportionately reduces the available 'pool' of those with exceptional qualifications, so that subsequent migrants must necessarily be drawn from those whose characteristics are more like the population of origin.

In the Mantaro valley in the central highlands of Peru, we found that a member of a richer household was relatively free to migrate because he could secure the labour of others to tend the farm while he was away; but poor villagers remained to provide that labour or to sharecrop the lands of the rich migrant. The situation changed as migration became a more generalized phenomenon in the central highlands. Wage labour in mines and plantations, work on construction projects and industrial work in Lima or in the provincial capital of Huancayo meant that more and more villagers became involved in the migration process. This, in itself, reduced the risks attending migration; friends of family members who had already migrated to work centres acted as bridgeheads facilitating the entry of those remaining in the village. The migration networks established soon encompassed the entire village populations. Furthermore, remittances from migrants and increasing numbers of returned migrants contributed towards a change in the village economy, generalizing the marketing of agricultural products and a money economy. Educational facilities at the village level also improved considerably in the period from about 1940 so that most young adults after that period were literate and had finished primary school. In the contemporary period there is no association between the economic and social status of a village family and the likelihood of its members either being migrants or having migrated (Laite, 1977; Roberts, 1976b; Long and Roberts, 1984). It is still the case, however, that those from the richer village families tend to obtain the better urban jobs; indeed, many of the sons of these families were educated to university level.

This emphasis on socio-structural factors in migration is not intended to be a substitute for an analysis of the spatial and economic variables that also determine migration. For example, the distance that a migrant must travel, the nature of his educational and occupational credentials and the relative importance of the economic centre to which he travels are variables whose interaction explains much of the variation between cities in the nature of the migrant 'pool' on which they draw. Such an analysis is, however, insufficient to provide an understanding of migration under the rural conditions of most underdeveloped countries, as can be appreciated by examining the issue of stage migration and its importance in contemporary migration movements. Taebur and his collaborators have described the stage migration process in the United States as follows: 'The aggregate shift from farm to large cities or suburbs is accomplished not by direct moves but by a series of less drastic moves – from farm to village, from village to town, from town to city ... Many persons participate in these successive displacements, but the typical individual manages only one or two stages in his lifetime' (Taebur et al., 1968). Stage migration, with its implication that internal migration is predominantly short-distance migration, was the pattern identified by Ravenstein (1885) and Redford (1926) in the British Isles in the nineteenth century. In Brazil, Chile and Colombia stage migration has been seen as the typical pattern of cityward migration (Singer, 1973; Herrick, 1965; Morse, 1971b).

Browning (1971) makes the point that stage migration is most likely to predominate where there is a well-developed urban size hierarchy. This is the urban distribution to which we referred in the first chapter, where a hierarchical series of central places organize geographical space and are functionally interrelated by a set of relationships from the farming areas to local supply and service centres and to more specialized industrial and distributive centres. In this situation, potential migrants will be most familiar with the possibilities in the higher order centre next to them; the travel and social costs of movements to that centre are lower than for alternative centres.

This urban distribution is uncommon in Latin America as we have seen in the second chapter. The size of a country and extended communications produce approximations to this spatial organization and Brazil and Chile are good examples of this situation. Even in the case of Rio de Janeiro in Brazil, Perlman (1976) reports that most migrants among her sample of low-income families came directly to the city. In general, however, the development of primacy has meant that regional urban systems are often weakly developed and direct commercial, social and political relationships have arisen between even remote rural areas and the primate city. Thus, in a study of Guatemala City, I found that 60 per cent of migrants to the city came directly from a very large variety of small and intermediate size villages (Roberts, 1973a). Similarly, in the Mantaro valley of Peru, villages which were within several miles of each other differed considerably in the destinations of their migrants; some went predominantly to the provincial capital, other villages sent their migrants predominantly to Lima and others to mining centres (Roberts, 1976b). The observed differences were best accounted for by the commercial and social relationships already established between a particular village and a work centre. Browning (1971) also notes the predominance of direct migration in Mexico.

The understanding of both stage and direct migration in underdeveloped countries requires, then, a detailed analysis of the marketing and institutional organization of rural areas. Very few rural centres acquire sufficient strategic importance to become the focus of migration for an extended hinterland; instead, local marketing tends to increase dependence on, and linkages with, the major cities. This pattern is described by Johnson (1970) as a dendritic model of urbanization in which one or two urban places predominate and other centres are organized in vertical relationship with them.

Conning (1972) documents some of the institutional reasons for differential out-migration from rural villages in a study of seven villages in a poor region of the coastal plain of central Chile, equidistant from the major urban centres and metropolitan areas of Chile. He found that in the villages that were most dependent on agriculture (and most exposed to the crop blight which had impoverished the region), there was proportionately less migration to urban centres than in those villages which were more closely integrated into the national political and economic system. These latter villages he considered as more differentiated and with better communications and more commercial, educational and government facilities. However, in the most rural villages, the rate of rural to rural migration was higher than in the more differentiated villages. Thus, in the poorest villages, people seek local work opportunities, while in those villages with better contacts with national centres migrants are more likely to seek the better-paid jobs in urban centres.

The processes we have been examining result in one major uniformity in cityward migrations in Latin America: migrants, whatever their origins, arrive in the largest urban centres as a result of some prior contact or information. Many migrants have jobs or lodging assured them before arrival in the city. Married men will arrive before the rest of their families if job or accommodation is uncertain and exploratory visits to the city are common before final settlement (Roberts, 1973a; Lomnitz, 1977).

Most large city migrants have family or friendship contacts on arrival and these are often instrumental in obtaining work for the immigrant. Contacts developed between culturally and spatially distant places can result over time in a substantial flow of migrants, as Hirabayashi (1993) shows for mountain Zapotec Indians in the state of Oaxaca, Mexico. Though at first few in the villages had contacts beyond the provincial centre, Oaxaca City, by the 1970s contacts established through a few pioneers led to a process of chain migration that resulted in a substantial out-migration to Mexico City. By this time, most villagers had contacts in the capital and knew about life and job opportunities there. The characteristics of the out-migrants diversified in terms of age and marital status as the migration flows increased. Women were particularly numerous since it proved easy for them to find jobs as maids in the city.

The pattern of migration to Latin American cities has similarities with migration into the English industrial town of Preston in the nineteenth century. Anderson (1971) stressed the importance that kinship assumed in helping migrants adjust to the urban industrial situation; migration to Preston, as to other industrial towns in England, was predominantly short-distance. The one qualification to the predominance of short-distance migration in cityward migration in both Latin America and in nineteenth-century Europe is that the larger the city the more likely it is that its migrants come from greater distances (Morse, 1971a; Weber, 1899).

The importance of social networks in migration leads Tilly (1990) to make the point that migration is rarely determined solely by individual calculations but, instead, follows a collective logic. Thus, once someone from a village has moved to a city, there is a high probability that others from the same village will follow if only because the 'costs' of the move are lessened by the help and information that they can expect to receive from the one who preceded them. Furthermore, those who move are usually embedded in a set of social and economic relationships in their place of origin, such as rights to land, parents for whom they are responsible, prospective marital partners or spouses and children that they have left behind. These relationships are likely to cross-cut with those of other migrants so that, for example, cousins or brothers-in-law migrate together, reinforcing trust and their desire to help each other. Under these conditions, it is not suprising that migrants from the same place of origin tend to choose the same urban destinations, even the same neighborhood in a city, and may end up working in the same firms or type of occupation. The most complete account of the implications of this collective logic for migration is provided by Massey and his collaborators (Massey, 1990; Durand and Massey, 1992; Massey et al., 1987, 1992).

In their studies of a number of communities in the western area of Mexico they trace, over a period of 40 years, the evolution of internal and international migration. They show the logic of cumulative causation by which migrants from one place move to the same destination in the United States and through a sequence in which the first to undertake the move are male heads of families, then young, unattached males and, finally, unattached and even married women. As the volume of migration increases and substantial 'bridgeheads' are established in the places of destination, then it is less risky for others who do not have the resources or skills of the pioneers to follow. As a consequence, villages geographically close to each other may have sharply contrasting numbers of out-migrants. In the one, many villagers are absent or have experienced out-migration, whereas in the other there are a few migrants, even among those whose skills would make it relatively easy to find better-paying urban work abroad or at home. Thus, in estimating the likelihood that people with different levels of human capital or in different family situations will migrate, it is also necessary to take account of the historical factors that bind some places and not others into migrant networks.

This type of analyis has become increasingly relevant to understanding contemporary patterns of international migration. Various studies have reported the 'transnational communities' that Mexican migrants have established in the United States (Rouse, 1992; Smith, 1992). In these communities, established in cities such as New York or the San Fransisco Bay area, immigrants who consider themselves fairly permanently residents of the United States keep up active ties with their villages of origin. These villages and their ways of life remain an important reference point and source of identity. The immigrants may even participate actively in the politics of their villages of origin, attempting, as Robert Smith shows, to influence elections and helping to pay for infrastructure projects. Recent immigrants to the United States, who have come mainly from developing countries, have tended to keep contact with their countries and communities of origin. Remittances sent home by immigrants have become important sources of revenue for Mexico and the countries of Central America, often equalling or exceeding revenues earned from major exports (Lozano, 1993).

The Contribution of Migration to Urban Growth

The danger in the analysis of migration is that it sometimes leads to excessive emphasis on the city or, in the case of international migration, the foreign country as the inevitable and final destination for migrants. This ignores the possibility that cityward and even international migration are among several lifetime strategies that people adopt in underdeveloped countries to cope with the difficulties of pursuing stable careers in either rural or urban areas (Roberts, 1976b, 1995). In the last section, we noted that urban populations are often floating populations, seeking job opportunities at a particular stage in their lives but with the possibility of moving back to the village or on to another place if opportunities permitted. To provide an idea of the characteristics of these circular migration movements, I will use data drawn from a survey conducted in 1971 in the central highlands town of Huancayo in Peru, whose population was then 125,000.

In Huancayo over half the adult male population born in the town had migrated elsewhere to work or study for periods of more than a year; the adult male population is predominantly immigrant and some 60 per cent of that population was born outside the city. Of these immigrants about a quarter originated in Lima and in the coastal provinces near Lima; the majority of these adult males estimated that they would eventually return to their place of origin. These migrants from Lima and the coast were mainly employed in government administration, in the professions or in the larger trading establishments; some of them had arrived in Huancayo as part of an administrative or business career and would shortly move on. Others had come to take advantage of the active commercial life of the city and, when they had built up a little capital, they would leave for the coast.

A similar range of commitments is found among those who had migrated to Huancayo from the nearby villages of the central highlands of Peru. A higher percentage of such migrants expected to spend the rest of their lives in Huancayo than did migrants from Lima; however, a substantial percentage of these immigrants planned either to return to their home villages, investing any money saved in the city in building up their farms or in establishing a small rural business, or to move on to other work centres such as Lima. Lima was not a permanent destination even for these migrants. Our surveys in the small villages of the area indicated a high percentage of migrants who had returned from Lima, often in a late stage of their life cycle. Of Huancayo's present population, approximately 30 per cent of the adult males (excluding those born in Lima) have spent one or more years in Lima, indicating that migration to even a capital city should not necessarily be regarded as a definitive commitment.

Other studies, such as that of Chi and Bogan (1975) in four communities of the Chancay valley of Peru, also demonstrate that return migration is a frequent phenomenon and not simply confined to those who failed to find adequate work in the city. The village retains its attraction in the face of the city, especially when it continues to offer some basic security, such as access to land, housing or opportunities to trade. Such security acquires particular significance at certain periods of the life cycle such as old age or early child rearing, when the uncertainties of life in the large cities become more acute.

In recent years, return migration is likely to have become less feasible in the face of the stagnation of the rural economy. Instead, a more complex pattern of migration is appearing in which, for instance, the move from village to city may be followed by another move to another city or even abroad. Returning international migrants often do not go back to their village or even city of origin but choose another destination. In the case of Mexico, this has often been the northern cities bordering on the United States whose bustling economies provide job opportuniities and the advantage of proximity to the US.

In general, there are few underdeveloped countries in which there is, at present, a balanced urban growth based on a thriving regional network of small and medium sized urban service, commercial and industrial centres. This concentration of population is not simply the product of a desperate rural poverty but appears to be based, in part, on the attraction of the city and of its economic opportunities for the better-off members of rural society. For such people to move to the large cities and, by and large, to stay in them suggests that the city economy has some capacity to absorb the increasing numbers of the economically active population. Since the city economy is increasingly dominated by capital-intensive industry, with a low power to absorb labour, we need to look more closely at the structure of the urban economy to understand how employment opportunities continue to expand.

Conclusion

In Latin America, the counterpart to the concentration of economic activities in urban-industrial centres is an increasing diversification of the agrarian structure. The transformation of that structure by the infusion of capitalism remains a partial one, which is likely to be felt most sharply in the rural areas close to the most dynamic cities. Elsewhere, various forms of agricultural production coexist and complement each other: peasant farming expands as a means of colonizing new regions or of exploiting crops which are not commercially viable under other forms of production. The improvement of communications and the generalization of money wages have commercialized the village-level economy but without transforming it completely into capitalist production. Seasonal labour, often provided by peasant farmers or at times by agricultural workers residing in towns, powers plantations and commercial farms. The result is a situation in which, until recently, rural areas throughout Latin America have retained part of the natural increase in their population and their characteristic economic activities become those of petty trading, petty commodity production and labour-intensive farming. The household remains a significant unit in the local economy, but the migration of family members and the fragmentation of economic enterprise undermines its basis as a unit of production.

The forces acting upon the rural structure have dispersed population, resulting in substantial rural-urban migration and also some return migration. By the 1980s, rural-urban migration had lessened in importance as a factor in urban growth and rural-urban ties are likely to have attentuated compared with previous decades. However, the legacy of past movements and the commercialization of most rural areas mean that the distinction between rural and urban is often not a great one. Economic enterprise spans rural and urban locations. The patterns of consumption of the village may be different in scale from those of the town, but they are not different in kind. Transistor radios, television and refrigerators are found in villages. Canned foodstuffs, bottled drinks, detergents and insecticides are sold in village stores. This is the result of the type of industrialization discussed earlier. It is a sufficiently powerful force to undermine the basis for village craft production and to create wants that cannot easily be satisfied by subsistence farming, but industrialization has not expanded production and employment sufficiently to transform the structure totally. We will find that this uneven development appears in the cities also.

|5|

The Urban Economy and the Organization of the Labour Market

It is now time to examine more closely the workings of the urban economies of underdeveloped countries. So far the argument has concentrated on the macro-economic and political forces that have shaped contemporary industrialization. It is now necessary to look at the effects of this industrialization on urban employment and on the distribution of income. We can thus tackle the issue of the coexistence of wealth and poverty, modernity and traditionalism in cities of underdeveloped countries. The previous analysis has suggested that such apparent paradoxes can often be explained in terms of the way in which capitalism has expanded in underdeveloped countries.

In pursuing the argument, it will help if we keep in mind two factors that affect industrialization in Latin America. One of these is the presence of a strong, centralized state which, in many underdeveloped countries, has become one of the chief propagators of economic development. The other is that the industrial activities with which contemporary underdeveloped countries begin their industrialization are large scale and of a high technological level. The channels for transferring technology from advanced to less developed countries are richer than they were in the nineteenth century, leading to rapid transfer and, as we shall see, to a rapid displacement of craft production (Felix, 1977).

I shall focus my discussion on the organization of the urban labour markets of Latin America. The organization of the labour market provides a useful means to link the broader economic changes described in previous chapters with the ways in which the population is stratified socially, the topic of the following chapter. Occupations are the usual way of assigning people to different social strata and it is the labour market that regulates the number and type of occupations. I will discuss three features in urban economic organization that shape Latin American labour markets: the role of the state, the nature of the large-scale sector of the urban economy and the existence of an informal sector. We will also briefly review the key demographic factors that have affected the supply of urban labour: population growth and migration, the increase in female economic participation rates and household organization.

State Intervention and the Urban Economy

State intervention has been a powerful influence in shaping labour markets in Latin America. To understand how this takes place, we need first to examine the ways in which the state has become an important participant in the economies of underdeveloped countries. We saw earlier that the origins of this participation lie in the relative weakness of national bourgeoisies in the face of technological dependence on the advanced capitalist world and of the large-scale investments needed to acquire such technology.

In underdeveloped countries, the intervention of the state in the economy has been marked in the period of capital-intensive industrialization. Soares (1976b) brings together data from Latin America, Europe and the United States at the period of their industrialization to show that state intervention is greater in the underdeveloped world than it was in the advanced world at the time of its economic development. This intervention is also of a qualitatively different kind in contemporary underdeveloped countries to that of the state in developed countries. The state in underdeveloped countries invests a major part of its funds directly in economic enterprises (Baer et al., 1976). These range from works of economic infrastructure such as electricity, gas, water, roads and other communications such as telephones to direct investment in basic industries such as mining, oil and steel. This investment may diversify to include shares in petrochemical and even durable consumer goods industries. It is only in the 1990s that extensive privatization of state enterprises throughout Latin America is putting an end to the state's direct role in the economy.

The state influences labour markets in Latin America directly as an employer and indirectly through an extensive regulation of conditions of work. We can first consider the extent of its role as employer. As the state has taken on the prime responsibility for sponsoring economic development, so too employment has expanded within the state apparatus. The end result of the internal and external pressure to modernize is a substantial increase in state employment in administration, in state financed development agencies, in public enterprises and in social services such as health and education. The expansion of the police and armed forces in underdeveloped countries is also directly related to the political economy of underdevelopment. At one level, army personnel may serve as development agents in remote villages, helping to construct roads, build irrigation ditches and so on; all Latin American armies have this developmentalist side to them. More fundamentally, the expansion of police and armed forces has responded to fears of internal subversion and social discontent (Cotler, 1970/71).

The increase in non-military public employment is particularly significant in the non-manual strata in all countries of the region. In some countries, public employment becomes the major source of non-manual employment. By 1981, the public sector employed 57 per cent of non-manual workers in Peru and 52 per cent of non-manual workers in Argentina (*Censo de Población de Peru*, 1981, Resultados Definitivos Vol A, Tomo II, Cuadro 28; *Censo Nacional de Población de Argentina*, 1980, Serie D: Población Total de País, Cuadro A.10, p. 59).

The growth of public employment in Mexico appears to have been equally dramatic: central government employment in Mexico grew 12.5 per cent annually between 1970 and 1980 (Blanco, 1990). Whereas it was just over one million persons in 1970, by 1980 it was 3.2 million or 17 per cent of total employment. In Mexico, public enterprises, such as the state petrol monopoly PEMEX, accounted for about 24 per cent of public employment, administration 33 per cent and health and educational services 43 per cent (Rendon and Salas, 1987). In Brazil, jobs in public administration grew at an annual rate of 5.8 per cent between 1978 and 1985, whilst formal employment grew at only 0.9 per cent, making public employment the major new source of formal jobs in the country. By 1973, public administrative employees in Brazil numbered 3.4 million persons, with 40 per cent of these working in decentralized agencies such as regional development agencies or public enterprises. By 1980, public employment exceeded five million people, or 11.4 per cent of total employment, with 43 per cent of public employees working in decentralized agencies (Medeiros, 1986, Table 3).

State employment in Latin America has meant relatively secure jobs and a range of benefits such as health insurance, pension plans and loans for housing. State employees are amongst the first to receive these benefits, followed by workers in key industries of the private sector (Mesa-Lago, 1978). Thus, the growth of state employment introduces new elements into urban social stratification through contributing to a sizeable middle class with enough economic security to develop a comfortable lifestyle and to entertain long-term family strategies over housing or the education of children.

State Intervention and Economic Dualism

This degree of state intervention in the economy had, until recently, placed significant limits on the development of nationally-based private enterprise in underdeveloped countries. These limits already exist, as we have seen, in the nature of capital-intensive industrialization. The state reinforces monopoly tendencies by 'rationalizing' industrial investment to avoid wasteful use of scarce capital. State intervention has limited the development of private enterprise capitalism in another way also: it has meant the restriction of the crudest forms of exploiting labour. Minimum wage legislation and the extension of social security benefits to workers are common features of all Latin American economies.

Since the state has used its revenues to finance economic expansion, it has also tended to place the costs of social security and welfare on employers. In 1983, employees covered by social security contributed less than a third of total social security revenue in most countries, whereas their employers contributed over 40 per cent (Mesa-Lago, 1991, Table 6). Social security coverage is linked to employment throughout Latin America and those not insured receive only basic services such as primary health care and primary education.

Though expenditures on social security appear to be rising as a percentage of GDP in the majority of Latin American countries, the state spends only a small proportion of its non-payroll tax revenues on social services. Indeed, taxing of private sector enterprises through compulsory social security payments on behalf of workers is one source of state investment funds. This practice contributes to a potential crisis in pension funds as demographic change leads to an ageing population with payments to pensioners rising while worker contributions decline relative to the size of the dependent population (Mesa-Lago, 1991).

Naturally, large-scale private sector enterprises derive compensating advantages from protected markets and high productivity that, in part, are guaranteed by government subsidies or foreign exchange manipulation. Moreover, as McGreevey (1990) points out, when markets are protected the costs to employers of social security are likely to be passed on to the consumer through higher prices, in effect constituting an indirect tax that will fall indiscriminately on those who receive benefits and those who do not, mainly the poor. It is their oligopolistic dominance of the market that enables large-scale enterprises to pass costs on in this way and even they will seek to diminish their obligations. Thus, it is a frequently reported practice in Latin America for large-scale firms to employ workers casually and without contractual or social security in contravention of labour laws (Portes and Schauffler, 1993; Roberts, 1993).

In this context, state regulation of the labour market contributes to the formation of a class of workers outside the large-scale sector whose characteristics are almost the polar opposite of state employees – the workers of the informal sector who have little job security, fluctuating incomes and, consequently, relatively little economic capacity to plan other than in the short term. Following Castells and Portes (1989), I shall define the informal sector as those enterprises which avoid state regulation, such as fiscal obligations and labour standards, in contexts where similar activities are so regulated. In practice, the informal sector is mainly constitued of small-scale enterprises and the self-employed. Making profits in this sector depends on avoiding the costs that state regulation imposes, such as social security taxes or observing health and safety standards.

There is a relatively dynamic relationship between the formal and informal sectors of the urban economy whose consequences for social stratification we will examine in more detail in the next chapter. This relationship has depended, however, on the economic context created by import-substitution industrialization in which large-scale enterprises had a protected market for their relatively sophisticated products. In this context, the large, technologically advanced enterprise provides goods and services mainly to upper and middle-income groups. The urban low-income population represents a market of low profitability to large-scale enterprises, thus creating a space for the small-scale entrepreneur to offer low-cost services or goods.

Research is needed to establish whether the informal-formal relationship is changing as internal markets cease to be protected in the contemporary period of free trade and export-orientated industrialization. Changes in government policies are linked to this potential source of variation in the nature of urban economic dualism. Governments have differed both in the scale of their intervention in the economy and in their style of intervention, leading to differences in the size of the informal sector and in the nature of its links with the formal sector through subcontracting.

A way of understanding these variations is the analysis, outlined in Chapter 3, of the relative strengths and weaknesses of national bourgeoisies, of the industrial working classes and of state institutions. In Brazil, for example, there is a strong internal and foreign-linked bourgeoisie. State regulation of the economy in the 1970s suppressed workers wages to such an extent that there was relatively little difference between the wages of unskilled and semi-skilled workers in the large-scale sector and those in the informal sector. The same is true in the 1990s for the northern border region of Mexico where the mainly female workers in the *maquiladoras* (in-bond industries) earn less than the mainly male self-employed workers (Roberts, 1993). Chile provides an interesting case of what appears, at first sight, to be decline of the informal sector as a result of state policies that, by deregulating labour in formal firms, diminish the labour and overhead cost advantages of informality. Díaz (1993) documents the relative increase in Chile from 1983 onwards of waged labour and the relative decline in self-employment and unpaid family labour (a measure of the informal sector). He warns, however, that the increase in wage labour brings with it a new form of informality based on the growth of precarious waged employment, particularly among women. This precarious employment increasingly consists of full-time employment throughout the year, but on short-term contracts. The new labour law of the Pinochet military regime allowed employers considerable flexibility in the use of labour by removing contractual protections from the worker. Though precarious waged employment is most evident in small and medium size firms, it is found in large private companies, many of whom subcontract part of their operations to smaller companies.

In contrast, in the slowly developing, 'enclave' countries such as Peru, where the national bourgeoisie is weak, the state under nationalist pressures imposed strict labour regulations on the predominantly foreign-controlled large-scale sector of the economy. Until the 1980s, this regulation was so tight that there was a sharp difference in labour costs between these enterprises and the informal sector. This not only led to the proliferation of arrangements whereby large-scale sector firms farmed out work to the informal sector but created many opportunities for self-employment and for the small-scale entrepreneur to create economic niches for themselves and compete with the goods and services of the large-scale sector.

The greater readiness of the military governments of both Brazil and Chile to intervene radically in the urban economy is shown in the policies of regulating the squatter settlements of cities such as Rio in the later 1960s and 1970s and Santiago in the 1980s. Squatter settlements that once occupied the hillsides close to Rio's centre were pulled down and their inhabitants relocated to the periphery of the city. However, this programme ultimately failed in the face of continuing population pressure and the ending of military rule. In Santiago, the military government enforced policies that effectively segregated low-income, informal settlements from middle-class urban areas. In contrast, in Lima, the state, whether under military or civilian control, has sought to regulate and stabilize squatter settlements, granting such settlements legal recognition as 'young towns' (*pueblos jovenes*). Such differences between countries in state intervention remind us that the relative strength of central government and of the classes which compete for its attention continue to be important variables in determining the pattern of economic development.

The Large-Scale Sector

Large-scale, formally organized and regulated private sector enterprises have probably generated less than half of urban employment from 1940 to the present. Their demand for labour has been restricted, as we have seen, by their use of capital-intensive techology adapted from that used in the advanced industrial world. The labour market for the large-scale sector is a highly differentiated one. In part, this is due to the relative scarcity of the skills demanded by this sector. Despite the rapid increase in educational levels, particularly in the 1960s and 1970s, educational provision in Latin America has been inadequate for the needs of the modern economy. This has been the case both in vocational training and in educating people to secondary school or university standard. Shortages of skilled workers, technicians and professionals are often cited as major bottlenecks to the further industrial development of the continent.

It is also likely that, at some levels, these shortages are artificially created. Balan (1969) noted a tendency to credentialism by which firms demanded qualifications for entry (such as primary or high school certificates) that are not strictly necessary for the performance of the job. Indeed, until the 1980s, the recruitment practices of Latin American industries did not encourage a competitive labour market. In many countries, this results from agreements reached under populist regimes through which employers obtained protected markets and labour unions controlled access to jobs in the large-scale sector. In Mexico, for example, recruitment to a stable job in many large industries depends on the union's prior agreement. However, restrictions on the hiring and firing of certain categories of workers are also present in situations where unions are relatively weak, such as in Monterrey in Mexico. Aside from the question of skills, large-scale enterprises are, in fact, likely to prefer a stable and reliable labour force to one that is the cheapest that they can get, but highly transient. The low ratio of labour to capital costs in these enterprises means that industrialists are preoccupied less with keeping wages as low as possible than with having production disrupted by industrial strife or with the low level of commitment of the work force.

Wage and salary earners in the large-scale sector thus have had greater power than those outside it to negotiate better living conditions. They work under common conditions in large organizations whose economic potential is not only great but is known to those working within it. In contrast,

> at the other end of the scale, we can observe the opposite features. The labour force shows little capacity for organization owing to its fragmentation into a multiplicity of small units, to the low economic solvency of its organizations and its limited access (especially in rural areas) to adequate data and advisory services (Pinto and Filippo, 1976).

The most common practice of lowering labour costs within large-scale enterprises is that of maintaining large wage differentials between a skilled, permanent workforce and a more temporary semi-skilled or unskilled one. Kowarick (1975) shows that large-scale enterprises have a high rate of labour turnover and that even the most technologically sophisticated branches of production made extensive use of semi- and unskilled labour. Recent evidence from Mexico suggests that income polarization within firms has increased with industrial restructuring (Pozos, 1992; Carrillo, 1993). The temporary category is often used as a means to avoid social security obligations and to retain the firm's right to dismiss workers: a 'temporary' worker may, in fact, work many years for the same firm. The temporary workforce is often recruited through the family and friendship networks of the permanent workers, who are at times made responsible for the good behaviour of those whom they sponsor (Escobar, 1986; Roberts, 1978a).

The urban economy is thus organized in such a way that exceptional premiums are obtained by capital and by technical and skilled labour. This is one basis for urban income inequalities that I will review later in this chapter and for the widening of these inequalities in periods of economic growth. Capital-intensive industrialization thus produces significant income inequalities in the urban sphere, first by the differences in income between the large modern sector firms and small enterprises and, second, by the wide income differences found *within* modern sector enterprises.

The Informal Economy

One of the most debated issues in the literature on economic development is whether or not an informal economy exists that plays a dynamic role in wealth and employment generation (See Bromley's, 1994, review of these debates, focusing on Hernan de Soto's championing of the virutes of small- and medium-scale enterprise when these are freed from government bureaucratic regulation). Since the informal economy is mainly defined in terms of self-employment, ownership of small-scale enterprises and workers in such enterprises, those within it are, as we will see, not easily analysed by the normal class categories. Some understanding, then, of the dynamic of the informal economy is necessary in order to fully appreciate the emerging pattern of stratification in Latin American cities.

The argument that a dynamic informal sector can exist alongside a modern one has old roots in Geertz's (1963b) distinction between the bazaar economy and the firm economy in Indonesia. The bazaar economy is made up of a large number of small enterprises which are highly competitive among themselves, which rely on the intensive use of labour, often drawn from the family, and which seek to minimize their risks rather than seek profit maximization. Geertz's point is that the bazaar economy prevents capital accumulation and represents a way of life and a means of absorbing surplus labour; it is not conducive to economic development. The firm economy is based on rationalizing production and capital accumulation for further investment and expansion.

This model of the bazaar economy is useful for understanding the early stages of rapid urbanization where the boundaries between city and countryside are often unclear (McGee, 1967; Pons, 1969). It also applies best to smaller urban places. The smaller places are more likely to develop interchanges with the peasant economy. Not only will transportation costs be lower between smaller urban places and peasant villages but peasant agriculture and crafts are more likely to flourish close to small provincial cities than to large centres. The size and income distribution of the large urban centre will encourage, as we noted with respect to Sao Paulo, the development of capitalist agriculture in its vicinity.

With increasing urbanization and larger city sizes, the independent basis of the bazaar economy will be eroded as a larger proportion of the consumption of even the poorest classes become dependent on the market. This change in the consumption pattern is closely related to an increase in the economic and spatial complexity of a city. With increasing complexity, it becomes less likely that work can be obtained close to the place of residence. This implies that the costs of the journey to work become a part of most families' budgets. Oliveira (1972) and Lopes (1979) both comment on the increasing commercialization of the budgets of low-income families in the large Brazilian cities.

Canned and other processed 'convenience' foods become an element in the diet of poor families when the wife or other female family members work outside the home and have less time to invest in lengthy food preparation (Gonzalez de la Rocha, 1988a, 1994). Other costs, such as educational and health expenses, begin to figure in the budgets of low-income families; entertainment such as television, cinema, sport and gambling become part of family budgets (Benería, 1991). The budgets of even low-income urban families are thus likely to include an increasingly large expenditure on goods and services which, directly or indirectly, are derived from the firm or modern sector of the economy. As Hart (1973) points out in the article on Accra, Ghana (perhaps the first to formulate the concept of the informal sector), some of these transfers may be illicit ones as in the case of robbery or prostitution, but the implication is the same, that the bazaar economy is closely interrelated to the modern economy and, over time, is less likely to have a significant, independent basis for subsistence.

The informal sector in Latin American cities does not, then, cater for the special wants of a segment of the population. There are no truly neighbourhood economies with markets based on goods and principles of organization distinct from those of markets catering to the 'modern' part of the city. Under these conditions, the informal sector in Latin America and elsewhere is an adjunct to the large-scale sector of the economy, producing those goods for which the market is so reduced and so risky that large-scale enterprises are not interested in entering (see for a general account of the significance of the informal sector Bromley, 1978, Bromley and Gerry, 1979, Portes and Schauffler, 1993, Roberts, 1993, Rakowski, 1994). Consequently, the small-scale sector is left with activities of low profitability that do not permit capital accumulation, making it unlikely that enterprises in this sector will develop into large-scale ones (Eckstein, 1975).

The small-scale economy is not traditional either in the techniques it uses or in its type of activity. Thus, in our studies of Huancayo and Lima in Peru, we found that the activities that predominated in this sector were complementary to the most productive and technologically sophisticated of the large-scale sector (Long and Roberts, 1984). In Huancayo, which is an important transport centre, automobile and truck repair workshops proliferated; these were small-scale, *informally* organized enterprises, but the repairs they undertook and the equipment they used were modern. These enterprises did not have the range of equipment of the repair workshops attached to the large car companies, such as Volkswagen but, between them, they assembled a range of equipment adequate to their tasks. One workshop might undertake general repairs and also have specialized equipment for welding and panel beating, another might specialize in installing mufflers and another in engine jobs.

Traditional activities, such as artisan production of cloth or pottery, are not significant components of the small-scale economies of Latin American countries, though certain types of artisan production, such as jewellery, 'craft' pottery and weaving may find a lucrative market among tourists and high-income families. In Guatemala City, the employment of squatter settlement inhabitants was, in the same way, anything but traditional; their jobs were in the construction of modern buildings, in transport, in repairing radios and televisions, in making modern clothes and shoes with the use of a sewing machine and with synthetic material, often imported from the United States (these points need not be laboured; readers can consult the extensive accounts of economic activity in the informal sector provided by Leeds, 1969, 1971, and Machado de Silva, 1971, for Brazil; by Peattie, 1968, for Venezuela; by Hart, 1973, for Ghana; by Eckstein, 1975, for Mexico; by Bromley and Gerry, 1979, for various countries; and by Perez Sainz and Menjivar, 1991, for Central America).

The place of the small-scale economy within the urban economy is similar to that of domestic outwork and petty commodity production in the early stages of the Industrial Revolution in England. Thus, in cities of the underdeveloped world, the self-employed worker or small family enterprise is often dependent on links with large-scale enterprises who provide the capital or the materials. These large-scale operators sell the product in their own shops or use it to complement their own production, as when a shoe factory commissions outworkers to trim shoe leather. Benería and Roldan (1987), for instance, show how female domestic outworkers in Mexico City are linked through a chain of subcontracting that leads ultimately to multinational companies.

Scott (1979, 1994) provides an informative account of the relationships between the large-scale economy and independent artisans, small-scale enterprises and casual workers. She points out that the independence of those working outside the large-scale economy is largely illusory. In the situation of Lima, Peru, very few of the self-employed or the small enterprises can survive without developing relatively stable relationships of dependence with larger enterprises to obtain credit or to secure a stable market for their products. Under these conditions, complex networks of production develop in which a modern factory may commission a small, family enterprise to undertake part of its production and, in turn, this enterprise may hire out-workers. Scott provides examples of these networks in the construction sector, in manufacturing and in transport, citing the assembly of refrigerators, the upholstery of microbuses and dressmaking. However, she stresses that, although the independence of these workers and small, family enterprises is largely illusory, they do retain a sense of control of their situation, based at times on ownership of the tools of their trade or of small amounts of factory equipment.

In contrast to the situation in nineteenth-century Britain, these forms of production do not appear to be disappearing in the face of the growth of the factory system (Hobsbawm, 1969b). The informal sector probably declined in importance in Latin America from 1940 to 1970 since estimates of the amount of urban self-employment show it decreasing from 29 per cent of the labour force in 1940 to a low of 20 per cent in 1970 (Oliveira and Roberts, 1994, Table 3). In the 1980s, the informal sector, defined as the sum of self-employment, unremunerated family employment and employment in enterprises of less than five workers (thus including domestic service), grew substantially both in numbers and as a proportion of the urban labour force. Initial PREALC (1988: Cuadro 1) estimates suggest that in the region as a whole urban informal employment grew rapidly, particularly in the mid-1980s. Using PREALC calculations, Portes and Schauffler (1993, Table 3) estimate that by 1989 informal employment made up 31 per cent of total urban employment in the region, compared with 30 per cent in 1980.

Data from Mexico and Central America provide a more detailed picture of these trends. In the three major metropolitan areas of Mexico there was an increase in employment in small-scale enterprises, in self-employment and in unpaid family employment. This increase was particularly marked in the repair services and in commerce (INEGI, 1988, 1977; Escobar, 1988; Gonzalez de la Rocha, 1988a; Roberts, 1991). Informal employment (including domestic service) was estimated at 33 per cent of the urban labour force in 1987. The self-employed and workers in small enterprises appear to have suffered a drop in real incomes. The informal sector had by 1989 become synonymous for many of its workers with bare subsistence. Only the owners of small-scale enterprises and informal workers with skills in demand earned significantly more than the minimum wage, but their enterprises were, in general, poorly equipped and showed little sign of capital accumulation.

Surveys showed that the urban labour markets of most Central American countries were highly informalized by 1989 in terms of the high numbers of the self-employed, unpaid family workers and workers and owners of firms with less than five workers (Perez Sainz and Menjivar, 1991). The percentages informally employed by these criteria were 33 per cent in Guatemala City, 30 per cent in Tegucigalpa, 28 per cent in San Salvador and 23 per cent in San José. In Managua, suffering the effects of the economic blockade and the war in the countryside and with a weak industrial base, the informally employed were 48 per cent of the urban labour force, not counting domestic servants (Chamorro et al., 1991). In Managua, the informal sector was already large by the time of the 1979 revolution, having expanded rapidly after the earthquake of 1972. From 1979 onwards, the informal sector was alternatively encouraged and discouraged by the Sandinista regime, though by 1989 it was viewed as providing essential services within the war-torn economy. Costa Rica, whose economy had been less affected than most Latin American economies by the recession of the 1980s, was the only one of the Central American countries not to have experienced increasing informalization in the 1980s.

Informal workers in the Central American cities are disproportionately drawn from the younger and older age groups, migrants, women and those with low levels of education. Informal employment is mainly in commerce, though about a quarter of the informally employed are in the industrial sector. In all the cities, the informal sector is socially and economically diverse with large differences in income between the owners of small-scale enterprise, their employees and the self-employed. Poverty is concentrated in the informal sector, though in all the cities, including San José, a substantial minority of formal workers earn incomes that place them below the poverty line. Case studies of samples of the self-employed and small-scale enterprises in these cities indicate that informality for the self-employed is basically a household survival strategy in the face of unemployment and declining real wages. Only the small-scale entrepreneurs earn a wage significantly above the minimum.

The difference in the underdeveloped situation is one of scale: since markets are more limited and uncertain than in the advanced capitalist world, an extensive informal economy is a necessary means of reducing risk and increasing profits for the formal sector of the economy. Under these conditions, it is premature to view the informal sector as simply an expedient and transitional form. The uncertain economic conditions of the 1980s have led, as we have noted, to an increase in informal sector employment due to the limited capacity of the formal sector to generate employment.

The Organization of the Informal Sector

To understand the significance of the informal sector for class situations, we need to explore the nature of social and economic relationships within the sector. The persistence of forms of labour other than that of wage labour creates a complex social situation within cities of the underdeveloped world. Jelin (1974), basing her analysis on data from Salvador in Brazil, has distinguished four main forms of economic activity outside the large-scale sector of the economy: competitive capitalism present in small and medium sized firms; family enterprises relying on the intensive exploitation of family members; self-employment in a variety of activities; and domestic service, which can be seen as complementing other forms of economic activity by substituting for the household work of family members whose skills can be devoted to other activities.

Access to the high-income sector of the economy provides the stimulus for entrepreneurial organization in the informal sector. Savings from work in the formal sector, indemnity payments after leaving work in the mines and the sale of a plot of land are some of the sources of capital which, in Peru, enabled people to set themselves up in small-scale enterprises. Those who achieved most developed stable relationships with the formal sector of the economy. One of the most successful market wholesale traders in Huancayo was a man who had once been a miner and now, on the basis of his previous work contacts, had secured contracts to supply the mines. Another was a family which had secured contracts to supply fruit to soft drinks firms in Lima.

To secure and build upon these advantages, the entrepreneurs of the informal sector need to cut their costs and provide highly competitive services. This is achieved, in part, by an intensive exploitation of available labour. Family labour is used to its fullest extent: young children run errands, mind the shop and check that loading or unloading is being carried out. Older relatives may sit for long hours minding a shop or selling small quantities of goods that are surplus to the main enterprise. This pattern of organization warns us against assuming too quickly that the individual engaged in what appears to be almost profitless activities is an isolated economic unit. Small scale market sellers, small shopkeepers, people offering to wash cars and so on, often appear to make little or no income and, in surveys of poverty, are classed among the desperately poor. They are undoubtedly poor, but it is important to examine the household and not the individual as a unit of economic enterprise. Many apparently unremunerative occupations are but the tip of an iceberg in which other members of the household earn the major incomes and the person in question simply contributes to his or her upkeep by minding the children, keeping an eye on the store and disposing of otherwise wasted products.

Entrepreneurship in the informal sector is also based on developing organization through personal relationships and trust (Portes and Sensenbrenner, 1993). The small-scale enterprise cannot afford to take on inflexible commitments: the risks and uncertainties of the competitive market in which it operates makes such commitments hazardous undertakings. For example, small-scale traders cannot commit themselves easily to delivering a fixed quantity of goods at a fixed price over a period of time when they have no control over production or transport. Such traders prefer to operate with tacit understandings with a variety of purchasers, producers and transporters. They will develop a wide network of contacts among all these categories to ensure that they can maintain a reasonable volume of business without running the risk of overextending their credit or liabilities.

These strategies are important elements in the dynamic of the informal sector, since those who operate within it are constrained to seek actively for new contacts to maintain and expand their businesses. Thus, it is useful to focus attention on the *network* of exchanges and obligations that develop in the small-scale sector. Unskilled workers anticipate the temporary nature of their work by seeking out other job opportunities weeks in advance of the likely end of their job (Machado da Silva, 1971). There are important elements of reciprocity in these work relationships since contacts for a job are repaid by providing information about sources of work in the future or by giving help on a specific project (Lomnitz, 1977).

Kinship ties, relationships with fellow villagers or with co-believers are thus important elements in the dynamic of the informal economy. In La Paz, Bolivia, Albo (1995) points to the symbiosis between a resurgent Aymara ethnicity and an informal economy whose transactions emphasize and make use of the common ethnic culture. These relatively intensive types of relationships provide a basis for trust in economic relationships. Since a great many of the transactions within the small-scale sector depend on tacit understanding and are not directly supervised by the entrepreneur, success depends on working with those one trusts. I am using trust in the sense of being able to anticipate behaviour and having the security of being related to the other by a set of interlocking relationships (Roberts, 1973a). Entrepreneurs, for example, may have to trust individuals with relatively expensive equipment, such as a tricycle vending cart. This trust is less likely to be broken when that individual is someone who interacts with the entrepreneur in other situations than the economic one – as a kinsman, member of the same church or supporter of the same football club. The costs of violating trust are higher in such situations, since the individual would have to forego other important activities of his urban life.

Social relationships provide the basis for quite sophisticated economic organization. Long (1973) has shown how what is in effect a large-scale trucking company in the highlands of Peru was built up through the social relationships of the individual owners. These owners formed a village-based fiesta association which included farmers and traders. They were also related to each other by kinship and marriage. The fiesta association provided a convenient framework for exchanging information about possible loads and coordinating strategy to fulfil contracts or reward important officials. In these ways, making a living in cities of underdeveloped countries gives vitality to the patterns of social organization.

This degree of organization and enterprise must not obscure the fact that even the most successful entrepreneurs in the informal sector are not very successful. There are important limitations on accumulation within enterprises of the small-scale sector. Since they are informal they have little access to government or private credit and thus little possibility of capitalizing the enterprise. Credits in underdeveloped countries go to the large enterprises. Thus, small-scale enterprises are labour-intensive and highly competitive with each other, while productivity and profits are relatively low. An accident to a truck or machine can effectively wipe out many small-scale sector entrepreneurs.

The expansion of enterprise is limited by the span of control of the entrepreneurs. They will usually prefer to proliferate their enterprises rather than increase any one enterprise in size. Increasing the size of an enterprise makes it liable to government regulation and reduces the possibility of trust developing between employer and employees. In Peru, we found that entrepreneurs in the small-scale sector preferred to invest spare capital in setting up another enterprise whose management they would delegate to a son or other relative. Some of these linked enterprises constituted quite impressive investments and in several cases merited listing the entrepreneur in the Peruvian *National Biography*. However, no single enterprise employed more than four or five people.

These forms of enterprise limit capital accumulation, but they do give the informal economy a high degree of flexibility. Linked enterprises mean, for example, that the failure of any one enterprise does not necessarily affect the others. Resources and labour can quickly be allocated to exploit new opportunities and shifted out of declining ones.

Participation in the Labour Market

Demographic factors interact with the features in urban economic organization that we have reviewed in the previous section to make urban labour markets in Latin America both highly competitive and also highly segmented. The rapid increase in the urban population is one of these factors since it creates a rapidly increasing supply of labour, often of the order of 5 or 6 per cent a year that can only be absorbed productively into the urban economy by sustaining high rates of economic growth. We should remember that the full impact of high rates of natural increase only occurs 16 years or so after they have occurred when those born at the time reach an age to enter the labour market. Thus, a high rate of population growth has a lagged effect on the labour market. In Latin America, the impact of the high population growth rates of the 1960s and 1970s are being felt in the 1980s and 1990s when economic growth has slowed.

The impact of rural-urban migration on urban labour markets is more immediate than that of natural increase since those migrating to the cities are disproportionately drawn from the young economically-active age groups. The contribution of rural-urban migration to urban growth is greatest in the period from 1940 to 1970, though even in this period it varied, as we have seen, according to the stage of urbanization of individual countries. The combined impact of natural increase and rural-urban migration is to increase the labour supply in Latin American cities by rates in excess of 5 per cent for most of the years from 1940 to 1970. The rural component of this labour supply is, in general, low-skilled and with low educational levels. In the years up to the 1970s, the Latin American urban economies showed a suprising capacity to absorb this rapidly growing labour supply into employment (see Gregory, 1986, for an analysis of this trend in Mexico). Self-employment declined in these years and unemployment rates remained low. Naturally, much of the employment was at very low wages and the ready supply of cheap labour was a major factor in the viability of the informal sector and contributed, directly and indirectly, to the profitability of the formal sector (see the analysis in Portes and Walton, 1981).

Another result of economic diversification and increasing urbanization is the rapid growth of female participation in Latin American labour markets in the 1970s and 1980s. The increase in female participation rates is due to changes in the demand for labour, particularly the expansion of non-manual occupations and, to a lesser extent, of employment in industries such as assembly plants that prefer female labour. Increasing educational levels delay the age of entry into the labour force, but also increase female participation. Highly educated women become more likely to seek work outside the household. Low levels of fertility, already present in Argentina and Chile and being rapidly reached in Brazil and Mexico, also encourage the growing labour force participation of women.

Female participation rates are highest in the large metropolitan areas. These areas grew markedly, as we noted above, through natural increase and rural-urban migration. The occupational structures of these metropolitan areas are particularly open to female employment: in domestic service, in other personal services, in commerce and in the expanding ranks of office workers. Female employment became part of the increasing polarization of the urban occupational structures. Women have had more job opportunities than in the first half of the twentieth century in 'middle-class' occupations such as teachers or skilled secretaries, but they also entered informal employment, in increasing numbers, as personal service workers or as domestic outworkers.

The concentration of women in certain types of work had little effect on the gender division of labour. Women remain segregated in the labour market despite the changes in occupational structures. Opportunities for women were restricted not as a result of competition in the labour market but by factors such as the possibility of combining domestic with extra-domestic work and by social norms which fixed which occupations were accepted as suitable for women (Jelin, 1978; De Barbieri, 1984; Humphrey, 1987).

Women's employment in manufacturing industry has not increased to the same extent as it did in the services. It also differed between countries.

In Argentina, Chile, Brazil and Peru, women's employment in industry declined absolutely between 1960 and 1980, mainly due to the decline in craft industry (CEPAL, 1986). Female manufacturing employment increased in Mexico from the 1960s due to the expansion of assembly operations by multinational companies, the persistence of industries (such as the garment industry) that traditionally were heavy users of female labour, and the spread of domestic outwork (García and Oliveira, 1994). Brazil showed a slight expansion of female manufacturing workers and craft workers between 1970 and 1980.

In the 1980s, the economic crisis made it even more necessary for the urban poor to use various monetary and non-monetary resources to make ends meet. A single salary became increasingly inadequate to maintain a family in the face of the decline in real wages. Even the low salaries of the young and women became necessary to sustain the household, along with increased domestic work. This has been the major factor increasing female labour force participation in the poorest households, but has also contributed to increasing employment among women with high levels of education and married to men with high status jobs, the married female category that has the highest levels of participation in the labour force (De Barbieri and Oliveira, 1987; Gonzalez de la Rocha, 1988a; García and Oliveira, 1990). Also, mutual help networks increased among relatives and friends (Ramos, 1984; Raczynski and Serrano, 1984; De Barbieri and Oliveira, 1987; González de la Rocha and Latapi, 1988).

In the metropolises of Latin America, women's paid work had become an essential part of the domestic budget by 1980. There are no detailed studies of the changes in the female labour market from 1980 to 1990, but data from Mexico and Brazil can be used to illustrate the trends. In Mexico there was a marked expansion in female employment during the 1980s, with an increase of 6.5 per cent per year in the participation rate of economically active women between 1979 and 1987. The equivalent rate of increase between 1970 and 1979 was 3.5 per cent annually (García and Oliveira, 1994; Pedrero, 1990). The trend in Brazil was similar with an increase of 7.6 per cent in female participation between 1980 and 1985, as opposed to one of 4.6 per cent between 1970 and 1980 (Bruschini, 1989).

Economic recession in the 1980s led in Mexico to the mobilization of a potential supply of labour mainly made up by adult women (35–49 years) of low levels of education, married and with young children. In contrast, young, single women (20–34), with middling or high levels of education showed a relative decrease in their relative participation in the labour market. This contrast is likely to have been produced by the contraction in non-manual employment opportunities and the increase in informal employment (Garcia and Oliveira, 1994). The Brazilian data indicate a similar tendency in terms of educational levels and age of the female labour force. Women with low levels of education increased their participation rates by 56.3 per cent between 1980 and 1985, whilst women with five or more years of study showed more modest increases. Women between 30 and 49 had higher increases in participation in the same period than younger women (Bruschini, 1989).

The changes in the characteristics of women entering the labour market occurred in conjunction with changes in the types of jobs that they take. In Mexico, the percentage of non-manual workers (professionals, technicians and clerical workers) in the female economically active population decreased significantly. Only the most qualified workers succeeded in obtaining the few non-manual jobs that were created. Data for the years 1982 and 1987 show that fewer women with low levels of education participated in manual wage work, but those with middling levels of education increased their presence (García and Oliveira, 1994). Both these trends show greater credentialism and stricter requirements for contracting labour in periods of recession.

Domestic servants became a significantly smaller proportion of the female economically active population, as did manufacturing workers. Only manual wage workers in the services increased their share of female wage work. The female self-employed increased their share of employment, especially those with low levels of education living in common-law unions with young children. The increase in self-employment occurred not only in the tertiary sector – the sector with the most female employment – but in manufacturing (García and Oliveira, 1994). This expansion of self-employment is not only due to survival strategies on the part of poor families but to the restructuring of manufacturing activity through the use of subcontracting to workshops and to domestic workers (Escobar, 1986; Tokman, 1987; Benería and Roldan, 1987; Roberts, 1989; Marshall, 1987; Arias, 1988; García, 1988; Portes, Castells and Benton, 1989).

For the large majority of the population, participation in the labour market, and even the type of job, is closely associated with household position. When wages are uniformly low with few prospects of improving them through internal or external promotion or through an occupational career, the changing needs of households for income and the responsibilities of different household members become important determinants of the jobs that people take.

This can be appreciated by contrasting the 1989 employment profiles of households at different stages of the household cycle in two border cities in Mexico, Matamoros and Ciudad Juarez, and in the three major metropolitan cities, Mexico City, Guadalajara and Monterrey (see Roberts, 1994, for a fuller analysis of these Mexican data). There is a close association between household position, the stage of the household cycle and job position. Among a sample of working class households, workers – the proletariat – are concentrated in unmarried children and young married couples without children. This is true of both the metropolitan areas and the border cities, and in the border cities there is a high concentration of manufacturing workers among young, unmarried adults. The border cities are major locations of the new export-orientated industrial plants and these have recruited young, unmarried adults, mainly women. In the metropolitan cities, in contrast, heads of household are still likely to be employed in manufacturing even at older ages. The metropolitan cities still retain much of the older style of industrial organization with its unionized workforce and job security in the large manufacturing plants. In the metropolitan cities and particularly on the border, heads of household, both men and women, are more likely to be employed entrepreneurially (as owners of small-scale enterprises, as self-employed or family workers) as the household cycle advances. At the last stage of the household cycle, there is a sharp contrast between parents, almost half of whom are engaged in their own enterprise, and their children, who are predominantly employees of large-scale enterprises.

The changes in economic opportunities available to different cohorts of workers account only in part for these contrasts. The high rates of own enterprise amongst parents are, for example, much greater than would be true of this cohort when it first entered the labour market some 30 years ago. The cohort-specific effect is more evident on the border in that the higher proportions, at all stages, in large-scale manufacturing reflects the recent growth of jobs in that sector. The concentration of female children in manufacturing is no higher than that of males, reflecting the trend in *maquiladora* employment whereby males now average about 45 per cent of that employment compared with some 30 per cent at the beginning of the 1980s (see Fernandez Kelly, 1994).

The high proportions of own enterprise among heads of household is most convincingly explained by the convergence of two factors: the employment policies of large-scale enterprises that favour young workers, and the preference of older workers for autonomy. Support for this argument is given by Despres (1991) in his report on a Brazilian sample of the self-employed from Manaus, who have a strong preference for autonomy. He also finds that industrial workers are concentrated among the young and unmarried.

A further reason for the high percentage of heads of households with their own enterprise in the Mexican sample is apparent in their average incomes. Almost without exception, the average self-employed income of heads of households is higher than their incomes as employees in either large- or small-scale enterprises. Particularly notable are the low earnings of manufacturing workers relative to other workers in large-scale enterprises. It is especially marked in the border cities, suggesting the low rates of pay in export-orientated industries. Conversely, self-employment is lucrative work on the border, in part reflecting the economic dynamism of the region and the possibilities of cross-border transactions. For this reason, it is not surprising that, on the border, self-employment is more heavily concentrated among male heads of household while it is concentrated mainly among women in the metropolitan cities. Indeed, the low incomes of self-employed women in the metropolitan centres and of those employed in small-scale enterprises is the only evidence of the 'informal' sector as a subsistence sector. On average, the highest incomes earned by the Mexican sample are in two categories of the 'informal' sector: small-scale entrepreneurs and the self-employed. Note, however, that the types of employment included in the informal sector are highly differentiated by income: small-scale entrepreneurs earn on average three times more than their workers and 50 per cent more than the self-employed. There is further differentiation by economic sector: own enterprise is more profitable in commerce and certain services, such as transport and repair services, than it is, for example, in manufacturing or other personal services.

In general, incomes decline with age after peaking when the heads of household are young. As in the case of Manaus workers, reported by Despres (1991), neither children nor spouses in the Mexican sample earn, on average, more than the male heads of household. This occurs despite the fact that their educational levels are, on average, higher, as is the occupational status of their jobs. By the end of the household cycle, children are contributing almost as much to household income as are the heads of household. At this stage, the declining incomes of household heads and their spouses, and their lower rates of employment, are offset by their children's participation, resulting in a recuperation of per capita household income. When children leave home, the loss of their earning power is likely to be severe for households at the end of the household cycle since household heads will find it increasingly difficult to find work as they grow older. Also, only a minority of households headed by the elderly are likely to have rights to pensions.

Conclusion

This discussion warns us of the difficulties of analysing employment and class relationships in cities of the underdeveloped world from the viewpoint of individual members of the labour force. Both poverty and class relationships are determined by the structure of the economy and, in particular, by the relationship between the large-scale sector and the small-scale sector. The small-scale sector is one of unstable employment and low incomes, but it is a highly organized sector which creates opportunities for economic survival for most city dwellers. These opportunities are distributed on the basis of household membership and of other relatively intimate social relationships. It is a small minority of the labour force which is totally isolated from these relationships.

This circumstance does not make poverty a benign condition, but it does help us understand the economic activism of the poor. Declining real standards of life in cities lead families to expand household employment using all available labour; the networks of the small-scale economy facilitate these strategies. Poverty under the conditions of the small-scale economy means a constant struggle, but it does not imply passivity in the face of overwhelming difficulties, nor does it imply social isolation (Lewis, 1952).

The heterogeneity of low-income groups and their job and geographical mobility prevent the development of strong class consciousness and class organization. Poor households are not homogeneous in their social and economic characteristics. It is common for workers of different types to be present in the same household: workers in the manufacturing sector, service workers, white collar and blue collar workers, workers in the formal and informal sectors and so on. Studies in Mexico City and Guadalajara indicate that in households headed by manual workers, the sons are usually also manual workers, whilst the daughters and wives – when they work for a wage – work in a variety of occupations (García et al., 1981; González de la Rocha, 1994). The types of economic arrangements which have been described in previous sections individualize the problem of making a living: they obscure, on one hand, the exploitation that the working class suffers at the hands of the bourgeoisie and, on the other hand, they create the sense of economic opportunity for the enterprising individual.

Open unemployment is rarely the major problem, the poverty of these cities consists of the very large numbers of people who are underemployed either because of the small amount of work they can get or because of extremely low wages in jobs of very low productivity. In this way, the urban economies of underdeveloped countries create ambiguous job statuses: a worker is not simply employed in the large-scale sector or unemployed, there are a variety of intermediate statuses (Kritz and Ramos, 1976). The source of the poverty of the working class is obscured: it does not appear as a direct result of the employment practices of the bourgeoisie or of the state.

These issues will be pursued in the next chapter from the perspective of the social stratification and mobility that have characterized the cities of Latin America in recent decades.

|6|

The Nature of Urban Stratification

Urbanization and industrialization radically altered the social divisions of Latin American society, making some, such as possession of land, less salient and others, such as professional qualifications, more important. In 1940, Latin American cities had a heterogeneous social structure with some containing a substantial industrial proletariat, while others remained mainly commercial and administrative centres in which the worker-employer relationship was not the dominant one (Oliveira and Roberts, 1994). In the early period of industrialization in Latin America, from the 1940s to the 1970s, the transformation of this urban social structure through extensive opportunities for social mobility were factors that contributed to reducing the class militancy of urban low-income workers. The economic situations of the 1980s and 1990s are, in most cities, very different ones: urban incomes are becoming more unevenly distributed and the opportunities for good jobs are expanding less fast than is the urban, economically active population. In this chapter, we take up these issues and consider the changing nature of social stratification in urban Latin America. Consequently, we need to consider the types of social mobility and class conflict that are produced by the uneven urban economic growth described in previous chapters.

I will depart from the historically-based class analysis that has been used so far to concentrate on the themes of social stratification and social mobility. This change in focus enables us to examine how urbanization and industrialization affect the life chances of different social groups and to address the question of whether the class structure becomes more open with urbanization so that those born in the lower strata have greater opportunities than before to move to higher strata. The theme of a society 'open' to talent is a familiar one in the developed world with studies of whether the exchanges between occupational strata increase over time so that, for example, children born to manual workers are more likely to attain professional or managerial positions (Kurz and Muller, 1987).

After the seminal work of Germani in Argentina (1987 [1955], 1968, 1969/70, 1981), these issues were to receive relatively little attention in the literature on Latin America. They were overshadowed by the debates over dependency, by the use of a class analysis that derived from Marx rather than Weber and by their seeming irrelevance to a region mired in poverty. However, I shall argue that the stratification perspective captures, as few others do, the relations between economic change and social identity that underlie the political changes of the last 40 years in Latin America.

We can begin with the research agenda that Germani and his colleague, Di Tella (1962, 1974), developed to examine the relationship between urbanization, changes in occupational structures and political stability. Their focus is the changes in aspirations and in group identities that accompany urbanization and industrialization, and they seek to take into account the particular mismatch in Latin America between the rapid mobilization of a population resulting from urbanization, the slow extension of economic opportunities and an exclusive political structure. From their perspective, stability depends on two key groups increasing their sense of participation through social mobility and political organization: one is a politically and socially fragmented working class employed mainly in small and medium size firms and competing fiercely for jobs as a result, in part, of large-scale rural-urban migration; the other is a 'new' middle class made up mainly of employees in professional, technical and office work that replaces the 'old' middle class of independent professionals, traders and craftspeople.

In a study that is a useful point of comparison with the data that we will shortly review, Germani (1987 [1955]) examines the changes in occupational structure in Argentina up to the census of 1947. He identifies the most intense period of social mobility in Argentina as having occurred prior to the 1940s. There is a substantial increase in the urban middle classes, particularly the new middle classes of office workers (many of them government employees) and sales clerks, who are concentrated in the capital, Buenos Aires. However, the independent middle-classes of liberal professionals and owners of small-scale businesses also had expanded in number by 1947. Germani distinguishes between the social mobility of the native born, who move upwards by becoming white collar employees, and the immigrant, whose social mobility is through setting up a business in commerce or manufacturing. He identifies two major tendencies in the composition of the working classes: their continuing fragmentation since just over 70 per cent work in enterprises of less than ten workers and an increase in the proportion of manufacturing workers who are employed in large enterprises (Germani, 1987). Manufacturing workers were, however, only a third of the Argentine working classes in 1947, though their political significance was accentuated by the concentration of manufacturing in the metropolitan area of the capital, Buenos Aires.

Argentina in 1947 was the most highly urbanized and industrialized

Latin American country and the patterns of stratification found there were unlikely to be replicated elsewhere in Latin America at that time. To provide a means of understanding the variation in stratification, Di Tella outlines four basic types of urban stratification in Latin America by the 1950s, based on the degree of concentration of the working-class and on the possibilities of social mobility to the middle class (1965b). First, there are the large, industrializing cities in which the class pyramid broadens at its base through the increasing numbers of manual workers. The decline in the relative importance of the middling strata is offset, and education-linked mobility opportunities created, by the emergence of a 'new' middle class of dependent professionals and office workers needed to meet the demands of administration and of more complex business organization. Examples of this type are cities such as Buenos Aires in Argentina, Sao Paulo in Brazil and Mexico City. Secondly, there are the plantation or mining towns, such as those of the sugar producing areas of Argentina or the mining regions of Chile, Peru and Bolivia, dominated by a mass of workers with few intermediate occupations and few opportunities for upward mobility. Thirdly, there are the towns and cities in regions once economically important but that had declined or stagnated. Examples are towns in the north-east of Argentina, the Los Altos region of Jalisco in Mexico, the towns of north-eastern Brazil, the 'gold' towns of Minas Gerais and Popayán in Colombia. All these were economically isolated by the 1940s as a result of the stagnation of regional economies and new trade routes that by-passed the old commercial centres. Such towns retained a substantial upper and middle class, but its members have limited local prospects of retaining their relative status. They will become important sources of middle-class migration to the large cities. Lastly, there is the pattern of stratification found in dynamic agricultural regions, such as that of Santa Fe in Argeninta, Sonora in north-west Mexico or the coffee region of Antioquia in Colombia, where entrepreneurship in commerce and the services begins to replace large-scale landowning and craft industry as the basis of the town and region's social and economic structure.

The industrialization and economic growth of the period after the 1940s reinforced these regional differences in social stratification. It resulted, in most countries, in marked differences in the nature of class organization between capital cities and provincial regions. The size of the major cities and their importance as centres of economic and political power meant that the aspirations and preoccupations of their inhabitants often had an overwhelming influence on national politics, as Davies (1994) shows for Mexico City. Since working-class concentration and the relative weight of the middling class differs between countries and between their major cities, broad national contrasts also appear in the overall patterns of stratification contributing to the differences in political regimes between the Latin American nations.

The Emerging Pattern of Occupational Stratification

Economic, demographic and social changes resulted by the 1970s in a pattern of urban stratification that in certain crucial respects is increasingly similar throughout Latin America. The most salient divisions within this class structure can be identified in terms of several criteria: the degree of control over the means of production, control over labour power and type of remuneration (Portes, 1985). These criteria approximate the major divisions of collective interest that are likely to be found in Latin American cities: between those who depend on the profits of enterprise and those who are employed by them, between those who manage the labour of others and those who do not, between those on stable incomes and those who are casually employed. A further division needs to be added, that between manual and non-manual work, differentiating those whose jobs and lifestyle depend on relatively high levels of schooling and those who do not.

In the cities of Latin America, education becomes the single most important factor in obtaining higher status and better paid occupations than their parents. Family status continues to be a significant factor in childrens' occupational attainment, but its impact occurs mainly through its effect on childrens' education. As a determinant of childrens' educational attainment, the socio-economic status of the family is more important than place of origin (whether born in rural or urban areas) and continues to influence attainment even with the rapid expansion of educational opportunities in the 1960s and later (Balan et al., 1973).

A distinctive characteristic of educational levels in Latin America affecting occupational stratification and income inequality is their polarization (Tedesco, 1987). Alongside a persistently large percentage of those failing to finish primary school are growing numbers with secondary and university education. Though the trend is obscured, to some extent, by the lack of comparable classifications between the censuses, the increase of those with seven or more years of education is marked between 1960 and 1980, rising in Peru, for example, from 15 per cent of the economically active population to 45 per cent (Oliveira and Roberts, 1994, Table 5.4). Whereas literacy was a sufficient qualification for most skilled manual jobs in the 1960s, primary education became essential by the 1970s. Similar increases in required educational qualifications occurred for non-manual jobs. Though part of the demand for higher qualifications arose from the requirements of new jobs based on advanced technology in the services or industry, even the same jobs required higher levels of education in 1980 than in 1960 (Balan, 1969; Roberts, 1973b; CEPAL, 1989).

There are, in fact, indications that the increase in private (usually religious) education at primary and secondary levels, in the 1960s and later, reflected the importance placed on education by middle-class parents and their dissatisfaction with overcrowded urban public schools (Roberts,

1973b). The 1960s and 1970s also saw an expansion of private universities, both religious and secular, catering for the increased demand for higher education and providing a more privileged educational environment for those with money than did the mass public universities (Levy, 1986).

The class divisions include, firstly, a proportionately small dominant class based mainly on ownership of large-scale enterprises concentrated in the service and manufacturing sectors. These business elites begin to alter in composition and organization with economic change and industrialization. Foreign direct investment brings a managerial group of expatriates, mainly North American, but also European. These are counted among the elite, although their period of residence in any one place is usually only a few years and although their social contacts are mainly confined to the circles of their own nationality. An example is Imaz's (1964) account of the expatriate business elite in Argentina, who often do not speak Spanish, live in segregated neighbourhoods and use the schools and clubs of their nationality.

The size and complexity of the urban economies, increasingly externally linked through investment and technology, make the family-type enterprise of the 1930s difficult to sustain. The business elites adopt more impersonal styles of management and obtain technical training either through the private technological institutes that develop apace in many parts of Latin America or by going abroad. Winn (1986) reports this as happening to the owners and managers of the Yarur textile enterprise in Chile after 1954. Lomnitz and Perez Lizuar (1987) provide a detailed account of this change as it affects the Gomez industrial empire in Mexico. They show the tensions between maintaining a family-based enterprise, the need to develop social relations with government officials and the limits placed on the Gomez enterprises by the refusal of the patriarch to forgo his particularistic style of control (see Muñoz and Suarez, 1989, for the case of Monterrey in Mexico).

These trends, along with the growing importance of the state to business through contracts, subsidies, licenses to import new technology and labour regulation, undermine family and paternalism as the basis of elite ideology and practice. Business elites increasingly seek alliances on a class basis and extend these to include government officials and the military. In interviews with Argentinean and Brazilian industrialists in the 1960s, Cardoso (1971) documents the importance for them of intra- and inter-class alliances to achieve economic development, including landowners, bankers, military, politicians and workers. Brazilian industrialists are less likely than their Argentinean counterparts to place importance on alliances with workers. Also, in both countries, the industrialists with the highest external dependence are those most likely to discount the need to include workers in such alliances. The economic power of the state means that a career in government service became a means of entry into the urban elites and an increasingly acceptable career for children of traditional elite families.

The trends in the nature of urban elites can be summarized in three broad tendencies. First, urban elites become more interconnected in their interests and social networks. Family ceases to be the main basis of economic as well as social power. Access to credit, to technology, usually externally based, and to political and economic information become more important to the success of an enterprise irrespective of the sector of the economy. In this context, the use of personal relationships as a means of furthering economic and political interests remains as salient as in the past but, especially in the most dynamic urban economies, social networks begin to include a wider range of national and international elite positions than hitherto. The media, politics, bureaucracy, financial and professional services acquire a new salience for the maintenance and furthering of elite careers. Leeds (1964), for instance, argues that such elite networking is likely to be more dynamic in those regions with high rates of economic development, such as Sao Paulo and Minas Gerais, than in more economically stagnant states, such as Bahia and Pernambuco. Secondly, the importance of the state as economic entrepreneur as well as manager and the relative weakness, until the 1970s, of the private entrepreneurial sector make high government officials co-equal members of urban elites. Thirdly, the increase in the foreign economic presence, whether through multinationals or technology transfer, attenuates the national character and independence of urban elites (Evans, 1979; Cardoso, 1971).

These trends are most evident in the largest metropolitan centres, especially in those which are also national capitals, and will be modified in the 1980s as a result of the gradual withdrawal of state protection from national markets. In the 1990s, business elites in Latin America will be more international in their networks and alliances than previously, less dependent on the state and more assertive in taking overtly political stands on economic and social policy issues. Because of their lesser political and economic centrality and their particular histories, the elites of other cities are less exposed to these trends. The result is a degree of regional diversity in elite characteristics and ideologies which can be illustrated by reference to the elites of Monterrey and Guadalajara in Mexico and to those of Medellin and Cali in Colombia (Walton, 1977).

In Monterrey, the nature of the region, agriculturally poor but close to the United States and rich in minerals, is one factor in the consolidation of industrialization from the 1940s onwards through large-scale industrial combines which employ a large sector of the labour force. Monterrey's elite is small in numbers, cohesive and retains considerable independence and power of negotiation both with respect to foreign capital and central government and its local officials (see also Balán et al., 1973, and Vellinga, 1979, both of which stress the paternalist policies followed by the industrialists with respect their labour force). In the 1990s, the Monterrey elite has acquired major enterprises in the United States and extended its influence throughout Mexico through banking and finance ventures.

In contrast, Guadalajara, developing on the basis of a rich agricultural region and control over important trade routes, has an elite that is much more fragmented than that of Monterrey and is based on medium-scale enterprises in commerce and basic goods industries. Government officials are seen by informants as key members of the elite with power much greater than that attributed to them in Monterrey. External capital, whether foreign or based in Monterrey or Mexico City, is highly influential. Local elites have less of a sense of controlling their environment than do their counterparts in Monterrey. The contrast between Medellin and Cali illustrates other factors of variation. Cali, of the four cities, shows most elite factionalism. The city's rapid but uneven economic development has resulted in differences between a 'traditional' local elite, newcomers from other regions of Colombia and a powerful foreign presence. Medellin, like Monterrey, has an industrially-based and cohesive elite that retains considerable power of negotiation with central government or foreign capital. Unlike the Monterrey elite, but like that of Guadalajara, the Medellin elite is relatively numerous, based on medium-scale enterprise and committed to projects of civic betterment.

Below the elite class, a clearly defined bureaucratic-technical class emerges with high levels of education and employed in managerial and administrative positions in both public and private sectors. This class, like the elites, is concentrated in metropolitan centres and large urban areas. Portes (1985, Table 2) estimates that the dominant class and the bureaucratic technical class make up about 8 per cent of the economically active population. We can use the occupational categories of higher non-manual workers to provide some indication of the size of the bureaucratic-technical class in the urban population. Oliveira and Roberts (1994, Table 5.2) estimate that by 1980 higher non-manual workers made up approximately 16 per cent of the Latin American urban population.

The basis for making class distinctions among the rest of the urban population is complicated by the importance to life chances of whether economic activity and employment are formally regulated by the state or not. As noted in the previous chapter, the informal/formal distinction is an important factor in the stratification of the urban populations of Latin America. Both informal workers and informal employers have different sets of interests and levels of income than their formal counterparts. The partial extension of social security coverage to the Latin American population creates two classes of wage workers: those who receive a range of benefits, including contractual security, and those who do not. Workers in formal enterprises have, on average, higher levels of education than those in informal enterprises. However, formal workers also earn more than informal workers even when the differences in human capital are taken into account. Social security benefits constitute a premium for formal workers who further benefit through higher wages resulting from trade union negotiations and collective contracts. Portes (1985) categorizes wage workers covered by contract and social security as the formal working class and those not covered, including most self-employed and family workers, the informal working class.

Likewise, the partial extension of state regulation of economic activity and the uneven development of urban economies creates two classes of entrepreneurs. One group – mainly large-scale operators – are increasingly enmeshed in sophisticated credit, marketing and supply networks that necessitate their having legal status, which makes it more difficult to avoid fiscal and social security obligations. A second group of mainly small-scale entrepreneurs works so close to the margins of profitability, often in markets that fluctuate sharply, that savings on overheads, such as fiscal and social security obligations, become an important part of their survival strategies. The distinction between formal and informal entrepreneurs should, however, be seen as a continuum rather than a sharp break (Tokman, 1991). Most enterprises observe one or more of their legal obligations, though only a minority observe all of them. However, the small size of the enterprise, the low level of technology and precarious market position compared to larger and better endowed enterprises give the group of small-scale entrepreneurs, who can be labelled the informal petty bourgeoisie, an especial class position.

Both the informal petty bourgeoisie and the informal working class are likely to make up a larger proportion of the class structure in smaller cities and towns than in larger ones. The formal working class represents a more important share of the urban economically active population in the large cities (Pérez Sainz and Menjívar, 1991; Telles, 1988, Table 2.4; Roberts, 1991; SPP, 1979).

Portes (1985, Table 2) estimates the informal petty bourgeoisie in 1970 as 10 per cent, the formal proletariat or working class as 22 per cent and the informal proletariat (which includes the peasant population) as 60 per cent. Telles' (1988, Table 2.4) study of occupations, earnings and stratification in the six major metropolitan areas of Brazil in 1980 indicates that the formal working class averages just under a third of the economically active population of these cities and the informal proletariat about the same proportion.

A further stratum of lower non-manual workers needs to be added to Portes' (1985) characterization of the urban class structure. This lower middle class includes semi-professional occupations, such as teachers, nurses or other health workers, secretaries, bank clerks and sales clerks. Evidence from Mexico suggests that in the 1960s this stratum of the urban population earned more than a skilled industrial worker, but that the differential decreases or is eliminated by the 1970s (Reyes Heroles, 1983). In Brazil by 1980 the mean occupational income and prestige scores of semi-professional occupations such as teachers, nurses, secretaries and bookkeepers were higher than those of most manual workers in industry, construction and the personal services (Telles, 1988, Appendix B).

Though the differences are small between the incomes of this lower middle class group and that of the skilled, formal working class, four factors make it important to include this group as one of the six urban strata. Average levels of education of this class are higher than for the manual working class, with formal education being essential not only for carrying out the job but for reaching the better-paid positions. Conditions of work are generally better, with office workers, teachers and health workers enjoying more social security protection than the manual working class as a whole. Finally, this is the class most dependent on state employment. It represents most social mobility opportunities for women, i.e. female office workers earn significantly higher salaries than did females in the manual wage-earning categories of domestic and other personal services. However, the wages and working conditions of this stratum are somewhat heterogeneous. Sales clerks, who include the growing numbers of supermarket check-out workers, will often earn less than a factory worker and their levels of education may be lower. By the 1980s this lower middle class is likely to amount to about 21 per cent of the economically active urban population.

Non-Occupational Bases of Stratification

Factors other than occupation play a significant part in the stratification of Latin American cities and three, in particular, deserve especial mention: ethnicity, migration and gender. Racial and ethnic categories are, in some countries, the major bases of social cleavage and class inequality. There are considerable difficulties in estimating the ethnic mix of the Latin American populations. Few modern censuses ask populations to list their ethnicity or ancestry and questions about use of an Indian language are also rare. 1990 US government estimates of these ethnic differences put the highest proportions of Indians as 55 per cent in Bolivia, 45 per cent in Peru, 44 per cent in Guatemala, and between 20 per cent and 30 per cent in Ecuador, Colombia, and Mexico (CIA, 1990). The highest proportions of Blacks are 10 per cent in Ecuador and Venezuela, though in absolute numbers the Brazilian Black population is by far the largest. Ethnic and racial labelling is widely practised in Latin America, though its application depends on social context so that, for example, a relatively fair-skinned person dressed poorly by city standards may be labelled 'Indian' in a metropolis, a *mestizo* in a small provincial town and 'White' in the hamlet of his or her birth.

The labels 'White' or 'Spanish' are often used by urban and rural poor to categorize elites. Many members of the population consider themselves *mestizos*, while the categories of Indian and Black cover substantial minorities in several countries. Ethnic differentiation has also been affected by international migration. The predominantly 'White' populations of the southern cone countries of Argentina, Uruguay and Chile originated in the substantial European migrations at the turn of the last century. New international migrations have added to ethnic difference. At the elite level, this has happened through the immigration of entrepreneurs from the Middle East, Europe and Asia. In Argentina, the immigration of Bolivians and Paraguayans has added an ethnic dimension to poverty in both cities and countryside (Balan, 1981, 1985).

Indian ethnicity has remained an important factor in stratification in Latin America, but its significance is, in part, obscured by the rural residence of most Indian populations. To the city-based elites, Indians are often viewed as poor, economically backward and primitive. The army massacres of Indian populations in the 1970s and 1980s in Guatemala and in Peru in the 1980s during the war on *Sendero Luminoso* were prompted, in part, by the ethnic divides in both countries in which Indian opponents are viewed by the army elite as dangerous uncivilized 'others' not open to reason (Degregori and Rivera, 1993; Smith, 1990).

Until the 1970s, Indian ethnic identity was rarely a visible factor in the politics or social stratification of the cities of Latin America even in those countries with a considerable Indian population. This is partly because the permanent rural-urban migration of the mid-twentieth century drew first from the more commercialized rural areas inhabited by mainly *mestizo* populations (Roberts, 1978c). The clustering of migrants from the same village in an urban neighbourhood is a common feature of urbanization, but it is much rarer for these migrants to wear distinctive Indian dress or maintain other signs of their collective Indian identity (but see Arizpe, 1978, for an account of how Mazahua migrants to Mexico City retained certain aspects of their identity). Also, for the Indian populations, the move to the city means a conscious decision to abandon indigenous culture, a process known as *ladinization* in Guatemala. This situation is now changing, so that in Guatemala, for instance, the Indian population of the city had increased to almost 12 per cent of the total by 1986, but it is concentrated in precarious employment and is less likely to be covered by social security than the non-Indian population (Pérez Sainz et al., 1992). Indians are disadvantaged in all areas of urban stratification – income, housing, education and health – when compared to Whites. In Lima, Aymara- and Quechua-speaking migrants are among the poorest in the city (Altamirano, 1984, 1988). As we will see, ethnicity has become a more visible factor in collective identity in Latin America and is increasingly demanded as a citizen's right in various countries among urban as well as rural populations.

Being of African ancestry has also resulted in persisting disadvantage. The Black populations of Brazil have disproportionately concentrated in the poorest segments of the urban and rural population. Taking account both of levels of education, rural or urban origins and region of the country, Blacks are paid less than Whites, live in the worst housing conditions and suffer the worst health (Wood and Lovell, 1992; Wood and Carvalho, 1988). Thus, despite the claim that colour has less significance in producing inequality in Brazil than elsewhere, Blacks are the most disadvantaged among the urban population, though this inequality is lower in the most industrialized areas

(Telles, 1994). The flexibility in racial categories and the possibility of mobility from one category to another, particularly with migration, has, however, been a factor weakening collective identity and organization among Blacks.

Even in the largest and most industrialized cities, the rural population influences the formation of the urban classes through migration. This influence varies in strength from one country to another depending on the nature of the rural economies and whether, for example, out-migrants retain social and economic links with their places of origin. The continuing ties of migrants with their villages of origin, through property, visits and the exchange of goods, help to blur urban class distinctions; they give urban inhabitants political and economic interests that lie as much in the rural areas as with their urban neighbours or fellow workers (Altamirano and Hirabayashi, 1995).

The first rural-urban migrants appear to have been highly selective in terms of their educational and skill levels, with the skilled and 'middle-class' members of villages and small towns moving first to the cities (Balan et al., 1973). There is evidence from some cities that migrant selectivity declined after the 1960s, with those arriving in the cities possessing less education and skills relative to their populations of origin than had previous migrants. This was the case in Monterrey, Mexico, where migrants who arrived in the 1950s and 1960s were less skilled and were more likely to fill manual job positions than previous migrants (Balan et al., 1973). Likewise, from the 1960s there is an increasing migration of unskilled rural workers to Mexico City who took up unskilled urban positions (Oliveira, 1975). However, migrants play an important part in the expansion of the industrial labour force in Mexico City and of non-manual jobs (Oliveira and Garcia, 1984). In Buenos Aires, migrants, both male and female, are as likely to be found working in manufacturing and construction as those born in the city (Marshall, 1978).

Usually, rural migrants are disproportionately found in unskilled manual jobs in construction, manufacturing and services, whilst non-manual jobs – created by the rise of the modern services – which demand relatively high levels of education fall to those born in the city or in other cities with good educational facilities. The city-born and those urban migrants with at least primary education work, in general, in skilled or semi-skilled work in manufacturing, in service firms or in family workshops (Escobar, 1986).

Casual labour in personal services, in construction and in manufacturing has often been provided by temporary rural-urban migration, emphasizing the rural or ethnic distinctiveness of such workers. Examples are Smith's (1984, 1989) account of Peruvian highland villagers picking strawberries and selling fruit in Lima, and Arizpe's (1982) account of Mazua women in Mexico City. In general, however, the similarities in culture and physical appearance mean that rural migrants do not suffer substantial persisting disadvantage when compared with urban natives in most of Latin America.

Gender is also a contributing factor to inequality. Women earn significantly less than men even when their human capital endowments are similar. Female-headed households have increased in numbers in the region and represent the most impoverished group of households (Jelin, 1978). These households are, on average, smaller than those with male heads. The female head combines the tasks of earning a living with domestic ones and has also to maintain the networks that bring in non-monetary resources. The fact that female-headed households need to use all their available resources to survive means that they have less flexibility in the face of economic crises (González de la Rocha, 1988a). In the 1970s, households with female heads accounted for about 17 per cent of households in Mexico City and Buenos Aires, 22 per cent in Recife (in the north-east of Brazil), and 20 per cent in Santiago, Chile (García et al., 1982; Recchini, 1977, 1983; Pantelides, 1976; Garcia et al., 1983). Almost 45 per cent of female-headed households in Belo Horizonte, Brazil, were below the poverty line in the 1970s, whilst the equivalent figure for two-parent households was approximately 28 per cent (Merrick and Schmink, 1978).

The discussion of class structure and income inequality is complicated by needing to take account of the household in determining patterns of stratification. Most urban households in Latin America have more than one member who is economically active. Female participation rates have risen sharply, as we have seen. It is increasingly common for wives, and not just adult children, to work for a wage or help with the family business.

The distribution of extra wage-earners is not, however, even across the class strata both for economic and demographic reasons. Overall, households in the highest strata have smaller families and fewer members in the labour market. The lowest urban strata have larger families and more members in the labour market since, as data from Mexico show, children in these strata are more likely than children in the higher strata to enter the labour market rather than stay on at school (Selby et al., 1990). In general, members of very poor households are more likely than members of other households to be economically active (García et al., 1981).

In the higher strata, the income of the head of household is usually sufficient to maintain the family at its expected level of subsistence. Other members work to pursue a professional career and/or to increase the level of consumption which, at times, results in higher rates of participation in the labour force among married females. The Mexican Urban Employment Survey shows that married women from households whose male head has a professional, managerial or technical occupation are more likely to work for a wage than women whose husbands have working-class occupations, and this occurs at all stages of the household cycle (Roberts, 1993).

In Mexico, as elsewhere in Latin America, working-class wives are burdened with considerable domestic chores, and it is their sons and daughters who provide the supplementary income. Women with higher levels of edu-

cation can obtain much higher incomes than their working-class counterparts and can earn enough to substitute their own domestic labour with
paid domestic services (García et al., 1982, Table V.1; García and Oliveira,
1994). In the bottom deciles of income, the salaries of the heads of households are often insufficient to make ends meet or are close to the margin of
subsistence. In these cases, supplementary incomes earned by other family
members are an essential means of household survival.

The bottom income strata and the classes associated with them can, thus,
be identified not simply by occupational titles or by whether the job is formal or informal, but by the overall household strategy for obtaining an
income. These are the urban poor for whom pooling income and sharing
housing, food and other resources are essential means of urban survival.
Family and friendship networks are also crucial to urban subsistence strategies by providing help with housing, food and finding work. In the case of
Mexico City, 90 per cent of individual migrants were preceded or followed
by a family member (García et al., 1979). Poor households might contain
formally or informally employed workers, the self-employed or domestic
servants. They are less likely to have the spare resources to keep a child out
of the labour market, or a mother to devote herself solely to bringing up
children and keeping up the household. Thus, the consequences of income
inequality extend to inadequate standards of nutrition, health and general
welfare (Wood and Carvalho, 1988).

The regional differences in ethnic stratification and in the transfer of population from rural to urban areas as well as gender and household must be
kept in mind when interpreting the overall pattern of social mobility that
results from urbanization. We can begin with a very rough measure of social
mobility, the movement from farm labour to manual labour in the cities
and, within the cities, the move from manual to non-manual occupations.
These movements, whether within generations or between them, are likely
to entail important changes in lifestyle, consumption and aspirations. The
direction of change need neither be linear nor in an upward direction since,
for example, the increased costs of subsistence in the city can offset any
monetary or status advantages accruing to urban jobs.

The Pattern of Social Mobility

In general, the four decades from 1940 to 1980 have been years of a high
degree of social mobility because of the massive transfer of labour from
agriculture to urban jobs (Filgueira and Geneletti, 1981). The extent and
pace of change in the occupational structure in Latin America varies from
country to country and, consequently, social mobility differs also. CEPAL
(1989) estimates that between 1960 and 1980 the combined shift from agri-

cultural work to manual non-agricultural work and from manual non-agricultural to non-manual ranged from a low of −1.1 per cent in Uruguay to a high of 41 per cent in Honduras. Of the ten countries surveyed, Uruguay and Argentina have little or no occupational mobility because urbanization and industrialization is already well advanced; whereas those countries with the largest changes are those that are rapidly urbanizing: Honduras, Bolivia, Brazil and Ecuador.

Basing itself on a comparison of the occupations of the 24–34 year old age cohort in 1960 with those of the 45–54 cohort in 1980 (who, arguably, are the same people 20 years later), CEPAL suggests that much occupational mobility is likely to have occurred during the lifetime of a generation (CEPAL, 1989). However, comparing the 24–34 year old age cohort in 1980 with the 24–34 year old cohort in 1960, CEPAL shows that intergenerational mobility is higher than that occurring within the lifetime of a generation. The new occupational opportunities tend to be seized by those entering the labour market.

We can further explore the nature of the changes by using data on occupational stratification in six countries of Latin America that categorize urban occupations into five groups: (a) higher non-manual occupations, such as professionals and managers; (b) lower non-manual such as clerks; (c) manual workers in manufacturing and transport; (d) workers in construction and the services, including domestic service; and (e) the self-employed (Oliveira and Roberts, 1994, Appendix Tables 2–7). The reason for distinguishing categories (c) and (d) is that the former is likely to represent the more 'established' urban working class while the latter represents the types of jobs that rural migrants are most likely to enter when they come to the city. Both its size and its ambiguous relation to economic growth make it interesting to distinguish the self-employed category as separate in the analysis of structural mobility. The self-employed form a substantial sector of the economically active urban population, ranging between 20 and 30 per cent in these years. Furthermore, the extent of self-employment indicates, in certain respects, the failure of the large firm to absorb the increase in the urban labour force and, as we noted in the last section, self-employment is often synonymous with the informal economy. We should remember that the limitations of the data mean that these five categories do not correspond closely to the class strata outlined in the previous section. The self-employed will include, for instance, the informal petty bourgeoisie, though the majority of the self-employed are subsistence workers who belong to the category of informal proletariat. Despite this *caveat*, the categories are sufficiently close to the class strata to give us a broad outline of the major patterns of urban class mobility between 1940 and 1980.

In the six countries represented in Table 6.1, the relative decline in agricultural employment varies by period and by country. It is lowest in Argentina, which by 1940 already had a mainly urban population, and highest in Brazil and Mexico, both of which were predominantly rural

Table 6.1. Overall structural mobility in six countries, 1940–1980

Country & time period	Percentage increase/decrease in share of total employment					
	Higher non-manual occupations	Lower non-manual occupations	Manual workers in manufacturing & transport	Manual workers in construction & services	Urban self-employment	Agriculture
Argentina						
1940–60	1.6	0.3	-2.1	1.1	4.9	-5.8
1960–80	3.6	4.0	-3.4	-1.2	4.6	-7.5
Brazil						
1940–60	2.6	1.5	1.9	5.0	2.4	-13.4
1960–80	7.4	4.1	3.0	5.2	1.3	-20.9
Chile						
1940–60	3.9	3.8	-0.9	8.3	0.9	-16.0
1960–80	4.3	7.9	-1.2	2.7	-0.2	-13.5
Colombia						
1940–60	2.5	3.8	3.9	5.8	-1.3	-14.6
1960–80						
Mexico						
1940–60	3.2	5.3	4.9	4.9	-2.6	-15.8
1960–80	4.7	5.0	-1.4	5.8	5.7	-19.9
Peru						
1940–60	1.2	2.6	1.6	5.2	1.5	-12.0
1960–80	4.1	7.7	0.3	-2.5	2.7	-12.2

Source: Calculations based on Oliveira and Roberts, 1994, Tables 2–7.

countries in 1940 but urbanized rapidly thereafter. The decline in the importance of agriculture is compensated for by the increasing importance of non-agricultural, predominantly urban, employment. This trend is the fundamental element in social mobility in all six countries. This type of occupational mobility is directly associated with spatial mobility as people who have worked on the land migrate to the cities and take jobs as construction labourers, domestic servants or factory workers. Even for those born in the cities, however, there is considerable structural mobility as indicated by the increasing importance of non-manual occupations between 1940 and 1980. The increasing importance of 'white collar' work and the declining importance of 'blue collar' work is a feature of job opportunities in the developed world in this period, and this structurally induced occupational mobility results in similar patterns of occupational mobility as between the USA and Europe in the 1950s and 1960s (Lipset and Bendix, 1959).

The changes in the structure of urban employment differ between countries. In Argentina, the increasing share of non-agricultural occupations in total employment occurred almost entirely in self-employment and non-manual occupations. This is a similar trend to that reported by Germani in the work citied above and we should remember that self-employment in Argentina is, for most of this period, more 'middle-class' than is the case elsewhere in Latin America and consists of owners of small, formal businesses. Manual occupations, particularly manufacturing and transport, declined in importance in these years. Manufacturing and transport only increased their importance substantially in Colombia and Mexico between 1940–60 and in Brazil between 1960–80. In all countries, with the exception of Peru between 1960–80, the main increase in manual non-agricultural occupations occurred in construction and the services, including domestic service. In all these countries, again with the Peruvian exception, self-employment was less important in absorbing the urban labour force than were construction and the services. For most of these countries, then, during the years of their rapid growth, the urban economies appear to have been relatively successful in generating enough jobs to absorb both migrants and the increasing numbers of those born in the city. The capacity to absorb labour through employment rather than self-employment appears, however, to be higher in the first period (1940–60) than in the second period.

Taken at face value, the degree of social mobility occurring in Latin America between 1940 and 1980 suggests a period in which the negative side of the dislocations produced by urbanization and industrialization were offset by a substantial improvement in peoples' life chances. Large numbers of people exchanged the arduous toil of peasant farming and the lack of amenities in the rural areas for the somewhat less arduous jobs of the cities and their more extensive amenities. Within the cities, manual labour was increasingly replaced by the less physically exhausting and more socially prestigious non-manual labour. Also, the close links in this period between literacy and being able to obtain good urban jobs were likely to have encouraged families to emphasise their childrens' education and be optimistic about their future prospects. Though I shall argue that this scenario is broadly correct, it must be modified to take into account not only variations between countries, but the unevenness of occupational change, particularly the relatively weak development of stable work careers.

The Changing Nature of Urban Inequality

In general, in the period up to the mid-1970s, there was a rise in real incomes for all strata of the urban populations (Iglesias, 1983). This general trend was interrupted by economic cycles and by political conjunctures, such as the 1964–78 decline in real wages in Sao Paulo, Brazil, resulting from the policies of the military government to contain inflation. During this same period, income concentration increased slightly in Latin America with the top 10 per cent of households by income receiving 47.3 per cent of total income in 1975 compared to 46.6 per cent in 1960 (Portes, 1985, Table 3). Table 6.2 shows that income inequality is still high in Latin America in 1990 with some of the most economically dynamic countries, such as Brazil and Chile, showing levels of income concentration higher than that reported for Latin America in 1975. The levels of income concentration are also much higher than in the United States and the difference is as sharp as the one Portes noted for 1975.

High levels of income inequality have been accompanied by increasing poverty among the urban population as is shown by the estimates of the Economic Commission for Latin America (Table 6.2). The Commission's estimates suggest a sharp rise in urban poverty during the 1980s so that 34 per cent of urban households in the region fell into the poverty category by 1990, although in some countries, such as Chile, the increase in poverty was marked in the 1970s. Note the contrasts with the United States. Although poverty has been rising in the United States, its levels there are far below those common in Latin America.

The national figures on income distribution when related to class differences enable us to explore the significance of occupational mobility for changes in urban inequality. The social strata that have been described above are likely to be differentiated by sources of income and by the amounts they receive. The highest income levels, that of the top 10 per cent, are likely to correspond to the dominant and bureaucratic-technical class. They have monopolized the income benefits of economic growth. The contrast with the bottom 40 per cent of the income distribution is acute since, as Table 6.2 indicates, their incomes are, on average, up to 30 times less than those in the top 10 per cent. These strata are mainly rural but they

Table 6.2. Income distribution and poverty in Latin America

Country	Percentage share of income or consumption c. 1990[A]					Urban households in situation of poverty[B]		
	Lowest 40%	Third quintile	Fourth quintile	Highest 20%	Top 10%	1970	c. 1980	c. 1990
Argentina	nd	nd	nd	nd	nd	5	7	12
Brazil	7.0	8.9	16.8	67.5	51.3	35	30	39
Chile	11.0	10.3	16.2	62.9	48.9	12	37	34
Colombia	11.0	12.6	20.4	55.8	39.5	38	36	35
Costa Rica	13.0	14.3	21.9	50.8	34.1	15	16	22
Guatemala	7.9	10.5	18.6	63.0	46.6	nd	41	nd
Honduras	8.7	10.2	17.6	63.5	47.9	40	53	65
Mexico	12.0	12.3	19.9	55.9	39.5	20	na	23
Peru	14.0	13.7	21.0	51.4	35.4	28	35	45
Uruguay	nd	nd	nd	nd	nd	10	9	10
Venezuela	14.0	14.4	21.9	49.5	33.2	20	18	33
Latin America	nd	nd	nd	nd	nd	26	25	34
United States	16.0	17.4	25.0	41.9	25	10	10	11

[A]The proportion of income or consumption held by the lowest 40%, the next three quintiles, and the highest 10% of the distribution respectively.
[B]In the case of the Latin American countries, the percentage of urban households having incomes amounting to less than twice the cost of a basic basket of food. In the case of the United States, the Bureau of the Census' estimate of that proportion of urban and rural households that cannot afford the food and other necessary goods and services needed for adequate subsistence.
Sources: For income distribution, World Bank, 1994a, Table 30; For poverty, ECLA, 1993, Table 22; and Statistical Abstract of the United States, 1994, Table No. 735.

include urban workers in industry, construction and the services who are formally employed but semi- and unskilled, together with most self-employed workers and informally employed workers. These are the workers whose households are most likely to belong to the 34 per cent of urban households that were in poverty in 1990 (Table 6.2). The self-employed and skilled informally employed workers are, in the 1990s, likely to be in the upper end of these strata, especially the craftworkers, while those in personal services are at the bottom end.

The remaining 50 per cent of the income distribution will be almost entirely urban. These are the strata where most social mobility is likely to have concentrated. The income differences between these strata are still considerable, but few within any of these strata are likely to earn enough to ensure a comfortable lifestyle by the standards of developed countries. The upper income levels of these intermediate strata are likely to be made up of aspiring members of the bureaucratic-dominant classes, just beginning their careers in government or in the private sector, some small-scale entrepreneurs in industry and the services and, in some countries, skilled workers of key industries, such as the petroleum or, in this period, the car industry.

The middle levels of these intermediate strata probably include the lower middle class: teachers, ancillary personnel in the health or welfare services, bank clerks and office workers in private and public sectors. The intermediate level also includes the less successful members of the informal bourgeoisie, the more successful among the self-employed and skilled workers in industry, transport and communications. The lower levels of the intermediate strata include the bottom end of the lower middle class – sales clerks and non-specialized office workers – skilled workers in basic goods industries, in construction and in the services and the self-employed in industry and certain of the services.

Studies from Mexico, Brazil and some other countries of Latin America suggest that, by the mid-1970s, urban income distribution, while demonstrating sharp inequalities, also evidenced an improvement in the position of the various strata (Portes, 1985, Table 3; Iglesias, 1983; Cortes and Rubalcava, 1991; Wood and Carvalho, 1988, Table 3.5; Escobar and Roberts, 1991). The bureaucratic-dominant group – who are likely to be synonymous with the richest 10 per cent of households in income – had clearly benefited from the rise in real salaries and in profits. In the period from 1960 to 1975, they probably increased their share of household income slightly (Portes, 1985, Table 3). However, the informal bourgeoisie, the lower middle-class and the formal working class also increased their real wages.

These gains reflected a series of factors in the pattern of economic development since the 1960s: the dominant groups and the informal bourgeoisie benefit from the general dynamism of the economies of the region and the entrepreneurial opportunities they generate; the lower middle class from the growth of state employment and the benefits given to state employees; and the formal working class from the power of organized labour to extract wage concessions. Up to 1980, all these groups, with the exception of the informal bourgeoisie, were also increasing their share of the population as waged and salaried work increased as a proportion of the urban labour force. While the unskilled and informal workers appear to have decreased their share of total income, thus creating a certain polarization in the class structure, this is offset by a rise in real incomes even among these strata.

These trends in income change from about the 1970s onwards. My assessment of these trends is necessarily speculative since more research is needed before long-term tendencies can be distinguished from short-term ones such as the temporary effects of economic crisis. One underlying element in the current situation is that the demand for workers in urban areas is negatively affected by technological changes that save on labour and by the economic crises that beset the Latin American economies. One consequence is a widespread decline in real wages that has important implications for the class structure, especially since it occurs in the context of a cut-back in state expenditures and employment.

In the 1980s, the decline in real wages was general and consistent throughout the region. Between 1980 and 1987, the real minimum wage declined by 14 per cent in Latin America, though with some recuperation between 1985–87 (International Labour Office, 1989, Table 1.10). The decline appears to have been most severe in public sector wages which dropped by 17 per cent, and least severe in manufacturing which dropped by 10 per cent. This overall trend conceals important variations by country and city. The declines were most severe in Peru and Mexico, while in Colombia real wages appear to have increased. Colombia is perhaps the only Latin American country to carry out an economic policy that, at one and the same time, permits the expansion of the volume of exports, the neutralization of the effects of the drop in international prices and an increase in real wages from the 1970s up to 1987.

In the 1980s, the Latin American economies increasingly adopted free market policies aimed at stimulating the private sector and reducing state intervention in the economy. These had a negative impact on the urban middle and working classes, especially the lower middle class, formal and informal working classes. The incomes of intermediate and lower level state employees, including teachers and health personnel, appear to have dropped sharply in these years, so that public sector workers in Uruguay, for example, earned 56 per cent of their 1975 wage by 1985 (International Labour Office, 1989). In Mexico, the decile of household incomes that mainly includes the lower middle class loses income relative to the one above. In terms of income and sources of income, the lower middle class decile became more similar to those below (Cortes and Rubalcava, 1991).

There is also a sharp decline in incomes at the top of income distribution relative to the period before the economic crises, but here there are signs of differentiation between the entrepreneurial section and high level administrators and professionals. The income from profits rises during the years of crisis, while salaries drop substantially. However, for the upper urban classes incomes are still substantially above those of other classes. One factor that maintains and even increases the income advantage of the professional and technical strata over those below is that high levels of training remain in demand as economies restructure and modernize. Pozas' (1993) case study of industrial restructuring in Monterrey, Mexico, shows that income polarization is likely to become marked as firms reduce the number of wage grades among workers while paying premium wages to technicians and professionals. Comparing labour market surveys of Monterrey with Guadalajara, Pozos also finds income polarization occurring, with Monterrey, where industrial restructuring is more advanced, having sharper polarization. This polarization occurs particularly between those with college education and those with primary or secondary education (Pozos, 1992). Though consumption may have diminished in these years, income remains adequate for a comfortable lifestyle. Escobar and Roberts (1991) indicate some of the monetary and non-monetary benefits that these upper strata continued to receive: company cars, productivity-linked bonuses, school fees and free travel.

The bottom end of the urban class structure appears to have also suffered from the crisis relative to the previous period, despite beginning with very low levels of income. The formal working class sees reductions in its income that are not offset by the increasing importance of non-wage benefits and by other sources of income, including remittances from abroad. Furthermore, the formal working class loses importance within the Latin American working classes in the 1980s as the informal working class grows substantially both in numbers and as a proportion of the urban labour force.

Because informal employment provided relatively easy access to incomes that could supplement household incomes, it facilitated a household strategy of placing more members on the labour market as a means of offsetting the declines in real wages (Gonzalez de la Rocha, 1988a; Selby et al., 1990; Oliveira, 1989). Households containing members of the informal working class may, as a consequence, have experienced a smaller reduction in overall income than other working-class families. Evidence from Mexico suggests that this was the case, with non-wage sources of income also having become more important: remittances, self-provisioning and renting out accommodation (Cortes and Rubalcava, 1991). The result of these various tendencies was a continuing polarization of incomes in Mexico despite a slight decline in income inequality. The poorest survived at the margins of subsistence through strategies, such as using child labour, mothers of young children seeking paid work or cutting food consumption, that were likely to perpetuate their disadvantages. Studies in Chile and Mexico show a worsening of nutritional levels in the late 1970s and 1980s and a general decline in welfare (Raczynski and Serrano, 1984; Tapia Curiel, 1984; Arizpe, 1990; Benaría, 1991)

Chile provides one of the most striking examples of the contradictions of the economic growth patterns of the 1980s. In terms of the decline in unemployment and the growth of waged employment, Chile is perhaps the success story of Latin America. By 1990, the rate of unemployment had fallen to 5.7 per cent and the proportion of waged workers in the labour force increased to 62 per cent from 49 per cent in 1982, a time when the majority of the employed population were self-employed, unpaid family workers, those in emergency work programmes or in military service (Díaz, 1993). Also, there was a substantial economic recovery in the second half of the 1980s with high rates of growth in Gross National Product. However, the favourable economic and employment trends were accompanied by an increase in social inequalities. Díaz reports a drop between 1978 and 1988 in the daily calorific consumption of the poorest 40 per cent of the population of about 7 per cent; whereas in 1978, the richest 10 per cent of the population controlled 37 per cent of all national income, their share had risen to 47 per cent by 1988. Thus, though more of the Chilean population was at work than previously, their relative poverty had increased. Poverty had become a working poverty based on low-waged, precarious jobs, often held by women. The Chilean data indicate that the proportion of families officially considered to be poor rose from 24 per cent to 26 per cent of the population between 1978 and 1988, and by 1990 the national household survey conducted by the new civilian government found that 40 per cent of the population of the country lived in poverty (Díaz, 1993).

Lustig's (1992) analysis of the social costs of adjustment in Mexico in the 1980s paints a similar picture. Between 1983 and 1988 there was a fall of real wages per worker of between 40 and 50 per cent. In this period, income concentration at the top 10 per cent of the population appears to have increased, while the share of the lowest 40 per cent declined as did that of the intermediate 50 per cent. The government reduced food subsidies and expenditures on the social services. Lustig provides evidence of deterioration in health standards as a result of malnutrition, pointing to the rise in infant mortality due to nutritional deficiencies. Families with incomes below two minimum salaries experience a decline in consumption as measured by the basic food basket. Even so, expenditures on food represented 52 per cent of the minimum salary in 1986, whereas in 1982 they only represented 34 per cent (Lustig, 1986).

The changes in the labour market tend to weaken the job as the central factor structuring daily life, redefining the bases for social stratification. The intensification of subcontracting by large-scale enterprises to domestic outworkers or workshops, the increase in unemployment, the casualization of much of the labour force and the increase in labour force turnover produces greater instability in employment. These processes work against the consolidation of the urban social classes in Latin America. An individual's occupation becomes a less useful indicator than in the past of social and class position. This is especially true for the working class, for whom the possession of skills is less likely to secure a stable work career and for whom the individual salary is usually insufficient to maintain a household.

The importance of occupation in defining life chances and social position is, to an extent, replaced by that of position within the household structure and stage in household cycle – heads of nuclear or extended households, with children or not, with or without spouse, or living alone – and by access to community and family help or to information networks. Stable occupational careers (characterized by remaining in the same enterprise, obtaining skills and promotion, benefiting from seniority and social security) become rarer than previously. The increase in interurban mobility is one indication of frequent changes of job. Increasing signs of residential mobility also imply that neighbourhoods become less stable than in previous decades, as does the neighbourhood basis for social solidarity. These themes will be taken up in the next chapter.

Conclusion

Growing income inequalities have not resulted in an increase in overt group and class conflict, partly because of the considerable geographical and occupational mobility that until recently has characterized the population of many underdeveloped cities. The occupational mobility between 1940 and 1980 was considerable with substantial numbers of children from peasant or manual working-class backgrounds finding non-manual jobs. There are, however, clear signs that this occupational mobility has slowed or is over. The major source of non-manual employment, the state, is contracting and informal and precarious employment appears to be on the rise throughout Latin America. The economic crises of the 1970s and 1980s have made life increasingly difficult not only for the urban poor but have eroded the lifestyle of the growing middle class. While the upper classes have consolidated their economic position, the middle class remains in a precarious situation, and large sectors of that class are only barely distinguishable from the urban poor. Unfortunately, there are too few studies available of the Latin American middle classes to enable us to continue with the analysis of their changing life chances in depth. In the next chapter, we focus on the low-income populations of Latin America and explore, in a more qualitative way, the nature of urban poverty.

7

Urban Poverty, the Household and Coping with Urban Life

So far we have concentrated mainly on the social and economic structures that accompany uneven urban development. Even so, political and social relationships have figured prominently in the discussion of the workings of the urban economy and in this chapter these relationships come to the forefront of the analysis. This account will be more ethnographic than previous chapters, attempting to provide some feeling for the quality of life in Latin American cities. The following description of social relationships, religious practices, the problems of housing and of local politics may seem far removed from our previous concerns, yet these details enable us to appreciate the extent to which all aspects of life are affected by the pattern of economic expansion that has occurred in underdeveloped countries.

There is also an analytic purpose since we need to explore the ways in which the sheer necessity of coping with urban life sets social and political forces in motion that may affect the path of economic development. This is our chance to bring the individual and the household back into our analysis as actors who are not simply puppets of forces beyond their control but forces contributing to shaping the course of events. The individuals and households will be, in this case, mainly from the low-income populations of the cities and we will explore the extent to which their activities, unplanned and unorganized as they may be, make up undercurrents of change in the political and social structure. We need, then, to see whether the class struggle in the cities of underdeveloped countries is manifest in other ways than through the actions of political parties and labour unions.

The account to follow will be organized around the theme of how the poor cope with their poverty and economic marginality. This has been an important issue in the literature on Latin American urbanization, beginning with the concern that urbanization would disorientate many of those who came to the city and result in a permanent social and cultural marginality and, in recent years, focusing on the severe challenges to family budgets posed by the economic crises of the 1980s.

Poverty and Social Marginality

On most indices of well-being, the situation of the urban poor in under-developed countries remains appalling. Though there has been some decrease in absolute levels of poverty and substantial increases in life expectancy and educational levels, malnutrition remains widespread and mortality rates are many times higher among these groups than among the middle classes or among the low-income populations of the developed world (see World Bank, 1990, for a review of the characteristics of poverty in developing countries that stresses the gains that have been made, but also the regional disparities). Conditions vary from one underdeveloped country to another with the highest levels of poverty found in India and sub-Saharan Africa, where about half the population is classified as living in poverty (World Bank, 1990, Table 2.1). In Latin America, estimates suggest that approximately 20 per cent of the population have incomes that are insufficient for adequate levels of food and shelter. Though poverty is concentrated in the rural areas of the developing world, the absolute numbers of the urban poor increased 75 per cent between 1970–85, with the highest increases occurring in Latin America and the Caribbean (United Nations, 1994).

Urban poverty is, however, not simply a matter of individual income; it is exacerbated by the spatial and physical organization of the cities. These cities are underurbanized in terms of the availability of housing and over-crowding is common. Though there have been improvements in the supply of electricity, water, and sewage disposal systems, there has been little improvement on one index of overcrowding, the number of people per room (ECLAC, 1993, Tables 32–3). In the large cities of developing countries, slums and informal settlements provide housing for between 30 and 80 per cent of the population. Estimates put such housing as 40 per cent of the total in Mexico City, 34 per cent in Rio de Janeiro and 32 per cent in Sao Paulo (United Nations, 1994, Table 42). Informal settlements are usually rudimentary housing of wood, thatch or even cardboard constructed by the residents on public and private land which they have illegally occupied (see Lowder, 1986, for an account of informal settlement in Latin America and elsewhere in the developing world). Even where land is legally settled with its owners subdividing and selling in small lots, the first residents often build the houses with their own labour and materials.

In most large cities of the underdeveloped world, there is also a severe shortage of public services. Many city roads, especially on the outskirts, are unpaved. Public water supply reaches low-income areas of the city through public hydrants servicing a large number of families, and adequate sewage disposal systems serve only a small proportion of the urban population. Health facilities are unevenly concentrated in the richer areas of the city; in low-income areas, a clinic with one doctor may serve over 10,000 people. Educational facilities are also unevenly distributed with the higher-income areas having private schools and better state school facilities; low-income areas such as shanty towns have rudimentary school buildings and over-crowded classes.

The various facets of capitalist development – land speculation, income concentration and capital-intensive industrialization – combine to exclude low-income populations from the benefits of economic growth. This issue has been discussed by Leeds (1974) in his account of the interlinked processes by which low-income urban populations are unable to obtain ade-quate housing, incomes and urban services in Brazilian and other Latin American cities. He points out that, despite the diversity of occupational, residential and family situations among the poor, they experience a common set of frustrations in which the 'exclusiveness' of the elites are apparent. These include the practices of public agencies or credit agencies in providing very limited access for low-income people; they must queue for services and are aware that they receive indifferent treatment (Roberts, 1973a).

Exclusion is also apparent in the uncertainty of tenure of low-income res-idents; informal settlements are always liable for demolition and those in rented and government assisted estates can easily be removed for default in payments or nuisances caused by children. Restrictive hiring practices in modern enterprises are, as we noted earlier, means by which large segments of the workforce are excluded from stable, high-income work opportunities. These common situations are linked through the activities of work, seeking and defending housing, householding and daily urban activities: no signifi-cant group of the low-income population is exempt from them.

The lack of adequate housing and of social services is, some would argue, directly related to the type of urban economic growth that was reviewed in Chapter 5. Wells (1976) points out that in Brazil the scarce investment in collective consumption (schools, public services) releases resources for pro-duction and for private consumption. Thus, in most Latin American cities, it is common to find radios, televisions and refrigerators even in the poorest informal settlements. The exclusion of the poor, then, is *not* an exclusion from the market for consumer goods.

Since these situations are part of the dynamic of the capitalist system, Leeds argues that it represents the proletarianization of the mass of the urban population. He claims (Leeds, 1974) that this proletarianization

is even more strongly delineated, less alleviated by 'affluence', less ameliorated by great masses of better-paid, highly skilled wage earn-ers, less softened by opportunities for upward mobility, less responsive to political protest and electoral expression, and generally more repressive in the 'underdeveloped' dependent societies than in the metropoles like Great Britain and the United States.

The exclusion of the poor from access to an adequate income and to urban services has given rise to what Perlman (1976) calls the myth of mar-ginality. In the following sections, I will review the data that show why it is inappropriate to see the poor as socially and politically marginal; but first I will outline the concepts of marginality that have perhaps most influenced the way the 'problem' of urban poverty is viewed generally and acted upon by governments. The first of these concepts is that which sees marginality as consisting of the lack of participation of low-income groups in politics, in their 'traditional' attitudes and in their lack of access to education, health care and adequate standards of consumption. From this perspective, marginality is an unfortunate and avoidable consequence of rapid urban growth in the situation of underdevelopment; marginality can be remedied through social welfare and educational programmes and through the creation of job opportunities. In Latin America, this concern with marginality became the basis of an extensive analysis, documenting the exclusion of substantial sectors of the population from the benefits of economic growth in the post-Second World War period (Desal-Herder, 1968; Giusti, 1971). It also became the basis for what amounted to political movements, often associated with Latin American Christian Democrat parties, aimed at remedying the dependence of Latin America *vis-à-vis* the developed countries.

This dependence was seen as remediable to the extent that the mass of the population could be organized to galvanize traditional structures (Vekemans and Giusti, 1969/70). The economic and political marginality of the mass of the population was seen to hinder this development process in several ways. Illiterate, poverty-stricken families living in urban slums, for example, were viewed as perpetuating from generation to generation feelings of hopelessness. Such populations were also seen as potential supporters of populist and authoritarian politicians and as constituting a barrier to stable democratic development. The remedy to marginality was seen to lie, in part, in the work of popular promotion: various types of cooperatives were to be set up among low-income populations as a means of engendering a spirit of self-help and as a means of promoting the internal integration of the poor. This perspective was one that emphasized the potential benefits to all social classes in ending the marginality of the mass of the population. Vekemans and Giusti (1969/70) expressed this hope as follows:

> The marginal sectors would function as pressure groups to accelerate the process of incorporation, while the ruling elites would provide the guidelines for action and control the general coordination for development. Only thus could the national states provide the basis for hemispheric integrations.

The second and more complex view of marginality is Lewis's (1961; 1968) attempt to describe the lifestyles of the poor by means of the culture of poverty thesis. Lewis developed the concept of the culture of poverty on the basis of intensive observation and interviewing in Mexico City and, subsequently, in San Juan, Puerto Rico and New York. He saw the culture of poverty as most likely to arise in the situation of underdevelopment, in which there is rapid urban growth without there being jobs in the modern sector of the economy and in which migration from the rural areas was an important component of that growth. He also stressed that his thesis applied to groups that had no strong basis of class or ethnic identity to sustain them in the face of the cumulative difficulties of urban poverty. Lewis argued that low-income casual work, poor living conditions and low levels of education made families and friendships unstable and unreliable. In this context, the culture of poverty develops through the generation of fatalistic orientations, emphasizing living for the moment. The culture of poverty is thus a subculture of the national one, enabling the poor to cope psychologically with a difficult environment.

The culture of poverty, according to Lewis, hinders people's attempts to escape from their impoverished situation even when some (limited) opportunities are provided: children brought up in the culture of poverty experience an unstable and often violent family life, have little chance of being educated and take on, at an early age, ill-paid and often illegal work. The culture of poverty thus acts to reinforce disadvantages from one generation to the next. Despite the self-perpetuating nature of the culture of poverty, Lewis viewed change as possible when structures are changed from above. At the time of his death, he was working in Cuba and argued that, under its communist government, economic and political structures had been changed sufficiently to destroy the basis for a culture of poverty (Lewis, 1968; Butterworth, 1974). In the Cuban research, Lewis and his collaborators showed that incomes were still low in La Habana, but that participation in economic and political life had changed dramatically, creating a sense of optimism about future possibilities among low-income families.

The basic problem with these two views of marginality is that they are elitist in conception: the poor tend to be viewed as being incapable of improving their situation by themselves and change originates from above. Until that time, the poor are relatively ineffectual actors in the urban political and economic scene. Such approaches underestimate the resourcefulness of the poor and the extent to which they participate actively in urban economic and political life. For example, despite the rich texture of his descriptions of the problems facing the poor, Lewis paid little attention to the workings of the urban economy and to the nature of the interconnections, which, as we shall see, exist between the poor and other more powerful members of the city.

The Household and Coping with Urban Life

Though at times the terms are used interchangeably, household and family are not synonymous concepts. Household refers to the basic unit of co-residence and family to a set of normative relationships. It is, however, within the context of the household that family strategies have usually been discussed and this is the usage here. When the basis of the household is a family unit, the actions of individual members are likely to be influenced, even if contrarily, by normative assumptions about the obligations of family members and by shared principles as to family priorities. These norms and principles do not guarantee that members of a household will act together to further some common goal. Individual members of a household are likely to have different interests based on their family status, their gender and their generation. Often what appears to be a household strategy turns out on closer inspection to be little more than the strategy of one member of a household, typically the male head of the household. This organization, particularly the domestic division of labour, is slow to change to accommodate new circumstances such as women's increasing importance as breadwinners (Morris, 1993).

Because of the normative component in household organization, there are likely to be cultural differences between countries in the degree of cohesion within households and in the expectations that members have of each other. There are, for example, continuing contrasts in the culture and operation of the family-based household unit as between Asian countries such as Japan or China and that of the Western world that have not been eroded by modernization (see Cornell, 1990). In the Latin American context, the family-based household is often thought to be more cohesive and with a higher emphasis on the responsibilities of family members than is the case in countries of the developed world, such as the United States.

Moreover, the legacy of Conquest with its forced conversion to Catholicism, coupled with the enforcement of patriarchal authority, has been linked to two cultural features of the Latin American family structure: *machismo* and *marianismo* (see Fernandez-Kelly, 1995, for a discussion of the use of these cultural terms). *Machismo* is the cult of the strong, irresponsible and fatalistic male who makes use of women and who subordinates family interests to his pleasures. It is thought to be especially prevalent in countries characterized by indigenous and *mestizo* populations. *Marianismo* is the mirror reflection of *machismo*, emphasising the virtues of female abnegation and suffering: the mother who will always be there for the children in contrast to the absent *macho* father figure (Stevens, 1973).

These cultural traits need, however, to be studied comparatively and placed within the changing social and economic context brought by urbanization, as is shown by Ehlers' account (1991) of *marianismo* among Guatemalan peasant women. There, *marianismo* reflects economic isolation as women's role in the family economy becomes marginalized with the growth of cash-crop farming. Likewise, in urban Latin America, cultural norms do not stop women leaving abusive or unreliable husbands and setting up their own single parent households when resources allow them do so. This is one conclusion of Chant's (1991) detailed study of female-headed households in the Mexican tourist centre of Puerto Vallarta where women can find jobs relatively easily.

Despite variations due to cultural and contextual factors, family-based households are likely to have some common strategies. Individual family members may have conflicting interests, but each is likely to derive some advantage from the enhancement of their collective welfare. Some members may gain more than others. Coalitions may emerge between members of a household to secure a greater share of resources for themselves. Yet, in Latin America, the family-based household has remained for its members the basic resource for coping with the environment whether rural or urban (Schmink, 1984).

This is particularly true for the poor in the absence of state-provided welfare. Individual survival in this situation depends upon family provision of care for the elderly and the infirm, the pooling of inadequate incomes and the sharing of shelter. The family, together with wider kinship and friendship networks, helps individuals find jobs and provides aid in emergency. The strategies that households employ to get by in the cities of the developing world, based mainly on the intensive use of household and community relationships, are well-documented (see Lomnitz, 1977, and Gonzalez de la Rocha, 1994, for particularly rich case studies). They differ little from those used during industrialization in Europe and are affected by similar variables, such as type of work, and whether the family is self-employed or proletarian (Tilly and Scott, 1978; Anderson, 1971).

Tilly and Scott (1978) argue that it is not urbanization nor even factory employment per se, that makes the basic difference to household organization but the general changes in context created by proletarianization and the increase in opportunities to earn wages and to spend them. It is these changes that lead to the family economy of the early industrial period being replaced by the family wage economy and, finally, by the family consumer economy, altering the expectations attached to the different family roles. The move from one type of family economy to another entails a lessening in the collective coordination of family strategies. The family economy is based on a common enterprise, typically a small farm, and the life plans of individual members are subordinated to that enterprise. The family-wage economy lessens that subordination even though having more than one wage-earner in the family is essential to family survival. Absent children can, for instance, support their parents monetarily from afar. Finally, in the family-consumer economy, coordinating the contributions of individual family members is not essential to survival since the wage of the main breadwinner is enough to ensure the subsistence of the whole family. Children are thus 'released' to pursue their formal education and the spouse may specialize in managing the household. Extra wages, whether of spouse or children serve to enhance consumption.

This approach can usefully be applied to understanding the effects on urban family organization of the changes in the urban economy that we have reviewed. In Latin America, in the period of import-substitution industrialization from the 1940s to the 1970s, there are differences in the strength of social organization between cities with dynamic economies and in those with stagnant ones, as suggested by the contrast between Lomnitz's (1977) account of strong household and community organization in Mexico City, and my own emphasis (1973a) on relatively weak organization in Guatemala City. However, in this period, households have economic opportunities that contrast positively with those of the past and encourage aspirations for further social mobility. Even among the working class, there are the beginnings of a 'family wage'. Households whose male heads have stable jobs could survive on a single income with the wife attending to domestic work and the children in school. In the new order from the 1970s onwards this, admittedly slow, emergence of a family wage is halted and reversed. When women work it is not to expand consumption and build up resources but to maintain a basic subsistence. With the exception of the privileged few, most members of the household, men as well as women, young and old, earn supplementary wages.

The dilemma for family strategies is an acute one. For the young, they are likely to be better off if they leave the parental household and set up independently, provided that they can find housing. A young married couple without children are in the best financial position. Finding housing is not easy, however, and there will be considerable pressure from parents for them to stay at home and to continue to contribute financially, particularly when the parents have no other source of income. The stage at which individuals or couples are free from responsibilities to parents or children is, under these conditions, likely to be a brief one. Indeed, a couple are most likely to set up an independent household when they are expecting children, and will soon enter the second stage of the household cycle with its sharp drop in income.

Multiple earner households survive better than those dependent on one earner, but the crucial determinant is family size. As Despres (1991) shows for his Manaus sample, the small amounts of income supplement coming from non-heads of households mean that extra earners can only partially offset the increased consumption of larger families. This is especially the case when the supplement comes from children, not all of whose income will be contributed to the family pot. Multiple earners are unlikely, then, to be the basis for accumulation and social mobility strategies among Latin American working-class households. Among the sample from the Mexican urban employment survey reviewed in Chapter 5, it is only professional, managerial and technical households that appear to have some capacity for accumulation. Among these households, spouses are more likely to be employed than in the working-class households, where the earnings of spouses are high and family size is smaller.

There is evident tension within households, as husbands expect their wives to fulfil their domestic chores as well as take in work for pay. Though members of the household pool resources, the pooling is often perceived to be inequitable, with women providing more of their income than men and the young feeling that they have a right to a greater share of their income for their personal needs. There is some evidence that women are better off alone with their children than when husbands are also present (Chant, 1991). At the community level, the economic pressures fragment as well as unify. Households work long hours, with little time to give to community affairs, and their members have different jobs to those of their neighbours.

The most difficult period in family life is usually that of the early part of the household cycle when the children are young, their mother takes care of the household and the youth of the father results in a low wage. The principal family strategy has been for households to add members to the labour force, with children delaying their exit from the household and wives increasing their participation in the labour force (Gonzalez de la Rocha, 1991, 1994). However, married women have had low employment rates in Mexico, partly as a result of cultural biases against married women working outside the home and partly as a result of the preferences of employers for single women. Thus, as the family cycle advances, the supplementary earners in the household will be the children. The situation is similar to that described by Lamphere (1987) for immigrants in New England in the early part of this century when it is 'working daughters' not 'working mothers' who provide the additions to family income.

Both households and community survival strategies generated tensions which led to household break-up and community fragmentation (De la Peña et. al., 1990; Gonzalez de la Rocha et al., 1990). The pressure on family relationships is considerable, particularly for women. Women, as mothers and housewives, carry a double responsibility: they have to look after the house and care for other household members, whilst seeking income sources through domestic outwork or employment outside the home. Male heads, though unable to maintain the household on their low salaries, often remain resistent to their wives working outside the home. Males are reluctant to contribute their entire income to the family budget, increasing the potential for family conflicts. Fathers expect both their sons and daughters to contribute to the family pot, while they, in turn, wish to use their earnings for individual needs. The gender and generational conflicts that arise within households were a marked characteristic of urban life in Latin America by 1990.

The Significance of Social Relationships within the City

In this section, I shall examine the extent to which the urban poor, including rural migrants, are socially isolated and are given to 'traditional' patterns of behaviour. There have been frequent reports of the lack of trust and interpersonal hostility within low-income neighbourhoods (see Jesus, 1963, and Levine, 1994, for an account of Jesus's subsequent history, emphasising the disadvantages she faced because of class and racial prejudice). Likewise, in some Latin American cities, such as Lima, and more markedly, in African and Asian cities, ethnic identities and customs survive in low-income areas, appearing to ruralize the city. In Brazilian cities, magical rites have an extensive following among low-income populations in even the largest and most modern cities.

These and other 'marginal' features must be placed within the context of the patterns of development that characterize cities in the underdeveloped world. We have noted how, in the past, ethnic customs and 'traditionalism' are often the product of capitalist development: this argument can also be applied, with modifications, to the contemporary urban situation. For example, the importance of ethnic identity in urban situations is not simply a survival of rural practices but a direct response to the exigencies of survival in a competitive urban economy where economic opportunities are scarce. Ethnic identity permits a certain monopoly of jobs and clients and provides a basis for trust. This type of analysis has been used by Cohen (1969) in describing the significance of religious identification for a particular group of traders in Ibadan in Africa. Such an analysis is in the tradition of those British social anthropologists who show that it is the urban situation, including its conflicts, anxieties and social interactions, that selectively reinforce rural traits or identities, as for tribalism in African cities (Mitchell, 1966, 1957).

There is, then, little to be gained in categorizing behaviour as 'traditional', 'rural' or 'fatalistic'. It is more interesting to examine how, in the face of an uncertain economic environment, individuals use the cultural and social resources available to them and adopt a particular pattern of coping with the difficulties of urban life. The uneven development of the urban economy often implies a diversity of means by which people struggle, culturally and socially, not simply to survive but to better their position. There are a number of highly informative ethnographic accounts of these daily struggles and readers can consult, among others, Lomnitz's (1977) account of Mexico City, González de la Rocha's (1994) account of Guadalajara, Mexico, and the various Brazilian community studies, such as Caldeira's (1984) study of neighbourhood organization in Sao Paulo and Zaluar's studies (1985, 1994) of crime and neighbourhood organization in Rio de Janeiro.

From this perspective, there is no reason to assume that rural migrants will have inherent problems in adjusting to urban life and to urban occupations. A more interesting approach is to look at the resources, such as capital, social relationships, educational and other skills, that different groups of migrants and city-born are able to marshall to cope with urban life. The relative significance of the different types of resources will vary depending on the size of the city and its stage of economic development.

Among low-income families, the strength of kinship will vary with the urban situation of the individual and of the family. Thus, among small-scale entrepreneurs operating extended domestic enterprises, kinship relationships are important. Family events will be celebrated and there is intensive interaction between kin members both within the city and outside it. In contrast, those with jobs that do not require collaboration with trusted others are perhaps less likely, as Smith (1975a) reports for Lima, to maintain kinship ties. In the extreme case, a high degree of poverty and job instability in a city may undermine the stability of the nuclear household. Eames and Goode (1973) review a series of studies in the Caribbean and Central America that indicate that single-parent families and unstable households are the result of economic uncertainty. They suggest that, under conditions of poverty and job instability, men may be unwilling to commit themselves to relatively permanent obligations; likewise, women may be unwilling to take on the liability of a permanent attachment when the man might prove a drunkard, unable to earn a living or prone to violence.

This explanation for marital instability in cities of underdeveloped countries emphasizes the elements of rational calculation entering into arrangements that, to the casual observer, may seem to be the result of individual and social disorganization. In my study in Guatemala, I found that 58 per cent of couples living together in the shanty town and 46 per cent in the legally settled neighbourhood were not married by either church or state. Guatemala is a Catholic country and many of these couples living in consensual unions were active church members. These unions were, on average, very stable and, when I questioned families about marriage, I was often told quite explicitly that it was not worth being legally married since, apart from the expense, it meant that it would be more difficult to separate. The women, in particular, emphasized the risk of attachment to a man who drank too much, brought in no money and consumed her earnings. While these women were satisfied with their present union, they stressed that in a place like Guatemala the future was always uncertain.

Likewise, the number of social relationships which an individual or family maintains with non-kin, both inside and outside their neighbourhood of residence, depends on factors such as the level of income of a family, the location of their neighbourhood, age and the type of work of family members. Other factors are recency of arrival in the city and number of prior contacts in the city. For example, in my Guatemala study I found that older people travelled less frequently outside the neighbourhood, relied on neighbours or were dependent on others visiting them; likewise, poverty inhibited external visits because of the expenses of travel but increased reliance on neighbours (Roberts, 1973a). Those living in more centrally located neighbourhoods found it easier to visit outside the neighbourhood than did those in peripheral locations; from peripheral locations, travel to the centre involved considerable time and expense. More recent migrants and those without prior contacts in the city had less opportunity to develop extended relationships.

Despite these qualifications, both neighbourhood-based and city-wide networks are maintained by low-income families and it is rare for families not to have people on whom they can rely for help and information. Similar conclusions have been reached by, among others, Perlman (1976) for Rio de Janeiro, Peattie (1968) for Ciudad Guayana in Venezuela, Lomnitz (1976, 1977) for Mexico City, Gonzalez de la Rocha (1994) for Guadalajara, Mexico, and Degregori and his colleagues (1986) for Lima. Among the Guatemalan sample, the large majority of informants were able to cite people who would help in illness, give small loans, advice or help with a job (Roberts, 1973a). In my observations of these families and in my trips with them around the city, I found that they had a relatively detailed knowledge of where kin, fellow villagers and friends were living.

The networks of low-income families provide a basis for inter-neighbourhood linkages whereby, for example, carnival or betterment committees in one low-income neighbourhood collaborate with those in quite distant parts of the city. There are examples of such linkages for Guatemala and Brazil (Roberts, 1973a; Leeds, 1974). Low-income families put much effort into maintaining and creating these social networks. Someone who happens to be in another part of the city on a job or errand, for example, will take the opportunity to call on an old friend and kinsman and exchange information about jobs, housing and the like (Roberts, 1973a).

Kin living in different parts of the city will visit each other on holidays or meet in some public park or at a sporting event. Commentators on urban life in Latin American have frequently observed the vitality of social relationships and the extent to which kinsmen, friends, or fellow villagers living in different parts of a city will maintain contact with each other (Kemper, 1974, 1977; Smith, 1984, 1989). The social relationships of urban low-income families often include friends and kin in the provinces and, also, in foreign countries. Cornelius (1976) and Massey and his collaborators (1987) report on the extensive network of relationships maintained by Mexican urban and rural families with friends and kin who have migrated to the United States (see also the description of transnational communities in Rouse, 1990, and Smith, R. 1994).

Indeed, the few studies of the behaviour of the middle and upper classes in Latin America indicate considerable particularism in their use of social relationships. The existing reports emphasize the significance of both kinship and friendship relationships for these classes, arguing that it is through the maintenance and manipulation of their social networks that the class advantages of upper- and middle-class families are maintained whether in Puerto Rico (Caplow, 1964), Brazil (Leeds, 1964), or Chile (Lomnitz, 1971). Lomnitz and Perez-Lizuar (1988) provide a detailed account of the social relationships of the Mexican elite Gomez family from 1880 to 1980, showing how kinship ties based on the continuing immigration of family members from Spain have served to consolidate a large business empire. The importance of government for business makes it important for business dynasties, such as that of the Gomez family, to forge social ties with government officials through friendship or marriage. In many countries of Latin

America, Middle Eastern immigrants, such as the Lebanese, have used kinship as a basis for developing the trust relationships needed for successful entrepreneurship. In the case of the Lebanese, as in that of peninsular Spanish immigrants, kin are the obvious business partners since political and economic uncertainties made it difficult to rely on local businessmen and politicians to fulfil agreements.

It is also the wealthy in cities of the underdeveloped world who may often develop 'provincial' attitudes to urban space. Most middle- and upper-income families confine their activities either to the centre of the city or to the relatively isolated residential suburbs in which many of them now live. Special recreational clubs provide additional enclaves for these families. The increasing reliance on the automobile reinforces this tendency for the middle and upper classes to avoid any use of public facilities or public urban space; thus, such classes rarely use public transportation, rarely walk streets outside the fashionable business areas and rarely shop in places used by low-income families.

Even those families without many social relationships may find ways of obtaining social support. Religion is one of the most important of these ways. I attributed the development of Pentecostal and other sects in predominantly Catholic Guatemala to the attempts of those without extensive social relationships to develop the basis for such relationships (Roberts, 1968b). In the two low-income neighbourhoods I studied, members of the sects were often those without kin in the city and included women separated from their husbands or whose husbands were alcoholic. The self-employed were frequently found in these sects. The relationships established in the sects were reinforced through frequent meetings and travel, on church business, throughout the city, and were often the basis of business partnerships or the exchange of economically useful information. I also found that the Catholic *hermandades* (voluntary religious groups) performed similar functions for other low-income residents. They provided the opportunity for single women with children, for example, to have a stable basis of interaction with others who could help them find work or obtain some benefits from social welfare agencies (Roberts, 1973a).

De la Peña and De la Torre (1990) compare the role played by parish associations, ecclesiastical base communities and Pentecostal sects in Guadalajara, Mexico, in developing community identity and cooperation. Despite the differences in the organization and ideology of these religious groups, they have a similar effect in helping the neighbours organize themselves to obtain urban services or to meet their individual needs, such as finding jobs. The success of religious associations is, in part, due to the fact that they are untainted by identification with traditional political manipulation, a point that Lehman (1990) also makes when he reviews Brazilian neighbourhood-based religious groups. Also, all the Guadalajara religious groups provided a stable basis for cementing friendships and opportunities for their members to express themselves and feel that their voices were being heard. Mariz (1992) reports similar

findings for Brazil when she compares the significance for their members of
Catholic base communities and Pentecostal churches. Despite the sharp differences in ideology, both types of religious community provide the poor with
social support and increase their self-esteem, making them more active in
resolving urban problems (see Burdick, 1993).

Fry's (1978) analysis of Pentecostalism and Umbanda (a spirit cult of
Afro-Brazilian origin) in urban Brazil and of Methodism in nineteenth-
century Manchester takes this kind of argument further. He stresses that
urban religious movements are not simply means of obtaining social
support or of integrating people into urban life. Such movements also
provide a framework for interpreting daily events in ways that are broadly
congruent with an individual's social and economic position and prospects.
Fry suggests that movements like Umbanda challenge the dominant ethos of
economic development while others, like Pentecostalism and Methodism,
support that dominant ethos.

Pentecostalism in urban Brazil has certain similarities with Methodism,
providing a stable congregation, hierarchically organized into federations,
and a unified cosmology in which clear-cut notions of good and evil lead to
a rigorous moral ethic emphasizing the values of hard work, thrift and absti-
nence. For many of the middle class, and for the skilled working class of
both Manchester and of urban Brazil, such values are congruent with the
possibilities of material improvement. These values served besides to provide a standard of behaviour by which to judge the less fortunate classes.

Fry contrasts this religious affiliation with that of Umbanda, which has a
large and growing following among low-income groups, often drawn from
the small-scale sector of the urban economy. Umbanda is organized around
cult centres which are controlled autocratically by cult leaders. It has an
eclectic and variable cosmology in which good and evil are necessary parts
of ritual efficacy and by which individuals develop particularistic relations
with their spirits. The devotees demand help against malevolent forces that
have been inflicted on them undeservedly, such as ill-health, unemployment,
frustrations in love or other basic problems of urban living. Umbanda, then,
is organized by clientage and specializes in short-term ritual solutions to the
difficulties and insecurities of life in the cities and rural areas.

Umbanda represents one, and in underdeveloped countries, often the predominant face of capitalist development: thus, alongside the large-scale sector of the economy, based on 'rational' principles of organization and
allocation of resources, there exists a cruder form of economic exploitation
based on a combination of authoritarianism and particularism. Fry shows
how the organization of Umbanda, such as the entrepreneurial nature of
individual cult centres, its rivalries and schisms, fits the Brazilian urban environment in which people seek individual solutions to their problems:

> Umbanda thrives ... as magic thrives in social relations and magic
> thrives in such relations where formal power is wielded autocratically

and apparently illogically over those who suffer its consequences and, who having no formalized channels of influencing the exercise of these powers . . . continue to 'make out' in urban Brazil by a cunning conjunction of the obtaining of professional qualifications and . . . by the manipulation of personal relationships.

Despite initial repression, the Sao Paulo state government has begun to sponsor Umbanda festivals. However, the newspapers and business journals that reflect the view of the Sao Paulo bourgeoisie, continue to denounce Umbanda as a source of perversion and corruption and criticize government sponsorship of the cult. As Fry points out, the government could not afford to ignore this mass movement which, in any event, was playing the same kind of game as the politicians. It was left to the bourgeoisie to imply that the movement was contrary to the moral and political behaviour needed by a modern capitalist state.

The many bases on which the urban poor can develop a sense of collective identity mean that they do not live in an anomic situation. Neighbours may have different sets of values, but they usually share in a popular urban culture based on the importance placed on close personal relationships as a means of survival, whether through solidarity or dependence. Such a culture can create a strong sense of common identity, despite the apparent rootlessness of urban careers, as De la Peña (1994) shows in his analysis of urban identity in low-income neighbourhoods of Guadalajara, Mexico. He points out, however, that this urban culture can both inhibit collective action and, under different circumstances, promote it.

The capacity of the poor to retain a strong sense of their own identity and worth, even in the most unfavourable circumstances, is brought out in Zaluar's (1994) studies of crime and poverty in Rio de Janeiro neighbourhoods. Many neighbourhoods are controlled by drug traffickers and their assistants and jobs with the drug cartels are among the few good economic opportunities available to youths in the neighbourhood. However, neighbours make clear distinctions between themselves as hard-working workers, even in times of unemployment, and the easy-living drug traffickers and other criminals. Neighbours get on with their daily lives, trusting to personal relationships, but fearing the impersonality of the street where they face the double danger of attacks from both criminals and police.

Living Conditions and Neighbourhood

To obtain a fuller understanding of the significance of social relationships for low-income groups, we need to look more closely at the living conditions generated by urban growth and especially at housing. The trends in urban spatial organization are a necessary component of the changes in social organization in the Latin American cities (see Hardoy, 1975, Gilbert and Ward, 1985, Gilbert, 1992b, and Portes et al., 1994, for overviews of these trends). Urban land use patterns in Latin America are rarely neatly ordered by such market factors as urban land rent gradients tied to the costs and benefits of central location (Yujnovsky, 1976). Spatial organization, and the changes therein, provide only a loose framework channelling social and economic interaction.

Part of the dynamic of urban settlement comes from the efforts of the poor to survive in an unfriendly economic environment. Coping with urban spatial organization, like other aspects of urban living that we have reviewed, requires considerable energy and the helping hand of kin and friends. The original establishment of informal settlements is often based on prior social relationships among the invaders: subsequent settlement also depends on having some relationship with the existing squatters. The characteristics of informal settlements, such as their illegality, their densities and the predominace of owner-occupation, make it unlikely that people settle in them simply as a result of an individual search for rented or purchasable accommodation. Also, the search for housing is complementary to the other attempts of low-income families to secure a living in the city: individuals and families often prefer to locate near friends or kin who can help them find work or assist in times of emergency. This is especially apparent, as we have seen, among recent migrants to Latin American cities. This argument applies to other low-income settlements also. In cities of the underdeveloped world there are few public, 'impersonal agencies' to which those in search of housing can go to obtain information or to be placed on a waiting list.

The search for shelter takes place in a housing market in which there is little purpose-built accommodation available for low-income groups. In any urban economy in which there is a considerable amount of casual and low-paid work, private housing provision is unlikely to be adequate for the needs of the population, mainly because there is no profit incentive for private builders to build low-income housing. Thus, in late nineteenth-century London where casual employment and sweatshops abounded, the working-class housing market was also highly restricted and complex (see the account of this market in Stedman Jones, 1971).

In Latin America, there is little or no house building for the poor by the private sector. Even in the few cities where such housing appears – such as Buenos Aires, Sao Paulo, and Monterrey in Mexico – this housing covers only a fraction of the low-income population. Budgetary constraints and the high cost of building new housing have also limited the supply of public housing for low-income populations. The exception to this is government-financed housing designed for occupations which are in well organized labour unions or which have a special relation to the government. Thus, in Mexico, the government subsidizes housing for workers in the major unions; housing colonies are constructed for workers belonging to the same enterprise or branch of industry (Araud et al., 1975). In Rio, there are high-rise housing blocks for bank clerks, sailors, industrial workers and public functionaries. Various studies have shown that state projects to provide affordable housing for the poor usually result in housing that only middle-income families can afford (see Shidlo, 1990, and Batley, 1983, for an account of low-income housing projects in Brazil and Schteingart, 1989, for data on public housing in Mexico).

In this situation, the poor find what housing they can – through the sub-division of the abandoned mansions of the rich as in some of the *vecindades* of Mexico City or through the intensive occupation of other central spaces. As the cities grew in the 1950s and 1960s, they increasingly sought out alternative forms of cheap shelter, such as self-construction, after invading land, or semi-legal purchases from property speculators. An example of this process is Ward's (1990) account of the spatial development of Mexico City. By the 1980s, even peripheral land was becoming densely settled resulting in some cities in the re-concentration of low-income groups in the centre of the city as the cost of peripheral housing rose, as Rolnik and Somekh (1990) describe in Sao Paulo.

Leeds (1971) provides an account of the diversity of low-income settlement types in Latin American cities that remains a useful guide to conditions in the 1990s. He stresses diversity and the social heterogeneity with which it is associated as part of his critique of the culture of poverty thesis. He distinguishes several very different types of low-income living environment. These include the central city tenements which are often formed from the subdivision of former elite residences. This type of housing is made up of a large number of rooms, many of which accommodate transients or single people. Other housing, in contrast, may have more of a communal organization, such as the *callejones* of Lima and *vecindades* of Mexico (the type described by Oscar Lewis) which are smaller units organized around an interior courtyard and sharing facilities. This type of low-income housing, though sometimes labelled 'slums of despair' because of the alleged transient nature of its population and their lack of social cohesion, can become the basis for lively community organization, as Eckstein (1990a, b) shows for Mexico City. They are likely, however, to be under pressure from the attempts of developers to gentrify the inner city as a place of residence for high-income groups (Benton, 1986). Economic crises and uneven urban development have, however, made gentrification a slow and halting process in Latin America cities.

Other types of housing are usually found on the periphery of the city, often at one or two hours' commuting distance from the centres of work. The most frequent type of government-sponsored housing for low-income groups is in such locations. Another peripheral type is the subdivision of land by government or private developers for privately owned houses. These houses are usually built by the first purchasers of the land in a variety of shapes and sizes. Much of this development is semi-legal in that, though the developers may have title to the land, they do install the infrastructure required by law. Thus, 'legal' peripheral developments are often indistinguishable from informal settlements, lacking adequate supplies of water, electricity and without a sewage disposal system.

Finally, there are the informal settlements, where land is occupied illegally and the squatters erect their own housing, though subsequently this housing may be sold or rented. Informal settlements are usually legalized after a period a time, particularly when neighbourhood organization coincides with a government's seeking popular support. Settlements appear at whatever point of the urban landscape there is empty space that, for one reason or another, is not in great demand. Usually these spaces are also on the periphery of the city and in undesirable locations such as swampy land, but they also exist close to the centre when topography discourages other uses, such as in the ravines of Guatemala City or on the steep hillsides of Rio de Janeiro. Informal settlements are of physically diverse types. In some of the oldest settlements of Rio de Janeiro, the process of housing improvement has reached a point where the settlements are hardly distinguishable from legal housing areas with a reasonably good standard of housing. Neighbours in informal settlements will often, over time, install basic urban services through both cooperative and individual enterprise (Turner, 1967; Mangin, 1967; Leeds, 1969; Perlman, 1976). In cooperative ventures, neighbours combine to install sewage and water supplies, petitioning government and international agencies for aid.

I provide a case study of such attempts in a Guatemala informal settlement in which, over a period of eight years, neighbours, through their own initiative, succeeded in building a church, a community centre, a small school, and in installing sewage disposal and piped water (Roberts, 1973a). They were helped by the municipal and national governments of Guatemala and also by the United States Agency for International Development. This assistance was granted after considerable and sophisticated lobbying from squatters. A more recent account is that of Degregori (1986) and his collaborators who describe the development from the 1950s to the 1980s of a neighbourhood in one of Lima's largest peripheral settlements, San Martín de Porres. They describe, using the testimonies of neighbours, the extensive initial community organization that successfully constructs the neighbourhood through self-help. Later, the cohesion of the neighbourhood declines as it becomes legally integrated with the city; but organizational activity remains intense as extra-local associations, such as clubs of fellow migrants, trade unions and religious groupings, become more important.

By these processes, informal settlements acquire a distinct character: the major variables that contribute to this character are the age of the settlement, the average income of the residents and the size of the settlement. Leeds (1969) has provided a detailed study of the importance of such variables in analysing the range of informal settlements in Rio de Janeiro. He points out that large informal settlements are likely to generate their own economic activity, providing clients for small storekeepers, craftsmen and so on; other smaller settlements are more likely to be dormitories, dependent on surrounding legal neighbourhoods for needed services.

Leeds is careful to emphasize that such factors in informal settlement organization do not acount for all the variation that is found. The major point about informal settlements is that they cater for diverse housing and settlement needs (Turner, 1967; Frankenhoff, 1967). Squatting is attractive to people whose familes are growing in size and who find themselves increasingly inconvenienced by the cramped quarters of the inner-city tenements. For such people, squatting may provide the only cheap alternative that is also near to their work. Other squatter types are people with unstable jobs who wish to avoid the difficulties of constantly having to pay rent or who cannot afford to put the money down for a house or a legal plot of land. In the Guatemala informal settlements, I found a disproportionate number of single women with children. These women worked outside the settlement in domestic or other low-paying services, often leaving the children to look after themselves in the shanty town. They valued the security that their shack gave them.

Even people with stable, relatively well-paying jobs may prefer to settle in informal settlements because such housing allows them to save income for alternative investments. Thus, in Guatemala small businessmen might locate temporarily in a informal settlement while building up capital. In Mexico, wealthy professionals have been known to appropriate land in illegally settled neighbourhoods, offsetting the poor facilities of the area by building large houses protected by high walls. In the studies of informal settlements in different parts of the world there has been a similar emphasis on the diversity of these settlements. Laquian (1971), for example, emphasizes the range of informal settlements in Asia and also argues strongly against the idea that these settlements are the refuges of the most poor or the most recent migrants. Instead, he surveys the range of economic activity found within informal settlements and stresses the many forms of social, political and economic participation found in such settlements. Consequently, low-income settlements are internally heterogeneous in terms of the occupations of residents, stages in their life cycles and length of residence in the city

Finding housing is a bewildering and complex operation which often constitutes the basic problem of city residents. Consider this report (Roberts, 1973a) by one of my Guatemalan informants who is now a relatively prosperous small businessman but continues to live in a informal settlement:

'I went searching in all of Zone 12 and there would be a sign saying this room is for rent. When I asked, "how much is the apartment, ma'am?", she says to me, "It's only seventy-five *quetzales* a month." I was astonished, and not to shame myself I said to the lady that I would come back. We continue looking for humbler little houses ... we asked how much is the rent of this room. "This is worth twenty-five *quetzales*", she says to me. I did not think that this one was the one for me either, since I was going to earn forty-five *quetzales* and to pay twenty-five *quetzales* did not suit me. Eventually we came to a little house, shack like the one we are living in now [in an informal settlement] and I asked the lady, "how much is the little room?" "Eight *quetzales*," she says, "do you have children?" "Yes", says I, "I have four." "Ah, we don't want anyone with children."'

Despite the importance of self-construction, renting continues to be the major means of access that the poor have to shelter, with its incidence probably increasing by the 1990s as even informal settlements became a 'normal' part of the city and the original owners rent out space as a means of supplementing their incomes (Edwards, 1982; Gilbert and Varley, 1990; Gilbert and Ward, 1985; Eckstein, 1989a; Gilbert, 1993). Though substantial progress has been made in the provision of basic urban services, such as water, electricity and sewage disposal, a substantial part of the urban population in most of the major Latin American cities still remains without adequate access to basic urban amenities (Edel and Hellman, 1989; Ward, 1990).

Land occupation is not ordered neatly since while most unoccupied space is on the urban periphery, its availability depends on political factors such as whether it is public or private, the capacity of popular organization to seize and defend it and the speculative intentions of its owners. The resultant pattern of urban spatial organization obeys what Kowarick (1977) calls the 'logic of disorder' (see Kowarick, 1979, for a detailed account of this logic as it affects Rio de Janeiro and Sao Paulo).

This outcome is not an inevitable result of population pressures, but has political dimensions related to the specific ways in which the urban populations of developing countries cope with their environment. Many of the economic opportunities of cities in developing countries, particularly in the informal sector of small-scale enterprises and self-employment, are based on the spatial heterogeneity of the city that enables, for example, the food vendor, street trader or domestic servant to live close to their clients. The highly effective organization of residents of a central Mexico City slum to defend themselves against relocation was based, in part, on the community networks and commitments of informal sector workers whose businesses depended on their central location (Eckstein, 1990b).

The absence of effective zoning regulation permits workshops to be established in residential areas, either in their own building or in part of a dwelling. This occurs in middle-class as well as in working-class neighbourhoods as entrepreneurs save the cost of renting space by using part of their family residence to conduct their business. Even large-scale manufacturing enterprises contribute to this 'logic of disorder'. Located on the outskirts of the city, distant from existing working-class areas, these industries stimulate the irregular settlement of nearby areas and a mix of housing types.

Schmink (1979) describes the social heterogeneity that results from a mix of government-subsidized housing, private building and illegal squatting in a study of a peripheral industrial neighbourhood of Belo Horizonte, Brazil. There is considerable mobility within the neighbourhood and between the neighbourhood and others parts of Belo Horizonte as changes in the household cycle or occupational mobility lead people to seek housing best suited to their needs.

Land speculators often encourage squatters to occupy land in the expectation that government will subsequently provide infrastructure. In the face of a speculative and poorly developed land market, bureaucratic politics, and the often desperate attempts of both the working and the middle classes to find suitable accommodation, overall urban planning fails (Batley, 1983). One important consequence is that the ecology of most Latin American cities is heterogeneous and the uses of urban space constantly contested by different social groups and economic interests, as Gilbert and Ward (1985) show for Colombian and Mexican cities, Valladares (1989) for Rio de Janeiro, Kowarick et al. (1991) and Kowarick and Campanario (1994) for Sao Paulo, and Rolnik (1989) for Brazilian cities in general. Residential neighbourhoods, with housing of different standards, coexist side by side and there is only a partial emergence of neighbourhoods clearly differentiated around social class lines.

To the extent that zoning is absent, the mix of uses in the same local space is likely to increase the exposure of the population to industrial pollution, waste and contamination. Food vending in this environment, whether done formally or informally, is likely to constitute a health hazard. Note, also, as Schteingart (1989) points out for Mexico City, that this mix of uses is likely to be most pronounced for low-income populations, whose housing is located in and around industrial areas, exposing these populations to the highest concentrations of pollution.

In these ways, the built environment is constructed by the interplay of state, land speculators, construction and real estate companies and low-income populations searching for cheap housing. Schteingart (1989) documents the process whereby Mexico City's largest slum, Ciudad Nezahuacoyotl, was put together by a combination of illegal subdivision by landowners, by illicit deals with the *ejiditarios* (small-scale farmers whose land is social property and intended for agricultural use) and, to a lesser extent, by invasion. The various administrations of Mexico City connived in these illegal processes. For them, as for other city administrations in developing countries, informal settlement is, as Mangin (1967) put it, both problem and solution at the same time. Government priorities are heavily orientated to economic infrastructure as a means of attracting and encouraging industry, and the provision of cheap housing has a much lower priority.

Schteingart (1989) shows that the provision of public housing also involves a heterogeneous and uncoordinated group of actors. In Mexico

City, public housing provision has mainly occurred indirectly through sub-sidized loans from state agencies. The cost of this housing in Mexico City is such that it has to be rented or sold only to those who earn more than twice the minimum salary, thus excluding the urban poor. The construction of this subsidized housing is undertaken by private consortia on government-owned land that is distributed unevenly throughout the city. Its marketing is also administered by private development companies.

The disorder of the city is matched by the disorder of the transportation systems. These have been put together by a combination of government and private initiatives, but with little coordination. The dispersion of low-income populations throughout the city and the fact that most workers have little choice over where they work, but must take what jobs they can find, means that the distance between home and work is often considerable. Urban resi-dents tend thus to face long journeys to work, often involving changes in bus, train and underground, on equipment that is often antiquated and breaks down frequently. Selby and his colleagues (1990) provide an evocative description of the journey that many residents of Ciudad Nezahuacoyotl must make to get to their places of work, a journey that can take up to two hours and involve several changes, queuing, crowding and long waits.

The logic of disorder means that government planning for the urban environment is, at best, ineffectual and, at worst, hypocritical. Though in the 1980s the government of Mexico city moved to decentralize administra-tion and advocated local participation, in reality the only effective partici-pation came from middle-class neighbourhoods, mainly intent on protecting their space against encroachment by low-income populations (Aguilar, 1988). Pezzoli (1991) looks at the development of the Ajusco area to the south of Mexico City. This area is a designated green belt, containing some of the city's last remaining forest cover. Over the years, however, it has been subject to the types of piecemeal occupation that were described earlier: the semi-legal sale of *ejidal* land to developers for commercial, industrial and residential property, invasion by squatters and appropriation by powerful private and public agencies. The planning authorities attempted to clear some of the irregular settlements, and Pezzoli (1991) reports the organiza-tional efforts of residents to counter this threat. In one of these low-income neighbourhoods, residents, with the help of outside assessors, developed their own counter-proposals for protecting the environment based on a novel system of waste disposal. Their case was made stronger by the city government's practice of using the green belt for ecologically harmful waste disposal practices. However, in the end, the proposals came to nothing due to the expense involved and to the difficulty of sustaining local organization. Since the government came to a compromise with the residents, their efforts finally ended with the situation almost where it had begun.

The flight of the middle and upper classes from the city centres has been tempered by poor communications and inadequate infrastructure in prospec-tive suburban areas. Also, the proximity of informal settlements to most middle-class suburban subdivisions diminishes their social exclusivity. Consequently, conflicting tendencies are apparent in urban spatial organization with varied consequences for social segregation. Portes (1989) points to a 'qualitative leap' in class polarization in Santiago when he contrasts its patterns of spatial polarization with those of Bogota and Montevideo. In Santiago, polarization is a result of the land market and urban administrative policies of the military government. In contrast, though patterns of residential segregation according to occupation and income had clearly emerged by the 1970s in Montevideo and Bogota, they were partially reversed in the 1980s as economic crisis led most classes to seek affordable shelter irrespective of location. In other cities, such as Rio de Janeiro and Sao Paulo, the occupation of space has become more socially and economically mixed as high-rise middle-class housing is built in poor areas. Poor squatters are expelled to make way for new middle-class subdivisions, while the poor seek whatever niche they can find within established residential neighbourhoods.

Paradoxically, the diverse patterns of urban social segregation are the result of the fact that the urban land market is an integrated one, to which even the supposedly 'marginal' informal settlements belong (Gilbert and Ward, 1985). It is this integration that underlies spatial heterogeneity. Over time, land and housing will be bought and sold in informal settlements, or housing rented, at prices that reflect, though imperfectly, factors such as distance from centres, space, facilities, as well as the social 'cachet' of an area. This land market is only likely to segregate spatially low and middle-income groups when absolute prices of segments of the residential land market are sharply differentiated (Gilbert and Ward, 1985; Ward et al., 1993). Piecemeal urban development creates, however, a mosaic of tenure and infrastructural conditions even within a relatively small urban area.

The heterogeneity of most urban areas and the relatively low incomes earned by most urban households mean that middle-income households are likely to make trade-offs in space or in convenience of location against the low status and poor services of an irregular settlement. The money saved can, in any event, be used to purchase services, such as private education for the children, that may be seen as more crucial to mobility aspirations. This phenomenon of the middle-income raiding of low-income neighbourhoods has been reported throughout Latin America.

The argument can be illustrated by a comparison over time of spatial segregation, incomes and land prices in three Mexican cities. Toluca, Queretaro and Puebla (Ward et al., 1993). In all three cities, the trend in land prices has been cyclical, with current prices similar to those 20 years previously. The factors that have most impact on urban land prices in the three cities are the macro-economic conditions, notably the expansion or contraction of the economy and wage trends. Land and housing affordability is a problem even for middle-income households as a result of the declining real incomes of the 1980s. And for the poor, the problem becomes severe.

Only in Queretaro, however, is there substantial spatial segregation between middle- and low-income classes. This is explained by the greater availability of blocks of low-priced and poorly serviced land in Queretaro due to the inability of *ejidatarios* to resist encroachment and to set their own terms of sale. The availability of low-priced land means that the differential with middle-income land prices is marked, entailing that while the poor have access to land, they have little possibility of mobility into middle-income subdivisions. Conversely, middle-income households are less likely in Queretaro than in the other two cities to trade off a larger plot for a lower status settlement since these settlements are more homogeneously poor than in Puebla and Toluca.

Local-level Politics

The final type of marginality to consider in this chapter is political marginality, or the extent to which low-income familes are ignorant of urban or national political issues and are unable to organize themselves to influence decision-making. Most studies have agreed that it is incorrect to view low-income urban populations in underdeveloped countries as politically passive and unaware of issues. Thus, Perlman (1976) documents the complex political organization of *favelas* in Rio de Janeiro and points out that the level of political awareness among *favelados* is higher than that found in rural areas of Brazil. Their level of direct participation in politics, through demonstrations or political meetings, is comparable with that of poor people in United States cities, as is their level of contact with local and national administrative agencies.

The poor are not politically marginal in the sense of not participating in or affecting urban politics in Latin American cities. When the political structure permits, the poor enter readily into the electoral game, organizing on behalf of middle-class candidates and extracting what benefits they can for themselves or their neighbourhoods. Even where authoritarian regimes severely restrict party politics or abolish them altogether, the poor are still active in bureaucratic politics, seeking to lobby the various branches of urban and national government and to develop patronage relationships with influential military and civilian leaders (see Dietz, 1980, for an account of politics among the poor under Peru's military regimes of the 1970s). The political opportunities created by organizing the urban poor leads Collier (1975) to observe that the creation of informal settlements in Lima was based to a large extent on the desire of politicians to obtain political support.

For the mass of the urban population, the neighbourhood remains as it was in the past the main basis on which their grievances and deprivations are articulated. As Cornelius points out, there are few other agencies for developing political organization and consciousness in Latin American cities. Other city-wide bases for organization do not include significant proportions of low-income families. Voluntary associations or movements based on ethnic, regional or other issues have, on the whole, been relatively weak. One major exception to this has been the importance of regional associations in Lima, Peru, in La Paz, Bolivia, and, to a lesser extent, in Quito, Ecuador, and Mexico City (Altamirano and Hirabayashi, 1995). In these cases, such associations have been vehicles of political organization at both local and national levels.

Political parties, even under populist regimes, have rarely attempted to organize low-income families on a permanent basis. There have, however, been important exceptions, such as the government of the *Unidad Popular* under Allende and, more recently, the rise of the Workers Party (*Partido do Trabalho*) in Brazil. The Workers Party owes its origins in 1982 to the union activities of its leader, Lula, based on the automobile plants in the industrial suburbs of Sao Paulo (Alves, 1992; Kowarick and Singer, 1994). The Workers Party worked closely with neighbourhood organizers and, by the 1990s, had acquired a national presence with its candidate, Lula, obtaining second place in the Presidential campaign of 1994 to Fernando Henrique Cardoso.

Furthermore, among low-income families, the neighbourhood is a highly salient basis for political organization. Most low-income neighbourhoods are deficient in many basic services such as water, electricity and transport services. In informal settlements, land tenure is also uncertain, requiring residents to organize themselves to press government to legalize their settlement or, at least, to take no action against it. There have been, as we will see in the next chapter, a large number of urban social movements in Latin American cities based on neighbourhood issues and often expanding to become city-wide movements.

But political mobilization over specifically urban demands is difficult to sustain, partly because it is relatively easy for government to buy off or placate these demands. Although no government could afford to accede to *all* demands for improved services from low-income families, it can provide some of the services demanded to some of the neighbourhoods demanding them. Unlike labour union demands for improved wages, government agreement to a demand for urban services does not entail an across-the-board settlement. In practice, Latin American urban authorities have tended to alternate repression and concession over demands for improved urban services and the legalization of informal settlements. When a neighbourhood obtains a needed service after a degree of struggle, its own militancy declines and it does not contribute to the struggles of those neighbourhoods still in need of urban services. Community leaders tend to be more politically aware and sophisticated than the majority of urban inhabitants, but their visibility makes them liable to be coopted by government. These processes have for long been the basis for the clientelism that has often been seen to characterize the political systems of Latin America and other under-developed areas. Although patron-client relationships exist under most political systems, they flourish under the conditions of an unevenly developed economy in which neighbourhoods are occupationally heterogeneous and access to resources is not determined by standard administrative procedures.

Conclusion

The poor in cities of Latin America are not socially or politically isolated. The activities in which they must engage to make a living mean that they develop complex patterns of social interaction that are not confined to neighbourhood. The urban poor also find ways of interpreting the uncertainties of their economic and social position which are compatible with an active attempt to cope with the day-to-day problems of urban living. Thus, the religious practices of the urban poor can be viewed in this way and also demonstrate the cultural heterogeneity that accompanies uneven economic development.

Social relationships are crucial to survival in these cities. Obtaining housing as well as jobs is a question of developing an effective social network. Indeed, the striking feature about the urban poor is their activism in the face of seemingly appalling conditions. The study of informal settlements shows what can be achieved by people who have few material resources. Although informal settlements are not social problems, neither are they a solution to resource scarcity in cities of the underdeveloped world. Indeed, informal settlements are often used by governments as a means of patronizing low-income populations at little cost. Expenditures on housing or social services, which need to be made if existing income inequalities are to be remedied, are thus avoided.

Exclusion on many fronts from the benefits of urban economic growth places the bulk of the population in a similar situation. Although they are skilful participants in local politics, the poor have been unable to sustain protests or political organization enough to constitute a serious threat to government. Their protests against the inadequacy of urban services are rendered ineffective because urban issues offer a fragile basis for political organization. Protests can be bought off cheaply and one neighbourhood set against another by government provision of partial services. The activism of the poor is, however, a factor in urban politics since their behaviour constitutes an unknown element which is alternatively feared and sought after, depending on the strength and political complexion of the government of the day.

The urban poor receive few benefits from the dominant form of economic organization and have little reason to accept as a norm any one standard of family life, social and political behaviour or moral worth. They also have few opportunities to participate in a sustained way in organizations, such as trade unions or associations of the self-employed that help influence their conditions of work, or in the government of their neighbourhoods or cities. This means that in Latin American cities there is a weak civil society in the sense of urban residents having the means to influence state actions and sharing some consensus over appropriate values and behaviour for citizens. In the absence of such consensus, governments and the dominant classes are deprived of one of the most valuable bases of potential support, that of legitimacy. The development of citizenship is the topic of the concluding chapter.

8

The Development of
Citizenship

Citizenship and the contests over its meaning have been key themes in Latin American development since the Independence movements of the nineteenth century. Citizenship is a concept that has a variety of meanings. It refers, in narrow terms, to formal membership of a nation and the individual rights and obligations, such as that of voting or military service, which that membership entails. However, I am using the term in its broader sense of public, and hence collective, participation in exercising and changing rights and obligations (see Van Gunsteren, 1978, and Jelin, n.d., for a discussion of this definition of citizenship). For example, an individual citizen has the right to vote, but the broader definition of citizenship focuses on the ways in which and the extent to which people exercise that right collectively to make changes in the way resources are allocated. Citizenship is, from this perspective, always negotiated since by their participation citizens can change their rights and obligations and, equally, governing elites may seek to limit or influence these changes as a means of consolidating their power.

Latin American states have been strongly nationalistic and determined to make their members forswear parochial loyalties, whether of community, region or ethnicity, in favour of the central authority. Moreover, the liberal constitutions that were adopted throughout the continent, often directly influenced by the example of the US constitution, created the basis for a civil society independent of the state. Constitutions throughout Latin America established the inviolability of private property and the equality of all citizens before the law, ending status privileges and restrictions such as those attached to aristocratic status, slavery or to community and church lands (Pérez and Gonzalez, 1927). The constitutions protected a variety of freedoms – from arbitrary arrest to travel inside and outside the country, of association and of speech – and established both the right and the duty of free public education. They enacted a division of powers between executive, legislature and judiciary. Most countries had male universal suffrage by the early twentieth century. Women's suffrage came later, and it was not until the 1950s that women had the vote throughout Latin America (Nohlen, 1993).

The rights attached to citizenship have, however, often been of little practical value to the inhabitants of the region. The extension of citizenship rights from the nineteenth century onwards has had the effect of classing the native Indian populations of Latin America as suspect members of the new nations since, in practice and often in law, citizenship has required literacy in Spanish or Portuguese and a forswearing of indigenous practices and loyalties. Violations of basic human rights, such as through arbitrary arrest, have been widespread up to the present. Voting and democratic politics have been interludes within a recurrent theme of authoritarian government. Governments have, however, been more ready to extend the social benefits of citizenship: education, health care and social security.

Citizenship in Latin America appears, then, to have primarily served the purposes of elites as they have struggled with each other over the making of the modern nation. Citizenship has been used by elites to rally support for projects that have varied with time and place. In the twentieth century, these elite projects have, as we have seen, often assigned the state a directing role in economic development, particularly as the Latin American economies shifted towards industrialization and tried to reduce dependence on the export of primary materials. These projects sought, however, to curtail popular participation in state-led development. They ranged from simple appeals to nationalism against an external or internal enemy, as in the many justifications of military rule, to the more complex projects of populist regimes seeking to incorporate sectors of the working class with the offer of welfare benefits or job security.

In these respects, the evolution of citizenship in Latin America has been closer to that in the authoritarian monarchies of Europe, particularly Germany, than to Marshall's (1992 [1950]) case of the United Kingdom where he noted the sequential development first of civil rights then political rights, and, finally, social rights. Flora and Alber (1981) note the conditions explaining the early development of social rights, such as social insurance, in the authoritarian monarchies: the need to co-opt a working class generated by industrialization and urbanization which, if independently organized, might threaten the legitimacy of the regime; the existence of strong state bureaucracies capable of administering welfare from above; and the domination of landed interests that could shift the costs of social expenditures to the urban classes by taxes on income and profit and by employers' insurance contributions. Mann (1987) notes that the European authoritarian monarchies used citizenship to consolidate their rule in the face of change and raises the counterfactual possibility that, had not military defeat intervened, the authoritarian monarchist strategy would have survived into advanced postindustrial society. In postindustrial society, opposition is weakened by the tertiarization of economies, resulting in heterogeneous urban groupings differentiated along manual/non-manual lines, by labour market dualism and by the variety of the service industries.

Contemporary Latin America presents a test case of this counterfactual possibility. It blends some of the socio-economic conditions characteristic of the European authoritarian monarchies of the late nineteenth century with features of postindustrial society. Agrarian structures in Latin America are diverse and include a substantial peasantry. The bourgeoisie is weakly consolidated, yet urban economies are postindustrial with highly developed service sectors, a substantial white-collar segment of employment, few concentrations of manufacturing workers and marked labour market dualism based on a sizeable 'informal' sector.

I shall argue, however, that the authoritarian strategy, though prevalent, is not a consistent limit on the evolution of citizenship in twentieth-century Latin America. Moreover, it is a strategy that is proving to be increasingly irrelevant to contemporary conditions in the region. Countering top-down strategies to limit citizenship are popular pressures that, while weakly organized, exercise a cumulative force for change against even the most consolidated authoritarian elite strategies. In practice, citizenship in Latin America has been defined by a combination of elite and popular pressures that varies historically and from country to country.

The cumulative force for change occurs, I argue, on several fronts. First is over the meaning of citizenship. Neither elites nor the general population have immutable concepts of what are the rights and duties of citizenship. Secondly, change occurs in the practice of citizenship, particularly the exercise of rights and duties. This exercise is not automatic, but depends on people wanting to exercise their rights, as is shown by the wide variation in the proportions of a population who exercise the right to vote in those countries where suffrage is universal. Participation, in turn, depends on people feeling that they have reason to participate. Thus, citizenship involves the dual process of defining and redefining rights and of broadening the basis of participation. New rights and duties are defined, such as those concerning the environment, but also the social basis for participation can change. People come to recognize new bases for their participation in society in terms of gender, age and ethnicity. Thus, though women have long had the formal right to vote in most countries, their participation in politics changes in intensity and nature as they become active over women's issues.

Social movements in Latin America are the most visible signs of the struggle to define and redefine citizenship. Their field of action differs from what it is in the advanced industrial countries because in Latin America the project of modernity is far from accomplished, particularly in terms of formal democracy and an adequate standard of living for the majority of the population. As Schuurman and Heer (1992) argue, social movements in Latin America, whether 'new' or 'old', are more likely to seek political participation within the state, not autonomy from it, with the aim of making government more responsive to citizens' needs. However, social movements are part of broader societal transformations and their individual successes or failures should not distract attention from the underlying current of change. The mass media, along with the internationalization of economics and politics, give people means of communication that change perceptions of rights and duties. Above all, perhaps, the exigencies of daily life in the face of poverty, an inadequate material infrastructure and an unresponsive state continue to engender vigorous, if piecemeal, grass roots organization to demand new and defend old rights, as Jelin (n.d.) shows in her review of urban social processes in Latin America from 1930 to 1990. These experiences slowly shape the predominant views of what are the legitimate rights and duties of citizens and the measure of whether states are seen as fulfilling legitimate expectations.

The liberal legacy in Latin America and the strains of a rapid urbanization and industrialization made the limited expansion of citizenship through education, health and social security a central element in the development projects of Latin American elites. In turn, increased aspirations and economic needs made non-elites question the limitations on citizenship, particularly in the political sphere. Also, the change in the global context within which nations develop, particularly trade and market integration on a world scale, has altered the meaning of citizenship both for elites and for non-elites. An important issue is the close involvement of international agencies and non-governmental organizations in the internal debates over citizenship in Latin America. Though elites are likely to contest the further expansion of citizen rights, they are handicapped, as we will see, by the logic of their own neo-liberal development projects that have come increasingly to emphasize individual, market-based rights and obligations and the withdrawal of the state.

The Context of Citizenship in the Post-Second World War Era

Simplifying a complex history, I argue that the more diversified the internal social and economic structure of a Latin American country, as measured by urbanization and economic growth, the more powerful are the 'new' class interests of the industrial bourgeoisie, the salaried middle classes and industrial workers. In this situation, class alliances became more complex as traditional classes defended their interests or sought accommodation and the civil, political and social attributes of citizenship became one of the major issues over which these conflicts and accommodations took place.

The justifications for using urbanization as a key variable in the development of citizenship are various. From an old, but still relevant, sociological perspective, urbanization shifts population from rural areas where local allegiances and community and family ties predominate. It relocates them to urban areas whose size, density and heterogeneity promote individuality, a sense of individual rights and impersonal forms of order, particularly the direct dependence of the individual on the state. Urban living is also likely to create a new and wide range of demands on the state to provide services that, in the rural situation, were either provided by family and community or were less necessary under rural subsistence conditions. Reality often departs from these hypothesized conditions. Rural wage workers can be subject to highly impersonal and exploitative forms of authority, as in the case of plantation workers. Also, urban residents can be just as enmeshed in dense networks of kin and community as the rural peasant population. Likewise, they can be controlled by urban political bosses akin to rural political *caciques* and can be self-employed or work in family businesses.

Economic growth influences the development of citizenship through the indirect effect of the expansion of the market economy. The growth in wage employment and in dependence on the market for survival have brought to the fore key elements in contemporary citizenship, such as labour rights and social security. Indeed, the development of social rights is likely to be a direct response to the inequities and insecurities of the market as a means of allocating resources. Urbanization and economic growth, however, create contradictory pressures to advance and to retract rights. An economically developed state has the resources to satisfy a wide range of citizen demands, but economic growth and urban residence create new expectations and new demands and these will be seen by elites as hindering further growth.

The distinction made in Chapter 3 between early, fast and slow developing countries provides a first approximation to understanding the evolution of citizenship in Latin America. The early developers have the most extensive set of citizenship rights and of supporting institutions, such as trade unions, political parties and civil associations. The middle classes early became an important force in politics, followed by substantial sectors of the urban working class (Cardoso and Faletto, 1979). It is also in these countries that the social rights of citizens became most extensive due to their long history of confronting urban employment and welfare problems. The extension of citizenship among fast developers will be later and less complete than among the early developers, but considerably more advanced than among the slow developers.

However, the evolution of citizenship in Latin America is not linear, nor did the extension of one set of rights, whether civil, political or social, necessarily entail the extension of others. The evolution was complicated by the uneven pattern of economic growth and especially by the particular relationship between urbanization and industrialization. Even in the early developing countries, population concentration in the cities did not result in patterns of urban residence and occupational stratification that incrementally fostered class consciousness and organization to extend and defend rights. Though the strength of citizen organization in Argentina and Chile explains, in part, the violence of the dictatorships that sought to eliminate that organization, it is still the case that civil and political rights in these countries were effectively suppressed in the 1970s and earlier. Also, despite the destruction of political opposition by the Chilean military after 1972, social rights with respect to health, education and family welfare continued under the dictatorship, though at lower levels. To explain these developments, we need to explore further the nature of the urban culture that arose during the rapid urbanization of Latin America.

The Myth of Marginality Revisited

In the 1950s and 1960s, commentators in various countries of Latin America emphasized the social and economic marginality of a major part of the region's urban population. They emphasized the recent rural origin of many urban inhabitants, their low levels of education, their lack of familiarity with urban culture and their failure to find stable wage work, particularly in large and medium size firms. The analysis of urban marginality was based on two persisting trends in the region. First, cities were growing at unprecedented rates with a notable contribution coming from direct migration from even the smallest rural places. United Nations (1980, Table 11) estimates of the contribution of migration and reclassification to urban growth show that migration contributed 51 per cent of urban growth in Argentina from 1947 to 1960, 50 per cent of urban growth in Brazil from 1950 to 1960, 42 per cent in Peru from 1961 to 1972, 37 per cent in Chile from 1952 to 1970, 37 per cent in Colombia from 1951 to 1964 and 32 per cent in Mexico from 1960 to 1970.

Secondly, though peasants became proletarians in the cities, the extent of proletarianization was not as great as it had been in the United Kingdom at its comparable period of urbanization. In this respect, Latin American cities are closer to those of the Italian south and with similar consequences, as we will see, in terms of the weakness of class-based politics (Mingione, 1992). In 1940, some 35 per cent of the economically active Latin American urban population was self-employed or unpaid family labour and we have noted that this proportion declined only slightly by 1990 (Oliveira and Roberts, 1994).

Several of the analysts of marginality worked in countries of early development, such as Argentina and Chile. Their preoccupation with urban marginality was that it entailed conditions that prevented people participating effectively in the political process. Working in Chile, Vekemans and Giusti (1969/1970) viewed illiterate, poverty-stricken families living in urban slums as perpetuating from generation to generation feelings of hopelessness. These populations were seen as potential supporters of populist or authoritarian politicians and, thus, a barrier to stable democratic development. The Argentinean, José Nun (1969), pointed to the political and economic fragmentation of the poor in city and countryside, viewing their social and economic marginality as posing little threat to the dominant system. In the cities, the poor are rarely proletarians, are beyond the reach of worker organizations and make a living in ways in which they exploit each other. In Nun's (1969) words, the marginal mass is 'afunctional' to capitalism because it does not even serve as an industrial reserve army. Their labour is not needed now, nor will it be in the future given the capital-intensive nature of contemporary capitalist development.

This focus on the marginality of the urban poor in Latin America was to be rejected by subsequent analysts, many of whom worked in Brazil (Faria, 1976; Kowarick, 1975; Cardoso, 1971; Oliveira, 1972; Perlman, 1976; Portes and Walton, 1981; Roberts, 1978a). Instead, these analysts emphasized that the apparent marginality of much of the urban population was little more than the conditions that industrial capitalism creates in its initial stages of expansion. These are exaggerated in terms of economic disruption and poverty in unevenly developed countries but resemble those, for instance, in British cities in the early nineteenth century. Moreover, the urban poor are integrated into the capitalist economy in a multitude of ways through, for example, the types of goods that they purchased or through subcontracting work from large firms. Also, the urban poor were shown, in various studies, to be resourceful economically and politically and fully attuned to the opportunities as well as the dangers of urban politics (Leeds, 1971; Roberts, 1973; Perlman, 1976).

The debate over marginality was influenced by the countries in which the analysts worked. Those in the southern cone countries were reacting to a situation in which the early promise of development and modernity had become stalled as urban economies faltered, no longer absorbing the increase in the urban labour force, and as democracy failed to consolidate. Those working in Brazil and other fast developing countries reacted to the scale of transformation in their countries in which a predominantly rural and traditional social and economic structure was being replaced by an urban, modern one without signs of serious breakdown.

In terms of citizenship, both positions identified important trends. In both city and countryside, urbanization had increasingly mobilized populations in the sense of weakening old patterns of livelihood and making people seek new ways of coping, both politically and economically (Di Tella, 1990). These new patterns of coping often were embedded in apparently traditional practices, such as the use of kinship or community of origin networks to survive in the cities. Now, as never before, networks had to be used to manage relationships with the state, not indirectly as through a rural *cacique*, but directly over the multitude of everyday ways in which state policies and practices affected urban inhabitants. In the cities, these populations were attuned to national politics, were directly affected by economic cycles and were aware of the impact of economic policies on their lives.

Mobilization did not mean, however, that the popular classes were able to organize themselves to exercise effective and consistent pressure on the state. The political pessimism of the early analysts of marginality was, in that sense, well founded. The overwhelming impression derived from reports of organization among the mass of the urban populations of Latin America up to the 1980s is of their fragmentation. They were fragmented economically by urban labour markets in which employment failed to concentrate in large firms. The heterogeneous sector of the services increasingly predominated over manufacturing as a source of employment. By 1980, manual employment in manufacturing industry had declined to approximately 16 per cent of Latin American urban employment (Oliveira and Roberts, 1994, Table 5.2). Even the informal economy contained a heterogeneous series of statuses and income levels that differentiated the interests and lifestyles of its members. The working classes were fragmented socially because to survive they needed to adopt individual household strategies, including networking throughout the city.

The issue is not one of lack of interest in collective solutions on the part of the popular classes, but of the structural conditions that foster individualism. The poor are rarely in a similar life situation to their neighbours but are differentiated by type of employment, by stage in the life cycle and, above all, by the importance of the individual household and its labour resources as a means of survival. The main coping device used by the poor in Latin America was to increase the number of household members in the labour market, either from within the nuclear family or by adding members to the household. Social and economic fragmentation encourages vertical, rather than horizontal, political relationships as individuals seek patronage and protection from above as a means of securing what little they have gained in housing or as a means of obtaining more benefits for themselves and their neighbourhood. Degregori and his collaborators (1986) describe this process as it affects politics among residents of San Martín de Porrés in Lima. Heterogeneity prevents, they claim, the formation of clear class identities in this poor sector of the city; instead, a more diffuse popular identity is formed.

The pressure to resolve everyday necessities did, however, generate cooperation as well as fragmentation. Jelin (1993a), referring to Campero's (1987) assessment of the neighbourhood movements in Santiago, points to the tension between an individualistic differentiation among the urban poor and the shared difficulties in subsisting in the city. The first undermines collective identity, while the second generated collaboration and created a basis for collective action. Also, rural-urban migration frequently grouped kin and fellow villagers in the same neighbourhood and united them in reciprocal favours (Lomnitz, 1977). Formal associations of migrants from the same village or region were organized in certain cities, most notably in Lima, but

also in Mexico City, some of them from areas of predominantly Indian culture (Altamirano, 1988; Doughty, 1970; Hirabayashi, 1993; Kemper,
1977).

Under these conditions, collective, neighbourhood-based strategies to
cope with economic difficulties had a limited development. In most countries, collective neighbourhood-based movements to seize land, subsequently defend it and provide it with infrastructure attained a degree of
success (Roberts, 1978a). These movements frequently developed a city-
wide organization, as has been reported for Chile (Castells, 1983), Peru
(Blondet, 1991), and Mexico (Bennett, 1992).

The success of movements often depended on the patronage they received
as a result of intra-elite conflicts, as in the case of the *Frente Popular Tierra
y Libertad*, a coalition of neighbourhood movements in Monterrey, Mexico
(Castells, 1983). When patronage was withdrawn, the movements weakened (Tamayo, 1994). Another reported alternative was the co-option of the
movement leadership by governing elites, leading eventually to a distancing
of the organization from the people it represented. Even where a movement's leadership was committed ideologically to increasing participation,
as in the case of the leadership of the Chilean squatter settlement, *Nueva
Havana*, a distancing occurred based, in part, on the priority that the leadership gave to the interests of their political party, the MIR, over the interests of the neighbourhood, and, in part, to the exigencies of surviving under
poverty that divided members of the neighbourhood from each other and
gave them different preoccupations than had their leadership (Castells,
1983).

Perhaps the major source of independent organization for the population
were trade unions. Industrialization from the 1940s onwards gave a certain
bargaining power to workers in key sectors of the economy. Workers in
transport were early organized, as were workers in sectors such as oil and
public utilities. Large-scale manufacturing industry, in branches such as textiles, steel, engineering and automobiles, were organized into trade unions
throughout the region. In most countries, trade unions exercised an important influence at the national level for most of the period, often interrupted,
however, by military government. Registered trade union membership had
reached relatively high levels by the 1980s, but varied in coverage between
countries. In the early developing countries, union coverage remained extensive, though interrupted by periods of military dictatorship. Union coverage
was lowest in the slow-developing countries. Thus, in the early 1980s,
Argentina, Chile, and Venezuela were estimated to have between 30 and 40
per cent of the economically active population affiliated with unions,
Colombia and Mexico between 20 per cent and 30 per cent, while El
Salvador and Guatemala had less than 10 per cent (International Labour
Office, 1985, Table 1.2; Latin American Bureau, 1980).

Trade unions represented only a limited form of citizenship participation
for two reasons. One is that they mainly covered workers in large firms, not

reaching the informal sector nor many workers in the services. The other was the hierarchical organization of many of the unions in Latin America. The incorporation of unions in the governing structures of Brazil and Mexico often made them unresponsive to the demands of their members and vehicles for the imposition of government policies. However, despite these caveats, labour relations were an important arena in which citizenship was contested and redefined. Despite the appearance of the tight control from above of labour relations in Latin America, there is also a long history of grass roots activism. Jelin (1975) pointed out that this activism, based on 'bread and butter' issues, is more common than is supposed and, at various times and places, has escalated into broader-based movements questioning labour relations and the lack of worker participation. In the 1970s, the importance of grass roots activism became clear in the case of the independent union movement in Mexico (Roxborough, 1984) and in the automobile workers' unions of Sao Paulo (Humphrey, 1982; Moises, 1982). In the Sao Paulo case, union activism was reinforced by community participation since the automobile plants employed a large part of the population of the townships in which they were located. In a comparative study of Sao Paulo and South African workers' movements, Seidman (1994) shows how neighbourhood and community concerns reinforced the solidarity of the workers in both situations.

The majority of the urban poor were not members of unions and rarely participated, in the 1950s and 1960s, in associations or organizations that gave them a basis of collective organization independent of the state. Political parties throughout Latin America made explicit appeals to the poor, but there were few parties with national importance whose policies explicitly catered for all the poor. Populist parties such as Peron's in Argentina and the APRA party in Peru were dominated by the middle classes and organized labour. When a party had a strong presence in low-income settlements, as in the case of the PRI in Mexico, this served as a means to organize patronage and secure top-down control by the state. Otherwise, political parties were often little more than temporary coalitions of elites or around populist figures that made expedient appeals to the poor and were regarded equally expediently by the poor. Thus, Perlman (1976) documents the support that *favela* inhabitants in Brazil gave to the military regime that overthrew the left-leaning civilian government of Goulart. That support, Perlman makes clear, was not due to political ignorance based on marginality but to a reaction to the economic anarchy of the previous regime and a calculation that military rule would improve the economy. The major exception to this absence of grass roots, community-based politics linked to political parties was Chile from the end of the 1950s to the military coup of 1972 (Valdes and Weinstein, 1993).

Under these conditions, both political and civil rights were in jeopardy in Latin America for much of the period from 1940 to 1980. Put plainly, with the partial and brutal exception of Chile, there was little organized capacity on the part of the masses to defend or exercise political and civil rights and little interest on the part of elites. The urban populations, increasingly mobilized and politically aware, had other priorities. In the next section, we turn to an analysis of these priorities and to the lopsided emphasis on social rights in citizenship practice.

The Predominance of Social Rights

There were several forces making political and civil rights less salient in Latin America during the period of import-substitution industrialization from the 1940s to the 1970s. Chief amongst them, I suggest, was the social mobility that accompanied the urbanization and economic development reviewed in Chapter 6.

These were the years when, as described in the last chapter, the Latin American cities were constructed largely by the efforts of their own inhabitants. The invasion of land and the self-construction of housing enabled even the urban poor to obtain a sense of improving their situation, as reported in their published testimonies (see, for example, those collected in Lima by Degregori et al., 1986). At first sight, it might seem that the rudimentary living conditions in which people existed in the proliferating shanty towns of Latin America would promote class-consciousness and a political involvement designed to remedy their situation. This was, in general, not to be the case. These were 'slums of hope', as Peter Lloyd (1979) put it, not slums of despair. The poor co-operated with their neighbours to defend land or to obtain services, but this co-operation was subordinate to each family's attempts to better its position.

The other factor that helped lessen the urgency that people felt for political and civil rights is the key role that the state played in these economic transformations. In the 1960s and 1970s, we have seen how the state became a major employer in Latin America, particularly in the cities and particularly for non-manual workers. This state dependence did not prevent the formation of worker organizations but it is clear that it reduced their independence. Like the professional associations, they were being formed in the shadow of the state and, often, under its guidance.

In this context, it is not surprising that the citizens' rights that were most securely developed during this first period were social rights. First, social rights were salient both to elites and non-elites. In the developmentalist ideologies of the period, the key to development was linked to the improvement of education and of health. International agencies as well as local governments sponsored programmes throughout Latin America aimed at raising both educational and health standards. Education and health were rights that the population could easily and visibly appreciate. Health clinics appeared in squatter settlements, as did schoolrooms, often built by the local inhabitants. The quality of the service provided was, of course, often low and inferior to that of the services used by the middle and upper classes. There was a substantial increase in private education in Latin America at all levels, including university. Education was, as we have seen, a key to occupational mobility.

By and large, countries throughout Latin America were successful in raising both health and educational standards. In Mexico, for example, rising enrolments in higher education in the 1950s and 1960s met the demand for highly trained professionals and managers in the economy (Lorey and Mostkoff, 1991). Also, the capacity to extend these social rights bore little relation to a country's relative economic performance. Consider the case of Peru. We noted in Chapter 3 that Peru's rapid urbanization was not matched by its economic growth. There was even less of a match between economic growth and the rise in educational standards. By 1980, Peru had one of the highest reported proportions in Latin America of its economically active population with some university education. In that year, Peru was reporting 64 per cent of the age group as enrolled in secondary education, a proportion double that reported by Brazil. Yet, not only was Peru's economic growth a slow and faltering one but the jobs available for those with high educational levels were not particularly good ones. In most cases, they were low-paid jobs working as state employees in capacities such as teachers, petty bureaucracy and so on. A broadly similar picture can be seen with respect to a health-related measure, that of life expectancy. The improvement in life expectancy was dramatic in Latin America, irrespective of the level of economic development of the country. To be sure, the earliest developing countries still had the highest life expectancies by the 1980s, but the gap between them and both the fast and slow developing countries had narrowed considerably. In Nicaragua, Honduras, Guatemala, El Salvador and Peru, life expectancy at birth had increased from between 40 and 45 years in 1950 to averages of between 60 and 65 years by 1985 (ECLAC, 1983, Table 9; 1993, Table 10).

The extension of social security to the economically active population and their dependents was another area in which social rights were advanced during the period of import-substitution industrialization (Mesa-Lago, 1978, 1991). The timing of this extension varied according to the sector of employment. In general, those occupational groups who received pensions and health protection earliest were effective pressure groups because of their political or economic importance. They also received the widest coverage (Mesa-Lago, 1978). The military were usually top of the list, followed by civil servants, other government workers, such as teachers and a labour aristocracy of workers in key sectors, such as the railroads, petroleum, electricity, mining and, in some countries, workers on modern plantations. Workers in large-scale manufacturing industry tended to receive coverage next, followed by those in commerce. Agriculture had the lowest coverage.

The countries of early development had the first and most complete extension of social security. Mesa-Lago (1991, Table 3) groups Latin American countries according to the degree of development of social security by 1980 into an upper, intermediate and lower group. The upper group had the earliest pensions legislation and the most population covered. In this upper group, between 62 and 96 per cent of the economically active were covered by a pensions programme compared to between 18 per cent and 50 per cent in the intermediate group, and between 2 per cent and 19 per cent in the lower group. These groupings correspond, with some exceptions, to the three groups of early, fast and slow developers. All three early-developing countries, Argentina, Uruguay and Chile are in the upper group and they spend the highest amount of their GDP on social security, including health. Brazil is also in the upper group, showing very high rates of coverage, though a relatively low GDP expenditure. The other fast growing countries, Mexico and Colombia, are in the intermediate group with respect to the development of social insurance. All four countries of slow development, Guatemala, El Salvador, Nicaragua and Honduras, are in the lower group. These differences persist when the extent of coverage is considered. Thus, in the upper group, health and pension benefits are extended to all categories of the economically active population including domestic servants and the self-employed, while in the lower group benefits tend only to cover workers in formal enterprises (Mesa-Lago, 1991, Tables 11–12).

Two circumstances limited the extension of social security in Latin America. First, social security was dependent on employment. In no single Latin American country were pensions and full health care given to all citizens as a right. Secondly, even in those countries in which all the economically active had the legal right to coverage, a substantial proportion of them were not covered in practice. Most of this lack of coverage occurred amongst the self-employed, workers in very small enterprises, and domestic servants: the informal sector both in urban and rural areas (Mesa-Lago, 1991). However, even among workers in very large-scale enterprises, there was a proportion who were not protected by social security (Roberts, 1993). Throughout Latin America, large-scale enterprises reduced their costs by employing, often illegally, temporary workers or domestic out-workers for whom they did not make social security payments.

Despite these gaps, social security had become a major fiscal obligation in Latin America by 1980. The fiscal burden was highest in those countries that had extended social security earliest. Argentina, Uruguay and Chile all had substantial accounting deficits in their social security systems. These were also the countries that had the highest proportion of their population aged 65 and older. Their low rates of population increase relative to other Latin American countries resulted in their having the highest ratios of the population aged 60 or more to the population aged 20 to 59 (McGreevey, 1990, Annex Table 50). These dependency ratios were 24.1 for Argentina in 1980, 29.5 for Uruguay, and 16.7 for Chile. In comparison, Brazil and

Mexico had dependency ratios of between 13 and 14; while, in contrast, Guatemala had a dependency ratio of 11.1.

The lower rates of social mobility in the early developing countries combined with the higher levels of organization of both middle and working classes helps explain why this group of countries experienced some of the most violent political confrontations in the 1970s. Argentina and Chile, for example, were to experience a radical repression of both civil and political rights. Though military dictatorships replaced civilian governments in many countries during this period, as happened in Brazil after 1964, repression was less severe, partly, it can be suggested, because the level of organized opposition was less than in the early developing countries. Also, the demands of the population for the extension of social welfare began to reach levels, particularly in the early developing countries, that threatened capital accumulation and the fiscal stability of the state. In this context, the notion of the 'bureaucratic-authoritarian' state was formulated as a stage in Latin American development (O'Donnell, 1975). Ruling elites, it was argued, viewed the suppression of civil and political rights as a necessary aid to economic development. Unfettered by demands from below, the state could sponsor rapid economic growth with the aid of an increasingly technocratic bureaucracy.

The Changing Definition of Citizenship

From approximately the mid-1970s, macro-level forces created a new context for the development of citizenship in Latin America by reducing the saliency of social rights, while increasing that of civil and political rights. Furthermore, micro-level forces linked to the macro changes altered some of the bases for participation, particularly amongst women and in relation to changes in household and community organization.

Macro-level forces

By the end of the 1980s, the urban systems of most of Latin America were mature. Natural increase accounted in the 1980s for most of the growth of cities and rural-urban migration for only a small proportion. Though the generalization needs to be tempered by differences in the stage of urbanization, it is likely that by 1990 the period of 'making the city' was over in much of Latin America. Land invasions and the self-construction of houses continued but, increasingly, the priorities of urban residents turned to consolidating and defending on an individual basis the gains that had been made. Eckstein (1990a) provides an account of this process in a peripheral squatter settlement of Mexico City which changes from a 'slum of hope' to one of 'despair' in the period from the 1950s to the 1980s. She reports how the increase in renting rather than home ownerhsip, the regularization of the situation of the shanty town as a normal subdivision of the city and the installation of urban services led to a decline in collective organization, noting a reliance on individual household strategies, rather than community ones, to resolve the increasing problems of poverty, underemployment and crime which the neighbourhood experienced in the 1980s.

As citizens gained the basic right to shelter but faced the more intractable problems of urban poverty so, too, their demands posed a more complex problem for the authorities. Patronage, the old stand-by of Latin American governments, is not enough to buy off opposition since it is no longer a case of buying off particularly well-organized neighbourhood groups but of satisfying a general urban need. Also, the chaos and pollution of the major cities pose problems for elites also. In the new economic ideologies of the 1980s, poor urban infrastructure was seen as an obstacle to modernization likely to deter foreign investment and hold countries up to ridicule in an international community committed, at least on paper, to environmental concerns.

A new emphasis becomes apparent, stronger in some countries than in others, on the technical efficiency of government in delivering services. Though budgets remain inadequate to meet all demands, one widely practised solution to this excess of demand-making is to base service delivery on impersonal criteria of need and community contribution (Ward, 1993). This service delivery might still have political ends, but it marks a new non-patronage stage in state community relations, as Eckstein (1990b) argues in her analysis of the Mexican government's implementation of a social pact in 1986 (*Convenio de concertación democrática*) to resolve the housing needs of the earthquake victims of Mexico City.

The maturing of the cities coincides with the ending of the dramatic changes in the occupational structures of Latin America. The major shift from agricultural to non-agricultural occupations is over for all but the slow developing Latin American countries and, within the cities, the shift to non-manual occupations, particularly higher non-manual occupations, has decelerated. The 1980s were, by and large, years of economic crisis in Latin America in which most of the region's economies had either negative rates of economic growth or rates lower than 1 per cent annually.

Open unemployment became an issue to an extent that it had not been previously. In the 1960s and 1970s, unemployment was often characterized as a condition most likely found among the better educated and wealthier sections of the population who could afford the 'luxury' of waiting until a suitable job appeared. In contrast, in the 1980s, data from Brazil and elsewhere suggest that open unemployment is concentrated among the poor and least skilled (Humphrey, 1994). Even the informal economy cannot easily absorb the unemployed of the formal economy because many of the opportunities within it, such as self-employment, require some capital and because its own dynamic is closely linked to that of the formal economy.

As the decline in social mobility and the increasing complexity of the city begin to shift the priorities of the population to civil and political issues, so too events move the state in a similar direction. Throughout Latin America, with some exceptions, the state reduced its directive role in the 1980s. The external debt and the need to attract foreign investment exercise a fairly uniform effect on the countries of Latin America. They make governments unusually sensitive to the requirements of the international lending agencies. These requirements include fiscal austerity to reduce government deficits and counter inflationary pressures. Governments are urged to privatize state industries, make administration more efficient, reduce subsidies for consumption and production and cut back state employment. They are also urged to reduce tariff protection for local industries and to ease restrictions on foreign ownership of local resources.

Chile was one of the first to follow this road to economic growth under the Pinochet military dictatorship from the mid-1970s onwards. Civilian regimes in other Latin American countries followed suit in the 1980s, Mexico, Argentina and Peru being some of the foremost examples. The change in state policies meant that nationalism became less important as a state ideology. Governments from Mexico to Argentina talked less in the 1980s about the need to protect national sovereignty and more about the need to open up their markets to the outside. In Mexico, even symbols of the state's revolutionary origins, such as the *ejido* (a form of social property in land belonging to village-based peasant farmers and their heirs), was permitted to be sold as a means of increasing private investment in agriculture. The corporate features of many Latin American states are undermined in this situation since neither entrepreneurs, unionized workers nor peasants can any longer count on protection from external competition. Indeed, to attract foreign investment, governments throughout the continent seek to weaken labour protection and to give more freedom to firms to determine work organization.

The Bismarckian model of economic development, with the state taking a directive role, becomes less appealing to the elites that control the Latin American states. The extension of social rights had, as we noted above, become burdensome for some states and promised soon to be burdensome for others. Instead of co-opting groups by extending them social protection, governments in various Latin American countries seek ways of shifting some of the burden to the different groupings of civil society, urban residents, employers and workers. Thus, urban neighbourhoods and rural communities are asked to contribute part of the costs if they are to receive help under the *Solidaridad* programme in Mexico. Employers are urged to pay the real cost of their workers' social security. Self-reliance and community caring are stressed as possible substitutes for state-provided welfare.

By throwing more of the responsibility for social and economic welfare onto the populace, states, both directly and indirectly, promote the independent organization of citizens. Neighbours, for example, are encouraged to organize and take fiscal responsibility for their neighbourhood affairs. Degregori et al. (1986) show the gradual growth of citizenship among residents of San Martín de Porrés in Lima. Significant in this process is the sponsorship of neighbourhood organization under the reform military government of Velasco in the early 1970s. However, the crucial stage occurs when economic crisis and the state's withdrawal of welfare lead residents to identify themselves with others in similar situations throughout the city. They talk in terms of defending their *rights* to a reasonable standard of living. Particularistic identities, such, for instance, as migrants from specific provincial regions, remain important but take second place in political organization to the concerns they share with other urban inhabitants.

Fiscal austerity also means that some of the state's key supporters, the multitude of government health, educational and administrative workers, feel that their interests are in jeopardy. A wide range of groups are stimulated to organize in order to cope with the new rules of the game. Entrepreneurs are amongst the first to do so. Where previously they could rely on tacit agreements with the state to protect their economic interests in the face of competition, they now find themselves facing fierce competition from manufactured imports. Also, though free trade brings export opportunities, these require organization on the part of entrepreneurs to generate the resources and information to compete in new markets. In Mexico, entrepreneurial organizations became more active in the 1980s, particularly to lobby government and influence politics (Tamayo, 1994). Also, small- and medium-scale entrepreneurs, under severe pressure from foreign imports, organized themselves independently of larger entrepreneurs and took a different political stance. In Brazil, Gunn (1994) describes a similar pattern occurring amongst regional entrepreneurs in the state of Ceará who enter politics through the Brazilian Social Democratic party. They wrest control from what they see as a corrupt and inefficient oligarchy with the explicit aim of modernizing and democratizing the state administration.

The significance of this entrepreneurial organization is that it emphasizes civil and political rights. Entrepreneurs' ability to influence government begins to depend more on their political weight than on their economic power. Governments, after all, can now rely on the free market to stimulate investment and productivity and are not committed to any one set of entrepreneurs. For entrepreneurs, political opening gives them their best chance to influence government. Thus, in Mexico, the conservative party, PAN, became reinvigorated in the 1980s as a party supporting entrepreneurial interests and opposed to the lack of civil and political rights. PAN's platforms in the late 1980s and early 1990s were basically in agreement with the PRI government's economic policies, but opposed the government's lack of democracy and respect for civil rights (Tamayo, 1994).

By the 1980s, citizens had access to sophisticated media, newspapers and especially radio and television, that provided information over which states had little control. The media are often controlled by governing elites, as in the case of *Televisa* in Mexico, but their influence on public opinion is broader than their political propaganda since it includes images of lifestyles and family practices, national and international, conveyed through the *telenovelas* (soap operas) that are avidly watched by an estimated half or more of the region's population. The presence of the national and international media covering the *Zapatista* uprising in Chiapas was an important factor giving it national and international visibility and a degree of protection from state repression. Indeed, the media has become the forum through which an independent public opinion is being formed. Opinion polls have become routine in Latin America in the 1980s, even for authoritarian governments. Published widely during the 1994 Mexican and Brazilian Presidential elections, they include analyses of the social bases of the different parties and their regional strength and reported respondents' evaluations of presidential performance.

The increasing presence of non-governmental organizations (NGOs) is also a key factor in broadening and protecting citizenship. In the 1970s and 1980s, NGOs expanded their presence in Latin America as they did in other regions of the developing world (Livernash, 1992). They became means of channelling humanitarian aid and of promoting community self-help in the face of the indifference or hostility of authoritarian governments towards citizens' rights. NGOs can bypass national governments because they have powerful international backers. Under the Pinochet regime, the Catholic and other churches in Chile sponsored a range of NGOs concerned with human rights issues and with collective organization to improve living conditions such as neighbourhood associations, soup kitchens and craft workshops (Valdes and Weinstein, 1993). International civil rights associations, with the backing of the United Nations, Western European and United States governments, begin to make their presence felt even under dictatorships. International relief organizations, such as OXFAM, and international charitable foundations sponsor a host of community development and community self-empowerment projects in Latin America. The relations between the international sponsors, the local NGOs and the communities they serve are often difficult because of differences in power and agenda, but NGOs have helped train and provide opportunities for leadership for large numbers of the Latin American poor, rural and urban, men and women (Schuurman and Heer, 1992). By the end of the 1980s there were an estimated 700 organizations in Chile linked to international donor funds, highly concentrated in Santiago (Schuurman and Heer, 1992).

The Formation of Identities

The increasing openness of markets and state reluctance to protect the victims of economic competition provide an impetus to ethnic identity in many parts of Latin America. The spread of commercial farming, ranching and improved road infrastructure brought, by the 1980s, even remote areas of Latin America into close economic dependence on national and international trends. Indian communities in the Chiapas area of Mexico became more economically differentiated and more sensitive to economic cycles, experimented with new cash crops, engaged in various forms of seasonal labour and produced handicrafts (Wasserstrom, 1983). Though differentiation produces class divides within communities, it does not override the sense of Indian identity. Instead that identity acquires new potential as a basis of ethnic alliance in the face of increasingly complex and pressing external relations. Similarly, Hirabayashi (1993) points out that ethnic alliances among mountain Zapotec in Oaxaca, Mexico, increase in order to defend their rights and autonomy against the intrusion of large businesses, Protestant missionary groups and the state.

As the Mexican state withdraws its protection of the *ejido*, ending the possibility of new grants of land, so, too, through the North American Free Trade Agreement it threatens the livelihood of the Indian farmer unable to compete with cheap imports of grain and fodder crops. Ethnicity becomes, in this situation, a basis of collective action through the *Zapatista* movement that shook Mexico in January 1994. This movement is both a 'new' and an 'old' social movement. It represents the long struggle of Indian farmers against *mestizo* and 'White' landowners. It is partly based on a sense of being abandoned by a corrupt and uncaring government and an age-old grievance of Indian rebellions in Latin America. But it also has new elements, such as an emphasis on democratic reform and a degree of regional autonomy as a solution to local injustice, rather than a reliance on the beneficence of central authority.

The cumulative consequences of economic transformation in Latin America have their effects on the formation of ethnic identity even when there is no substantial change in the relations of state and civil society. Thus, the Guatemalan state, dominated by its military, continues to repress independent organization. Its policies of combining repression and top-down community development result, however, in a more widespread sense of pan-Indian identity than existed previously (Smith, 1990). In Bolivia, the declining significance of the mining sector and the abolition of the traditional *hacienda* as a result of the 1953 agrarian reform appears to have made class a less significant basis of collective organization, and ethnicity a more significant one, though not in new areas of colonization where the peasantry have adopted *mestizo* culture (Albó and Barnadas, 1984). Territorially-based Indian political organizations have recently acquired national political significance, as in the case of the CIDOB (the Indigenous Confederation of the East of Bolivia) founded in 1982.

Making ethnic rights a national political issue owes much to increasing Aymara self-awareness as they migrated in large numbers to La Paz in the 1970s and 1980s. Despite the considerable pressures to adopt Spanish, Aymara ethnic consciousness is strengthened by their common life situations, such as residence in the higher sections of the city, poverty, participation in the informal economy and the availability of both radio and television in Aymara (Albó, 1990).

Age becomes a more important political identity as the demographic structures of societies mature. In the southern cone countries, pensioners become increasingly strident in defence of incomes that are severely eroded by inflation. Even in a country with a younger age structure, such as Mexico, pensioners demonstrate publicly against inadequate pensions. The young are particularly hard hit by economic change. Just as in the 1950s and 1960s, they are the first to benefit from the new occupational opportunities, so too in the 1980s, they are the first to be hit by the declining opportunities. Youth (15–24 years) unemployment became an important issue in the Latin America of the 1980s, with levels estimated at between 25 and 30 per cent (International Labour Office, 1989). Unemployment is likely, however, to have highly ambivalent and negative effects on the political participation of the young, as Zaluar (1994) indicates in her accounts of youths in Rio's poor neighbourhoods who are drawn into organized crime.

The frustration of the young occurs at all educational levels. Indeed, it may be highest in the highest levels of education. This frustration is a factor in the appeal of *Sendero Luminoso* to university students in the Peruvian highlands (Gianotten et al., 1985). University education was widespread by the 1980s in Latin America and not simply the privilege of a small economic and social elite. However, the number of professional or managerial jobs available to university graduates was probably in decline in the 1980s. Lorey and Mostkoff's (1992) data for Mexico show, for example, that the production of university trained people far exceeds the rate of job creation for professional and equivalent jobs. Students, always a politically active group in Latin America, thus have new reasons to organize politically. University budgets have not kept up with inflation nor with enrolment in the years of crisis. Moreover, government sponsorship of private higher education is seen by students in state universities to be a direct attack on public education. Throughout Latin America in the 1980s, students are to supply much of the organization for social movements in both urban and rural areas. Popular grievances there are aplenty, but students often supply the organizational catalyst. Faith in education as a means of mobility out of the working class appears to endure even in countries such as Peru where the prospects of mobility are low. Thus, Degregori et al.'s (1986) young informants still retained a certain optimism about their futures, despite their disillusionment with the existing political structure.

Perhaps the most significant social trend changing the nature of citizenship in Latin America is the altered status of women in the economy and in the family (see Alvarez's, 1990, analysis of the social, economic and political factors leading to the increasing participation of women in social movements in Brazil in the 1970s and 1980s). We have seen in Chapter 5 how changes in the occupational structure combined with economic crisis to increase women's economic participation throughout the region. This increase in women's economic participation has ambiguous results for their status. Various studies report that women feel that having their own source of income gives them more independence within the family (Benería and Roldan, 1987). Yet, working for pay also increases the burden on women since studies also report that there is little reduction in the time they spend on household chores. Women in effect work the *doble jornada* of paid and unpaid work. The economic crises of the 1970s and 1980s increase the burden on women and lead many to become active in community organization as a means of securing the welfare of their families (see the testimonies of Lima women in Degregori et al., 1986, and Caldeira, 1984, for an account of women's participation in local organizations).

Though most women in Latin America still pursue their traditional roles as wives and mothers, there are clearly some changes in the way women see their role in society. This is particularly true of countries, such as those of the southern cone, in which women's economic participation is higher and had increased earlier. There, too, non-traditional forms of the family, such as single parent households, are more common. Throughout Latin America, however, women appear to be taking a more independent role not only economically but in community affairs. Blondet (1991), for example, describes the importance of women to the neighbourhood movements in Peru from the early 1970s onwards. Her case study of women's organizations in Vila El Salvador, a huge low-income settlement in Lima, shows the growth of a women's movement, successfully organized around the collective provision of food through soup kitchens. The active leadership in this movement is disproportionately taken by women who are single parents and who are economically independent.

Valdes and Weinstein (1993) provide a comprehensive and detailed study of neighbourhood movements in Chile and of women's role in them (see also Lehman, 1990, for a comparison of neighbourhood movements in Brazil and Chile stressing the different roles of the church and state in the two countries). Women gained experience of organizing during the 1970s and 1980s and this experience, along with the economic pressures on them, made women and women's organizations increasingly important in community and national politics. Women's demands tend to be somewhat different to those of men, more orientated to ensuring that the welfare of the family is secured. Thus, women organize to reduce the cost of food, gain needed services, including education, and improve their living environment. While men tend to dominate the more directly political organizations, women dominate those concerned with subsistence issues (Valdes and Weinstein, 1993). Jelin (1993), discussing the movement of the *Madres de Plaza de Mayo* in Buenos Aires, makes the general point that Latin American women who are active in the struggle for civil rights are not necessarily feminist since they are responding to the specific issues that affect them and, consequently, differ from country to country in their form and rationale of action. In Argentina, the *Madres* used maternity, their traditional role within the family, as both a defence against repression and as a means of attacking the dictatorship.

The increased political participation of women broadens the basis of political participation. To traditional male issues, usually tied to the workplace, are added a range of issues to do with the management of daily life. These issues give salience to civil and political rights. Freedom to associate, not to be subject to arbitrary arrest and to be able to express dissatisfaction through voting against a government become more important rights when the state loses its capacity to co-opt through the extension of social rights. In the face of rising unemployment, arbitrary violence and rising prices, people may still value the social security attached to certain types of employment. But the extension of social rights is a less immediate prospect than the regaining of civil and political rights.

Changes in community organization, particularly in the cities, but also apparent in the villages, erode some of the safety valves that had made viable the authoritarian strategy of social rights. Though there is no conclusive evidence on this point, it is likely that there is a weakening of the networks of kin and fellow villagers that have provided much of the mutual aid that enabled people to cope with urban life. The increase of inter-urban mobility is likely to combine with intra-urban mobility to fragment support networks. Thus, when a son or daughter leaves a city to seek work elsewhere, it is unlikely that they will be helped in adjusting to the new place to the extent to which their parents were when they moved from village to city. The common interests in property and the communal traditions of reciprocity that give village-based networks their strength are barely present in the cities and are fast disappearing in the countryside.

Argentina, an early-developing country, demonstrates some of the problems of urban social isolation that can arise from high urban residential mobility. Thus Redondo (1990) reports the difficulties faced by the elderly in *La Boca*, a port neighborhood of Buenos Aires. When they first settled in the neighbourhood, it was a bustling centre of port activity. They still remember the cohesion of the mainly Italian origin community. With the years, their children had moved away and the neighbourhood became increasingly filled with new immigrants from the interior of Argentina, from Bolivia and from Paraguay. Redondo's elderly informants reported their feelings of isolation both from their neighbours and from their children and other relatives. They must make do on their own and feel that there is little community support.

Any reduction in the community's capacity to care will give rise to more demands on the state to provide substitute services. Remember that a similar process is likely to be occurring in the villages of Latin America as children leave for the cities or migrate internationally, and those who are left become increasingly dependent on state services. In the current period of fiscal austerity in Latin America, meeting increasing demands cannot readily be resolved by the state extending social rights. The issue thus becomes a political one around which various groups lobby to advance their interests. In this situation, political rights and civil rights become a more attractive focus for economic elites as well as the mass of the population. Democratic politics involves a competition for resources which remains biased in favour of the wealthy, one way of handling the problem of not having enough resources to meet demand.

Conclusion

The increase in demand-making at the bottom combines with a partial withdrawal of the state from providing rights from above. Social rights attached to employment, the Bismarckian model, becomes less feasible as a means of co-opting opposition in Latin America given the enormity of the fiscal burden. Social rights thus become in the 1980s and 1990s another basis of conflict between elites and the population. As market integration on a world scale makes the nationalist, authoritarian state less attractive to economic elites, so, too, they are taking a renewed interest in the original liberal project of Latin America. Associations and political parties become more acceptable ways of advancing their interests. Elite control of crucial institutions, such as the media, gives them some assurance that politics can be directed as they wish. The general population is also more participant, though not perhaps in terms of traditional movements, such as trade unions. There is the emergence of powerful public opinion. This is fed by the difficulties that most of the population face in making ends meet and is partly articulated by the media. More groups are ready to organize themselves to defend their interests: women, the young, the old, ethnic and neighbourhood groups. No single social movement covers these various interests or has successfully and consistently articulated any one of them nationally. But their constant appearance, disappearance and emergence in new forms increases citizen awareness and participation.

It is the cumulative effect of these different trends that underpins the current 'transition to democracy' in Latin America. The transition is unlikely to result in stable two-party politics. Interests are too volatile and unorganized for that. However, it is equally unlikely that the transition will be stalled and return to the authoritarian/corporatist practices that have been common in Latin America for much of the twentieth century. The economic basis for that model – the import-substitution phase of Latin America's development – has gone and, with it, its limited conception of citizenship. Instead, there are now multiple bases for citizen participation in Latin America and active contests over the nature of citizens' rights and duties.

Epilogue

In reviewing the changes in urban organization from the mid-1970s to the mid 1990s, my overall impression is that of a strong thread of continuity despite the changes in direction brought by the end of import-substitution industrialization. In several important ways, however, the 1980s and 1990s mark a break with the past. Gone are the protected markets, economic nationalisms and interventionist states that characterized Latin America from the 1940s to the 1970s. The relations of the cities with each other and with their hinterlands are different also. The flow of rural migrants into the sprawling metropolises of Latin America has diminished and even less than before are these cities of peasants. The primacy of urban systems is less as intermediate size cities begin to challenge the predominance of the major metropolis. Yet, the continuities are as important as the differences. The urban landscapes of Latin America are as disordered in the 1990s as they were in the 1970s and earlier. There have been improvements in the provision of basic urban services but their levels remain far below those of the cities of the developed world. Also, to the old contrasts between shanty towns and skyscrapers are added the newer ones of modern export industry arising amidst a landscape of urban poverty. Thus, many of the thousand modern factories of the *maquiladora* (in-bond) industry of Ciudad Juarez, Mexico, are as sumptuous in outward and internal appearance as the palaces of the merchant princes of bygone eras, but they pose a sharp contrast to the squatter settlements, with their shacks, lack of basic services and unpaved roads, that house many of their workers.

Urbanization and industrialization have brought no diminution in income inequality or poverty to Latin America. Indeed the connection between economic growth and urban poverty is, if anything, more evident in the 1990s than in the 1970s. Economic success stories, such as that of Chile, brought an increase in income inequality in the 1980s, as did Mexico's economic restructuring policies in the same period. The Mexican economic crisis of 1995, itself a direct result of hasty policies of export-led growth, is likely to decrease real wages and further add to already high levels of poverty.

The new, free market economic policies have excluded most of Latin America's population from the benefits of growth. This population is now predominantly urban and solutions to the problems of urban poverty are as distant now as they were when masses of rural migrants struggled to find whatever work and shelter they could in the city. Increasingly, the problems are those of working poverty, of the shortage of jobs that pay an adequate subsistence wage. Economic restructuring has increased income polarization, generating some highly-paid jobs and many lowly-paid ones, but not enough jobs to enable a worker, male or female, to maintain a family. At the same time, the policies associated with restructuring have reduced the subsidies that the state previously provided for urban low-income families.

The contrasts among the countries of Latin America are almost as sharp in the 1990s as they were in the 1970s. The legacy of their particular histories continues to shape their trajectories in the present. Thus, the current differences in democratic practices, such as the greater strength of political institutions in Chile as compared to the more personalized politics of Argentina or Brazil, reveal their particular histories of populist or liberal-democratic politics. These histories, as noted, reflect differences in their patterns of social and economic development that have shaped the strength of working- or middle-class organization.

On some measures of economic development, the differences among countries have narrowed somewhat. Thus, Brazil and Mexico are beginning to overtake the countries of the southern cone in per capita income, are now broadly similar in their levels of urbanization and have narrowed the differences on such social measures of development as educational attainment and life expectancy. Yet, the gaps in economic development between the countries of Central America, Peru and Bolivia and the most developed countries of Latin America remain large. Moreover, there is little sign of convergence in paths of economic development. Indeed, in many respects, import-substitution industrialization resulted in greater uniformities in Latin American societies than does export-orientated industrialization, promoting a similar concentration of population in large cities and the development of strong central states. The current focus on industrial exports and open markets potentially creates divergence amongst countries as each seeks a particular niche in the new international division of labour as exporters of manufactures, of primary materials, or of labour power.

These new patterns of insertion into the world economy are likely to have contradictory consequences for the political and economic unity of Latin America. InterAmerican trading blocks, which were tried and failed in the 1960s and 1970s, are now being revived with greater chances of success in a global economy which forces small economies to unite if they are to compete effectively. However, the dominant trend is not towards Latin

American economic integration, but towards hemispheric integration in which the United States and Canada form a trading block with the countries to the south, a process that has begun with Mexico but will soon include Chile. This trading bloc is not an alliance of equals and the preponderant economic power of the United States, its corporations and investors, is likely to determine economic policies to the south even more completely than in the past.

How, then, do the people of Latin America, or for that matter, people of other developing areas, participate politically in an increasingly globalized economy in which their life chances are shaped by external decisions? The political options have been considerably narrowed by the fall of Communism in the former Soviet Union and its satellites. The idea of alternative forms of economic management to that of capitalism has, for the time being, been discredited. The political events of the 1980s in Central and Eastern Europe gave credibility to the claims made by a range of Latin American politicians that there is no alternative to neo-liberal economic policies and to reducing the role of the state. Furthermore, the interdependence of the global economy makes it difficult to formulate distinctive national policies around which opposition politics can organize.

The re-emergence of democracy in Latin America in the 1980s and 1990s has thus occurred in unpropitious circumstances. Cheresky (1992) uses the example of the short-lived democratic effervescence in Argentina that followed the fall of the military government in 1983. He notes how this widespread collective political activity gave way to political apathy and a readiness on the part of the population to trust absolutely to the will of the President, even though he went back on electoral commitments. O'Donnel (1991) has termed this type of political participation 'delegative democracy'. He suggests that the absence of well-entrenched democratic political institutions means that liberal democracy in Latin America takes on some of the characteristics of the non-liberal democratic past, whether populist or authoritarian. Particularly important is the central role of the leader, now an elected President, who governs as he or she sees fit and with little consultation other than through plebiscite.

This is where the issues of citizenship discussed in the last chapter become significant. Cheresky's (1992) fear is that, in the absence of strong democratic institutions, citizens' rights in Argentina will become individualized with the decline of the social movements that had defended and enlarged them in the period of the transition to democracy. He sees society as becoming fragmented around local issues, resulting in a decline in the quality and intensity of public debate and, consequently, no limits on Presidential caprice. My position is somewhat different. The development of political institutions is, I agree, important if people are to participate effectively in decision making and in limiting arbitrary power. However, the emphasis on institutions neglects the social and economic changes that have taken place in Latin America in the last 40 years. These changes make the practice of citizenship very different today to what it was in the period of Populism or of Bureaucratic-Authoritarian regimes.

We have noted the many ways in which the basis of political participation has broadened as issues of age, gender and ethnicity have been added to those of work and living conditions. Also, my sense is that the networks of participation are denser now than in the past and less tied to family. The amount and quality of information available to the citizen through the media has increased dramatically and the failures of the powerful are rapidly communicated, as witnessed by the current crisis of confidence in Latin America's longest-standing example of delegative democracy, Mexico's presidential system. Since there is a basis for the effective exercise of citizenship, I do not see the problems besetting democracies in Latin America as fundamentally institutional ones. Moreover, changes in the political economy of the world system mean that the market forces that once undermined Latin American democracies will, in the 1990s, now act to strengthen the institutions that are central to liberal democracy: an impartial judiciary, part of whose function is to ensure a stable legal environment for national and international business, an independent central bank that will diminish political interference in the market and a separation of powers between President and Congress that allows not only for policy debate, but the opportunity for powerful economic interests to influence policy making.

To my mind, the focus of attention should be on the social policy challenges that are arising as Latin America, now a predominantly urban society, remains embedded in poverty, with severe social inequalities, and without the opportunities for social mobility that, in the past, provided some hope of a better future for its rural and urban population. These issues are not the dramatic choice between the reform of corrupt administration or archaic structures of land tenure and making revolution, but more basic ones of employment generation, the safeguarding of small- and medium-scale enterprise in the face of transnational competition, welfare safety nets and local control of services and administration. Around these issues, different political platforms can and will form.

Bibliography

Abu-Lughod, J. 1971: *Cairo: 1001 Years of the City Victorious*. Princeton, NJ: Princeton University Press.

Abu-Lughod, J. 1980: *Rabat: Urban Apartheid in Morocco*. Princeton, NJ: Princeton University Press.

Adams, R. 1959: *A community in the Andes: problems and progress in Muquiyauyo*. Seattle and London: University of Washington Press.

Adams, R. 1991: Strategies of ethnic survival in Central America. In Urban, G. and Sherzer, J. (eds.), *Nation-States and Indians in Latin America*. Austin, TX: University of Texas Press, 181–206.

Adams, R. and Heath, D. (eds.) 1965: *Contemporary cultures and societies of Latin America*. New York: Random House.

Aguilar Martinez, G. 1988: Community participation in Mexico City: a case study. *Bulletin of Latin American Research* 7, 1: 22–46.

Alavi, H. 1972: The state in post-colonial societies: Pakistan and Bangladesh. *New Left Review* 74 (July–August).

Albo, X. 1995. La Paz/Cukiyawu: The Two Faces of a City. In Altamirano, T. and Hirabayashi, L. (eds.), *Migrants, Regional Identities, and Latin America Cities*. Society for Latin American Anthropology.

Albo, X. and Barnadas, J. 1984: *La Cara India y Campesina de Nuestra Historia*. La Paz: Unitas/Cipca.

Altamirano, T. 1984: *Presencia Andina en Lima Metropolitana*, Lima: Fondo Editorial, Pontificia Universidad Católica.

Altamirano, T. 1988: *Cultura Andina y Pobreza Urbana: Aymaras en Lima Metropolitana*. Lima: Pontificia Universidad Catolica del Peru.

Altamirano, T. and Hirabayashi, L. (eds.), 1995: *Migrants, Regional Identities, and Latin America Cities*. Society for Latin American Anthropology.

Alvarez, S. 1990: *Engendering Democracy in Brazil: Women's Movements in Transition Politics*. Princeton, NJ: Princeton University Press.

Alves, M. H.M. 1992: In Corradi, J.E. Fagen, P.W. and Garreton, M.A.

(eds.), *Fear at the edge: state terror and resistance in Latin America,* Berkeley: University of California Press 184–211.

Amin, S. 1973: *Neo-colonialism in West Africa.* Harmondsworth: Penguin.

Amin, S. 1974: *Accumulation on a world scale.* New York and London: Monthly Review Press.

Anderson, M. 1971: *Family structure in nineteenth–century Lancashire.* Cambridge: Cambridge University Press.

Araud, Ch., Boon, G.K.G., Rocha, A., Ricon, S., Strassman, W.P. and Urquidi, V.L. 1975: *La contruccion de vivienda y el empleo en Mexico.* Mexico City: Colegio de Mexico.

Arias, E.P. 1971: *Las empresas multinacionales y sus efectos sobre la economia.* Buenos Aires.

Arias, P., 1988: La pequeña empresa en el occidente rural. *Estudios Sociologicos.* 6, 17, 405–436.

Arizpe, L. 1978: *Migración, Etnicismo y Cambio Económico: Un Estudio sobre Migrantes Campesinas a la Ciudad de México.* Mexico City: El Colegio de México.

Arizpe, L. 1982. Relay migration and the survival of the peasant household, in Helen Safa (ed.), *Towards a Political Economy of Urbanization in Third World Countries,* Delhi: Oxford University Press, 19–46.

Arizpe, L. 1990: Fin de epoca: Nuevas opciones, in *México en el Umbral del Milenio,* Mexico, DF: Centro de Estudios Sociológicos, El Colegio de México, 459–74.

Armstrong, W. and McGee, T.G. 1985: *Theatres of Accumulation.* London & New York: Methuen.

Arroyo, A.J. 1989: *El abandono rural: Un modelo explicativo de la emigración de trabajadores en el occidente de México.* Guadalajara: University of Guadalajara.

Assadourian, C.S. 1973: Sobre un elemento de la economia colonial: produccion y circulacion de mercandias al interior de un conjunto regional. *Revista Lationamericana de Estudios Urbanos Regionales* (EURE) 3 (December), 135–81.

Assadourian, C.S. 1977: *La produccion de la mercancea dinero en la formacion del mercado interno colonial.* Documentos CEED, Colegio de Mexico.

Assadourian, C.S. 1982: *El Sistema de la Economía Colonial: Mercado Interno, Regiones, y Espacio Económico.* Lima: Instituto de Estudios Peruanos.

Assadourian, C.S. 1992: The Colonial Economy: the transfer of the European system of production to New Spain and Peru. *Journal of Latin American Studies* 24, Supplement, 55–68.

Baer, W. 1962: The economics of Prebisch and the ECLA. *Economic Development and Cultural Change* 10, 169–182.

Baer, W., Trebat, T. and Newfarmer, R. 1976: State capitalism and economic development: the case of Brazil. Paper presented at conference on

Implementation in Latin America's Public Sector: Translating Policy into Reality. University of Texas at Austin, April/May.

Balan, J. 1969: Migrant-native socio-economic differences in Latin American cities: a structural analysis. *Latin American Research Review* 4 (1), 3–29.

Balan, J. 1973: Migracoes a desenvolvimento capitalista no Brazil: ensaio de interpretacao historico–comparativa. *Estudos* CEBRAP 5 (July– September), 5–80. Sao Paulo.

Balan, J. 1976: Regional urbanization under primary sector expansion in neo-colonial societies. In Portes and Browning, 1976.

Balan, J. 1981: Estructuras agrarias y migración en una perspectiva histórica: estudios de casos latinoamericanos, *Revista Mexicana de Sociologia*, 43, No 1, 141–192.

Balan, J. 1985. *International Migration in the Southern Cone,* Buenos Aires: Centro de Estudios de Estado y Sociedad.

Balan, J., Browning H.B. and Jelin, E. 1973: *Men in a Developing Society,* Austin, TX, and London: ILAS/University of Texas Press.

Banck, G.A. 1974: The war on reputations: the dynamics of the local political system in the state of Espirito Santo, Brazil. *Boletin de Estudios Lationoamericanos y del Caribe* 17, 69–77.

Banton, M. (ed.), 1966: *The social anthropology of complex societies.* London: Tavistock.

Barkin, D. 1975: Regional development and interregional equity: a Mexican case study. In Cornelius and Trueblood, 1975, 277–99.

Barratt Brown, M. 1974: *The economics of imperialism.* Harmondsworth: Penguin.

Bartra, R. 1974: *Estructura agraria y clases sociales en Mexico.* Mexico, DF Serie Popular, editorial Era.

Batley, R. 1983: *Power through Bureaucracy: Urban Political Analysis in Brazil.* New York: St Martin's Press.

Benería, L. 1991: Structural adjustment, the labour market, and the household: The case of Mexico. pp. 161–183 in Guy Standing and Victor Tokman (eds.) *Toward Social Adjustment: Labor Market Issues in Structural Adjustment.* Geneva: International Labor Office.

Benería, L. and Roldan, M. 1987: *The Crossroads of Class and Gender.* Chicago: University of Chicago Press.

Bennett, V. 1992: The evolution of urban popular movements in Mexico between 1968 and 1988. In Arturo Escobar and Sonia Alvarez, *The Making of Social Movements in Latin America,* Boulder, CO: Westview Press, pp. 240–259.

Benton, L. 1986: Reshaping the urban core: the politics of housing in authoritarian Uruguay. *Latin American Research Review,* 21(2): 33–52.

Berlinck, M.T. and Cohen, Y. 1970: Desenvolvimento economico, crescimento economico e modernizacao na cidade de Sao Paulo. *Revista de Administracao* de Empresas 10, 1 (Jan/Mar), 45–64. Rio de Janeiro.

Berry, B.J.L. 1967: *Geography of market centers and retail distribution.* Englewood Cliffs, NJ: Prentice–Hall.

Blanco S.M. 1990: *Empleo en México: Evolución y Tendencias,* PhD Dissertation in Social Sciences, El Colegio de México, México, DF.

Blondet, C. 1991: *Las Mujeres y El Poder.* Lima: Instituto de Estudios Peruanos.

Boeger, A. 1994: Tradition and Revolution: the Struggle for Community Control at Bolivia's Chojlla Mine, 1944–1964. PhD Dissertation, University of Texas at Austin.

Bornschier, V. and Chase-Dunn, C. 1985: *Transnational Corporations and Underdevelopment.* New York: Praeger.

Bourricaud, F. 1970: *Power and society in contemporary Peru.* New York: Praeger.

Boyer, R.E. 1972: Las ciudades Mexicanas: perspectivas de estudio en el siglo XIX. *Historia Mexicana* 22, 2 (October/December), 142–59.

Brading, D.A. 1971: *Miners and merchants in Bourbon Mexico, 1763–1810.* Cambridge: Cambridge University Press.

Brading, D.A. 1976: The city in Bourbon America: elite and masses. Paper presented at 42nd International Congress of Americanists, Paris.

Bradshaw, Y.W. 1987: Urbanization and underdevelopment: a global study of modernization, urban bias, and economic dependency. *American Sociological Review* 52: 224–39.

Bromley, R. 1978: The urban informal sector: why is it worth discussing? *World Development,* 6: 1033–9.

Bromley, R. (ed.). 1979: *The Urban Informal Sector: Critical Perspectives on Employment and Housing Policies.* Oxford: Pergamon Press.

Bromley, R. (ed.). 1985: *Planning for Small Enterprises in Third World Cities.* Oxford: Pergamon Press.

Bromley, R. 1994: Informality, de Soto style: from concept to policy. In Rakowski, C.A. (ed.), *Contrapunto: The Informal Sector Debate in Latin America.* Albany, NY: State University of New York.

Bromley, R. and Gerry, C. (eds.). 1979: *Casual Work and Poverty in Third World Cities.* London: John Wiley.

Brookfield, H. 1975: *Interdependent development.* London: Methuen.

Brown, R. (ed.), 1973: *Knowledge, education and cultural change.* London: Tavistock.

Browning, H.L. 1958: Recent trends in Latin American urbanization. *Annals of the American Academy of Political and Social Science* 316 (March), 111–20.

Browning, H.L. 1968: Urbanization and internal migration in Latin America. Paper delivered at the Undergraduate Conference on the Population of Latin America, Cornell University, January 24–7.

Browning, H.L. 1971: Migrant selectivity and the growth of large cities in developing societies. In National Academy of Sciences, 1971, 273–314.

Browning, H.L. 1972a: Primacy variation in Latin America during the twentieth century. *Acta y Memorias del XXXIX Congreso Internacional de Americanistas, Lima 1970* 2, 55–77.

Browning, H.L. 1972b: Some problematics of the tertiarization process in Latin America. Paper presented to the 40th Congress of Americanists, Rome, September.

Browning, H.L. and Feindt W. 1971: The social and economic context of migration to Monterrey, Mexico. In Rabinovitz and Trueblood, 1971, 45–70.

Browning, H.L. and Singelmann, J. 1975: The development of the service sector in Latin America: an international historical perspective. Mimeo, Population Research Center, Austin.

Bruschini, C. 1989: *Tendencias da Forca de Trabalho Feminina Brasileira nos Anos Setenta a Ochenta.* Comparacoes Regionais, 1/89. Sao Paulo, Brazil, Departamento de Pesquisas Educacionais-Fundacao Carlos Chagas.

Bulmer–Thomas, V. 1994: *The Economic History of Latin America since Independence.* Cambridge: Cambridge University Press.

Burdick, J. 1993: *Looking for God in Brazil.* Berkeley: University of California Press.

Bureau of the Census, 1975: *Historical statistics of the United States.* Washington, DC: Government Printing Office.

Butterworth, D. 1974: Grass roots political organization in Cuba: the case of the committees for the defense of the revolution. In Cornelius and Trueblood, 1974, 183–206.

Caldeira, T. 1984: *A Política dos Outros: O Cotidiano dos Moradores de Periferia e o que Pensam do Poder e dos Poderosos.* Sao Paulo: Brasilense.

Caldwell, J.C. 1969: *African rural–urban migration: the Movement to Ghana's towns.* Canberra: Australian National University Press.

Caldwell, J.C. 1976: Towards a restatement of demographic transition theory. *Population and Development Review* 2, 3–4 (September/December).

Campero, G. 1987: *Entre la Sobrevivencia y la Acción Política. Las Organizaciones de Pobladores en Santiago.* Santiago: ILET.

Canak, W.L. 1989: Debt, austerity, and Latin America in the New International Division of Labor. In W.L. Canak (ed.), *Lost Promises: Debt, Austerity and Development in Latin America.* Boulder: Westview Press, 9–30.

Caplow, T. 1964: *The urban ambiance: a study of San Juan, Puerto Rico.* Ottowa, New Jersey: Bedminster Press.

Cardoso, F.H. (ed.), 1968: *Cuestiones de sociologia del dearrollo de America Latina.* Santiago de Chile: Editorial Universitaria.

Cardoso, F.H. 1971: Comentários sobre os conceitos de superpopulação relativa e marginalidade, *Estudios CEBRAP* 1: 99–130.

Cardoso, F.H. 1973: Dependency revisited. Hachett Memorial Lecture, Institute of Latin American Studies, University of Texas at Austin.

Cardoso, F.H. 1975a: The city and politics. In Hardoy, 195, 157–90.

Cardoso, F.H. 1975b: *Autoritarismo a democratizacao*. Pas e Terra: Rio de Janeiro.

Cardoso, F.H. 1977: The consumption of dependency theory in the United States. *Latin American Research Review* 12, 3, 7–24.

Cardoso, F.H. and Reyna, J.L. 1968: Industrializacion, estructura ocupacional y estratificacion social en America Latina. In Cardoso, 1968.

Cardoso, F.H. and Faletto, E. 1969: *Dependencia y desarrollo en America Latina*. Mexico: Siglo Veintiuno.

Cardoso, F.H. and Faletto, E. 1979: *Dependency and Development in Latin America*. Berkeley: University of California Press.

Carillo, J. (ed.). 1990: *La Nueva Era de la Industria Automotriz en México* Tijuana, B.C: El Colegio de la Frontera Norte.

Carillo, J. (ed.). 1993: *Condiciones de Empleo y Capitación en las Maquiladoras de Exportación en México*. Mexico: El Colegio de la Frontera Norte/Secretaría del Trabajo y Previsión Social.

Castells, M. 1972: La urbanizacion dependiente en America Latina. In M. Castells (ed.), *Imperialismo v urbanizacion en America Latina*. Barcelona: Editorial Agusto Gilli.

Castells, M. 1976: *La cuestion urbana*. Mexico, Madrid and Buenos Aires: Siglo Veintiuno.

Castells, M. 1977: *The urban question: a marxist approach*. London: Edward Arnold.

Castells, M. 1983: *The City and the Grassroots*. London: Edward Arnold.

Castells, M. and Portes, A. 1989: World underneath: the origins, dynamics, and effects of the informal economy. In Portes A., Castells M., and Benton L.A. (eds.), *The Informal Economy: Studies in Advanced and Less Developed Countries*, pp. 11–37. Baltimore: The Johns Hopkins University Press.

Castles, S. and Kosack, G. 1973: *Immigrant workers and class structures in Western Europe*. London: Oxford University Press for Institute of Race Relations.

Censo General de la Población de Bolivia, 1900. 1904. Tomo II. La Paz: Oficina Nacional de Inmigración, Estadística y Propaganda Geográfica.

Censo Nacional de Población y Ocupacion (Peru) 1940: Vol. 1. Lima: Ministerio de Hacienda y Comercio, Direccion Nacional de Estadistica, 1944.

Censos, N. (Peru) VII de Poblacion, II de Vivienda, 1972: Vol.1. Lima: Oficina Nacional de Estadistica y Censos, 1974.

Censo Nacional de Población y Vivienda (Argentina), 1980. Buenos Aires: Instituto Nacional de Estadistica y Censos, 1982.

Censo, N. (Peru) VIII de Poblacion III de Vivienda, 1981: Vol.1. Lima: Oficina Nacional de Estadistica y Censos, 1983.

Census of England and Wales, 1901: Census Office, 1902–3. London: HMSO.

Central Intelligence Agency (CIA), 1990: *The World Factbook 1990.*Washington DC: US Department of Commerce.

CEPAL, 1986. *América Latina: las mujeres y los cambios socio-ocupacionales 1960–1980,* Documento LC/R.504, División de Desarrollo Social. Santiago: United Nations.

CEPAL. 1989. *Transfomación Ocupacional y Crisis Social en América Latina,* Santiago: United Nations.

Chamorro, A., Chávez, M. and Membreño, M. 1991: El sector informal en Nicaragua. in Pérez Sainz J.P. and Menjivar Larin R. (eds.), *Informalidad Urbana en Centroamérica,* pp. 217–257. San José, Costa Rica: Editorial Nueva Sociedad.

Chant, S. 1991: *Women and Survival in Mexican Cities: Perspectives on Gender, Labour Markets and Low-Income Households,* Manchester: Manchester University Press.

Cheetham, R. 1973: El sector privado de la construccion: patron de dominacion. *Revista Latino Americana de Estudios Urbano Regionales* 1, 3 (October).

Cheresky, I. 1992: La emergencia de los derechos humanos y el retroceso de lo politico. *Punto de Vista,* No.43 (Agosto), pp. 42–48.

Chi, P.S.K. and Bogan, M.W. 1975: Estudio sobre migrantes y migrantes de retorno en el Peru. Notas de Poblacion. *Revista Latinoamericana de Demografia* 3, 9 (December), 95–114.

CIDA, 1970: *Estructura Agraria v Desarrollo Agricola en Mexico.* Vols 1–3, Mexico: Centro de Investigaciones Agrarias, Comite Interamericano de Desarrollo Agricola.

Cliffe, L. 1977: Rural class formation in East Africa. *Journal of Peasant Studies* 4, 2, 195–224.

Cohen, A. 1969: *Custom and politics in urban Africa.* London: Routledge and Kegan Paul.

Collier, D. 1975: Squatter settlements and policy innovation in Peru. In Lowenthal, 1975, 138–78.

Collins, J. 1988: *Unseasonal Migration.* Albany, NY: State University of New York.

Conniff, M.H., Nohlgren, S and Melvin, H. 1971: Brasil. In Morse, 1971c.

Conning, A. 1972: Rural-urban destinations of migrants and community differentation in a rural region of Chile. *International Migration Review* 6, 2 (summer), 148–57.

Cornelius, W.A. 1971: The political sociology of the cityward migration in Latin America: towards empirical theory. In Rabinowitz and Trueblood, 1971.

Cornelius, W.A. 1974: Urbanization and political demand-making: political participation among the migrant poor in Latin American cities. *American Political Science Review* 68, 3, 1125–46.

Cornelius, W.A. 1975: *Politics and the migrant poor in Mexico City.* Stanford, Calif.: Stanford University Press.

Cornelius, W.A. 1976: Mexican migration to the United States: the view from rural sending communities. Paper presented at conference on Mexico and the United States, the Next Ten Years. School of International Service, The Amercian University, Washington, DC, 18–19 (March).

Cornelius, W. 1991a: Labour migration to the United States: development outcomes and alternatives in Mexican sending communities, In S. Díaz-Briquets and S. Weintraub (eds.), *Regional and Sectoral Development in Mexico as Alternatives to Migration,* Washington, DC: Commission for the Study of International Migration and Cooperative Development, pp. 89–131.

Cornelius, W. 1991b: *Los migrantes de la crisis*: the changing profile of Mexican migration to the United States. In Mercedes González and Agustín Escobar (eds.), *Social Responses to Mexico's Economic Crisis of the 1980s,* pp. 91–113. San Diego, CA: Center for US–Mexican Studies, University of California, San Diego.

Cornelius, W. and Trueblood, F. (eds), 1974: *Latin American urban research* 4. Beverly Hills and London: Sage.

Cornelius, W. and Trueblood, F. (eds), 1975: *Latin American urban research* 5. Beverly Hills and London: Sage.

Cornell, L.L. 1986: Taking reproduction seriously: an essay on the modern family in China, Japan, and the United States. Paper presented at 81st Annual Meeting of the American Sociological Association, New York, NY, August 30–September 2, 1986.

Cornell, L.L. 1990: Constructing a theory of the family. *International Journal of Comparative Sociology,* 31(1–2): 67–78.

Cortes, F. and Rubalcava, R.M. 1991: *Autoexplotacion Forzada y Equidad por Empobrecimiento.* Mexico, DF: El Colegio De Mexico. Jornadas 120.

Cortes Conde, R. and Gallo, E. 1967: *La formacion de la Argentina moderna.* Buenos Aires: Paidos.

Cotler, J. 1970/71: Political crisis and military populism in Peru. *Studies in Comparative International Development 6,* 5.

Cowell, B. Jr. 1975: Cityward migration in the nineteenth century: the case of Recife, Brazil. *Journal of InterAmerican Studies and World Affairs 17,* 1 (February).

D'incao e Mello, M.C. 1976: O *'Boia-Fria': acumulacao e miseria.* Petropolis, Brazil: Editora Vozes.

Dalton, G. (ed.), 1971: *Studies of economic anthropology.* Washington, DC: American Anthropological Association Studies 7.

Dandler, J. Havens, E., Samaniego, C. and Sorj, B. 1976: La estructura agraria en America Latina. *Revista Mexicana de Sociologia 38,* 1 (January–March), 29–50.

Davis, D. 1994: *Urban Leviathan: Mexico City in the Twentieth Century.* Philadelphia: Temple University Press.

Davis, K. 1965: The urbanization of the human population. *Scientific American* 214 (September), 40–53.

Davis, K. 1972: *World urbanization, 1950–70* 1 and 2. *Population Monograph Series* 9. University of California, Berkeley.

De Barbieri, T. 1984: *Mujeres y Vida Cotidiana.* Mexico, DF: SEP-Fondo de Cultura Económica.

De Barbieri, T. and Oliveira, O. 1987: *La Presencia de las Mujeres en Amercia Latina en una Década de Crisis,* Santo Domingo: Centro de Investigación para la Acción Femenina (CIDAF), Editora Bho.

De Janvry, A. and Garramon, C. 1977: The dynamics of rural poverty in Latin Amercia. *Journal of Peasant Studies* 4, 3: 206–216.

De Janvry, A., Sadoulet, E., and Wilcox Young, L. 1989: Land and labor in Latin American Agriculture from the 1950s to the 1980s. *Journal of Peasant Studies* 18: 3–35.

De la Peña, G. 1994: Estructura e historia: La Viabilidad de los nuevos sujetos. In María Luisa Tarrés et al. *Transformaciones Sociales y Acciones Colectivas: América Latina en el Contexto Internacional de los Noventa.* Mexico: El Colegio de México, pp. 141–159.

De la Peña, G. and De la Torre, R. 1990: Religión y política en los barrios populares de Guadalajara. *Estudios Sociológicos,* 24: 571–602.

De la Peña, G., Durán, J.M., Escobar, A. and De Alba, J.G. (eds.). 1990: Crisis, Conflicto y Sobrevivencia: Estudios Sobre la Sociedad Urbana en México. Guadalajara, Jalisco: Universidad de Guadalajara, and Tlalpan, Mexico DF: CIESAS.

De la Torre, C. 1992: The ambiguous meanings of Latin American Populisms, *Social Research,* 59(2): 385–414.

De Soto, H. 1989: *The Other Path: the Invisible Revolution in the Third World.* New York: Harper Row.

Dean, W. 1969: *The industrialization of Sao Paulo, 1880–1945.* Latin American Monographs 17. Institute of Latin American Studies, Austin and London: University of Texas Press.

Degregori, C.I. and Rivera, C. 1993: *Peru 1980–1993: Fuerzas Armadas, Subversión y Democracia,* Documentos de Trabajo No. 53, Lima: Instituto de Estudios Peruanos.

Degregori, C.I., Blondet, C. and Lynch, N. 1986: *Conquistadores de un Nuevo Mundo: De Invasores a Ciudadanos en San Martín de Porres.* Lima: Instituto de Estudios Peruanos.

Desal-Herder, 1968: *La Marginalidad en America Latina: Un Esayo de Diagnostico.* Barcelona.

Despres, L.A. 1991: *Manaus: Social Life and Work in Brazil's Free Trade Zone,* Albany: State University of New York.

Deyo, F.C. 1986: "Industrialization and the structuring of Asian labor movements: the 'gang of four'." In Hanagan, M. and Stephenson, C. (eds.), *Confrontation, Class Consciousness and the Labor Process.* New York: Greenwood Press, pp. 167–198.

Di Tella, T. 1962: Estratificación social e inestabilidad política en Argentina y Chile. *6th Conference of the Instituto de Desarrollo Económico y Social,* September 1962, Buenos Aires.

Di Tella, T. nd. (c.1965). *La Teoria del Primer Impacto del Crecimiento Economico.* Santa Fe, Argentina: Universidad Nacional del Litoral, Instituto de Sociologia.

Di Tella, T. 1965a: Populism and reform in Latin America. In Veliz, 1965, 47–74.

Di Tella, T. 1967: *Sindicalismo y comunidad.* Buenos Aires: Editorial del Instituto Torcuato di Tella.

Di Tella, T. 1974: *Classes sociales y estructuras políticas.* Paidos: Buenos Aires.

Di Tella, T. 1990: *Latin American Politics.* Austin, TX: University of Texas Press.

Díaz, A. 1993: *Restructuring and the New Working Classes in Chile: Trends in Waged Employment, Informality and Poverty, 1973–1990.* Discussion Paper 47, United Nations Research Institute for Social Development, Geneva.

Dietz, H. 1977: The office and the *poblador*: perceptions and manipulations of housing authorities by the Lima urban poor. Malloy, 1977.

Dietz, H. 1980: *Poverty and Problem-Solving under Military Rule: the Urban Poor in Lima.* Austin, Texas: University of Texas Press.

Dirección General de Estadística (DGE), 1943. *Sexto Censo de Población, 1940.* Resumen General. Mexico, DF: DGE.

Diskin, M. 1991: Ethnic discourse and the challenge to Anthropology. In Urban, G. and Sherzer, J. (eds.), *Nation-States and Indians in Latin America.* Austin: University of Texas Press, pp. 156–180.

Doughty, P. 1970: Behind the back of the city: provincial life in Lima, Perú. In W. Mangin (ed.) *Peasants in Cities,* Boston: Houghton Mifflin, pp. 30–46.

Doughty, P. 1972: Peruvian migrant identity in the urban milieu. In Weaver and White, 1972.

Drake, M. (ed.), 1973: *The process of urbanization.* Bletchley: Open University Press.

Dutra Fonseca, P. 1989: *Vargas: O Capitalismo em Constuçâo.* Sâo Paulo: Editora Brasiliense.

Durand, J. and Massey, D.S. 1992: Mexican migration to the United States: a critical review. *Latin American Research Review,* 27: 3–42.

Dyos, H.J. (ed.), 1971: Greater and greater London: notes on metropolis and provinces in the nineteenth and twentieth centuries. In Bromley and Kossmann, 1971, 89–12.

Dyos, H.J. and Aldcroft, D. 1969: *British transport.* Leicester: Leicester University Press.

Eames, E. and Goode, J.G. 1973: *Urban poverty in a cross-cultural context,* New York: Free Press; London: Collier-Macmillan.

Eckstein, S. 1975: The political economy of lower-class areas in Mexico City: societal constraints on local business opportunities. In Cornelius and Trueblood, 1975, 125–45.

Eckstein, S, 1990a: Urbanization revisited: inner-city slum of hope and squatter settlement of despair. *World Development*: 18, (2): 165–81.

Eckstein, S. 1990b: Poor people versus the state and capital: anatomy of a successful community mobilization for housing in Mexico City. *International Journal of Urban and Regional Research*, 14(2): 274–296.

ECLA, 1957: Change in employment structure in Latin America. *Economic Bulletin for Latin America* 2, 1 (February), 15–42.

ECLA, 1965: Structural changes in employment within the context of Latin America's economic development. *Economic Bulletin for Latin America* 10, 2 (October) 163–87.

ECLA, 1970: *Development problems in Latin America*. Austin: University of Texas Press.

Economic Commission for Latin America (ECLAC), 1983: *Statistical Yearbook for Latin America and the Caribbean, 1983* Chile: United Nations.

Economic Commission for Latin America (ECLAC), 1993: *Statistical Yearbook for Latin America and the Caribbean, 1993* Chile: United Nations.

Edel, M. and Hellman, R.G. (eds.). 1989: *Cities in Crisis: The Urban Challenge in the Americas*, New York: Bildner Center for Western Hemisphere Studies.

Edmonson, M.S. Carrasco, O. Fisher, G. and Wolf, E. 1957: *Synoptic studies of Mexican culture*. Tulane University: Middle Amercian Research Institute, publication 17.

Edwards, M. 1982: Cities of tenants: renting among the urban poor in Latin America. In Hilbert, A. Hardoy, J. and Ramírez, R. (eds.), *Urbanization in Contemporary Latin America*, London: John Wiley, pp. 129–58.

Effrat. M.P. (ed.), 1974: *The community: approaches and applications*. New York: Free Press.

Ehlers, T.B. 1991: Debunking marianismo: economic vulnerability and survival strategies among Guatemalan wives. *Ethnology*, 30 (1): 1–16.

Elizaga, J.C. 1972: Internal migration: an overview. *International Migration Review* 6 (summer), 121–46.

Escobar, A. 1986: *Con el Sudor de tu Frente*, Guadalajara: El Colegio de Jalisco/CIESAS.

Escobar, A. 1988: The rise and fall of an urban labor market: economic crisis and the fate of small-scale workshops in Guadalajara, Mexico. *Bulletin of Latin American Research*, 7, 2: 183–205.

Escobar, A. and Roberts, B. 1991: Urban stratification, the middle classes, and economic change in Mexico, in Gonzalez de la Rocha, M. and Escobar, A. (eds.), *Social Responses to Mexico's Economic Crisis of the 1980s*. San Diego: Center for US-Mexican Studies, UCSD, pp. 91–113.

Evans, P. 1979: *Dependent Development: The Alliance of Multinational, State and Local Capital in Brazil*. Princeton, NJ: Princeton University Press.

Evans, P. 1989: Predatory, developmental, and other apparatuses: A comparative political economy perspective on the Third World State. *Sociological Forum*, 4(4): 561–587.

Fajnzylber, F. 1990: *Unavoidable Industrial Restructuring in Latin America*. Durham and London: Duke University Press.

Faria, V. 1976: Occupational Marginality, employment and poverty in urban Brazil. PhD dissertation, Harvard University.

Faris, R.E.L. (ed.), 1964: *Handbook of modern sociology*. Chicago: Rand McNally.

Fausto, B. (ed.), 1975: *O Brasil Republicano* 3, Sao Paulo: Difel.

Fausto, B. (ed.), 1976: *Trabalho urbano e conflito social, 1890–1920*. Sao Paulo and Rio de Janeiro: Difel.

Feagin, J.R. 1988: *Free Enterprise City*. New Brunswick: Rutgers University Press.

Feldman, A. and Moore, W. 1962: Industrialization and Industrialism: convergence and differentiation. *Transactions of the Fifth World Congress of Sociology* 2, International Sociological Society.

Felix, D. 1977: The technological factor in socio-economic dualism: toward an economy-of-scale paradigm for development theory. In Nash, 1977, 180–211.

Fernandes, F. 1969: *The negro in Brazilian society*. New York: Columbia University Press.

Fernandez-Kelly, Patricia, M. 1994: Broadening the scope: gender and the study of international development. In Kincaid, D. and Portes, A. (eds.), *Comparative National Development*, pp. 143–168. Chapel Hill: University of North Carolina.

Fernandez-Kelly, Patricia, M. 1995: Political Economy and gender in Latin America: the emerging dilemmas. In Roberts, B. Cushing, R. and Wood, C. (eds.), *The Sociology of Development, Vol 2*. Cheltenham: Edward Elgar.

Ferner, A. 1977: The industrial bourgeoisie in the Peruvian development model. PhD thesis, University of Sussex.

Filgueira, C. and Geneletti, C. 1981: *Estratificación y Movilidad Ocupacional en América Latina*, Cuaderno de la CEPAL, No. 39, Santiago: CEPAL.

Fishlow, A. 1973: Some reflections on post-1964 Brazilian economic policy. In Stepan, 1973, 69–118.

Fitzgerald, E.V.K. 1976: Peru: the political economy of and intermediate regime. *Journal of Latin American Studies* 8, 1 (May).

Flinn, W.L. 1971: Rural and intra-urban migration in Colombia: two case studies in Bogota. In Rabinovitz and Trueblood, 1971.

Flora, P. and Alber, J. 1981: Modernization, democratization, and the development of Welfare States in Western Europe, in Flora, P. and Heidenheimer, A. (eds.), *The Development of Welfare States in Europe and America*, New Brunswick, NJ: Transaction Books, pp. 37–80.

Foster, J. 1974: *Class struggle and the Industrial Revolution.* London: Weidenfeld and Nicolson.

Fox, R.W. 1975: *Urban population growth trends in Latin America.* Washington, DC: Inter-American Development Bank.

Foxley, A. (ed.), 1976: *Income distribution in Latin America.* London: Cambridge University Press.

Frank, A.G. 1971: *Capitalism and underdevelopment in Latin America.* Harmondsworth: Penguin.

Frankenhoff, C.A. 1967: Elements of an economic model for slums in a developing economy. *Economic Development and Cultural Change* 16, 1, 27–35.

Franklin, S.H. 1965: Systems of production, systems of appropriation. *Pacific Viewpoint* 6, 2, 145–66.

Friedel, E. and Jimenez, M.F. 1971: Columbia. In Morse, 1971c.

Frieden, B.J. and Nash, W.W. (eds), 1969: *Shaping an urban future.* Cambridge, Mass.

Friedlander, J. 1975: *Being Indian in Hueyapan.* New York: St. Martin's Press.

Friedmann, J. 1969: The role of cities in national development. *American Behavioral Scientist* 12, 5, 13–21.

Freidmann, J. 1969/70: The future of urbanization in Latin America. *Studies in Comparative International Development* 5, 9.

Friedmann, J. 1972a: The spatial organization of power in the development of urban systems. *Comparative Urban Research* 1 (spring), 5–42. New York.

Friedmann, J. 1972b: A general theory of polarized development. In N.M. Hansen (ed.), *Growth Centers in Regional Economic Development.* New York: Free Press.

Friedmann, J. 1989: The dialectic of reason. *International Journal of Urban and Regional Research.* 13: 217–236.

Friedmann, J. and Sullivan, F. 1974: The absorption of labor in the urban economy: the case of developing countries. *Economic Development and Cultural Change* 22 (April) 385–413.

Fröbel, F., Heinrichs, J. and Kreye, O. 1980: *The New International Division of Labour.* Cambridge: Cambridge University Press.

Fry, P. 1978: Two religious movements: Protestantism and Umbanda. In Wirth, 1978.

Furtado, C. 1976: *Economic development of Latin America.* Cambridge: Cambridge University Press.

Galey, J. 1971: Venezuela. In Morse, 1971c.

Gallo, E. 1974: *El 'boom' cerealero y cambios en la estructura socio-politica de Santa Fe (1870–1895).* Documento de trabajo 88, Centro de Investigaciones Sociales. Instituto Torcuato Di Tella.

Gamio, M. 1930: *Mexican Immigration to the United States*. Chicago: University of Chicago Press.

Gans, H.J. 1965: *The urban villagers*. New York: Free Press.

García, B. 1988: *Desarrollo Económico y Absorción de Fuerza de Trabajo en México: 1950–1980*, Mexico, DF: El Colegio de México.

García, B. and Oliveira, O. 1994. *Trabajo Femenino y Vida Familiar en México*. México, DF: El Colegio de México.

García, B., Muñoz, H. and Oliveira, O. 1979: *Migración, Familia y Fuerza de Trabajo en la Ciudad De México*, Cuadernos del CES, No. 26, México, DF: CES/El Colegio de México.

García, B., Muñoz, H. and Oliveira, O. 1981: Migration, family context and labour-force participation in Mexico City, in Balan, J. (ed.), *Why People Move*, Paris: UNESCO.

García, B., Muñoz, H. and Oliveira, O. 1982: *Hogares y Trabajadores en la Ciudad de México*, Mexico, DF: El Colegio de México e Instituto de Investigaciones Sociales, UNAM.

García, B., Muñoz, H. and Oliveira, O. 1983: *Familia y Mercado de Trabajo: un Estudio de dos Ciudades Brasileñas*, Mexico, DF: El Colegio de México e Instituto de Investigaciones Sociales-UNAM.

Garza, G. 1985: *El Proceso de Industrialización en la Ciudad de México, 1821–1970*. México, DF: El Colegio de México.

Garza, G. (ed.), 1989: *Una Década de Planeación Urbano-Regional en México 1978–1988*. México, DF: El Colegio de México.

Garza, G. and Departamento del Distrito Federal, 1987: *Atlas de la Ciudad de México*, DF: Departamento del Distrito Federal and El Colegio de México.

Garza, G. and Sobrino, J. 1989: *Industrialización Periférica en el Sistema de Ciudades de Sinaloa*. México, DF: El Colegio de México.

Geertz, C. 1963a: *Agricultural involution: the process of ecological change in Indonesia*. Berkeley and Los Angeles: University of California Press.

Geertz, C. 1963b: *Peddlers and princes: social development and economic change in two Indonesian towns*. Chicago: University of Chicago Press.

Gereffi, G. and Korzeniewicz, M. (eds), 1990: *Commodity Chains and Global Capitalism*. Westport, CT: Greenwood Press.

Germani, G. 1966: Social and political consequences of mobility. In Smelser and Lipset, 1966, 364–94.

Germani, G. 1968: *Política y sociedad en una época de transición*. Buenos Aires: Paidos.

Germani, G. 1969/70: Stages in modernization in Latin America. *Studies in Comparative International Development* 5, 8.

Germani, G. 1981: *The Sociology of Modernization*. New Brunswick, NJ: Transaction Books.

Germani, G. 1987 [1955]: *Estructura Social de la Argentina*. Buenos Aires: Ediciones Solar.

Gershrenkron, A. 1962: *Economic backwardness in historical perspective*. Cambridge, Massachusetts.: Belknap Press.

Gianella, J. 1969: *Marginalidad en Lima Metropolitana*. Lima: Cuadernos, DESCO.

Gianotten, V., de Wit, T. and de Wit, H. 1985: The impact of *Sendero Luminoso* on regional and national politics in Peru. In David Slater (ed.), *New Social Movements and the State in Latin America*, Amsterdam: CEDLA, 171–202.

Gibbs, J.P. and Browning, H.L. 1966: The division of labor, technology and the organization of production in twelve countries. *American Sociological Review* 31, 1 (February).

Gilbert, A. 1974: *Latin American development: a geographical perspective*. Harmondsworth: Penguin.

Gilbert, A. 1992a: Urban agglomeration and regional disparities. In Gilbert, A. and Gugler, J. (eds.), *Cities, Poverty and Development: Urbanization in the Third World*, 33–61. Oxford: Oxford University Press.

Gilbert, A. 1992b: The housing of the urban poor. In Gilbert, A. and Gugler, J. *Cities, Poverty, and Development*, New York: Oxford University Press, 114–154.

Gilbert, A. 1993: *In Search of a Home*. London: University College London Press.

Gilbert, A. and Ward, P. 1985: *Housing, the State and the Poor: Policy and Practice in Three Latin American Cities*, Cambridge: Cambridge University Press.

Gilbert, A. and Varley, A. 1990: Renting a home in a third world city: choice or constraint? *International Journal of Urban and Regional Research*, 14: 89–108.

Giusti, J. 1971: Organizational characteristics of the Latin American urban marginal settler. *International Journal of Politics* 1, 1, 54–89.

Glade, W. 1969: *The Latin American economies: a study of their institutional evolution*. New York: American Books, Van Nostrand, Reinhold.

Goldthorpe, J. 1978: The current inflation: towards a sociological account. In Hirsch and Goldthorpe, 1978.

Gonzalez Casanova, P. 1965: Internal colonialism and national development. *Studies in Comparative International Development* 1, 4, 27–37.

González de la Rocha, M. 1988a: De por qué las mujeres aguantan golpes y cuernos: un análisis de hogares sin varón en Guadalajara, en Gabayet, Luisa et. al., *Mujeres y Sociedad: Salario, Hogar y Acción Social en el Occidente de México*. Guadalajara: El Colegio de Jalisco/CIESAS del Occidente.

González de la Rocha, M. 1988b: Economic crisis, domestic reorganization and women's work in Guadalajara, Mexico. *Bulletin of Latin American Research*, 7(2): 207–223.

González de la Rocha, M. 1994: *The Resources of Poverty: Women and Survival in a Mexican City*. Oxford: Basil Blackwell.

González de la Rocha, M. and Escobar, A. 1988: Crisis and Adaptation: Households of Guadalajara. Texas Papers on Mexico, pre-publication working papers of the Mexican Center, Institute of Latin American Studies University of Texas at Austin.

González de la Rocha, M., Escobar, A. and De la O Martínez Castellaños, M. 1990: Estrategias versus conflicto: reflexiones para el estudio del grupo doméstico en época de crisis. In De la Peña, G., Durán, J.M., Escobar, A. and De Alba, J.G. (eds.), *Crisis Conflicto y Sobrevivencia: Estudios Sobre la Sociedad Urbana en México*, Guadalajara, Jalisco: Universidad de Guadalajara and Tlalpan, México DF: CIESAS, 355–388.

González-Aréchiga, B. and Barajas Escamilla, R. (eds.) 1989: *Las Maquiladoras: Ajuste Estructural y Desarrollo Regional*. Tijuana, BC: El Colegio de la Frontera Norte? Fundación Friedrich Ebert.

Goodman, D. and Redclift, M. 1977: The 'Boias-Frias': rural proletarization and urban marginality in Brazil. *International Journal of Urban and Regional Research* 1, 2, 348–64.

Gordon, D.M. 1972: *Theories of Poverty and Unemployment*. Lexington Massachusetts: DC Heath.

Graham, D. 1970: Divergent and convergent regional economic growth and internal migration in Brazil. *Economic Development and Cultural Change* 18 (April), 362–82.

Graham, D. 1972: Foreign migration and the question of labor supply in the early economic growth of Brazil. Mimeo, Economic History Workshop, Instituto de Pesquisas Economicas, Universidade de Sao Paulo.

Graham, R. 1973: *Britain and the onset of modernization in Brazil*. Cambridge: Cambridge University Press.

Graham, R. and Smith, P. (eds.), 1974: *New approaches to Latin American history*. Austin and London. University of Texas Press.

Greaves, T.C. 1972: The Andean rural proletarians. *Anthropological Quarterly* 45, 2, 65–83.

Gregory, P. 1986: *The myth of market failure: employment and the labour market*. Baltimore: John Hopkins University Press.

Griffin, K. 1969: *Underdevelopment in Spanish America: an interpretation*. London: Methuen.

Griffith-Jones, S. and Sunkel, O. 1986: *Debt and Development Crises in Latin America: the End of an Illusion*. Oxford: Clarendon Press.

Grondin, M. 1978a: *Comunidad Andina: Explotación calculada*. Secretaría de Estado de Agricultura de la República Dominicana. Santo Domingo.

Grondin, M. 1978b: Peasant cooperation and dependency: the case of the electricity enterprises of Muquiyauyo. In Long, N. and Roberts, B. (eds.), *Peasant Cooperation and Capitalist Expansion in Central Peru*, 99–127. Austin, TX. University of Texas Press.

Gugler, J. 1992: The urban-rural interface and migration. In Gilbert, A. and Gugler, J. *Cities, Poverty, and Development*. New York: Oxford University Press.

Gugler, J. and Flanagan, W.G. 1978: *Urbanization and Social Change in West Africa*. Cambridge: Cambridge University Press.

Gunn, P. 1994: *Social or Enterpreneurial Innovations in the Geography of Production: the case of Ceará in Brasil*. Paper presented to the XIII World Congress of Sociology, Bielefeld, Germany, 19–23 July.

Gutiérrez, L.H. and Romero, L.A. 1992: Ciudadanía política y ciudadanía social: los sectores populares en Buenos Aires, 1912–1955. *Indice*, No. 5, 77–101, Buenos Aires.

Haber, S.H. 1992: Assessing the Obstacles to Industrialization: The Mexican Economy, 1830–1940, *Journal of Latin American Studies*, 24 (1).

Hall, M. 1974: Approaches to immigration history. In Graham and Smith, 1974.

Halperin, D.T. 1963: La expansion ganadera en la compania de Buenos Aires (1810–52). *Desarrollo Economico* 111, 1–2 (April–September). Buenos Aires.

Halperin, D.T. 1970: *Historia contemporanea de America Latina*. Madrid: Alianza Editorial.

Handelman, H. 1975: The political mobilization of urban squatter settlements. *Latin American Research Review* 10, 35–72.

Hanke, L. 1956: *The imperial city of Potosi: an unwritten chapter in the history of Spanish America*. The Hague: Hijhoff.

Hansen, N.M. (ed.), 1972: *Growth centers in regional economic development*. New York: Free Press.

Hardoy, J. (ed.), 1975: *Urbanization in Latin America: approaches and issues*. Garden City, NY: Anchor.

Hart, K. 1973: Informal income opportunities and urban employment in Ghana. *Journal of Modern African Studies* 11, 61–89.

Hart, K. 1987: Rural-urban migration in West Africa. In Eades, J. (ed.), *Migrants, Workers and the Social Order*: 65–81. London: Tavistock.

Harvey, D. 1973: *Social justice and the city*. London: Edward Arnold.

Harvey, D. 1990: *The Condition of Postmodernity*. Cambridge, MA and Oxford, UK: Blackwell.

Hauser, P.M. and Schnore, L.F. (eds), 1965: The study of urbanization. New York: Wiley.

Hawley, A. 1950: *Human ecology*. New York: Ronald Press.

Hawley, A. 1971: *Urban Society: an ecological approach*. New York: Ronald Press.

Hayter, T. 1971: *Aid to imperialism*. Harmondsworth: Penguin.

Henderson, J. 1986: The new international division of labour and urban development. In David Dukakis-Smith, *Urbanisation in the Developing World*. London: Croom Helm, 63–81.

Hermansen, T. 1972: Development poles and related theories: a synoptic review. In Hansen, 1972.

Herrick, B.H. 1965: *Urban migration and economic development in Chile*. Cambridge, Massachusetts. and London: MIT Press.

Hill, R.C. 1977: Two divergent theories of the state. *International Journal of Urban and Regional Research* 1, 1, 76–99.

Hill, R.C. 1986: Crisis in the motor city: the politics of economic development in Detroit. In Fainstein, S. et al. *Restructuring the City*: 80–125. New York: Longman.

Hirabayashi, L. 1993: *Cultural Capital: Mountain Zapotec Migrant Associations in Mexico City*. Tucson, AZ: University of Arizona Press.

Hirsch, F. and Goldthorpe, J.H. (eds), 1978: *The political economy of inflation*. London: Martin Robertson.

Hirschman, A.O. 1977: A generalized linkage approach to development with special references to staples. In Nash, 1977, 67–98.

Hobsbawm, E. 1964: The nineteenth-century London labour market. In Centre for Urban Studies (ed.), *London: aspects of change*. London: Macgibbon and Kee, 3–28.

Hobsbawm, E. 1969b: La marginalidad social en la historia de la industrializacion europea. *Revista Latinoamericana de Sociologia* 5, 2 (July), 237–49.

Horowitz, I.L. 1967: The military elites. In Lipset and Solari, 1967, 146–89.

Horowitz, J. 1990: Industrialists and the rise of Peron, 1943–1946: some implications for the conceptualization of Populism. *The Americas*, 47 (2): 199–217.

Humphrey, J. 1982: *Capitalist Control and Workers' Struggle in the Brazilian Auto Industry*. Princeton, NJ: Princeton University Press.

Humphrey, J. 1987: *Gender and Work in the Third World: Sexual Divisions in Brazilian Industry*. London and New York: Tavistock Publications.

Humphrey, J. 1994: Are the unemployed part of the urban poverty problem in Latin America? *Journal of Latin American Studies*. Forthcoming.

Iglesias, E. 1983: La crisis economica international y las perspectivas de América Latina, in Centro Latinamericano de Economía Humana, *América Latina y la Crisis Internacional*. Montevideo: Serie Estudios CLEH No. 29, 53–76.

ILPES-CELADE, 1968: Elementos para la elaboracion de una politica de Desarrollo con intergracion para America Latina. Sintesis y Conclusiones. Mimeo.

Imaz, J. 1964: *Los que Mandan*. Buenos Aires: Eudeba.

Inkeles, A. 1960: Industrial Man: The Relation of Status to Experience, Perception, and Value. *American Journal of Sociology*, 66: 1–31.

Instituto Nacional de Estadística, Geografía e Informática (INEGI). 1977: *Encuesta Nacional de Empleo Urbano: Indicadores Trimestrales de Empleo*, México, DF: INEGI.

Instituto Nacional de Estadística, Geografía e Informática (INEGI), 1988: *Encuesta Nacional de Empleo Urbana Indicadores Trimestrales de Empleo (Enero-Marzo de 1987)*, Aguascalientes: INEGI.

InterAmerican Development Bank, 1989: *Economic and Social Progress in Latin America, 1989 Report*. Washington, DC: InterAmerican Development Bank.

International Labour Office, 1985: *World Labour Report, 2.* Geneva: International Labour Office.

International Labour Office, 1989: *World Labour Report, 6.* Geneva: International Labour Office.

Jacobson, L. and Prakash, V. (eds), 1970: *Urbanization and National Development.* Beverly Hills, Calif.: Sage.

Jelin, E. nd *De la Clase al Movimiento: Procesos Sociales Urbanos en América Latina, 1930–1990.* Mimeo, CEDES, Buenos Aires, Argentina.

Jelin, E. 1974: Formas de organización de la actividad económica y estructura ocupacional: el caso de Salvador, Brazil. *Desarrollo Económico 53,* 14 (April–June), 181–203.

Jelin, E. 1975: Espontaneidad y Organización en el Movimiento Obrero. *Revista Latinamericana de Sociología,* no. 2, 77–118.

Jelin, E. 1978: *La Mujer y el Mercado de Trabajo Urbano,* Estudios CEDES, Buenos Aires: CEDES.

Jelin, E. (ed.), 1987: *Ciudanía e Identidad: las Mujeres en los Movimientos Sociales Latino-Americanos.* Geneva: UNRISD.

Jelin, E. (ed.), 1990: *Family, household, and gender relations in Latin America.* London: Kegan Paul International.

Jelin, E. 1993a: Prólogo para un texto comprometido. In Teresas Valdés and Mariza Weinstein (eds.), *Mujeres que Sueñan: Las Organizaciones de Pobladoras 1973–1989.* Santiago: FLACSO, 13–22.

Jelin, E. 1993b: *Ante, De, En, Y?: Mujeres, Derechos Humanos.* Lima, Peru: Red Entre Mujeres/Diálogo Sur-Norte.

Jenkins, R. 1984: *Transnational Corporations and Industrial Transformation in Latin America.* London: Macmillan.

Jesus, C.M. de. 1963: *Child of the dark.* New York: Signet/E.P. Dutton.

Jimenez, R. and Velasquez, A. 1989: Metropolitan Manila: a framework for its sustained development. *Environment and Urbanization,* 1, 1: 51–58.

Johnson, E.A. 1970: *The organization of space in developing countries.* Cambridge, Massachusetts: Harvard University Press.

Kang, M-G. 1989: Political Economy of Urbanization: Industrialization, Agrarian Transition and Spatial Change in South Korea and Mexico. PhD Dissertation, Department of Government, University of Texas at Austin.

Katz: F. 1974: Labor conditions on *haciendas* in Porfirian Mexico: some trends and tendencies. *Hispanic American Historical Review 54,* 1 (February), 1–47.

Katzman, M.T. 1977: *Cities and frontiers in Brazil: regional dimensions of economic development.* Cambridge: Harvard University Press.

Katzman, M.T. 1978: São Paulo and its hinterland. In Wirth, 1978.

Kaufman, R.R. 1974: The patron-client concept and macro-politics: prospects and problems. *Comparative Studies in Society and History* 16, 284–308.

Kay, C. and Silva, P. (eds.), 1992: *Development and Social Change in the Chilean Countryside.* Amsterdam: CEDLA.

Kemper, R.V. 1974: Family and household organization among Tzintzuntzan migrants in Mexico City. In Cornelius and Trueblood, 1974, 23–46.

Kemper, R.V. 1977: *Migration and adaptation: Tzintzuntzan peasants in Mexico City*. Beverly Hills and London: Sage.

Kemper, R.V. and Foster, G.M. 1975: Urbanization in Mexico: the view from Tzintzuntzan. In Cornelius and Trueblood, 1975, 53–75.

Kentor, J. 1985: Economic development and the world division of labor. In Michael Timberlake, Urbanization in the World-Economy. Orlando: Academic Press, 25–39.

Kirsch, H. 1973: Employment and the utilization of human resources in Latin America. *Economic Bulletin for Latin America* 18 (2), 46–94.

Klaren, P. 1973: *Modernization, dislocation and aprismo*. Austin and London: Institute of Latin American Studies/University of Texas Press.

Kowarick, L. 1975: *Capitalismo e marginalidade na America Latina*. Rio de Janeiro: Paz e Terra.

Kowarick, L. 1977: The logic of disorder: capitalist expansion in the metropolitan area of greater Sao Paulo. *Discussion Paper*, Institute of Development Studies at the University of Sussex, Falmer, United Kingdom.

Kowarick, L. 1979: *Espoliacáo Urbana*, Rio de Janeiro: Editorial Paz e Terra.

Kowarick, L. and Campanario, M.A. 1994: Industrialized underdevelopment: In Lucio Kowarick (ed.), *Social Struggles and the City: the case of Sao Paulo*. New York: Monthly Review Press, 45–59.

Kowarick, L. and Singer, A. 1994. The Worker's Party in Sao Paulo. In Lucio Kowarick (ed.), *Social Struggles and the City: the case of Sao Paulo*. New York: Monthly Review Press, 225–255.

Kowarick, L., Rolnik, R., Somekh, N. and Amaral, A.L. (eds.), 1991: *São Paulo: Crise e Mudança*. São Paulo: Editorial Brasiliense.

Kritz, E. and Ramos, J. 1976: The measurement of urban underemployment: a report on three experimental surveys. *International Labour Review* 113, 1 (January/February), 115–127.

Kurz, K. and Muller, W. 1987: Class mobility in the industrial world. *Annual Review of Sociology*, 13: 417–442.

Laclau, E. 1971: Feudalism and capitalism in Latin America. *New Left Review* 67 (May-June), 19–38.

Laite, A.J. 1977: The migrant worker: a case study of industrialization and social stratification in highland Peru. PhD thesis, University of Manchester.

Laite, A.J. 1981: *Industrial Development and Migrant Labour*. Manchester: Manchester University Press.

Lake, N. 1971: Argentina. In Morse, 1971c.

Lampard, E.E. 1965: Historical aspects of urbanization. In Hauser and Schnore, 1965, 519–54.

Lampard, E.E. 1968: The evolving system of cities in the US: urbanization and economic development. In Perloff and Wingo, 1968.

Lamphere, L. 1987: *From Working Daughters to Working Mothers: Immigrant Women in a New England Industrial Community*. Ithaca, NY: Cornell University Press.

Landes, D. 1970: *The unbound prometheus*. Cambridge: Cambridge University Press.

Laquian, A.A. 1971: Slums and squatters in South and Southeast Asia. Jakobson and Prakash, 1971.

Lasuen, J.R. 1969: On growth poles. *Urban Studies* 6, 2 (June).

Latin American Bureau, 1980: *Unity is Strength*. London: Latin American Bureau.

Lawton, R. 1962: Population trends in Lancashire and Cheshire from 1801. *Transactions of the Historical Society of Lancashire and Cheshire* 114, 189–213.

Leacock, E. (ed.), 1971: *The culture of poverty: a critique*. New York: Simon and Schuster.

Lee, J.Y. 1992: Economic Development and Earnings Inequality in South Korea. PhD Dissertation, University of Texas at Austin.

Leeds, A. 1964: Brazilian careers and social structure: an evolutionary model and case history. *American Anthropologist* 66, 6, 1321–47.

Leeds, A. 1969: The significant variables determining the character of squatter settlements. *America Latina* 12, 3, 44–86.

Leeds, A. 1971: The culture of poverty concept: conceptual, logical and empirical problems, with perspectives from Brazil and Peru. In Leacock, 1971, 226–84.

Leeds, A. 1974: Housing-settlement types, arrangements for living, proletarianization and the social structure of the city. In Cornielius and Trueblood, 1974.

Leff, N. 1972: Economic development and regional inequality: origins of the Brazilian case. *Quarterly Journal of Economics* 86 (March), 243–62.

Lehman, D. (ed.), 1974: *Agrarian reform and agrarian reformism: studies of Peru, Chile, China and India*. London: Faber.

Lehman, D. 1990: *Democracy and Development in Latin America: Economics, Politics and Religion in the Post-War Period*. Philadelphia, PA: Temple University Press.

Lerner, D. 1958: *The passing of traditional society*. New York: Free Press.

Levine, R.M. 1994: The cautionary tale of Carolina Maria de Jesus. *Latin American Research Review*, 29 (1): 55–83.

Levy, D. 1986: *Higher Education and the State in Latin America: Private Challenges to Public Dominance*. Chicago: University of Chicago Press.

Lewis, O. 1952: Urbanization without breakdown: a case study. *Scientific Monthly* 75, 1, (July).

Lewis, O. 1961: *The children of Sanchez*. New York: Random House.

Lewis, O. 1968: *La vida: a Puerto Rican family in the culture of poverty–San Juan and New York*. New York: Vintage Books, Random House.

Lewis, R.A. 1973: Employment, income and the growth of the *barriadas* in Lima, Peru. PhD thesis, Cornell University.

Lieberson, S. 1980: *A Piece of the Pie*. Berkeley: University of California Press.

Lipietz, A. 1988: Accumulation, Crisis, and Ways Out. *International Journal of Political Economy*, 10–43.

Lipset, S.M. and Bendix, R. 1959: *Social Mobility in Industrial Society*. Berkeley: University of California Press.

Lipset, S.M. and Solari, A. (eds), 1967: *Elites in Latin America*. New York: Oxford University Press.

Lipton, M. 1977: *Why Poor People Stay Poor: Urban Bias in World Development*. London: Temple Smith.

Livernash, R. 1992: The growing influence of NGOs in the Developing World. *Environment*, 34: 12–43.

Lloyd, P. 1979: *Slums of hope? Shanty towns of the Third World* (Harmondsworth). Manchester: Manchester University Press.

Lomnitz, L. 1971: Reciprocity of favors among the urban middle class of Chile. In Dalton, 1971.

Lomnitz, L. 1974: The social and economic organization of a Mexican shanty town. In Cornelius and Trueblood, 1974, 135–56.

Lomnitz, L. 1976: Migration and network in Latin America. In Portes and Browning, 1976.

Lomnitz, L. 1977: *Networks and marginality: life in a Mexican shanty town*. New York and London: Academic Press.

Lomnitz, L. and Perez-Lizuar, M.P. 1987: *A Mexican Elite Family: 1820–1980*. Princeton, NJ: Princeton University Press.

London, B. 1980: *Metropolis and Nation in Thailand: the Political Economy of Uneven Development*. Boulder, CO: Westview Press.

London, B. 1987: Structural determinants of third world urban change. *American Sociological Review*, 52: 28–43.

London, B. and Smith, D.A. 1988: Urban bias, dependence, and economic stagnation in non-core nations. *American Sociological Review*, 53: 454–63.

Long, N. 1973: The role of regional associations in Peru. In Drake, 1973, 173–91.

Long, N. 1977: *An introduction to the sociology of rural development*. London: Tavistock.

Long, N. and Roberts, B. (eds), 1978: *Peasant cooperation and capitalist expansion in the central highlands of Peru*. Austin and London: University of Texas Press for Institute of Latin American Studies.

Long, N. and Roberts, B. 1984: *Miners, Peasants, and Entrepreneurs*. Cambridge: Cambridge University Press.

Long, N. and Roberts, B. 1994: The Agrarian Stuctures of Latin America:

1930–1990. In Bethell, L. (ed.), *The Cambridge History of Latin America*, Vol VI, 325–390. Cambridge: Cambridge University Press.

Lopes, J.B. 1961: Relations industrielles dans deux communautes brasiliennes. *Sociologie du Travil* 4, 61, 18–32.

Lopes, J.B. 1976: Do latifundio a empresa: unidade e diversidade no campo. *Caderno*, CEBRAP 26, Editors Brasiliense, Sao Paulo.

Lopes, J.B. 1977: Developpement capitaliste et structure agraire au Bresil. *Sociologie du Travail* 19, 1, 59–71.

Lopes, J.B. 1979: Capitalism in the periphery: notes on the development of the proletariat in Sao Paulo. *International Journal of Urban and Regional Research*, forthcoming.

Lopreato, J. 1967: *Peasants No More*. San Fransisco: Chandler Publishing.

Lorey, D. and Mostkoff, A. 1991: Mexico's 'lost decade,' 1980–90: Evidence on class structure and professional employment from the 1990 Census. In Wilkie, J. Contreras, C. and Weber, C. (eds.), *Statistical Abstract of Latin America*, Vol 30, Pt 2, Los Angeles: UCLA Latin American Center Publications.

Love, J. 1975: Autonomia e interdependencia: Sao Paulo: e a Federacao Brasileira, 1889–1937. In Fausto, 1975.

Love, J. 1994: Economic ideas and ideologies in Latin America since 1930. In Bethell, L. (ed.), *The Cambridge History of Latin America, Vol VI, Part 1*, 393–460. Cambridge and New York: Cambridge University Press.

Lowder, S. 1973: Aspects of internal migration in Peru. PhD dissertation, University of Liverpool.

Lowder, S. 1986: *Inside Third World Cities*. London and Sydney: Croom Helm.

Lowenthal, A. (ed.), 1975: *The Peruvian experiment*. Princeton and London: Princeton University Press.

Lozano, F. 1993: *Bringing it Back Home: Remittances to Mexico from Migrant Workers in the United States*. San Diego, CA: Monograph Series, 37, Center for US – Mexican Studies, University of California, San Diego.

Lustig, N. 1986: Economic Crisis and Living Standards in Mexico: 1982–1985, Documento preparado para el proyecto sobre. The impact of global recesion of living standards in selected developing countries UNUWIDER.

Lustig, N. 1992: *Mexico: The Remaking of an Economy*. Washington, DC: The Brookings Institution.

Lyons, R.F. (ed.), 1965: *Problems and strategies of educational planning*. UNESCO.

McGee, T.G. 1967: *The South East Asian city*. London: G. Bell.

McGee, T.G. 1971: Catalysts or cancers? the role of cities in Asian society. In Jakobson and Prakesh, 1971, 157–82.

McGreevey, W.P. 1971a: *An economic history of Colombia, 1845–1930*. New York: Cambridge University Press.

McGreevey, W.P. 1971b: A statistical analysis of primacy and lognormality in the size distribution of Latin American cities, 1750–1960. In Morse, 1971c.

McGreevey, W.P. 1990: *Social Security in Latin America*, World Bank Discussion Paper No. 110, Washington, DC: World Bank.

Machado da Silva, L.A. 1967: A politica nas favelas. *Cuadernos Brasileiros* 9, 3.

Machado da Silva, L.A. 1971: *Mercados metropolitanos de trabalho manual e marginalidade*, MA dissertation presented to the postgraduate programme of social anthropology of the National Musuem, Rio de Janeiro.

Mallon, F. 1983: *The Defense of Community in Peru's Central Highlands: Peasant Struggle and Capitalist Transition, 1860–1940*, Princeton: Princeton University Press.

Mallon, F. 1992: Indian communities, political cultures, and the state in Latin America, 1780–1990. *Journal of Latin American Studies*, 24, Supplement: 35–53.

Malloy, J.M. (ed.), 1977: *Authoritarianism and corporatism in Latin America*. Pittsburgh: University of Pittsburgh Press.

Manchester University Economics Research Section, 1936: *Readjustment in Lancashire*. Manchester: Manchester University Press.

Mangin, W.P. 1965: The role of regional associations in the adaptation of rural migrants to cities in Peru. In Adams and Heath, 1965, 311–23.

Mangin, W.P. 1967: Latin American squatter settlements: a problem and a solution. *Latin American Research Review* 2, 3, 75.

Mann, M. 1987: Ruling class strategies and citizenship. *Sociology*, 21, 3:339–354.

Mariz, C. 1992: Religion and poverty in Brazil: a comparision of Catholic and Pentecostal Communities. *Sociological Analysis*, 53:S:S63–S70.

Marshall, A. 1978: *El Mercado de Trabajo en el Capitalismo Periférico: el Caso de Argentina*, Santiago: PISPAL.

Marshall, A. 1987: Non-standard Employment Practices in Latin America, Discussion Paper OP/06/1987, Geneva: International Institute for Labour Studies.

Marshall, J.D. 1961: The Lancashire rural labourer in the early nineteenth century. *Transactions of the Lancashire and Cheshire Antiquarian Society* 71, 90–128.

Marshall, T.H. 1992 [1950]: Citizenship and Social Class. In Marshall, T.H. and Bottomore, T. *Citizenship and Social Class*, London: Pluto Press, 3–51.

Martine, G. 1972: Migration, natural increase and city growth: the case of Rio de Janeiro. *International Migration Review* 6, 2 (summer), 200–15.

Martine, G. 1987: Exodo rural, concentraçao urbana e fronteira agrícola. In Martine, G. and Garcia, R.C. (eds.). *Os Impactos Sociais da Modernizacao Agrícola*. Sao Paulo: Editora Caetes, 59–79.

Martine, G. 1989: A urbanizaçao no Brasil. *Texto para Discussao No. 21.* Brasilia: Instituto de Planejamiento.

Martine, G. 1992: Procesos recentes de concentraçao e desconcentracao no Brasil. *Documento de Trabalho,* No. 11, Instituto SPN, Brasilia.

Massey, D. 1989: International Migration and Economic Development in Comparative Perspective. *Population and Development Review,* 14: 383–414.

Massey, D. 1990: Social structure, household strategies, and the cumulative causation of migration. *Population Index,* 56 (1): 3–26.

Massey, D., Alarcon, R., Durand, J. and Gonzalez, H. 1987: *Return to Atzlan* Berkeley: University of California Press.

Massey, D., Goldring, L. and Durand, J. 1992: Continuities in Transnational Migration: An analysis of 13 Mexican communities. Working Paper, Population Research Center, University of Chicago, 1992.

Maybury-Lewis, D. 1991: Becoming Indian in lowland South America. In Greg Urban and Joel Sherzer (eds.), *Nation-States and Indians in Latin America.* Austin, TX: University of Texas Press, 207–235.

Medeiros, A. 1986: *Politics and intergovernmental Relations in Brazil. 1964–1982.* New York: Garland Press.

Meillassoux, C. 1977: *Mujeres, graneros y capitales.* Mexico: Siglo Veintiuno.

Mellor, R. 1977: *Urban sociology in an urbanized society.* London: Routledge.

Merrick, T.W. and Schmink, M. 1978: Female headed households and urban poverty in Brazil, paper presented at the Workshop on Women in Poverty: What do we know? Belmont Conference Center, April.

Merrick, T.W. and Graham, D.H. 1979: *Population and Economic Development in Brazil.* Baltimore and London: The Johns Hopkins University Press.

Merrington, J. 1975: Town and country in the transition to capitalism. *New Left Review* 73, 71–92.

Mesa-Lago, C. 1978: *Social Security in Latin America: Pressure Groups Stratification and Inequality.* Pittsburgh: University of Pittsburgh Press.

Mesa-Lago, C. 1991: *Social Security and Prospects for Equity in Latin America.* World Bank Discussion Paper, No. 140, Washington, DC: The World Bank.

Miller, R., 1976: Railways and economic development in central Peru, 1880–1930. In Miller et al., 1976, 27–52.

Miller, R. Smith, C.T. and Fisher, J. (eds), 1976: *Social and economic change in modern Peru.* University of Liverpool, Centre for Latin American Studies, monograph series 6, 27–52.

Mingione, E. 1977: Pahl and Lojkine on the state: a comment. *International Journal of Urban and Regional Research* 1, 1, 24–36.

Mingione, E. 1992: *Fragmented Societies.* Oxford: Basil Blackwell.

Mingione, E. 1994: New forms of urban poverty in Italy. *International Journal of Regional and Urban Research,* 17(3) 415–428.

Mitchell, B.R. 1976: *European Historical Statistics, 1750–1970*. New York: Columbia University Press.

Mitchell, B.R. 1983: *International Historical Statistics. The Americas and Australasia*. Detroit: Gale Research Co.

Mitchell, J.C. 1957: *The Kalela dance: aspects of social relationships among urban Africans in Northern Rhodesia*. Rhodes Livingstone Paper 27, Manchester: Manchester University Press for Rhodes Livingstone Institute.

Mitchell, J.C. 1966: Theoretical orientations in African urban studies. In Banton, 1966.

Mitchell, W.P. 1991: *Peasants on the Edge: Crops, Cult, and Crisis in the Andes*. Austin: University of Texas Press.

Moises, J.A. 1982: What is the Strategy of the 'New Sindicalism'?, *Latin American Perspectives*, vol. 9, no.4, 55–74.

Moore, W. 1964: Social aspects of economic development. In Faris, 1964.

Moore, W. 1977: Modernization as rationalization: process and restraints. In Nash, 1977, 29–42.

Moreno Toscano, A. 1972: Cambios en los patrones de urbanizacion en Mexico, 1810–1910. *Historia Mexicana* 22, 2, 160–87.

Moreno Toscano, A. and Florescano, E. 1974: El sector externo y la organizacion espacial y regional de Mexico, 1521–1910. *Cuadernos de Trabajo del Departamento de Investigaciones Historicas*, Instituto Nacional de Antropologia y Historia, Mexico.

Moreno Toscano, A. and Aguirre, C.A. 1975: Migrations to Mexico City in the nineteenth century. *Journal of Interamerican Studies and World Affairs* 17, 1, (February), 27–42.

Morley, S.A. and Williamson, J.G. 1977: Class pay differentials, wage stretching, and early capitalist development. In Nash, 1977, 407–27.

Morris, L. 1994: Informal aspects of social divisions. *International Journal of Urban and Regional Research*, 18(1): 112–27.

Morse, R.M. 1962: Latin American cities: aspects of function and structure. *Comparative Studies in Society and History* 4 (July).

Morse, R.M. 1971a: Trends and issues in Latin American urban research, 1965–1970. *Latin American Research Review* 6, 1 (spring), 30–52.

Morse, R.M. 1971b: Trends and issues in Latin American urban research, 1965–1970 (Part II). Latin *American Research Review* 6, 2 (summer), 19–75.

Morse, R.M. 1971c: *The urban development of Latin America, 1750–1920*. Stanford University: Center for Latin American Studies.

Morse, R.M. 1974: Trends and patterns of Latin American urbanization, 1750–1920. *Comparative Studies in Society and History* 16, 4 (September), 416–417.

Morse, R.M. 1975: The development of urban systems in the Americas in the nineteenth century. *Journal of Interamerican Studies and World Affairs* 17, 1 (February), 4–26.

Morse, R.M. 1992: Cities as people, In Morse, R.M. and Hardoy, J.E.

(eds.), *Rethinking the Latin American City*. Washington, DC: The Woodrow Wilson Press, 3–19.

Moynihan, D.P. (ed.), 1970: *Towards a national urban policy*. New York: Basic Books.

Munoz, H.G. 1975: Occupational and earnings inequalities in Mexico City: a sectoral analysis of the labour force. PhD dissertation, University of Texas at Austin.

Munoz, H. and Oliveira, O. 1975: La mano de obra en America Latina. In CLACSO, *Fuerza de trabajo y movimientos laborales en America Latina*. Social Science Research Council and Grupo de Movimientos laborales del Consejo Latino-americano de Ciencias Sociales.

Munoz, H. and Suarez, H. 1989: *Educacion y Empleo: Ciudad de México Guadalajara y Monterrey*, Cuernavaca: UNAM/CRIM (Centro Regional de Investigación Multidisciplinaria), Serie: Aportes.

Nagengast, C. and Kearney, M. 1990: Mixtec ethnicity: social identity, political consciousness, and political activism. *Latin American Research Review*, 25, 2: 61–92.

Nash, M. (ed.), 1977: *Essays on economic development and cultural change in honor of Bert F. Hoselitz. Economic Development and Cultural Change* 25, supplement, Chicago: University of Chicago Press.

National Academy of Sciences, 1971: *Rapid population growth consequences and policy implications*. Baltimore and London: Johns Hopkins Press.

Nelson, R., Schultz, T.P. and Slighton, R. 1971: *Structural change in a developing economy*. Princeton: Princeton University Press.

Nemeth, R.J. and Smith, D.A. 1985: The political economy of contrasting urban hierarchies in South Korea and the Philippines. In Timberlake, M. (ed.), *Urbanization in the World-Economy*. Orlando: Academic Press, 183–206.

Nohlen, D. 1993: *Enciclopedia Electoral Latinoamericana y del Caribe*. San José, Costa Rica: Instituto Interamericano de Derechos Humanos.

Noyelle, T. 1987: *Beyond Industrial Dualism: Market and Job Segmentation in the New Economy*. Boulder: Westview Press.

Noyelle, T. and Stanback, T.M. 1984: *The Economic Transformation of American Cities*. Totowa, NJ: Towman and Allanheld.

Nugent, D. 1994: *Spent Catridges of Revolution*. Chicago: Chicago University Press.

Nun, José. 1969: Sobrepoblación relativa, ejército industrial de reserva y masa marginal, *Revista Latinoamericana de Sociología*, 4, 2: 178–237.

O'Donnell, G. 1975: Reflexiones sobre las tendencias generales de cambio en el Estado burocratico autoritario, Documento CEDES-CLACS0 No. 1, Buenos Aires: CEDES.

O'Donnell, G. 1977: Corporativism and the question of the state. In Malloy, 1977.

O'Donnell, G. 1992: *Delegative Democracy?* Working Paper No. 172,

Helen Kellogg Institute for International Studies, University of Notre Dame, Notre Dame, Indiana.

Oliveira, F. 1972: A economia brasileira: crítica á razäo dualista, *Estudios CEBRAP* 2: 5–82.

Oliveira, O. 1975: Industrialization, migration and entry labor force changes in Mexico City: 1930–1970. Based on 1971 sample survey of Mexico City (1,104 males), PhD dissertation, University of Texas at Austin, 15–64.

Oliveira, O. and Roberts, B. 1994: Urban growth and urban social structure in Latin America, 1930–1990, in Bethell, L. (ed.), *The Cambridge History of Latin America, Vol VI*. Cambridge: Cambridge University Press, 253–324.

Oliveira, O. 1989: Empleo femenino en México en tiempos de recesión económica: tendencias recientes, In Cooper, J. de Barbieri, T. Rendon, T. Suarez, E. and Tuñon, E. (comps.), *Fuerza de Trabajo Femenina Urbana en México*, Mexico, DF: Coordinacíon de Humanidades, UNAM/Porrúa, 29–66.

Oliveira, O. and García, B. 1984: Migración a grandes ciudades del Tercer Mundo: Algunas implicaciones sociodemográficas, *Estudios Sociológicos*, 2, 4: 71–103.

Pahl, R.E. 1971: Poverty and the urban system. In Chisholm and Manners, 1971.

Pahl, R,E. 1974: Instrumentality and community in the process of urbanization. In Effrat, 1974.

Pantelides, E. 1976: *Estudios de la Población Femenina Económicamente Activa en América Latina. 1950–1970*. Serie C, No. 16, Santiago: CELADE.

Peattie, L.R. 1968: *The view from the barrio*. Ann Arbor: The University of Michigan Press.

Peattie, L.R. 1975: Tertiarization and urban poverty in Latin America. In Cornelius and Trueblood, 1975, 109–24.

Pedrero Nieto, M. 1990: Evolución de la participación economica femenina en los ochenta, *Revista Mexicana de Sociología*, 52, 1: 133–149.

Pérez Sainz, J.P. and Menjivar Larín, R. (eds.), 1991: *Informalidad Urbana en Centroamérica: entre la Acumulación y la Subsistencia*. San José, Costa Rica: Editorial Nueva Sociedad.

Pérez, Sainz, J.P. Camus, M. and Bastos, S. 1992: ... *Todito, Todito es Trabajo: Indígenas y Empleo en Ciudad de Guatemala*. Guatemala: FLACSO.

Pérez, S.N. and Gonzalez, C. 1927: *Constitucciones de Europa y America, Tomo II*. Madrid: Librería General de Victoriano Suárez.

Perlman, J.E. 1976: *The Myth of Marginality*. Berkeley, CA: University of California Press.

Perloff, H.S. and Wingo, L. Jr 1968: *Issues in urban economics*. Baltimore and London: Johns Hopkins Press.

Petras, J. and Zeitlin, M. (eds), 1968: *Latin America: reform or revolution.* New York: Fawcett.

Pezzoli, K. 1991: Environmental conflicts in the urban milieu: the case of Mexico City. In Goodman, M. and Redclift, M. *Environment and Development in Latin America: the Politics of Sustainability,* 205–229. Manchester and New York: Manchester University Press.

Pickvance, C.G. 1976: On the study of urban social movements. In Pickvance, C.G. (ed.), 1976: *Urban sociology: critical essays.* London: Tavistock/Methuen, 198–218.

Pinto, A. and Di Filippo, A. 1976: Notes on income distribution and redistribution strategy in Latin America. In Foxley, 1976, 91–106.

Pons, V. 1969: *Stanleyville.* London: Oxford University Press for International African Institute.

Portes, A. 1971: Political primitivism, differential socialization and lower-class leftist radicalism. *American Sociological Review* 36 (October), 820–35.

Portes, A. 1985: Latin american class structures. *Latin American Research Review,* 20, No.3: 7–39.

Portes, A. 1989: Latin American urbanization during the years of the crisis, *Latin American Research Review* 24, 3: 7–49.

Portes, A. and Browning, H. (eds), 1976: *Current perspectives in Latin American urban research.* Austin and London: University of Texas Press.

Portes, A. and Walton, J. 1976: *Urban Latin America: the political conditions from above and below.* Austin and London: University of Texas Press.

Portes, A. and Walton, J. 1981: *Labor, Class and the International System,* New York: Academic Press.

Portes, A. and Schauffler, R. 1993: Competing perspectives on the Latin American informal sector. *Population and Development Review,* 19 (1): 33–60.

Portes, A. and Sensenbrenner, J. 1993: Embeddedness and Immigration: Notes on the Social Determinants of Economic Action. *American Journal of Sociology,* 98 (6): 1320–50.

Portes, A., Castells, M. and Benton, L.A. (eds.), 1989: *The Informal Economy: Studies in Advanced and Less Developed Countries,* Baltimore, MD: The Johns Hopkins University Press.

Portes, A., Itzigtsohn, J. and Dore-Cabral, C. 1994: Urbanization in the Caribbean Basin. *Latin American Research Review,* 29 (2): 3–37.

Pozas, M de los A. 1993: *Industrial Restructuring in Mexico.* San Diego, CA: Center for US-Mexican Studies, University of California San Diego.

Pozos, F. 1992: Economic Restructuring Employment Change and Wage Differentials: the Case of Guadalajara and Monterrey. PhD thesis, University of Texas at Austin.

PREALC, 1982: *Mercado de trabajo en cifras 1950–1980,* Santiago de Chile, OIT.

PREALC, 1988: La evolución del mercado laboral entre 1980 y 1987,

Working Document Series, No. 328, Santiago: International Labour Office.

Preobrazhensky, E. 1965: *The new economics*. Oxford: Clarendon Press.

Pressnell, L.S. 1956: *Country banking in the industrial revolution*. Oxford: Clarendon Press.

Quijano, A. 1968: Dependencia, cambio social y urbanizacion en America Latina. *Revista Mexicana de Sociologia*, July-September, 525–70.

Quijano, A. 1971: *Nationalism and capitalism in Peru*. New York: Monthly Review Press.

Quijano, A. 1973: Redefinicion de la dependencia y proceso de marginalizacion en America Latina. In Weffort and Quijano, 1973, 171–329.

Quijano, A. 1974: The marginal pole of the economy and the marginalized labor force. *Economy and Society* 3, 4 (November), 393–428.

Quijano, A. 1975: The urbanization of Latin American society. In Hardoy, 1975.

Quijano, A. 1983: Imperialism and marginality in Latin America. *Latin American Perspectives*, 10, 2/3: 76–85.

Rabinovitz, F.F. and Trueblood, F. (eds), 1971: *Latin American urban research* 1. Beverly Hills and London: Sage.

Raczynski, D. and Serrano, C. 1984: *Mujer y familia en un sector popular urbano: resultado de un estudio de caso*, Santiago: CIEPLAN.

Rakowski, C.A. (ed.). 1994: *Contrapunto: the Informal Sector Debate in Latin America*. Albany, NY: State University of New York Press.

Ramos, S. 1984: *Las relaciones de parentesco y ayuda mutua en los sectores populares urbanos: un estudio de caso*. Estudios CEDES, Buenos Aires: CEDES.

Ratinoff, L. 1967: The new urban groups: the middle classes. In Lipset and Solari, 1967, 61–93.

Ravenstein, E.G. 1885: The laws of migration. *Journal of the Royal Statistical Society* 48, 2, (June), 167–227.

Raza, M. et al. 1981: India: urbanization and national development, In M. Honjo (ed.), *Urbanization and Regional Development*. Nagoya, Japan: Maruzen Asia, 71–96.

Recchini de Lattes, Z. 1977: Empleo femenino y desarrollo económico: Algunas evidencias, *Desarrollo Económico*, 17, 66: 301–17.

Recchini de Lattes, Zulma, 1983. *Dinámica de la Fuerza de Trabajo Femenina en la Argentina*. Paris: UNESCO.

Redford, A. 1926: *Labour migration in England, 1800–1850*. Manchester: Manchester University Press.

Redondo, N. 1990: *Ancianidad y Pobreza*. Buenos Aires: Editorial Humanitas.

Reina, R. 1973: *Paraná: Social Boundaries in an Argentine City*. Austin, Tx: University of Texas Press.

Reissman, L. 1964: *The urban process: cities in industrial societies*. London: Collier-Macmillan, Glencoe: Free Press.

Rendon, T. and Salas, C. 1987: Evolución del empleo en México: 1985–1980. *Estudios Demográficos y Urbanos*, 2, 2 (México, DF), 189–230.

Reyes Heroles, J. 1983: *Política Macroeconómica y Bienestar en México*, Mexico, DF: Fondo de Cultura Económica.

RIIA, 1937: *The problem of international investment*. Royal Institute of International Affairs. London: Oxford University Press.

Roberts, B.R. 1968a: Politics in a neighbourhood of Guatemala City. *Sociology* 2, 2, 185–204.

Roberts, B.R. 1968b: Protestant groups and coping with urban life in Guatemala City. *American Journal of Sociology* 73, 6, 753–67.

Roberts, B.R. 1970: Urban poverty and political behaviour in Guatemala. *Human Organization* 29, 1 (spring), 20–28.

Roberts, B.R. 1973a: *Organizing strangers*. Austin and London: University of Texas Press.

Roberts, B.R. 1973b: Education, urbanization and social change. In Brown, 1973, 141–62.

Roberts, B.R. 1974: The interrelationships of city and provinces in Peru and Guatemala. In Cornelius and Trueblood, 1974, 207–36.

Roberts, B.R. 1975: Center and periphery in the development process: the case of Peru. In Cornelius and Trueblood, 1975.

Roberts, B.R. 1976a: The social history of a provincial town: Huancayo, 1890–1972. In Miller et al, 1976, 130–97.

Roberts, B.R. 1976b: The provincial urban system and the process of dependency. In Portes and Browning, 1976.

Roberts, B. 1978a: *Cities of Peasants*. London: Edward Arnold.

Roberts, B.R. 1978b: The bases of industrial cooperation in Huancayo. In Long and Roberts, 1978.

Roberts, B.R. 1978c: Agrarian organization and urban development. In Wirth, 1978.

Roberts, B.R. 1989: Employment structure, life cycle, and life chances: formal and informal sectors in Guadalajara. In Portes, A. Castells, M. and Benton, L. (eds). *The Informal Economy: Comparative Studies in Advanced and Third World Countries*: 41–59. Baltimore: Johns Hopkins Press.

Roberts, B.R. 1991: The changing nature of informal employment: The case of Mexico, in Standing, G. and Tokman, V. (eds.), *Towards Social Adjustment: Labor Market Issues in Structural Adjustment*, Geneva: International Labor Office, 115–140.

Roberts, B. 1993: The Dynamics of Informal employment in Mexico. In Schoepfle, G. and Perez-Lopez, J. (ed.) *Work Without Protections: Case Studies of the Informal Sector in Developing Countries*, Washington, DC: US Department of Labor, Bureau of International Labor Affairs, 101–125.

Roberts, B. 1994: Urbanization, Development, and the Household. In

Kincaid, D. and Portes, A. (eds.), *Comparative National Development*, 199–236. Chapel Hill: University of North Carolina.

Roberts, B.R. 1995: Socially expected durations and the economic adjustment of immigrants. In Ports, A. (ed.) *The Economic Sociology of Immigration*. New York: Russell Sage.

Rodriguez, D. 1987: Agricultural Modernization and Labor Markets in Latin America: The Case of Fruit Production in Central Chile. PhD thesis, The University of Texas at Austin.

Rolnik, R. 1989: El Brasil urbano de los años 80. Un retrato. In Lombardi, M. and Veiga, D. (eds.), *Las Ciudades en Conflicto*, 175–194. Montevideo: CIESU/Ediciones de la Banda Oriental.

Rolnik, R., Lucio and Somekh, N. (eds.). 1990: *Sao Paulo: Crise e Mudanca*. Sao Paulo: Brasilense.

Rosenstein-Rodan, P. 1943: Problems of industrialization in Eastern and Southeastern Europe. *Economic Journal* 53 (June-September), 202–11.

Rostow, W.W. 1956: *The Stages of Economic Growth*, 3rd edn. Cambridge: Cambridge University Press.

Rouse, R. 1992: Making sense of settlement: Class transformation, cultural struggle, and transnationalism among Mexican migrants in the United States. *Annals of the New York Academy of Sciences*, Vol. 645, 25–52.

Roxborough, I. 1984: *Unions and Politics in Mexico*. Cambridge: Cambridge University Press.

Sachs, W. (ed.). 1992: *The Development Dictionary: A Guide to Knowledge as Power*. Atlantic Highlands, NJ: Zed Books.

Sachs, W. (ed.). 1993: *Global Ecology: a New Arena of Political Conflict*. Atlantic Highlands, NJ: Zed Books.

Samaniego, C. 1974: Location, social differentiation and peasant movements in the central sierra of Peru. PhD dissertation. University of Manchester.

Sassen, S. 1993: *Cities in a World Economy*. Thousand Oaks, CA and London: Pine Forge Press.

Sassen, S. 1991: *The Global City: New York, London, Tokyo*. Princeton, NJ: Princeton University Press.

Sassen, S. 1995: Immigration and Local Labor Markets. In Alejandro Portes (ed.), *The Economic Sociology of Immigration*. New York: Russell Sage.

Sassen-Koob, S. 1985: Capital mobility and labor migration: their expression in core cities. In Timberlake, M. (ed.), *Urbanization in the World-Economy*. Orlando: Academic Press, 231–265.

Sassen-Koob, S. 1988: *The Mobility of Labor and Capital: A Study in International Investment and Labor Flow*. Cambridge: Cambridge University Press.

Saville, J. 1957: *Rural depopulation in England and Wales, 1851–1951*. London: Routledge.

Schmink, M. 1979: Community in Ascendance: Urban Industrial Growth and Urban Income Strategies in Belo Horizonte, Brazil. PhD dissertation, University of Texas at Austin.

Schmink, M. 1984: Household economic strategies: Review and Research Agenda. *Latin American Research Review*, 87–101.

Schmink, M. and Wood, C. 1992: *Contested Frontiers in Amazonia*. New York: Columbia University Press.

Schnore, L.F. 1961: The statistical measurements of urbanization and economic development. *Land Economics* 37, 229–45.

Schnore, L.F. 1965: On the spatial structure of cities in the two Americas. In Hauser and Schnore, 1965, 347–98.

Schnore, L.F. 1975: *The new urban history*. Princeton: Princeton University Press.

Schoenberger, E. 1988: From Fordism to flexible accumulation: technology, competitive strategies and international location. *Environment and Planning D: Society and Space*, 6: 245–262.

Schteingart, M. 1989: *Los Productores del Espacio Habitable: Estado Empresa y Sociedad en la Ciudad de Mexico*. Mexico, DF El Colegio de Mexico.

Schuurman, F. and Heer, E. 1992: *Social Movements and NGOs in Latin America*. Saarbrücken: Verlag Breitenbach.

Schuurman, F. and Naerssen, T.V. (eds.), 1989. *Urban Social Movements in the Third World*. London: Routledge, Chapman and Hall.

Schwartz, S.B. 1984: Colonial Brazil, c.1580–c.1750: plantations and peripheries. In Bethell, L. (ed,). *The Cambridge History of Latin America. Vol II: Colonial Latin America*, 423–499.

Scobie, J.R. 1964: *Revolution on the pampas: a social history of Argentine wheat, 1860–1910*. Austin: University of Texas Press.

Scobie, J.R. 1975: Patterns of urbanization in Argentina, 1869–1914. *Latin American Research Review* 10, 2, 132–4.

Scott, A.M. 1979: Who are the self-employed? In Gerry, C. and Bromley, R. (eds): *The casual poor in third world cities*. London and New York: John Wiley.

Scott, A.M. 1994: *Divisions and Solidarities: Gender, Class, and Employment in Latin America*. London and New York: Routledge.

Scott, C. 1976: Peasants, proletarianization and the articulation of modes of production; the case of sugar-cane cutters in northern Peru, 1940–1869. *Journal of Peasant Studies* 3, 3, 321–42.

Secretaría de Programación y Presupuesto (SPP). 1979. *La Ocupación Informal en Areas Urbanas*, Mexico, DF: SPP.

Seidman, G. 1994: *Manufacturing militance: workers' movements in Brazil and South Africa, 1970–1985*. Berkeley, CA: University of California Press.

Selby, H.A. Murphy, A.D. and Lorenzen, S.A. 1990: *The Mexican Urban Household Organizing for Self-Defense*, Austin, Texas: University of Texas Press.

Shaiken, H. 1990: *Mexico in the Global Economy: High Technology and Work Organization in Export Industries*. San Diego, CA: Center for US-Mexico Studies, UCSD.

Shidlo, G. 1990: Housing Policy in Brazil. In Shidlo, G. (ed.), *Housing Policy in Developing Countries*, 33–4, London and New York: Routledge.

Shirley, R.W. 1978: Legal institutions and early industrial growth. In Wirth, 1978.

Simmons, A.B. and Cardona, G. 1972: Rural-urban migration: who comes, who stays, who returns? – the case of Bogota, Columbia. *International Migration Review* 6, 2, 166–81.

Singelman, J. 1974: The sectoral distribution of the labour force in selected European countries. PhD dissertation, University of Texas at Austin.

Singer, P. 1973: *Economia politica da urbanizaçao*. Sao Paulo: Editora Brasiliense (Edicoes CEBRAP).

Singer, P. 1975a: O Brasil, no contexto do capitalismo internacional, 1889–1930. In Fausto, 1975, 347–90.

Singer, P. 1975b: Urbanization and development: the case of Sao Paulo. In Hardoy, 1975, 435–56.

Sjoberg, G. 1965: Cities in developing and in industrial societies: a cross-cultural analysis. In Hauser and Schnore, 1965, 213–63.

Skidmore, T.E. 1974: *Black into White*. New York: Oxford University Press.

Skinner, G.W. (ed.), 1977: *The City in Late Imperial China*. Stanford: Stanford University Press.

Sklair, L. 1993: *Assembling for Development: The Maquila Industry in Mexico and the US* San Diego, CA: Center for US-Mexican Studies, University of California, San Diego.

Slater, D. (ed.). 1985: *New Social Movements and the State in Latin America*. Amsterdam: CEDLA.

Slater, D. 1989: Territory and State Power in Latin America: the Peruvian Case. New York: St Martin's Press.

Smelser, N.J. and Lipset, S.M. (eds), 1966: *Social structure and mobility in economic development*. London: Routledge.

Smith, C. (ed.). 1990: *Guatemalan Indians and the State*. Austin: University of Texas Press.

Smith, J. and Wallerstein, I. (eds.). 1992: *Creating and Transforming Households: the Constraints of the World Economy*. Cambridge: Cambridge University Press.

Smith, G.A. 1975a: The social basis of peasant political activity: the case of the *huasicanshinos* of central Peru. PhD thesis, University of Sussex.

Smith, G.A. 1975b: Internal migration and economic activity: some cases from Peru, *woking paper* 17, Centre for Developing Area Studies, McGill University, Montreal, Canada.

Smith, G.A. 1984: Confederations of households: extended domestic enterprises in city and countryside. In Long, N. and Roberts, B. *Miners,*

Peasants and Entrepreneurs. Cambridge: Cambridge University Press, 217–234.

Smith, G.A. 1989: *Livelihood and Resistance: Peasants and the Politics of Land in Peru*. Berkeley and Los Angeles: University of California Press.

Smith, M.P. and Feagin, J.R. (eds.), 1987: *The Capitalist City: Global Restructuring and Community Politics*. Oxford: Basil Blackwell.

Smith, R.C. 1992: *Los Ausentes Siempre Presentes*: the imagining, making and politics of a transnational community between New York City and Ticuani, Puebla. PhD Dissertation, Columbia University.

Soares, G.A.D. 1976a: The web of exploitation: state and peasants in Latin America. Mimeo, University of Florida, Gainesville.

Soares, G.A.D. 1976b: The state in Latin America. Mimeo, University of Florida, Gainesville.

Soja, E. 1986: Taking Los Angeles apart. *Environment and Planning D*: 255–72.

Soja, E. 1987: Economic restructuring and the internationalization of the Los Angeles region, In Smith, M.P. and Feagin, J.R. (eds.), *The Capitalist City: Global Restructuring and Community Politics*: 178–198. Oxford: Basil Blackwell.

Soja, E. 1989: *Postmodern Geographies*. London: Verso.

Sorj, B. 1976: *The state in peripheral capitalism*. PhD dissertation, University of Manchester.

Souza, H. and Affonso, C.A. 1975: The role of the state in the capitalist development of Brazil. *Brazilian Studies* 7, York University, Toronto, Canada.

Spalding, K. 1984: *Huarochiri: An Andean Society under Inca and Spanish Rule*, Stanford: Stanford University Press.

Stavenhagen, R. 1965: Classes, colonialism and acculturation. *Studies in Comparative International Development* 1, 6, 53–77.

Stedman Jones, G. 1971: *Outcast London*. London: Oxford University Press.

Stepan, A. 1971: *The military in politics: changing patterns in Brazil*. Princeton: Princeton University Press.

Stepan, A. (ed.) 1973: Authoritarian Brazil. New Haven and London: Yale.

Stern, S.J. 1982: *Peru's Indian Peoples and the Challenge of the Spanish Conquest: Huamanga to 1640*. Madison: University of Wisconsin Press.

Stern, S.J. 1988: Feudalism, capitalism, and the world system in the perspective of Latin America and the Caribbean, *The American Historical Review*, Vol. 93, No. 4, 829–872.

Stevens, E.P. 1973: Machismo and Marianismo. *Society*, 10(6): 57–63.

Stolcke, V. 1988: *Coffee Planters, Workers, and Wives: Class Conflict and Gender Relations on Sao Paulo Plantations, 1850–1980*. New York: St Martin's Press.

Taebur, K.E. Chiazza, L. Jr. and Haenzel, W. 1968: Migration in the United States: an analysis of residence histories. *Public Health Monograph 77*, US Department of Health, Education and Welfare.

Tamayo, S. 1994: The 20 Mexican Octobers: Social Movements and Citizenship in Mexico, 1968–1988. PhD dissertation, University of Texas at Austin.

Tapia Curiel, J. 1984: *El Estado Nutricional en los Niños de Dos Grupos Sociales de Guadalajara*, Cuadernos de Difusión Científica, Serie Salud Pública, No. 2, Guadalajara, Mexico: Universidad de Guadalajara.

Taylor, C. 1948: *Rural Life in Argentina*. Baton Rouge, LA: Louisiana State University.

Taylor, P.S. 1932: *A Spanish-Mexican Peasant Community: Arandas in Jalisco Mexico*. Berkeley, California: University of California Press.

Tedesco, J.C. 1987: *El Desafío Educativo: Calidad y Democracia*, Buenos Aires: Grupo Editorial Latinoamericano.

Telles, E. 1994: Industrialization and Racial Inequality in Employment: The Brazilian Example. *American Sociological Review*, 59: 46–63.

Telles, E. 1988: The consequences of employment structure in Brazil: earnings, socio-demographic characteristics and metropolitan differences. PhD dissertation, University of Texas at Austin.

Thernstrom, S. 1964: *Poverty and progress: social mobility in a nineteenth-century city*. Cambridge, Massachusetts: Harvard University Press.

Thernstrom, S. and Knights, P.B. 1970: Men in motion: some data and speculations about urban population mobility in nineteenth-century America. *Journal of Interdisciplinary History* 1 (autumn), 7–35.

Thomas, B. 1973: *Migration and economic growth: a study of Great Britian and the Atlantic economy*. Cambridge: Cambridge University Press.

Thorp, R. 1992: A reappraisal of the origins of Import-Substituting Industrialization. *Journal of Latin American Studies*, 24: 181–195.

Thorp, R. and Bertram, G. 1976: Industrialization in an open economy: a case study of Peru, 1890–1940. In Miller et al., 1976.

Thorp, R. and Bertram, G. 1978: *Peru, 1890–1977: growth and policy in an open economy*. London and New York: Macmillan and Columbia University Press.

Tilly, C. 1984: Demographic Origins of the European Proletariat. In David Levine (ed.), *Proletarianization and Family Life*. New York: Academic Press.

Tilly, C. 1990: Transplanted Networks. In Virginia Yons-McLaughlin (ed.), *Immigration Reconsidered*, 79–95. New York: Oxford University Press.

Tilly, L. and Scott, J.W. 1978: *Women, Work, Family*. New York: Holt, Rinehart and Winston.

Timberlake, M. 1985: The World-system perspective and urbanization. In Timberlake, M. (ed.), *Urbanization in the World-Economy*. Orlando, Fla: Academic Press, 3–22.

Timberlake, M. 1987: World-system theory and the study of comparative urbanization. In Smith, M.P. and Feagin, J. (eds.), *The Capitalist City*. Oxford: Basil Blackwell, 37–65.

Tokman, V. 1987: El sector informal: quince años después., *El Trimestre Económico*, 215: 513–536.

Tokman, V. 1991: The informal sector in Latin America: from Underground to Legality. In Standing, G. and Tokman, V. (eds.), *Towards Social Adjustment: Labor Market Issues in Structural Adjustment*, Geneva: ILO, 141–57.

Turner, J.F.C. 1967: Barriers and channels for housing development in modernizing countries. *Journal of the American Institute of Planners* 32, 3 (May), 167–81.

Turner, J.F.C. 1970: Squatter settlements in developing countries. In Moynihan, 1970.

Unikel, L. 1975: Urbanism and urbanization in Mexico: situation and prospects. In Hardoy, 1975, 391–434.

United Nations, 1948: *National income statistics of various countries: 1938–1947*. New York: Statistical Office of the United Nations.

United Nations, 1964: *Statistical yearbook*. New York: Statistical Office of the United Nations.

United Nations, 1967: *Statistical yearbook*. United Nations.

United Nations, 1975: *Statistical yearbook*. United Nations.

United Nations, 1980: *Patterns of Urban and Rural Population Growth*. Population Studies, No. 68, Department of International Economic and Social Affairs, United Nations, New York.

United Nations, 1993: *World Urbanization Prospects, 1992 Revision*. New York: United Nations.

United Nations, 1994: *Population, Environment and Development*. New York: United Nations.

United States Department of Commerce, 1994: *Statistical Abstract of the United States 1994*. Washington, DC: United States Department of Commerce.

Urban, G. and Sherzer, J. (eds.), 1991: *Nation-States and Indians in Latin America*. Austin, TX: University of Texas Press.

Uzzell, D. 1972: Bound for places I'm not known to: adaptation of migrants and residence in four irregular settlements in Lima, Peru. PhD dissertation, University of Texas at Austin.

Uzzell, D. 1974: The interaction of population and locality in the development of squatter settlements in Lima. In Cornelius and Trueblood, 1974, 113–34.

Valdes, T. and Weinstein, M. 1993: *Mujeres que Sueñan: Las Organizaciones de Pobladoras 1973–1989*. Santiago: FLACSO.

Valladares, L. 1989: Rio de Janeiro. La visión de los estudiosos de lo urbano. In Lombardi, M. and Veiga, D. (eds.), *Las Ciudades en Conflicto*, 195–222. Montevideo: CIESU/Ediciones de la Banda Oriental.

Van Gunsteren, H. 1978: Notes of a theory of citizenship. In Birnbaum, P.

Lively, J. and Parry, G. *Democracy Consensus and Social Contract*, 9–35. London; Sage Publications.

Vanegas, S. 1987: Family Reproduction in Rural Chile: a Socio-Demographic Study of Agrarian Change in the Aconcagua Valley, 1930–1986. PhD dissertation, University of Texas at Austin.

Vapñarsky, C.A. 1975: The Argentine system of cities: primacy and rank-size rule. In Hardoy, 1975, 369–90.

Vekemans, R. and Giusti, J. 1969/70: Marginality and ideology in Latin American development. *Studies in Comparative International Development* 5, 11.

Veliz, C. (ed.), 1965: *Obstacles to change in Latin America*. London: Oxford University Press for Royal Institute of International Affairs.

Vellinga, M. 1979: *Economic Development and the Dynamics of Class: Industrialization, Power, and Control in Monterrey Mexico*. Assen: Van Gorcum.

Wade, R.C. 1959: *The urban frontier: the rise of western cities, 1790–1830*. Cambridge, Massachusetts: Harvard University Press.

Wallerstein, I. 1974a: *The modern world system*. New York and London: Academic Press.

Wallerstein, I. 1974b: The rise and future demise of the world capitalist system. *Comparative Studies in Society and History* 16 387–415.

Wallerstein, I. 1979: *The Capitalist World Economy*. Cambridge: Cambridge University Press.

Wallerstein, I. 1980: *The Modern World System II: Mercantilism and the Consolidation of the European World Economy*. New York: Academic Press.

Wallerstein, I. 1988: Comments on Stern's critical tests, *American Historical Review*, Vol. 93, No. 4, 873–885.

Walton, J. 1977: *Elites and economic development: comparative studies on the political economy of Latin American cities*. Austin and London: University of Texas Press for Institute of Latin American Studies.

Walton, J. and Ragin, C. 1989: Austerity and dissent: social bases of popular struggle in Latin America, In Canak, W.L. (ed.), *Lost Promises*. Boulder, Co: Westview Press, 216–232.

Ward, P. 1993: Social Welfare Policy and Political Opening in Mexico. *Journal of Latin American Studies*, 25: 613–628.

Ward, P. 1990: *Mexico City: the Production and Reproduction of an Urban Environment*, London: Belhaven Press.

Ward, P., Jimenez, E. and Jones, G. 1993: Residential land price changes in Mexican cities and the affordability of land for low-income groups. *Urban Studies* 30: 1521–1543.

Wasserstrom, R. 1983: *Class and Society in Central Chiapas*. Berkeley, CA: University of California Press.

Webb, R. 1974: Government policy and the distribution of income in Peru, 1963–73. PhD dissertation, Harvard University.

Webb, R. 1975: Public policy and regional incomes in Peru. In Cornelius and Trueblood, 1975.

Weber, A.F. 1899: *The growth of cities in the nineteenth century*. Ithaca, NW: Cornell University Press.

Weffort, F.C. 1973: Classes populares y desarrollo social. In Weffort and Quijano, 1973, 17–169.

Weffort, F.C. and Quijano, A. (eds), 1973: *Populismo, marginalización y dependencia*, San Jose, Costa Rica: Editorial Universitaria Centroamericana.

Wells, J. 1976: Subconsumo, tamanho de mercado e padroes de gastos familiares no Brasil. *Estudos* CEBRAP 17 (July–September), 5–60.

Whiteford, J. 1975: *Urbanization of rural proletarians and Bolivian migrant workers in northwest Argentina*. PhD thesis University of Texas at Austin.

Wibel, J. and De La Cruz, J. 1971: Mexico. In Morse, 1971c.

Wilheim, J. 1977: Sao Paulo 77: housing within the context of underdevelopment. Paper presented to conference of Manchester and Sao Paulo, The Crisis of Rapid Urban Growth, Stanford University, April.

Wilkie, J., Contreras, C. and Weber, C. (eds.). 1993: *Statistical Abstract of Latin America*, Vol. 30. Parts 1 and 2. Los Angeles: UCLA Latin American Center Publications, University of California.

Wils, F. 1975: *Industrialists, industrialization and the nation-state in Peru*. The Hague: Institute of Social Research.

Wilson, P. 1992: *Exports and Local Development: Mexico's New Maquiladoras*. Austin, TX: University of Texas Press.

Wingo, L. Jr. 1967: Recent patterns of urbanization among Latin American countries. *Urban Affairs Quarterly* 2, 1, (March), 81–109.

Wingo, L. Jr. 1969: Latin American urbanization: plan or process? In Frieden and Nash, 1969, 115–46.

Winn, P. 1986: *Weavers of Revolution: the Yarur Workers and the Chilean Road to Socialism*. New York: Oxford University Press.

Wirth, J. 1975: Minas e a Nacao: un estudo de poder e dependencia regional, 1889–1937. In Fausto, 1975.

Wirth, J. (ed.) 1978: *Manchester and Sao Paulo: problems of urban growth*. Stanford, Calif: Stanford University Press.

Wolf, E. 1957: The Mexican Bajio in the eighteenth century. In Edmonson et al., 1957, 180–98.

Wood, C.H. 1977: Infant mortality trends and capitalist development in Brazil: the case of Sao Paulo and Belo Horizonte. *Latin American Perspectives* 4, 56–65.

Wood, C.H. and Carvalho, J. 1988: *The Demography of Inequality in Brazil*. Cambridge, Cambridge University Press.

Wood, C.H. and Lovell, P.A. 1992: Racial Inequality and Child Mortality in Brazil. *Social Forces*, 70(3): 703–724.

World Bank, 1990: *World Development Report, 1990*. Oxford and New York: Oxford University Press for the World Bank.

World Bank, 1994a: *Population and Development*. Washington, DC: World Bank.

World Bank, 1994b: *World Development Report, 1994*. Oxford and New York: Oxford University Press for the World Bank.

Yepes, E. 1972: *Peru: 1820–1920: un siglo de desarrollo capitalista*. Lima: Instituto de Estudios Peruanos.

Yepes, E. 1974: Some aspects of Peruvian socio-economic history. PhD thesis, University of Manchester.

Yujnovsky, O. 1975: Urban spatial structure in Latin America. In Hardoy, 1975, 191–220.

Yujnovsky, O. 1976: Urban spatial configuration and land use policies in Latin Amercia. In Portes and Browning, 1976, 17–41.

Zaluar, A. 1985: *A Máquina e a Revolta*. Sao Paulo: Editora Brasiliense.

Zaluar, A. 1994: *Condomínio do Diabo*. Rio de Janeiro: Editora Revan/ UFRJ.

Index

Page references in italics refer to tables.

African/black ethnicity 143–4
agrarian development
  hindered by primary exports 70
  regional 81, 82–3
agrarian structure 186
  changes in 95–103
  diversification of 112
  and migration 87–112
  reform of and land shortage 92–3
  transformation of 28
agricultural regions, dynamic,
    stratification in 136
agriculture
  capitalist vs peasant 96
  commercial 37, 92, 95, 96
  decline in employment 147, 48,
    149
  decline of farm size 92
  effects of modernization 96–7
  exploitation of 37
  generational changes 103
  productivity 58, 70, 73
  small-scale, market-oriented 95–6
Argentina 39, 57, 58, 61, 76
  changes in occupational structure (up
    to 1947) 135–6
  changes in urban employment
    structure 149
  democracy and political apathy
    210–11
  expansion of livestock rearing 38,
    42–3

immigration opening up the interior
  43–4
nationalization 60
primacy and distribution of urban
  places 40
problems of high urban mobility 205
sugar industry 43
systems of production/rise of the
  state/class conflict 42–5
artisan industry, urban 34
automobile industry 75, 76

bazaar economy 120–1
Black ethnicity 53
Bolivia, ethnicity in 202–3
Brazil 35, 57, 58, 62, 66, 75, 76, 90
  1960s economic boom 73
  bi-city primacy 90
  black populations 143
  breakdown of peasant farming
    system 97
  changes in population distribution
    104
  diversification of the economy 46
  dominant classes 41–2, 46
  effects of Portuguese colonization 31
  female employment 129–30
  indigenous peoples in 52
  national populist industrialization
    63–4
  regional agrarian development 81
  rural out-migration 100

Brazil cont'd
  strong bourgeoisie 117
  systems of production/rise of the
    state/class conflict 45–7
  underdevelopment of north-east
    46–7
Britain, urban industrialization 20, *21*
Buenos Aires, growth of 44–5
bureaucratic-dominant class 152
bureaucratic-technical class 140
business elites 138, 139

capital flight 78
capital ownership, centralization of 14
capitalism 54
  and the problems of Latin America 9
capitalist development 13–14
  contradictions in 19
  low-income groups excluded from
    benefits 159–60
Catholicism 162, 169
centralization 89
centrifugalism 26, 27, 30, 33–5
change, determinants of 18–19
chemical industries, replacement
  products 59
child labour 93, 165
Chile 57, 61, 93, 189, 199
  1980s growth patterns 155
  differential out-migration 108
  effects of Santiago's dominance 11
  precarious waged employment
    117–18
  state sponsored industrialization
    64
  urban marginality 189–90
cities
  built by the poor 4, 194
  in declining or stagnating regions 136
  large, industrializing 136
  maturing of 198
  spatial heterogeneity of 176
  underurbanized 158
  see also colonial cities; informal
    settlements; primacy
citizens, responsibility for own welfare
  200
citizenship 210–11
  cf. authoritarian monarchies 185–6

changing definition of 197–201
development of 184–208
in early developing countries 188
evolution of 188–9
and force for change 186
post World War II 187–9
civil rights 193–4, 200–1
international associations 201
class 12, 188–9
  and low-income groups 133
class alliances 5, 187
class conflicts 5
class divisions 138
class interests 29, 38, 187
class relations, internal structure 8–9
class structure, and urbanization 134
class struggle 12, 13, 27, 29
clientelism 181–2
coercion 4, 18
coffee economy 45, 46
Colombia 58, 62, 140, 153
colonial cities 28, 29–30, 33–5
colonialism 29–36
  internal 80
colonization, by Spain and Portugal
  29–36
communications technology 78
community organization, changes in
  205
comparative advantage 69, 70, 78
competition/competitiveness 16, 38
constitutions, Latin American 184–5
convergence 7, 86, 88–9
  in migration patterns 88–9
core
  processes at 14–16
  see also periphery
core regions, dominance of 11–12
core-periphery 8, 11, 27
  implications of relationship 29
Costa Rica, balanced pattern of growth
  63
culture of poverty thesis 160–1

debt crisis 77–8
decentralization 18–19
democracy
  re-emergence of 210–11
  transition to 206–7

dependence
  economic, new pattern of 75
  export dependence 41
  external 72–9
  financial 17
  technological 85–6
dependency 7–9, 12
  theory 10–11
dependency ratios 196–7
deregulation 79
developing countries
  financial dependence of 17
  urbanization of 23
development 11
  dependent 27, 56
  national and regional, divergent
    trends in 41–51
  pace of 61
  and urbanization 6–10
diversification 112
  economic 58
  of exports 37–8
  of village economies 97–8, 99
diversity
  regional, in elites 139–40
  sources of 10–13
dominant classes 138
  Argentina 41–2, 44
  Brazil 41–2, 46

Economic Commission for Latin
    America (ECLA) 57, 58, 60
  analyses and policy
    recommendations 69–72
  income distribution and poverty in
    Latin America 150, 51
economic crises 156
  increasing women's burden 204
economic development 138
  different paths 60–9
  effects of post-1960s development
    152–3
  generating regional inequalities 80–5
  populism a strategy of 65–6
  and urban industrialization 6–7
economic dualism 115–18
economic enclaves 42, 95
economic expansion 87

economic growth, and development of
    citizenship 188
economic imperialism 23, 74
economic interdependence 74–5
economic liberalism 16–17
economic nationalism 77
economic transformation, and ethnic
    identity 202–3
economic uncertainty, affecting
    household stability 167
economies, opening of 78
economy, globalized, political
    participation in 210
Ecuador 62
education 140
  higher education 195
  inadequate for modern economy
    118–19
  linked to jobs 150
  and the lower middle class 141–2
  as means of social mobility 203
  qualification for jobs 137
  and socio-economic status 137
educational rights 194–5
elites 138–40, 142
  and citizenship 185
  local, and foreign interests 38
  urban, trends in 138–9
  see also dominant classes
employment
  agricultural 88, 89, 147, 48, 149
  female 128–9, 130
  growth patterns 73–4
'enclave' countries 118
enclave economy 64
enclave production 81–2
enterprises, family-based 138
entrepreneurial organization 200–1
entrepreneurs
  formal and informal 141
  immigration of 143
  in the informal sector 125–6
  rural 100
equity financing 17, 78
ethnicity 22, 166
  as a basis for stratification 142–4,
    146
  growth of 202–3
  and inequality 51–3

The Making of Citizens

Europe, exploitation of Latin America 28–9
exclusion, of low-income groups 159–60, 182
expatriates 138
export economy 38, 75
  and expansion of opportunities 42–51
exports 37–8, 61

family consumer economy 163
family labour, in the informal sector 125
family strategies 164–5
family wage 164
family wage economy 163
farming *see* agriculture
fiscal austerity 199, 200, 206
forces of change, local 11
Fordism 13
foreign (direct) investment 59, 76, 77
formal-informal sector relationship 117
fragmentation, internal, of Spanish America 35
France, economic development 20, *21*, 22
free market policies, adoption of 153

gender
  contributing to inequality 145
  see also women
global environmental issues 19
governments
  and international lending agencies 199
  pressures on 16–18
  strengthening of central control 38
grass roots activism, in labour movements 193
Guadalajara 47–8, 154
  elite in 139–40
  role of religious groups 169
Guatemala 202
  informal settlements 174
  marital instability 167 167
Guatemala City 94
  employment of squatters 122
  Indian population 143

health hazards 177
health rights 194–5
hinterlands, 'owned' by towns 31
household, cf. family 161–2
household enterprises 99
household position, and participation in the labour market 130–1
household strategies 162
  to offset declining real wages 154
households
  family-based 161–5
  and stratification 145–6
housing
  low-income, on city periphery 173–4
  search for 175–6
  see also informal settlements
Huancayo
  dependency of 84–5
  migration to 110–11
  small-scale economy 121–2
human rights 19

identities, formation of 202–6
immigration
  Argentina 43–4
  Brazil 45
  Lima 104–5
import-substitution industrialization (ISI) 4, 72–3, 117, 163–4
in-bond (maquiladora) industries 76–7, 78, 208
income, declining with age 132
income polarization 209
incorporation, into the world economy 23, 24, 25–6, 40
Indian ethnicity 51–3, 143, 202–3
indigenous populations, eliminated 52
industrial bourgeoisie 85
Industrial Revolution 36
industrialization 113, 208
  capital intensive 56, 72–9, 79–85, 114
  liberal 63
  and migrations 88–9
  national populist 63–4
  and regional development 79–85
  role of the state 64
  state-sponsored/-induced 64, 69

transition to second stage 69–72
twentieth century 57–60
and urbanization 55–86, 188
see also import-substitution
  industrialization (ISI);
  manufacturing/industry
inequality
  and ethnicity 51–3
  gender a factor in 145
  regional 80–5
  urban, changing nature of 150–6
  in urban incomes 120, 134, 156,
  208
informal economy/sector 116–17,
  120–4
  organization of 124–7
informal settlements 158, 174–6
  allow saving of income 175
  characteristics of 172
InterAmerican trading blocks 209–10
internal market 55–6, 61, 80, 89
interregional trade, and the colonial
  economic system 32
investment
  and primacy 39–40
  see also foreign (direct) investment
involution
  agricultural 98–9
  Brazil 47

jobs, high and low paid 15–16

kinship ties, important 166–7, 168–9

labour
  casual 144
  in the informal sector 124
  lowering of costs 119–20
  non-manual 149
  shortages of 118–19
  supply of, and immigration 44
  temporary 119–20
  see also migrants
labour force 45
  stable and reliable 119
labour market(s) 15
  effects of changes in 155–6
  and the informal economy 120–4
  and the large-scale sector 118–20

organization of 113–14
participation in 127–32
polarization in 15–16
role of the state 114–18
labour mobility 66
  consequences of global
  interdependence 15
labour relations 9–10
large-scale sector 116, 118–20, 132
Latin America, peripheral to Europe
  28–9
liberal democracy 210
life expectancy 195
Lima 94, 118, 121–2, 174
  immigration to 104–5
  survival of small enterprises 122–3
linked enterprises 127
living conditions, and neighbourhood
  171–80
local autonomy 18–19
'logic of disorder' 176–8
London 20
low-income families, and politics
  180–2
low-income groups, accommodation for
  172–6
low-income neighbourhoods, lack of
  trust and interpersonal hostility
  165–6
lower middle class 141–2, 152

machismo 162
macro-level forces 197–201
Manaus, dependency on central regions
  81–2
manual occupations 149
manufacturing/industry
  competitiveness in 16
  deconcentration of 90
  female participation in 128–9
maquiladora industries *see* in-bond
  (maquiladora) industries
marginality
  concepts of 160–1
  economic 189
  myth of 159–60, 189–94
  political 180–2
  social 158–61, 189
  urban 189–90

marianismo 162
marital instability 167
market forces 211
Medellin 62, 140
media, and public opinion 201
Mexican Urban Employment Survey
    145
Mexico 22, 58, 62, 93, 119, 130–1,
    154, 172–3, 199
  1995 economic crisis 208–9
  chain migration 108
  diversification of local economies 99
  economic crisis in 78–9
  employment of married women 165
  entrepreneurial organizations 200
  fastest growing cities 91
  female employment 129, 130
  growth of public employment 115
  impact of mining on the Bajio 32–3
  in-bond (maquiladora) industries
    76–7, 78, 117, 208
  Indian ethnicity 53
  migration, international and internal
    101, 109–10
  populism in 68–9
  regional development 82–3
  regional differentiation 47
  selectivity of migrants 106
  self-employment 131–2
  social costs of adjustment 155
  state sponsored industrialization 64
  systems of production/rise of the
    state/class conflict 47–9
  urban land prices and spatial
    segregation 179–80
  urban population growth 94
  working women 145–6
  see also Monterrey
Mexico City 16, 83, 105, 173, 198
  Ciudad Nezahuacoyotl slum 177
  growth of subsidized 84
  ineffectual government planning 178
  net out-migration 91
  primacy of 39
  public housing provision 177–8
Mexico–United States railways network
  48
middle class 135, 188
  importance of education 137–8

and upper class, importance of
    kinship/friendship relationships
    168–9
migrants
  associations of, same village/region
    191–2
  characteristics of 103–10
  rural 144, 208
  urban, origins of 102
migration
  and the agrarian structure 87–112
  contribution to urban growth
    110–11
  direct 107–8
  female 105–6, 108
  internal 95, 101
  international 43–4, 61–2, 89, 91,
    96–7, 142
  Latin America cf. Preston, UK
    108–9
  long-distance 100–1
  a permanent affair 102–3
  rural to rural 108
  selectivity of 105–6
  socio-structural factors 103–6
  temporary 98
  urban 89, 90
  and urban growth 94
  see also return migration; rural-
    urban migration; stage migration
migration movements, characteristics of
    103–10
mines 32–3, 34
mobility
  effects of 190
  of labour 15, 66
  occupational 150, 51, 152, 156
  social 134, 135–6, 146–50, 194,
    197, 203
  spatial 149
  structural 149
modern world system, concept of 9–10
modernization theories 6–7
Monterrey 48, 62, 154
  elite in 139, 140
  industrialization of 58–9
  migrants to 144
  neighbourhood movements 192
multinational corporations 2, 73, 77

developing countries producing for world markets 78
global strategies of 14–15
investment in Latin America 75–6
and new pattern of economic dependence 75

nation building, threatened by indigenous cultures 51–2
nationalism 60, 72
economic 77
natural increase, rates of 93
neighbourhood organization 200
neighbourhood-based movements 192
neo-colonialism 8
networking, by elites 139
networks
family and friendship 146
in the informal economy 125–6, 133
kin-based 101–2, 126
of low-income families 167–8
of participation 211
social, important in migration 109
used to manage relations with the state 190–1
see also kinship ties
new (international) division of labour 4–5, 16
non-governmental organizations (NGOs) 17, 201

occupational mobility 156
and changes in urban inequality 150, *51*, 152
occupational stratification 147, *48*, 149
emerging pattern of 137–42

Panama 62
Paraguay 62
patriarchal authority 162
patronage 18, 191, 198
patterns of consumption, changes in 36–7
peasant farms 99, 109
peasant population 96–7, 101–2
pension funds, crisis in 116
pensioners/pensions 196, 203
Pentecostalism 169, 170

peripheral housing developments 173–4
periphery 16
capital-intensive production in 81–3
role of 29
see also core; core-periphery
Peru 58, 64, 76, 99–100, 118
changes in migration 106
educational standards 195
overurbanization 62–3
regional inequalities in 83–4
sugar exports and class conflict 49–50
systems of production/rise of the state/class conflict 49–50
temporary migrants 98
see also Huancayo
petty bourgeoisie, informal 141, 147, 152
plantation economy, and major cities 39
plantation/mining towns 136
plantations 31, 34, 50
police and armed forces 114–15
political confrontations, violent 197
political participation, broadening of 19–20, 205, 211
political parties 206
populist 193
political rights 193–4, 200–1
politics, local-level 180–2
poor 191
coping with poverty and economic marginality 157–82
population, rural 89, 92
population growth
and the labour market 127
in underdeveloped areas 91–2
populism 67–9
middle-class or Peronist 64–6
poverty
fear of 19–20
increase in 155
and social marginality 158–61
urban 198, 209
primacy, in urban development 39–41
primary products, export of 59
private enterprise 3–4
limits on 115–16

privatization 114, 199
production costs, cheaper 74, 75
professional/technical strata, income
    advantage 153–4
proletarianization 159, 163, 189
public opinion 206
public services, shortage of 158–9

railway development 36, 38
    railway system, Mexico 48
recessions 77
    and female employment 129
recruitment practices 119
regional development 11, 44
    and industrialization 79–85
regionalization 37–8
regulation 13
    of squatter settlements 118
religion, and social support 169–71
remittances 106
renting (housing) 175–6, 198
repression, state 67
restructuring
    economic 72, 209
    financial 4
    industrial 78, 79
    of Latin American post-war
        economies 73
return migration 110–11, 112
Rio de Janeiro 46, 118, 173
    importance of natural increase 93–4
rural depopulation, lack of 92
rural migrants 208
    jobs for 144
rural-urban migration 4, 70, 88–112,
    144, 191–2
    change from temporary to permanent
        104
    impact on urban labour markets
        127–8
ruralization 37

Santiago 11, 118
    neighbourhood movements 191
Sao Paulo 16, 45, 46, 62, 173, 193
self-employment 128, 130, 131, 147,
    149, 152
    Mexico 131–2
Sendero Luminoso, appeal of 203

service sector 56, 58, 70, 191
    colonial times 34
    growth of 2–3, 72
services, and budget restriction 198
skilled workers 152
small-scale economy/sector 121–3, 132
    limits on accumulation 126–7
small-scale industry 100
    ECLA view 70, 72
social marginality 189
    and poverty 158–61
social mobility 134, 194
    in Argentina 135–6
    low in early developing countries
        197
    pattern of 146–50
social movements
    and definition/redefinition of
        citizenship 186–7
    urban 181
social policy challenges 211
social relationships
    and economic organization 126
    significance of within the city
        165–71, 183
social rights
    extension of burdensome 199–200
    predominance of 194–7
social security 140
    and employment 116, 196
    extension of 195–6
    a major fiscal obligation 196–7
social segregation, diverse patterns of
    179
South Korea 26, 79
spatial mobility 149
squatter settlements, regulation of 118
squatters/squatting 135, 177
stability 135
stage migration 107
state
    contributing to regional inequality
        83
    and economic development 113
    facing conflicting pressures 4
    of growing importance to business
        138
    as a major employer 194
    to provide substitute services 206

state intervention
  and economic dualism 115–18
  and the urban economy 114–15
structural changes *see* urbanization:
    industrialization
structural mobility 149
students, and social movements 203
subsistence farming/economy 96, 97,
    102–3
subsistence workers 147
systems of production 12
  expanding 12–13
  influencing class organization and
      struggle 12

technical training 138
technological change, affecting demand
    for workers 153
technological innovation 74
tenements, city-centre 173
trade unions 192–3
transition 7
transport, new forms of 36
trust, in economic relationships 126

Umbanda 170–1
underdeveloped countries 2, 3
  industrialization and new
      social/economic forces 56–7
underdevelopment 8, 54
  and population growth 91–2
  provincial 80
  regional 82
  and urbanization 33
underemployment 133
unemployment 128, 155, 198–9, 203
United Nations 57, 58
urban capitalist development,
    contemporary, inconsistencies of
    3–4
urban centres, provincial, employment
    in 84
urban economy(ies) 186
  capacity to absorb immigrants 111
  changes in affecting family
      organization 163–5
  place of small-scale economy 122
urban growth
  migration contributing to 110–11

and poverty 1–2, 3
rates of 93
significance of migration patterns
    88–95
urban incomes
  declining 153–4
  expenditure on goods and services
      121
  inequalities in distribution 152
urban industrialization, and economic
    development 6–7
urban life, coping with 166
urban organization, changes in 208
urban poor 146
  integration into capitalist economy
      190
  marginality of 189–90
urban population(s)
  fragmented economically 191
  permanent 56–7
urban poverty 198, 209
urban space 169
  and corporate strategies 14–15
urban spatial organization, conflicting
    tendencies in 179
urban stratification 134–56
  four basic types 136
  informal/formal distinction 140
  non-occupational bases of 142–6
  see also occupational stratification
urban systems
  centrifugal 33–5
  development of, Latin America 30–1
  diversified 62, 90
  mature 197–8
  primacy of (primate) 20, 22, 38, 208
urbanization 33, 208
  and citizenship 187–8
  contemporary patterns of 23, 24,
      25–6
  dendritic model 108
  in developing countries 4, 5–6
  and development 6–10
  historical and comparative
      perspective 20–7
  and industrialization 55–86, 199
  new stage in 13–20
  ninteenth century changes in patterns
      of 36–41

Uruguay 61
USA 23
  direct investment in Latin America
    76
  economic imperialism 74
  European immigration 22
  in-migration 91, 105
  labour for low-paid jobs 15
  regional inequalities 81
  tariffs and quota systems 59
  transnational communities 110
  urbanization in 21, 22

Venezuela 62
village economies, diversification of
    97–8, 99

wages, real, 152–3
women 165
  altered status of 204–5
  married, participating in the labour
    force 145–6, 164–5

migration by 108
participation in labour markets
    128–30
social mobility opportunities 142
work forces, militant 59, 67
working class 85, 135, 140, 152, 153,
    155–6, 188
  in Brazil 66
  fragmented socially 191
  informal 154
  political weakness of 66–7
  politically and socially fragmented
    135
  and populism 65
  reduction in income 154
World Bank 58

youth unemployment 203

Zapatista movement, Mexico 202
zoning regulations, absence of 176–7